Cabinets and Counselors

Cabinets and Counselors

The President and the Executive Branch

Washington, D.C.

Congressional Quarterly Inc.

Congressional Quarterly Inc., an editorial research service and publishing company, serves clients in the fields of news, education, business, and government. It combines Congressional Quarterly's specific coverage of Congress, government, and politics with the more general subject range of an affiliated service, Editorial Research Reports.

Congressional Quarterly publishes the *Congressional Quarterly Weekly Report* and a variety of books, including college political science textbooks under the CQ Press imprint and public affairs paperbacks on developing issues and events. CQ also publishes information directories and reference books on the federal government, national elections, and politics, including the *Guide to the Presidency*, the *Guide to Congress*, the *Guide to the U.S. Supreme Court*, the *Guide to U.S. Elections*, *Politics in America*, and *Congress A to Z: CQ's Ready Reference Encyclopedia*. The *CQ Almanac*, a compendium of legislation for one session of Congress, is published each year. *Congress and the Nation*, a record of government for a presidential term, is published every four years.

CQ publishes *The Congressional Monitor*, a daily report on current and future activities of congressional committees, and several newsletters including *Congressional Insight*, a weekly analysis of congressional action, and *Campaign Practices Reports*, a semimonthly update on campaign laws.

An electronic online information system, Washington Alert, provides immediate access to CQ's databases of legislative action, votes, schedules, profiles, and analyses.

Copyright © 1989 Congressional Quarterly Inc.
1414 22nd Street N.W., Washington, D.C. 20037

Printed in the United States of America

Library of Congress Cataloging-in-Publication Data
Cabinets and counselors : the president and the executive branch.
    p.   cm.
    Includes bibliographical references.
    ISBN 0-87187-519-5:
    1. United States. Executive Office of the President. 2. Cabinet officers--United States. 3. Executive departments--United States. 4. Executive advisory bodies--United States. 5. Independent regulatory commissions--United States. I. Congressional Quarterly inc.
JK518.C33 1989   89-17370
353--dc20   CIP

Authors: W. Craig Bledsoe, Harrison Donnelly, Richard A. Karno,
  Stephen L. Robertson, Margaret C. Thompson
Editors: Margaret Seawell Benjaminson, Michael Nelson,
  Sabra Bissette Ledent
Production Assistant: Jamie R. Holland
Indexer: Patricia R. Ruggiero
Cover Designer: Ed Zelinsky

WITHDRAWN

Table of Contents

Executive Office of the President: White House Office   1

Origins and Development of the White House Office   1
Structure of the White House Staff   12
Recruiting the White House Staff   15
Styles of Organization of the White House Office   16
Criticism of the White House Staff   21

Executive Office of the President: Supporting Organizations   25

Styles and Methods of Appointment   25
Office of Management and Budget   32
National Security Council   37
Office of Policy Development   39
Council of Economic Advisers   42
Office of the U.S. Trade Representative   47
Office of Science and Technology Policy   49
Council on Environmental Quality   51
Office of Administration   53

Cabinet   57

Origin and Development of the Cabinet   57
Role and Function of the Cabinet   61

Executive Departments   69

Styles and Methods of Appointment   69
Department of Agriculture   76
Department of Commerce   78
Department of Defense   80
Department of Education   82
Department of Energy   84
Department of Health and Human Services   86

Department of Housing and Urban Development   88
Department of the Interior   90
Department of Justice   92
Department of Labor   95
Department of State   97
Department of Transportation   99
Department of the Treasury   101
Department of Veterans Affairs   102

Government Agencies and Corporations   107

Regulatory Agencies   107
Independent Executive Agencies   110
Government Corporations   111
Styles and Methods of Appointment   111
Agency Profiles   113

Presidential Commissions   141

Types of Presidential Commissions   142
The Commissioners   145
Commission Staff   147
How Commissions Operate   149
Functions of Commissions   151

Index   155

Executive Office of the President: White House Office

In contrast to the early days of the presidency, when presidents had little or no staff to help them, the modern presidential establishment is a bureaucracy with thousands of employees, all of whom work for the president. The Executive Office of the President (EOP) is the president's tool for coping with Congress and the far-flung executive branch.

In no real sense is the EOP an "office"; rather, it is a collection of agencies whose only tie is their direct responsibility to the president. The components of the EOP have changed many times over the years as the needs of the presidency have changed. Today some of the major elements of the EOP are the National Security Council, Office of Management and Budget, Council of Economic Advisers, Office of Science and Technology Policy, Office of the Special Representative for Trade Negotiations, and White House Office.

Of these, perhaps the most important and surely the closest to the president is the White House Office. While all of the EOP does the president's business, the White House Office consists of the president's most intimate and trusted advisers. Of the entire presidential establishment, the White House Office is the most loyal to the president and has his or her particular interests most at heart.

A White House staff who knows the president's needs and desires and has political savvy can be a tremendous asset. They can advance the administration's programs to fruition and avoid the potential pitfalls that undermine a president's credibility. Indeed, much of a president's success depends on the ability of the White House staff, while many of a president's failures result from the staff's failures.

Examples of the importance of the White House staff abound. On the one hand, the vision and skill of President John F. Kennedy's staff were very important to his legislative success. The same was true in the early days of Lyndon B. Johnson's administration; the ability of Johnson's staff to deal with Congress was crucial in implementing the "Great Society." The disorganization and inexperience of President Jimmy Carter's staff, on the other hand, undermined his chances of achieving much in Congress. And it was the staff's failure to anticipate problems adequately and protect the president's interests that led to Watergate, which destroyed the presidency of Richard Nixon, and to

the Iran-contra affair, which haunted and weakened Ronald Reagan's second term.

Although the White House staff is important to the president, there is no set pattern for its selection or organization. In fact, the office itself has been in existence for only just over a half century.

Origins and Development of the White House Office

The problem of how to count the White House Office staff is a factor in any discussion of its growth. No universally accepted figures exist on the precise size of the White House staff, and published estimates vary considerably depending on who is counting and how. There are several reasons for this discrepancy: short-term fluctuations in staff size, placement of White House people elsewhere in government, use of detailees, and hiring of staff out of the discretionary funds (such as the Special Projects account) that are available to the president. Consequently, the figures that follow should be treated with caution; they are indicators of trends but are not necessarily exact.[1]

The existence of a large presidential staff is a relatively recent development. Early presidents had little or no staff to assist them, and what staff did exist was strictly clerical. There were no specialized or resident policy advisers, speechwriters, or liaison personnel. Believing that presidents should take care of their own business, Congress did not specifically appropriate funds for staff until 1857, when it provided an allowance for a presidential secretary.

Presidents who wanted more help were forced to hire it themselves and to pay for it out of their own pockets. George Washington hired his nephew to assist him in 1792 and paid him $300 a year from his own salary. Several later presidents followed Washington's lead and retained relatives or cronies in the White House. For most of those employed, however, the pay remained low and the jobs menial. Staff duties consisted almost exclusively of clerical work and scheduling the president's appointments.

Over the years the common practices of nepotism and cronyism resulted in the appointment of several advisers and presidential secretaries who proved hopelessly inadequate. For example, Andrew Johnson appointed his son Robert as secretary to the president even though the youn-

By Stephen L. Robertson

1

ger man was a womanizer and an alcoholic. Ulysses S. Grant's secretary, Gen. Orville E. Babcock, was a corrupt power-grabber who was involved in the Whiskey Ring, a group of liquor producers who were illegally avoiding federal liquor taxes. He eventually was indicted for fraud. And Rutherford B. Hayes chose William K. Rogers, an old classmate who had failed in three careers, as his secretary. Rogers proved inept at that job, too.

Given the limitations of the presidential pockets, as well as the small size of the government as a whole, the White House staff necessarily remained quite small throughout the nineteenth century. Presidents rarely could afford much staff, and they generally made more use of their cabinet as advisers than is true today. Benjamin Harrison was able to house his entire staff next to his living quarters on the second floor of the White House. Herbert Hoover doubled the number of his administrative assistants, increasing them from two to four (which caused a minor sensation). Besides them, Hoover had only military and naval attachés and about forty clerks and typists.

To some extent the small size of these staffs is misleading. Historically, presidents have resorted to "detailing," or borrowing, personnel from the executive departments to carry out various tasks. Thus, a president who needs assistance might requisition an aide or two from the War or State Department. Some presidents placed trusted advisers in positions within the executive branch to keep them available. Andrew Jackson named his close friend Amos Kendall as fourth auditor of the Treasury Department, but Kendall in fact did little work there, instead spending his time assisting Jackson. To keep his brains trust around him, Franklin D. Roosevelt appointed them not to his staff (which was still the size of Hoover's) but to posts in other departments: Raymond Moley became an assistant secretary of state, Rexford G. Tugwell was named assistant secretary of agriculture, and Adolph A. Berle, Jr., was appointed as counsel to the Reconstruction Finance Commission. They did almost no work for their departments, however.

Although the use of detailees was a great asset to presidents, the growing demands of the office meant that presidents needed more in-house advisers who were not encumbered by even minimal jobs elsewhere. As the nation and its government grew in the early twentieth century, the need for a larger presidential staff increased.

The potential value of a larger staff was indicated by the work of some of the presidential secretaries. Daniel G. Rollings, who was secretary to Chester A. Arthur, assisted the president in writing speeches and legislative proposals for Congress. Daniel Lamont was an able administrator, campaign manager, and public relations man for Grover Cleveland (who definitely needed the latter). Joseph P. Tumulty, secretary to Woodrow Wilson, was an all-purpose aide who "functioned as an appointments secretary, political adviser, administrative manager, and public relations aide" as well as a White House doorkeeper.[2] Calvin Coolidge's secretary, C. Bascom Slemp, proved to be an important liaison between the president and the Congress, as well as between the president and his own party. And Louis McHenry Howe was a highly important influence on Franklin Roosevelt until Howe's death in 1935.

Even more significant was the work of aides George B. Cortelyou and William Loeb, Jr. Cortelyou, who later became the first secretary of the Department of Commerce and Labor, was presidential secretary under William McKinley and Theodore Roosevelt. As secretary, particularly

to McKinley, he drafted speeches and messages, scheduled appointments, organized trips, ran the White House clerical staff, and tended to First Lady Ida McKinley, who suffered from poor health. He was also politically adept, working to defeat a possible move against Roosevelt as the vice-presidential nominee in the Republican national convention of 1900 and serving as the de facto president in the immediate aftermath of McKinley's assassination while greatly easing the transition for the vice president.

Loeb followed Cortelyou and was just as valuable while serving under Roosevelt. He too kept the White House and its occupants running smoothly. Loeb also served as the president's sounding board and had no small influence on Roosevelt and his policies. As a political operative, he was instrumental in pulling together support for William Howard Taft in the Republican national convention of 1908.

In the hands of aides such as Cortelyou and Loeb the position of secretary to the president was the crucial one on the presidential staff; indeed, to a large extent it *was* the staff. The presidential secretary was a jack-of-all-trades: legislative drafter, congressional liaison, press and public relations coordinator, appointments and junket scheduler, political manipulator, and White House manager. He was in fact a chief of staff with a very limited kingdom. By the 1930s, however, the responsibilities of the position had outstripped the abilities of any one person to fill them. When Franklin Roosevelt appointed Howe as his secretary in 1933, he also appointed Stephen T. Early as press secretary and Marvin H. McIntyre as appointments secretary. But when Howe died, the position died with him. Roosevelt never filled it, and its responsibilities were distributed eventually throughout a growing White House bureaucracy.

FDR: Beginning of the Present Staff System

The present staff system began during the administration of Franklin Roosevelt (1933-1945). The White House staff had been growing slowly for several years, but it still remained quite small. Like his predecessors, Roosevelt regularly borrowed help from elsewhere in the executive branch, using at least a hundred detailees in each year from 1934 to 1945. Unlike his predecessors, however, he concluded that such arrangements were hopelessly inadequate, and, as an activist president faced with an unprecedented economic crisis, he decided to change them. In his mind, dealing with the nation's problems required a larger permanent staff that worked solely for him. He was not alone in his belief; at least nine proposals for reorganizing the executive branch appeared between 1918 and 1937, and all recognized the need for more executive efficiency and planning capability.[3]

Roosevelt found the justification for his larger staff in the work of the Committee on Administrative Management, more popularly known as the Brownlow Commission. Created on March 20, 1936, the committee—consisting of Louis Brownlow, chairman, and members Charles Merriam and Luther Gulick—was directed to study the staffing needs of the presidency. Declaring that "the American Executive must be regarded as one of the very greatest contributions by our Nation to the development of modern democracy," the committee concluded that "the President needs help ... in dealing with managerial agencies and administrative departments of the Government" and recommended the creation of additional staff to assist him. The committee also recommended that

> these assistants ... not be interposed between the president and the heads of his departments. They would not be assistant presidents in any sense. Their function would be ... to assist [the president] in obtaining quickly and without delay all pertinent information possessed by any of the executive departments so as to guide him in making his responsible decisions; and then when decisions have been made, to assist him in seeing to it that every administrative department and agency affected is properly informed.... They would remain in the background, issue no orders, make no decisions, emit no public statements.... They should be men in whom the president has personal confidence and whose attitude and character are such that they would not attempt to exercise power on their own account. They should be possessed of high competence, great vigor, and a passion of anonymity. They should be installed in the White House itself, directly accessible to the president.[4]

The Brownlow Commission report was submitted to the president in January 1937. Immediately endorsing its findings, with which he completely agreed and over which he had had significant influence, Roosevelt quickly forwarded the report to Congress for authorization to implement the committee's recommendations. The Congress, however, was angry over Roosevelt's ill-fated attempt to pack the Supreme Court, and it refused to act upon the report. Not until April 1939 did Congress agree to most of the Brownlow proposals. (See Executive Office of the President: Supporting Organizations chapter.)

Under the congressional authorization the president was allowed to hire six new administrative assistants, although Roosevelt initially hired only three. Congress also permitted the president to undertake a partial reorganization of the executive branch. On September 8, 1939, Roosevelt issued Executive Order 8248, creating the Executive Office of the President and transferring the Bureau of the Budget (renamed the Office of Management and Budget in 1972) into it from the Treasury Department. The president

intended the EOP to be a more permanent and professional support staff than that of the White House. The White House staff was seen as the president's personal assistants; the EOP was the institutionalized infrastructure of the presidency.

Executive Order 8248 represents the birth of the modern presidency, including the modern White House Office staff. Roosevelt did not greatly increase the size of the staff, however. He preferred and was able to manage with a staff small enough to allow him to interact with all of his aides equally. Thus, the number of presidential aides never exceeded twelve, and the total number of full-time White House employees was fewer than sixty-five.[5] The latter figure stayed relatively low despite a huge increase in mail to the White House, which required hiring more clerical staff to handle it.

Roosevelt's staff remained not only small but also rather unstructured. Disliking flow charts and rigid hierarchies, the president preferred to work on an ad hoc basis, distributing assignments to whoever was then available. Few of his aides had specific titles. Aside from Press Secretary Early and Appointments Secretary McIntyre, only Harry L. Hopkins, who bore the title of special assistant to the president, and Samuel I. Rosenman, who was the counsel to the president, had special designations. Nevertheless, the first steps toward the differentiated structures maintained by other presidents were taken under Roosevelt. Hopkins, who had extensive influence over foreign affairs during the war years, was another forerunner of the chief of staff who would appear in later administrations. Rosenman's position was created just for him on the grounds that the president required an in-house legal adviser.

Thus, by the end of the Roosevelt administration the need for a larger staff had been recognized, and its expansion and differentiation had begun. The increasing role of the national government, both domestically and internationally, would fuel further staff growth over the next decades.

Franklin D. Roosevelt Library

Although FDR's staff remained small, unstructured, and free of specific titles, Harry Hopkins, left, a special assistant to the president, was a forerunner of today's White House chief of staff.

The Truman Staff:
The Beginnings of Growth

Roosevelt's White House staff had swelled to meet the demands of the war years. Distrusting the larger staff and fearing that it would impede his interaction with his cabinet and the rest of the government, President Harry S Truman (1945-1953) initially planned to return his staff to its prewar size. He quickly found that this was impossible, however. With Europe in ruins, the United States was the leader in the international community. At home the difficulties of restoring the economy to a peacetime status and repairing the dislocations caused by war created economic and political tensions for the federal government. The result was increasing pressure upon the Truman White House for action, which inevitably led to a staff size that exceeded that of the Roosevelt years. Furthermore, where Roosevelt had maintained a fairly small permanent staff and used a large number of detailees, by 1947 Truman had reversed that trend, employing an in-house staff of two hundred or more while detailing only a handful of other aides. The earlier practice of storing advisers in various government posts also came to an end. After Truman, presidents simply brought whatever advisers they wished into the White House, creating new positions for them if necessary.

The staff evolved in structure as well as size during the Truman years. When he became president, Truman inherited Roosevelt's relatively unstructured staffing system, which provided access to the president and allowed Roosevelt to play his advisers against one another. Truman valued the accessibility the open system allowed, but he found the intrastaff competition it fostered too chaotic and soon called for more structure.

To this end, Truman created the position of assistant to the president in 1946 and named John Roy Steelman to fill it. One of Steelman's duties was to serve as a link with the domestic agencies and to resolve many of their problems and disputes. As such, he too was a direct forerunner of the chief of staff who would emerge in later administrations. Unfortunately, Steelman was not very successful at keeping problems from the president; he was reluctant to bruise feelings, and Truman was unable to distance himself from the everyday problems of his administration.

Besides Steelman, Truman's staff consisted of a press secretary, an appointments secretary, a personnel director, a special counsel, a legislative drafter, a military aide and a naval aide, a special assistant, a minority liaison, a few speechwriters (who also doubled as general assistants), and the more institutionalized position of budget director. Clerical and subordinate aides made up the remaining staff.

During the Truman years Congress created two other bodies within EOP to assist the president. The National Security Act of 1946 established the National Security Council (NSC) to help the president deal with foreign policy problems. The NSC membership (as amended in 1949) consisted of the president, the vice president, the secretaries of state and defense, and anyone else the president wished to invite. The NSC was designed to insure coordination among the foreign policy agencies so that the president would be given the necessary facts and options about a problem quickly and efficiently.

Skeptical of a body that had been thrust upon him, Truman made little use of the NSC before the Korean War. Indeed, the decision to intervene in Korea was made with-

out formally consulting the NSC at all. During the war Truman found ways to use the NSC to his advantage and met with it more frequently, but the importance of the NSC as a personal staff remained minor.

The second body created to assist Truman was the three-member Council of Economic Advisers (CEA), intended to be the president's primary source of economic information and advice. As with the National Security Council, Truman rarely used the CEA at first, in part because under chairman Edwin G. Nourse it provided abstract advice devoid of any political considerations. It was only when Leon Keyserling replaced Nourse as chairman in 1949 that the CEA emerged as an important body. *(See Executive Office of the President: Supporting Organizations chapter.)*

The Truman administration also saw the emergence of staffers as policy advocates. Truman's special counsel, Clark M. Clifford, was a key figure in advocating liberal positions before the president. Such a role defied the original vision of the Brownlow Commission, which had proposed that aides be neutral facilitators of policy decisions; policy advocacy was to be left to the cabinet. Clifford's role of policy advocate represented a potentially major change in the role of the White House staff, but its extent would not be realized until later.

Thus, under Truman the White House staff increased in size and took on a more formal structure. Differentiation increased as particular staff members were assigned specific areas of responsibility, and White House staffers began to acquire small staffs of their own. In addition, Congress added two new bodies to the White House to assist the president. Finally, policy advocacy began to move into the White House and out of the cabinet where it theoretically belonged.

Despite these important developments, however, the Truman White House did not wield much power overall. With the exception of Clifford and W. Averell Harriman, who was in the administration only briefly, no major names or dominant personalities stood out on Truman's staff. Moreover, Truman preferred to use his cabinet as policy advisers; his staff was not allowed to gain much influence. The makings of a powerful staff were there but were not realized until later administrations.

Eisenhower and the Formalized Staff

Under Dwight D. Eisenhower (1953-1961) the staff grew in both size and complexity. As a former general and a career military officer, Eisenhower recognized the benefits of a properly structured staff. A well-organized staff could handle the simple problems and minor tactical details at the lower levels, allowing the commander to concentrate on the major problems and questions. Reacting to what he saw as confusion within the Roosevelt and Truman administrations, Eisenhower preached that organization could provide a more efficient, high-quality government. His message resulted in the most highly structured and diversified staff seen to that time in the White House.

Eisenhower's staff included many of the elements found in the Truman White House. His press secretary, James C. Hagerty, won a considerable reputation for his skillful handling of the position. Other staff members were an appointments secretary, a special counsel, and, of course, the much-needed clerks, typists, and messengers.

Several new positions were created as well. The Congressional Relations Office was established to facilitate interaction between the White House and Congress. The liaison aide was responsible for conveying the president's wishes to Congress, lobbying there for the president's programs, and relaying congressional feedback. This was not a completely new position; Matthew Connelly had fulfilled the same functions without the title under Truman, while others had acted in the same capacity for Roosevelt (including the president himself). Still, Eisenhower was the first to operate openly a congressional liaison office and to give it a formal place in the White House.

To improve the flow of paperwork through the channels of the administration, Eisenhower created the positions of staff secretary and secretary to the cabinet. In particular, the cabinet secretary's job was to improve the cabinet's ability to advise the president by coordinating meetings and facilitating communications between the two.

Eisenhower also used the position of special adviser to the president to bring in his own experts as needed. For example, he responded to the Soviet launching of *Sputnik* in 1957 by naming a science adviser. Many of these special advisers made a significant contribution to the Eisenhower administration. The president's Open Skies proposal of 1955, for example, which called for surveillance flights to allow each super power to monitor the other's military installations, was devised by Nelson A. Rockefeller, who was then serving as a special adviser.

All these additions, made in the name of efficiency, naturally swelled the White House staff. The number of professionals appointed by the president in the White House increased from 32 in 1953 to 50 by 1960.[6] Overall, the size of the permanent staff increased by some 90 people, to 355, during the same period.

Eisenhower also made important changes in the way some existing personnel were used. One major change concerned the National Security Council. Truman rarely met with the NSC before the outbreak of the Korean War in 1950 and never gave it much structure. To Eisenhower, however, the NSC appeared much more useful. He created an extensive apparatus that could examine problems and produce analyses and options for him. Under Eisenhower the NSC became an important element in the foreign policy process, although certainly not the dominant one. The lead in U.S. foreign policy remained with John Foster Dulles and the State Department. The president also created the post of national security adviser. This new adviser served as the administrative head of the NSC and as the president's personal aide in foreign policy matters. For Eisenhower, the national security adviser had the important job of coordinating America's foreign policy apparatus and providing him with timely information.

In one other major staff change Eisenhower elevated the role of the assistant to the president, which under Truman had not been very important. Believing in hierarchy and not wanting to be bothered with unnecessary details, Eisenhower sought an aide to manage the White House, much as his chief of staff had managed his headquarters staff in the army. In filling this post, Eisenhower's assistant, Sherman Adams, became the gatekeeper to the president during Eisenhower's first six years in office.

As presidential chief of staff, Adams was perceived as possessing enormous power; anyone wishing to do business with the president had to pass through Adams first. Given Eisenhower's distaste for routine matters, it seemed certain that a great many decisions were being made by Adams, not Eisenhower. Commentators described Adams as an "assistant president," particularly in domestic affairs in which Eisenhower had less interest. Indeed, some saw Adams as running domestic policy during his stint as assistant to the president. One contemporary observer noted that

> Adams has handled a considerable amount of the work that in past administrations has been done by the president himself.... While it has not been an inflexible rule, it has been the general practice that almost everything of importance in the White House bearing on domestic and political policy clears through Adams.... He is the channel through which many of the most important projects in domestic affairs reach the president ... [and] by the time [they] have reached the president they have already been shaped in part by Adams himself. Time and again when a caller or official springs an idea on Eisenhower, the president will tell him, "Take it up with Sherman." [7]

In reality, Adams probably did not have that much power. Witnesses within the administration have recalled that while Adams had great influence over administrative matters in the White House, he rarely was involved in policy discussions. Others remember considerable interaction among staff members, despite the staff hierarchy. In any case it is certain that Adams, in his role of official presidential choke point, possessed a degree of influence that was unprecedented for a White House staffer. It would pave the way for powerful staffs in the future.

Eisenhower thus introduced many changes in the White House staff; he increased its numbers, formalized its structure, and built a fairly strict operational hierarchy. With the exception of Adams, however, his staff remained largely anonymous and relatively uninfluential. Eisenhower believed that his staff should be subordinate to the cabinet and remain in the background, and he tried to operate his administration along those lines. To him, the staff was supposed to move information and help policy makers, not make policy itself.

Kennedy and Johnson: The Birth of the Activist Staff

John F. Kennedy (1961-1963) came to the presidency determined to eliminate the elaborate mechanisms that Eisenhower had created in the White House. Convinced that Eisenhower's staff structure was too restrictive and left the president too removed from his own administration, Kennedy deliberately attempted a return to a staff more akin to that of Franklin Roosevelt. He replaced the committees and secretariats that had supported the cabinet and the NSC under Eisenhower with a few senior aides who had distinct yet overlapping responsibilities. The overlap occurred because the staff structure was fluid, and because Kennedy tended to hand out assignments as they arose to whoever was available rather than channeling them to a predesignated individual.

Kennedy's staff included several of the now-established White House positions: press secretary, special counsel, appointments secretary, congressional liaison, and national security adviser. He had no formal chief of staff. Appointments secretary Kenneth P. O'Donnell doubled as White House administrator, while Kennedy himself controlled the paper flow, personally receiving reports from subordinates. He also had no designated speechwriters; as with Roosevelt, speech-writing duties were spread among his aides, most notably his special counsel, Theodore C. Sorensen.

In spite of the dismantling of Eisenhower's staff system, the Kennedy White House did not decrease in size. Under Kennedy the regular White House employees numbered between 300 and 350, which was less than during Eisenhower's second term (but not his first). Kennedy used far more detailees than Eisenhower, however. His White House employed between 429 and 476 full-time personnel—figures unmatched by any previous administration.

The continual growth of the White House staff reflected the increasing tendency of the public to look to Washington, and particularly the White House, for solutions to the nation's problems. This tendency was only accelerated by events such as the Berlin controversy and the Cuban missile crisis. As one scholar noted:

> The White House was allowed to keep growing because there was no resistance to growth. Indeed, creating another White House office was often the easiest way to solve a personnel or constituent problem, a conferring of high status with little effort. The White House was the only place in government where the president could totally control expenditures and was free to move personnel and establish units at will.[8]

The ease with which the White House staff could be expanded made such expansion irresistible.

The most significant development in the staff during the Kennedy years was not the increase in its size but in its responsibilities and influence. As a group, Kennedy's senior aides had far more influence than any previously. They meshed well with one another and with the boss. Because they thought along the same lines as Kennedy and often could anticipate him, they were readily able to speak for the president. This gave them a good deal of clout in Washington.

Beyond this, the influence of Kennedy's staff was increased by the governing style of the president himself. Kennedy was an activist president who wanted to get things done and to fulfill his campaign promise to get the country moving again. He sought actions and results. Inevitably, perhaps, he became frustrated with the permanent government, which was filled with elaborate standing routines and career bureaucrats who shared neither his goals nor his sense of urgency. He quickly came to regard the bureaucracy as "an institutional resistance movement . . . a force against innovation with an inexhaustible capacity to dilute, delay, and obstruct presidential purpose."[9] To prod and even avoid the bureaucracy, he turned to his staff, and, being activists like the president, they were eager to respond.

Like other presidents, Kennedy came into office intending to rely on his cabinet for policy innovations and advice. He quickly discovered, however, that cabinet meetings were dull and unproductive (he soon discontinued them) and that the loyalty of many of his department heads was open to question. He thus turned to other resources.

As a result, Kennedy's staff became involved in policy making to an unprecedented degree. Previous presidents had, with exceptions, prevented the White House staff from crossing the line that separated facilitating decisions from making decisions. The staff aided but rarely advised. Kennedy's senior staff became advisers and advocates more than aides. They were involved directly in many policy decisions, and as their importance swelled accordingly, they began acquiring larger staffs to assist them. Kennedy was in fact beginning to pull policy making, and thus power, out of the executive departments and concentrate it within the White House.

Kennedy's "New Frontier" was devised and advocated by his staff, largely under Sorensen's direction, not by the bureaucracy. Many other programs were handled similarly. Perhaps the staff's greatest influence lay in foreign policy. Having destroyed Eisenhower's elaborate NSC apparatus, and highly frustrated by the State Department, Kennedy turned to his national security adviser, McGeorge Bundy, and gave him a central role in the formulation and conduct of his foreign policy.

Kennedy's staff lacked that "passion for anonymity" that the Brownlow Commission had advocated. As the "president's men," they clearly stood apart from the rest of the government and were more visible than previous staffs. And while it was probably not anyone's conscious intent—for in theory the staff was still just a link between the president and the bureaucracy—the White House staff began to take on the characteristics of a shadow government, parallel to the bureaucracy.

When he became president on November 22, 1963, Lyndon B. Johnson inherited Kennedy's staff and its organization, which for various reasons he found acceptable and so left intact. Like Kennedy, he intended to follow the example of Franklin Roosevelt, and the fluid nature of Kennedy's staff suited him.

The White House staff continued to grow in influence during the Johnson administration (1963-1969). Johnson too was an activist president who wanted rapid access to the information and ideas needed to help him formulate new policies. He also wanted his staff to have sufficient authority to supervise policy implementation. LBJ found the cabinet departments to be too slow and ponderous to be truly useful, but he continued to hold cabinet meetings merely to obtain endorsement of his plans. This concentration of power in the White House was reinforced by Johnson's dominant personality, which led him to extend his control as much as possible. Later, the public outcry against his conduct of the Vietnam War caused him to withdraw into the sanctuary of the White House, relying on his staff even more.

Initially, Johnson kept Kennedy's people and staff arrangements, but as they gradually left he began clarifying the areas of responsibility within his staff. He maintained the usual press secretary, appointments secretary, special counsel (and deputy counsels), and congressional liaison offices. The latter received particular attention under Johnson, who had an extensive background in Congress. Speechwriters generally were drawn from other positions. Johnson also used his aides as links to groups outside the White House such as business, labor, and various religious and ethnic organizations. He was in fact operating a public liaison staff, although no formal structure or title was ever devised.

The major structural development of the Johnson administration was the creation of a domestic policy staff within the White House. The notion of a domestic policy adviser was not new; although he had had the title special counsel, Theodore Sorensen had performed a similar function for Kennedy. Johnson established the role as a separate position placed in the hands of Joseph A. Califano, Jr., and a small staff of assistants. Califano was responsible for isolating domestic problems, producing proposals for possible solutions, and assisting with the production of Johnson's legislative programs.

Although the president's activism and desire for control caused more authority to be vested in the White House staff, the staff's visibility decreased somewhat. Johnson preferred the public limelight for himself, particularly during the early days of his administration, and he downplayed his staff.

Overall, the White House staff increased in size and authority during the Johnson administration. Because the president used many detailees, his White House staff always numbered over four hundred, and in 1967 there were almost five hundred. The demands of his office and his own personality caused Johnson to concentrate more power within the White House than any previous president. Thus, the White House staff that Johnson passed on to Nixon was both the largest and most influential in history.

The Imperial White House: The Nixon Staff

By 1969 two major trends characterized the development of the White House staff. The first was a continuing trend toward increased size and complexity. The second was a tendency for presidents to consolidate resources and hence power within the White House. Eisenhower had demonstrated the virtues of a large and structured staff; Kennedy and Johnson had developed the staff to promote policy. These trends and characteristics came together in the Nixon administration (1969-1974).

The White House Office of Richard Nixon had by far the most elaborate structure seen to that time. As vice president during the Eisenhower administration, Nixon had observed firsthand the benefits of Eisenhower's staff hierarchy. Like Eisenhower, Nixon felt that he as president should deal with the broad policies, not the trivial details. He was also a private man who valued his time alone and preferred to make decisions solitarily, working from briefing papers. The staff he installed was designed to operate smoothly and to protect him from the outside distractions he disliked.

As originally constructed, Nixon's White House Office had four areas of operations: foreign policy, domestic affairs, congressional relations, and White House operations. *(See Figure 1.)* Each was headed by an administrative assistant responsible for its coordination and operation, assisted by a large number of specialists in various policy areas. The system was designed to channel expertise to the president and to facilitate the implementation of his decisions.

Nixon maintained the traditional offices of press secretary, appointments secretary, and special counsel, as well as a personnel office for staff selection and a small political operations staff. He also gathered a stable of designated speechwriters, something Kennedy and Johnson had abandoned.

Specialization was common on the Nixon staff. In his speech-writing operation, for example, Nixon had three primary speechwriters: Patrick J. Buchanan, William Safire,

Figure 1   Organization of the Nixon White House, 1972

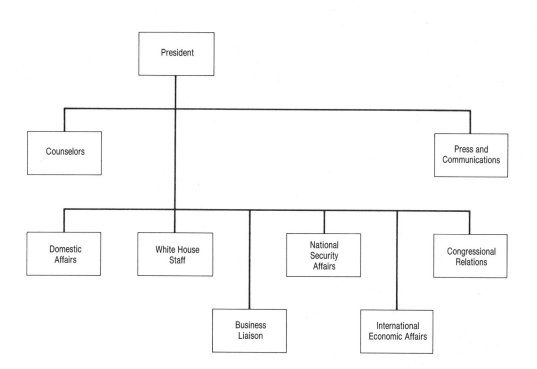

Source: Stephen J. Wayne, *The Legislative Presidency* (New York: Harper and Row, 1978), 48. Copyright © 1978 by Stephen J. Wayne. Reprinted by permission of the author.

and Raymond Price, who represented, respectively, the right, center, and left of the Republican party. Nixon never combined the talents of these men; rather, he used them selectively, depending on the nature of the speech he was to deliver. It was a highly specialized arrangement.[10]

The cornerstone of the structure was the chief of staff, a position Nixon resurrected and gave to H. R. Haldeman. Haldeman's task was to shield the president from unwanted paperwork, problems, or visitors, and to see that the business of the White House was carried out efficiently. He proved to be ruthlessly effective in his job. As the president's gatekeeper, he had as much or more authority than any staffer had ever possessed.

Staff innovations during the Nixon administration included a formalized Domestic Council. Unlike Kennedy and Johnson, who had maintained an untitled domestic adviser on their staffs (Sorensen and Califano, respectively), Nixon originally had two domestic advisory staffs, one under Daniel Patrick Moynihan and the other under Arthur F. Burns. Because Moynihan and Burns generally took opposing sides on policy questions, Nixon found himself being an arbitrator, a role he acutely disliked. Thus, he began using his special counsel, John D. Ehrlichman, as an intermediary.

Eventually, Ehrlichman replaced both Burns and Moynihan, and in November 1969 he was officially named as assistant to the president for domestic affairs. Eight months later Nixon established the Domestic Council, a counterpart to the NSC, and Ehrlichman became its director. The Domestic Council was supposed to coordinate the domestic policy-making apparatus, isolating and analyzing problems and providing possible solutions to the president. Several presidents had attempted to improve the domestic policy machinery, but the council was the most formal attempt to do so.

Nixon also originated the White House Communications Office, which essentially was a public relations arm of the White House. Other presidents such as Kennedy had been concerned with public relations, but they had left it to the press secretary's office, which rarely had much time for it. To Nixon, public relations was far more important; as much as one-fifth of his entire staff was dealing with press and public relations.[11] The Communications Office became a separate operation, a sister to the press secretary's office, and it continued to operate separately even after Nixon's press secretary, Ronald Ziegler, also became communications director.

This specialized structure naturally demanded still more personnel within the White House. In fact, Nixon had the largest White House staff in history. The number of detailees dropped dramatically after 1970, but the decrease was matched by an increase in permanent staff. In all, the Nixon White House never employed fewer than five hundred people, and in 1970 the number of staffers exceeded six hundred.

During the Nixon administration the White House Office became a small bureaucracy. The patterns of growth and formalization that had been developing for years culminated under Nixon, resulting in a largely depersonalized staff that was out of contact with the president it served. Franklin Roosevelt had worked closely with all his aides; in the Nixon White House there were assistants to the president who rarely, if ever, saw him. Nixon could not hope to supervise his staff; the staff had to control itself.

At the same time Nixon's staff had an enormous amount of power, to the extent that the White House largely became the government, rendering much of the regular government to a role of secondary importance. Problems were identified, options evaluated, and decisions made and implemented with minimal, if any, help from the traditional bureaucratic agencies. An increasing number of decisions and details formerly left to the executive departments were taken over by the White House staff. The White House bureaucracy mirrored and then overshadowed the permanent bureaucracy. Those who had problems learned to go not to the bureaucracy but to the appropriate official in the White House where the real power was. Interest groups, members of Congress, and even executive department officials had to take their business to the White House if they hoped to get decisions and actions. Sen. Ernest F. Hollings (D-S.C.) complained:

> It used to be that if I had a problem with food stamps, I went to see the secretary of agriculture, whose department had jurisdiction over that problem. Not anymore. Now, if I want to learn the policy, I must go to the White House to consult with John Price. If I want the latest in textiles, I won't get it from the secretary of commerce, who has the authority and responsibility. No, I am forced to go to the White House and see Mr. Peter Flanigan. I shouldn't feel too badly. Secretary [of Commerce Maurice] Stans has to do the same thing.[12]

For its part the staff frequently screened callers as it saw fit. To an unprecedented degree the White House staff was actually running the government's agencies.

The extent of the staff's power was seen most clearly in the role of the National Security Council under Henry A. Kissinger. The NSC structure resembled that of the State Department, with "desks" for the various world regions. All of the important foreign policy decisions originated in the NSC, which also played a key role in implementing them. For example, Nixon's China initiative was conducted without the knowledge of the State Department. Similarly, overtures toward the Soviet Union and Vietnam, among others, were largely devised and executed by the White House. The State Department generally was bypassed and the secretary of state reduced to a figurehead. At one point the world was treated to the spectacle of Secretary of State William P. Rogers publicly insisting that he really *did* have some role in the administration's foreign policy process.

While all the power amassed in the Nixon White House and the EOP allowed the presidency to operate the government almost autonomously, the same organization, having been designed to serve the president, was unable to distinguish between his best interests and those of the country. The staff's power, its zeal in serving Nixon, and its lack of outside supervision contributed to the political and legal excesses known collectively as Watergate. Watergate would cost many staffers, including Haldeman and Ehrlichman, their positions and eventually would drive Nixon from the White House. It also arrested, or at least slowed, the steady trend toward a larger and more powerful White House staff.

Ford, Carter, and Reagan: Trends in White House Staffing

The perceived power of Nixon's staff, with its tight shielding of the president, and the abuses stemming from its blind loyalty led to protests about the increasing authority gathered within the White House. Partly in response, both Gerald R. Ford (1974-1977) and Jimmy Carter

Figure 2 Organization of the Ford White House, 1976

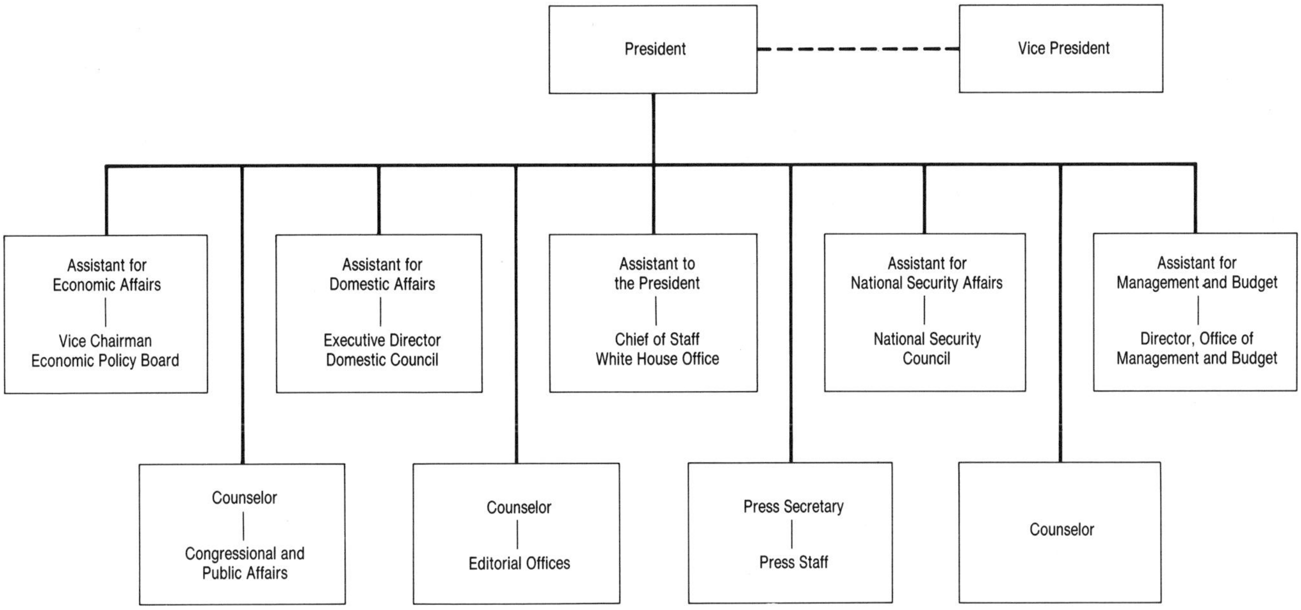

Source: Stephen J. Wayne, *The Legislative Presidency* (New York: Harper and Row, 1978), 53. Copyright © 1978 by Stephen J. Wayne. Reprinted by permission of the author.

(1977-1981) tried to create staff structures that avoided the excesses of the Nixon White House.

On paper, Ford's staff was structured much like the Nixon staff he had inherited, with its characteristic hierarchy and specialization. *(See Figure 2.)* Ford wanted more openness, however, and so he increased the number of advisers who had ready access to him. Whereas hardly anyone beyond Haldeman, Ehrlichman, and Kissinger had had easy access to Nixon, all of Ford's senior aides could see him at any time. In fact, Ford soon discovered that he had become too available and began to restrict access to better use his time.

Carter attempted a return to the Roosevelt-Kennedy models of White House staffing. Ford had tried to downplay the role of the chief of staff; Carter tried to eliminate it altogether. He wanted an informal structure in which a number of aides would have ready access to him, and he would be staff coordinator. The Nixon hierarchy was abandoned.

Like Ford, Carter found this arrangement unworkable. By 1976 the White House had become so large and complex that some hierarchical structure was essential. *(See Figure 3.)* Both Ford and Carter became bogged down in details and problems that swallowed up the time they needed for more important matters. They also found themselves settling turf disputes among their aides. Eventually, both turned to a chief of staff and reimposed hierarchy upon the White House.

Neither president was able to reduce the staff's influence as much as he wanted. Both sang the praises of cabinet government, but both found that it was confusing and ineffective. In what had become a very large and diversified White House, both Ford and Carter maintained the basic offices of press secretary, special counsel, appointments secretary, speechwriters, congressional liaison, cabinet secretary, staff secretary, public liaison, and domestic and national security advisers. Many of these offices had become rather large. For example, under Ford's press secretary, Ron Nessen, there were two deputy press secretaries, eight assistant secretaries (including ones for domestic affairs, foreign affairs, and administration), a personal photographer to the president, and the necessary clerical workers.

White House growth also reflected the rise of special-interest groups in American politics. Between 1975 and 1979 White House liaison offices were established for business and trade associations, minorities, Hispanics, civil rights, consumer affairs, youth, women, and senior citizens. There was also an assistant for human resources and a director of White House conferences.

Such specialization meant that the staff remained large, despite the efforts of Ford and Carter to reduce it. Ford's total staff remained at between 500 and 550, but Carter was able to reduce his staff to about 460 by 1978. By the end of his administration, however, it had returned to about 500.

By 1980 the White House had developed to such a size and complexity that major staff reductions had become difficult, if not impossible, to make. It also was impossible to operate the staff without a chief of staff and clear lines of authority. To structure the staff in the Rooseveltian manner would mean a loss of efficiency and control.

Figure 3   Organization of the Carter White House, 1980

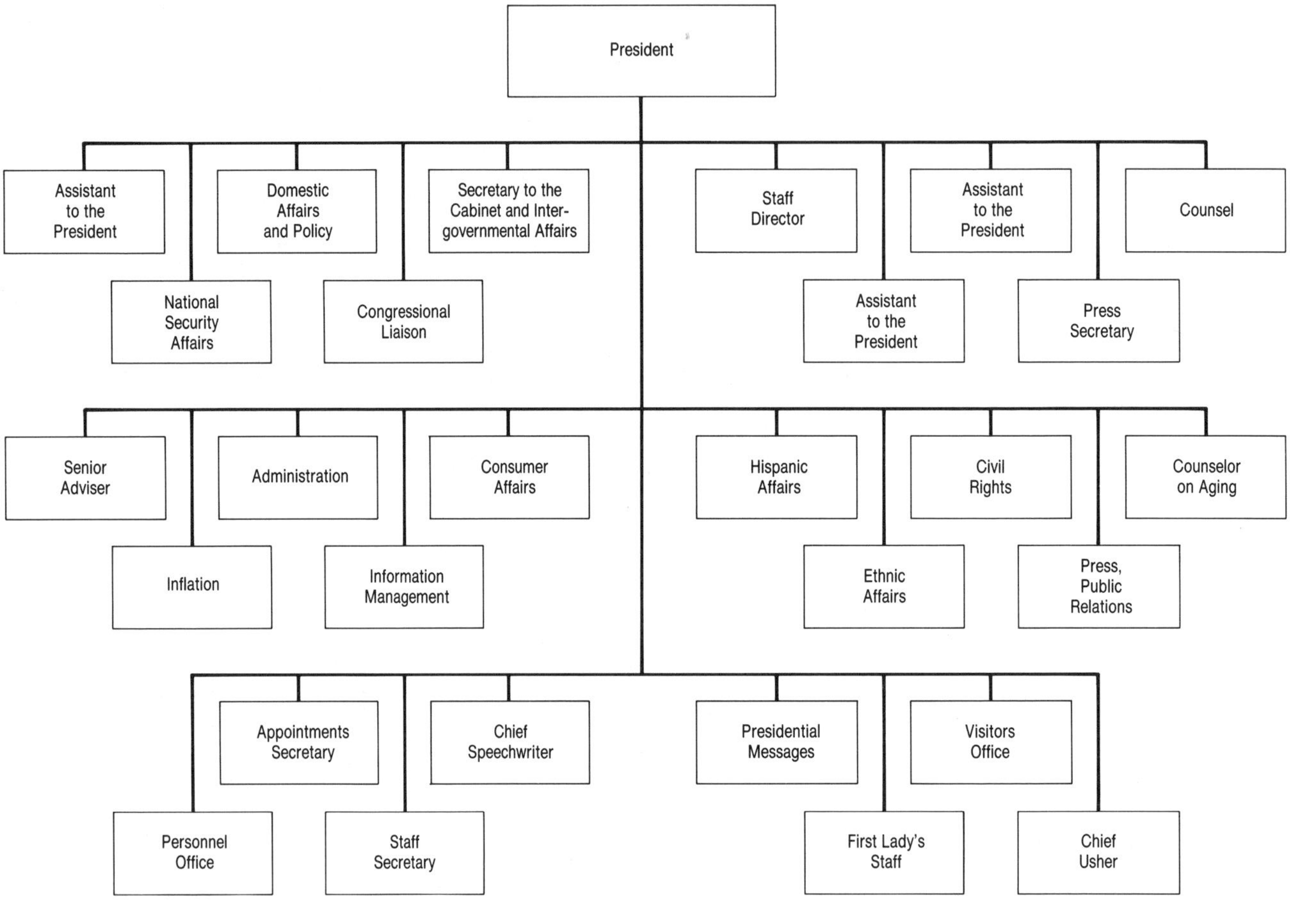

Source: Hugh Heclo and Lester M. Salamon, eds., *The Illusion of Presidential Government* (Boulder, Colo: Westview Press, 1981), 314.

Just as Ford and Carter organized their staffs in partial reaction to the Nixon experience, the Reagan administration (1981-1989) built a staff with one eye on the problems faced by its immediate predecessors. Moreover, Ronald Reagan saw no reason to tie himself up with technical details, preferring to concentrate instead on general strategies and broad policies as well as political leadership. In response to Carter's perceived obsession with details, President Reagan removed himself from the minutiae of governing perhaps more than any president in the modern era.

Thus, the Reagan staff was designed to implement the president's desire to avoid unnecessary details. It was carefully structured to work out policy specifics at lower levels; only the most important questions and broad outlines of policy were taken to the president. The staff was sufficiently specialized and hierarchical to ensure that Reagan could focus on his role as the "Great Communicator." He retained most of the offices that had become an institutionalized part of the White House, including a chief of staff, a special counsel, and a new position, counsellor to the president, which was created for Reagan's close adviser Edwin Meese III. *(See Figure 4.)*

One innovation in the Reagan White House was the Office of Planning and Evaluation (OPE), which coordinated the development of Reagan's policies with the public mood. The OPE used data from public opinion surveys to gauge public receptiveness to Reagan's programs and made long-range plans for their form and nature accordingly. This office represented the most sophisticated use of pollsters to date by the White House. While all presidents since FDR had used polling data, only Carter had a pollster as even an informal staffer, and none had institutionalized public opinion studies like the Reagan White House.[13]

Other innovations in the Reagan White House included the creation of a cabinet secretariat to coordinate interaction between the White House and the cabinet departments and an office of political affairs to work with political elements outside the White House such as the Republican party.

The Reagan staff was also original in its initial structure. As first created, the staff was subdivided to split policy formulation from political action. Separate units were charged with formulating administration policy and implementing it. A third section of the staff handled administrative details for the White House. The White House

Figure 4 Organization of the Reagan White House, 1981

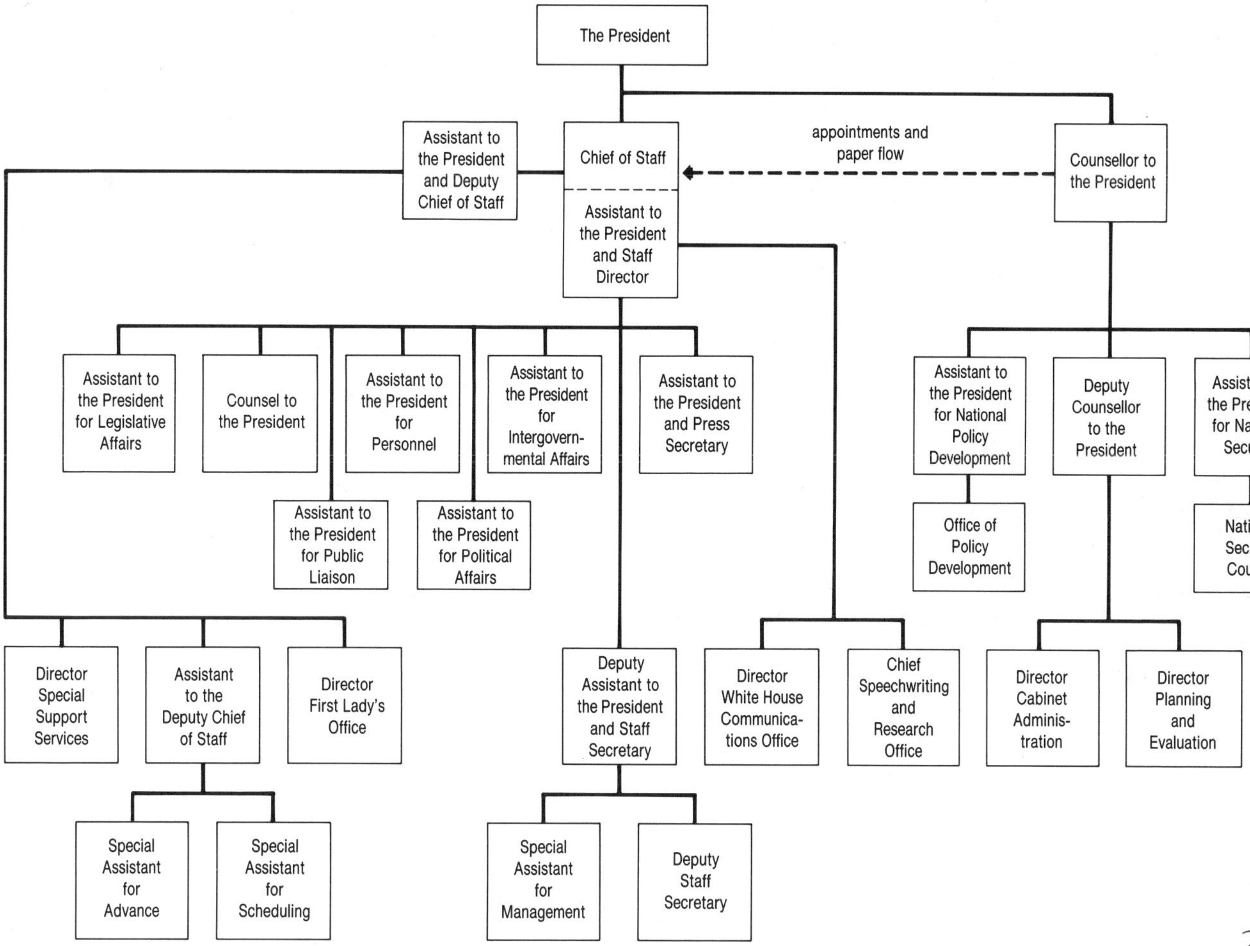

Source: Samuel Kernell and Samuel L. Popkin, eds., *Chief of Staff: Twenty-five Years of Managing the Presidency* (Berkeley: University of California Press, 1986), 202. Copyright © 1986 by the Regents of the University of California.

staff had for many years been engaged in both policy development and policy advocacy, but an institutionalized division between the two functions was unique in the evolution of the White House Office.

The Reagan White House remained large and specialized. President Reagan entered office declaring his love of cabinet government, but like Ford and Carter, he found that goal unattainable. Thus, his staff numbers did not greatly decline; he began with about 450 permanent employees and a budget of $21 million, and there was some minimal reduction.[14] The decline in size may have been largely an illusion, however. Presidential scholar Thomas E. Cronin has argued that the staff reduction was achieved on paper by moving the Office of Administration and the Office of Policy Development from the White House Office into the EOP, where they performed the same duties as before.[15]

Within the staff there was a shift as the roles of its most influential members—the national security and domestic advisers—were de-emphasized and the role of budget director was upgraded. Yet overall, despite another president's original desire to return to cabinet government, the White House staff remained an influential force in the federal government.

The Modern White House Staff

By 1989 the White House had evolved into an institutionalized bureaucracy with several hundred employees (several thousand if the EOP is included) and a multimillion-dollar budget, all of which exists solely to assist the president. Its influence remains formidable; even under Carter and Reagan, who sought to de-emphasize their staffs, the White House dominated the policy apparatus and monitored the bureaucracy. And it still had the ability to conduct operations on its own, as the Iran-contra affair indicated. It remains "the directing force of the presidential branch."[16]

Successive presidents have sought with little success to reduce the power and size of the White House, but today the White House bureaucracy has become a permanent fixture of American politics. Presidential scholars have noted several reasons for this. Perhaps the major reason is the public's tendency, in an era of ongoing crises, to expect the president to solve every problem from national defense and economic recession to drug addiction and AIDS. The president can respond only by appointing more staff to deal with all these expectations.

More presidential staff are also needed to coordinate

policy within the executive branch. Problems and the policies to deal with them now often spill across neat departmental divisions; farm policy, for example, may be the province of not only the Department of Agriculture but also the Departments of Treasury, Commerce, Labor, and even State. Coordination of all these agencies requires some direction from the top—and therefore more staff.

A correlation between the level of presidential skepticism about the performance of the permanent bureaucracy and the size of the White House staff is also evident. Either because they become impatient with the snail's pace maintained by the executive departments (Kennedy and Johnson), or because they see a bureaucracy filled with personnel left over from previous administrations and perhaps unsympathetic to their programs (Nixon), presidents often try to control within the White House as much of the development and implementation of their programs as possible. And the more activist presidents have the largest staffs.

The growth of the White House staff also parallels the growth of the congressional staff. In an effort to offset the capabilities of the executive departments, Congress has increased the size of both its personal and committee staffs over the last thirty years. In 1955 the total congressional staff (personal, committee, and support staff) was 5,585. By 1982 the number of total staff had swollen to 18,761, and either chamber had more staff than the entire Congress of 1955: the Senate staff numbered 6,800, while the staff of the House of Representatives numbered 11,961.[17] Since most of the contact between the president and Congress takes place at the staff level, an increase in congressional staff almost inevitably leads to a corresponding increase in presidential staff.

White House staff growth also has been prompted by the inclusion of special-interest representation within the White House. Since the Truman administration, presidential aides have been designated, at first unofficially but then more formally, as liaisons to certain groups in society such as labor or religious groups. The trickle of recognition has gradually grown into a torrent as literally dozens of groups have gained a voice within the White House. Cronin has noted that

> a partial listing of staff specializations that have been grafted onto the White House in recent years ... [forms] a veritable index of American society: budget and management, national security, economics, congressional matters, science and technology, drug abuse prevention, telecommunications, consumers, national goals, intergovernmental relations, environment, domestic policy, international economics, military affairs, civil rights, disarmament, labor relations, District of Columbia, cultural affairs, education, foreign trade and tariffs, the aged, health and nutrition, physical fitness, volunteerism, intellectuals, Blacks, youth, women, Wall Street, governors, mayors, "ethnics," regulatory agencies and related industry, state party chairmen.[18]

The multitude of interests with ties to the White House and the larger staff needed to deal with them helps explain the growth not only of the White House Office but also of the entire EOP.

A final factor in the growth of the White House staff is its increased concern with the president's public image. Every president has wanted to put forward the best image possible, but this concern took on greater sophistication beginning with the Nixon administration. The modern White House maintains considerable staff to manage the news and to handle public relations in an effort to "sell" the president and presidential programs to the people. Even pollsters have become a part of the presidential staff.

Structure of the White House Staff

As the president's personal staff, members of the White House organization provide the president with the advice and information needed to make decisions and try to ensure that presidential decisions are carried out. Their loyalty is to the president whose best interests are always in mind. Within the government the White House Office is the president's only exclusive domain.

Unlike other parts of the Executive Office of the President, the White House staff is not institutionalized and can change in size and form to suit a president's managerial style. Congress has been careful not to impose any structure upon it. Members of the White House staff are appointed solely by the president and are not subject to congressional confirmation. Staffers have no government status and no tenure in their position; they serve at the president's discretion and can be dismissed at any time for any reason.

While staffers may have enormous influence, that influence depends entirely upon their relationship with the president. With no independent power base, staff members may find that their influence will wax and wane according to their intimacy with the boss. Staffers with offices near the Oval Office, or those who have ready access to the president, are likely to be very powerful. Those who are stuck in the White House basement and see the president only by appointment are much less influential. Within the White House staff, proximity is everything. Thus, allotment of offices and the right to be the first or last to see the president each day become vital matters.

The following description of units within the White House staff must be prefaced with a caveat. In simple terms there is nothing fixed about the White House. Presidents can create, abolish, or reorganize its offices as they choose. Indeed, presidents are free to eliminate the entire staff if they wish. Similarly, the functions assigned to a given office may vary from one administration to another, and sometimes even within an administration. Presidents are free to change the job description of any office at any time, whether it is an office passed down from a previous administration or one of their own invention. Thus, titles do not always accurately indicate who does what in the White House.

Nor do titles always reveal whom the president consults on important matters. Presidents tend to seek advice from those assistants with whom they feel the most comfortable, regardless of the staffer's position or the subject matter. For example, President Carter consulted his special counsel, Lloyd N. Cutler, for advice on a variety of questions that were well outside Cutler's theoretical area of responsibility.

Chief of Staff

The most important position in the present-day White House is chief of staff. This person is responsible for the smooth operation of the White House, which is no small task. Materials must be made available to the president in a timely manner, and the president's requests and directives must be acted upon and implemented quickly. The swift and accurate flow of business is a primary goal.

The chief also acts as head gatekeeper to the president, and by reviewing all papers and visitors he or she funnels as many as possible around the president. Sherman Adams in the Eisenhower administration and H. R. Haldeman in the Nixon administration were very effective in this role. The gatekeeping function provides the chiefs of staff with a great deal of influence, since anyone wishing to bring an issue before the president must meet their approval.

Although most chiefs of staff have denied a role in policy making, the position has acquired a policy function as well. The close working relationship that most chiefs have with presidents means that it is only natural for presidents to seek and heed their opinions. Hamilton Jordan, who served as Carter's chief of staff, was an important voice in the administration, and James A. Baker III was an adviser as well as a political operative under Reagan. George Bush acknowledged even before taking office that his chief of staff, John H. Sununu, would be an administrator and a policy adviser. *(See Table 1.)*

Another important function of the chief is presidential hatchet wielder. All presidents have had jobs that they wanted to avoid, confrontations that they wished to dodge. Haldeman once noted that "every president needs his son-of-a-bitch" to do the dirty work.[19] The chief of staff is that person. Adams reprimanded or dismissed people to save Eisenhower the unpleasantness of doing it himself. Haldeman did the same for Nixon: after the 1972 election Nixon called a staff meeting and thanked everyone for their efforts in his behalf. Then, just before leaving, he turned the meeting over to Haldeman, who without preface immediately demanded everyone's resignation. The demand was really Nixon's and everyone knew it, but Haldeman had the task of carrying it out.

Finally, the chief often shoulders the blame for the president. Performing unpleasant jobs such as dismissals, which may have political significance, and taking credit for misstatements or other errors in fact made by the president are two cases in which the chief may act as presidential shield. Or the chief may act as a lightning rod to draw criticism away from the president. This function will not be found in any job description, but the possibility of being a scapegoat for the president is part of the job, and most chiefs know it.

Special Counsel

The position of special counsel has varied in importance over the years. In creating the position, Franklin Roosevelt argued that the White House needed its own lawyer because the attorney general, the nation's chief law officer and the government's first lawyer, was too busy to give the White House the necessary time. In reality, he envisioned a bigger role for his counsel.

The special counsel is the White House's private lawyer. This staff member provides legal advice on an assortment of topics, reviews legislation before it is sent to Congress, and may even check potential treaties for legal problems. The president also may seek the counsel's advice on the legality of certain actions. The counsel's office is concerned as well with "overseeing security clearances for

Table 1 Chiefs of Staff, 1932-1989

President	Chief of Staff	Years
Roosevelt	—	—
Truman	John R. Stedman[a]	1946-1952
Eisenhower	Sherman Adams[a]	1953-1958
	Wilton Persons[a]	1958-1961
Kennedy	—	—
Johnson	—	—
Nixon	H. R. Haldeman	1969-1973
	Alexander M. Haig	1973-1974
Ford	Donald Rumsfeld	1974-1975
	Richard B. Cheney	1975-1977
Carter	Hamilton Jordan	1979-1980
	Jack Watson	1980-1981
Reagan	James A. Baker III	1981-1985
	Donald T. Regan	1985-1987
	Howard H. Baker Jr.	1987-1988
	Kenneth Duberstein	1988-1989
Bush	John H. Sununu	1989-

Sources: Presidential libraries and the White House, 1989.

Note: The Roosevelt, Kennedy, and Johnson presidential libraries each reported that there was no chief of staff or even a presidential assistant who served in that role.

a. These aides carried the title of "assistant" rather than "chief of staff."

presidential appointees, supervising the selection of new federal judges, maintaining liaison with the Justice Department and the legal counsels in the other federal departments, and monitoring internal conflict-of-interest guidelines for employees" of the EOP.[20] Since Watergate, the special counsel's office also has been responsible for insuring the proper behavior of the presidential staff.

Beyond these duties the office has often served presidents as a place to put valuable aides. Franklin Roosevelt named a special counsel primarily to create a place for Samuel Rosenman, who served him as an adviser and a speechwriter. Clark Clifford filled a similar function while occupying the same post under Truman. Kennedy named Theodore Sorensen special counsel and used him as a speechwriter and domestic policy adviser. Under Carter, the office was used in two different ways: Robert J. Lipshutz confined himself to legal matters; his successor, Lloyd Cutler, advised the president on a wide range of issues, both foreign and domestic.

National Security and Domestic Advisers

The national security adviser is the president's primary adviser on foreign policy. Created originally as a largely administrative post, the national security adviser was responsible for overseeing the functioning of the National Security Council and coordinating the various elements of the foreign policy establishment, such as the State Department, Defense Department, and Central Intelligence Agency. Over the years the position has retained these administrative functions, and the Reagan administration, at least in its initial days, tried to reemphasize them. *(See Executive Office of the President: Supporting Organizations chapter.)*

Given the central location of the national security

adviser in the policy process, it was natural that presidents began turning to them for advice as well as coordination. National security advisers became important policy-making figures; men such as Bundy, Kissinger, and Zbigniew Brzezinski (under Carter) were major players, if not the crucial figures, in the development of their administration's foreign policy. Under these advisers the role of foreign policy designer began to overshadow that of administrator.

The prominence of the national security adviser has led to an occasional controversy about the position. The possibility that a national security adviser could dominate the execution of U.S. foreign policy has led to calls for congressional confirmation of appointees to the post. Demands for congressional approval have been particularly strident when evidence has surfaced of uncontrolled or excessive NSC activity, such as the Iran-contra affair.

The domestic policy adviser has existed under different names in several administrations. Some scholars have contended that Adams was a de facto domestic adviser under Eisenhower. Sorensen served as one under Kennedy. The title was first given to Califano in the Johnson administration, and the Domestic Council was formalized under Ehrlichman in the Nixon years. Carter rechristened it the Domestic Policy Staff, and Reagan renamed it yet again, designating it the Office of Policy Development. *(See Executive Office of the President: Supporting Organizations chapter.)*

By whatever name, the office of the domestic policy adviser has responsibilities that parallel those of the office of the national security adviser. The domestic adviser coordinates domestic policy making and acts as a policy adviser. The adviser's office settles disputes between domestic agencies and uses input from them to formulate legislative proposals. The president may also turn to the domestic adviser for advice on domestic problems.

The domestic adviser has not been as influential or as effective a coordinator as the national security adviser. This stems from the larger number of agencies and constituencies in the domestic adviser's domain, many of which are powerful and active. Thus, the domestic adviser cannot exercise the same degree of control as his or her foreign counterpart.

White House Liaison Offices

Several offices in the modern White House are concerned with its links with the world outside its gates. The oldest of these is the office of the press secretary. The press secretary manages the administration's relations with the news media. News summaries and daily briefings issued by the secretary for journalists provide information on the president's activities and decisions. The press secretary is regarded as the spokesperson for the administration, and his or her words often are taken to be the president's position.

Because of their proximity to the president, press secretaries may also become policy advisers. Hagerty functioned in that dual capacity for Eisenhower, as did the Nixon administration's Ronald Ziegler, who eventually was named as an assistant to the president as well.

Closely related to the press secretary is the Communications Office. The two offices were actually one through the Johnson administration, with the press secretary handling all press relations, but the increasing work load caused by the government's growth and the electronic era necessi-

tated a division of labor. The Communications Office was separated from the press secretary's office by President Nixon in 1969, and it has remained a separate entity since.

Like the press secretary's office, the Communications Office is concerned with the news media, but it is more involved in managing the news. The communications director responds to reporters' inquiries, provides information and briefings, and arranges interviews. The director also tries to get the administration's point of view across, using press releases, interviews, mailings, and other techniques to promote the president's side of a story. During the Nixon presidency, for example, the Communications Office sent out summaries of administration accomplishments to some five thousand journalists and commentators. During Watergate, it acted as a liaison between the White House and various groups opposing a possible Nixon impeachment.[21] The Communications Office functions as well as an advertising department and the public relations agency for the White House.

The White House also maintains offices to facilitate communication with important groups. One of the most important of these is the congressional liaison office, known under Reagan as the Office of Legislative Affairs. Used to control the interaction between the president and Congress, this office was formally established during the Eisenhower administration—previous presidents had unofficial liaison personnel, however. Subsequently, it has grown as Congress has grown.

The congressional liaison staff, with its components for the House and the Senate, tries to maintain a two-way flow of communication between the White House and the Congress. Staff members present the president's positions to Congress and sell presidential programs there. They also nurture good relationships with individual members of Congress who might support the administration on various bills. Information and materials are provided as well to help the administration's congressional friends persuade others in Congress and defend themselves back home.

In facilitating communications from Congress to the White House, the liaison staff relays and tries to resolve problems that members of Congress may be having with the administration. It is a channel through which Congress can talk to the president. The liaison staff also keeps the president informed on the mood in Congress and the chances of success there.

For specific bills the liaison staff must work with the president's congressional supporters to help determine when a bill should be introduced, how it should be worded, how it should be pushed and modified, and when it should be brought to a vote. Staff members also must keep accurate counts of the number of votes available to the president for a bill. They then know exactly who is wavering, and either can be won over or must be reinforced, and what incentives are needed to gain a member's vote. The staff also must know when and to what degree direct presidential involvement is needed to save a bill. Any slip-up may mean losing a salvageable bill or wasting valuable presidential resources.

The public liaison office was established during the Nixon administration, and it has remained a White House fixture. Its goal is to build support for the administration's policies within the general public. Liaison staffers contact constituency groups and try to educate them about the administration's goals and actions. One of President Carter's assistants for public liaison, Anne Wexler, invited influential groups to the White House to hear administration officials, including the president, explain the administration's positions on particular issues. Her goal was increased public support for the president. Other White House liaison offices maintain ties with various specific constituency groups.

The White House also has a staff of presidential speechwriters. Unlike earlier staffs, recent staffs have had distinct speechwriter positions. Presidential speechwriters are the administration's wordsmiths: they compose the addresses, statements, and messages that the president delivers to Congress and the general public, both at home and overseas. Much of President Kennedy's famed inaugural address, for example, was actually written by Theodore Sorensen. Many phrases that have defined an administration were created by speechwriters, not the president who spoke them. Because words define policy, speechwriters also may have a role in policy making. Indeed, in the Roosevelt, Truman, and Kennedy administrations speechwriters were policy advisers as well.

Personnel Office

Throughout every administration numerous vacancies occur in the executive branch, and all presidents' staffs maintain a personnel office to find people to fill them. This office locates potential officeholders, checks on qualifications and conducts interviews, and along with the special counsel's office arranges for background checks, often by the Federal Bureau of Investigation. If all is in order, the office presents the nominee to the president for approval and submission to the Senate, if necessary. It also might brief the appointee on the questions he or she may face from that body. The rigor with which the personnel office does its business varies from administration to administration, ranging from using computer data banks to informal queries.[22]

Recruiting the White House Staff

Because the success or failure of an administration may depend largely upon the abilities of the White House staff, the problem of how to find good people is of major concern to presidents. Unfortunately, few studies have examined critically how presidents choose their staffs and what factors determine how and why staffers are selected.

Recent presidents have had both an inner and outer staff. In a bureaucracy that includes hundreds if not thousands of people (depending on whether one includes the EOP), not everyone can have the ear of the president. The inner staff refers to those senior aides who are close to the president and can reasonably expect admission to the Oval Office when needed. The outer staff refers to the other members of the presidential establishment who perform specialized functions in the lower echelons of the White House but see the president rarely, if ever. The distinction between the two staffs is of some importance, for presidents may choose personnel for each in different ways.

Historically, the senior inner staff is chosen from among the president's close friends and cronies. To fill these staff positions, presidents usually look to the people with whom they have worked closely in the past, tending to select campaign workers or old friends to take the top staff positions. In 1968, for example, President Nixon chose his campaign manager as his White House chief of staff. Technical qualifications thus may not matter as much as a good relationship with the president.

Presidents often bring their inner staff to Washington with them. Truman appointed a number of old cronies from Missouri to various staff positions. Kennedy had his "Irish Mafia," staffed by men from Harvard and the Northeast; Carter's Mafia was drawn from his native Georgia. Johnson brought old Texas associates such as Jack Valenti and Bill Moyers, while Reagan brought William P. Clark, Edwin Meese III, and Michael K. Deaver from California to serve in his new administration.

Presidents tend to choose their inner staff from close friends and associates for good reasons. In the first place, these people are nearby when a new president starts forming the White House team. In the crush of a presidential transition period the new president has a multitude of details to worry about, and a serious search to fill staff appointments is often not really possible. Indeed, because a new president needs help immediately after the election, the only way to get that help is to call on friends and associates to fill staff positions.

More important, the president usually chooses the inner staff from among close associates because these are the people the president can trust when seeking political or personal advice. The need for trustworthy confidants is particularly keen for a president. For example, when FDR's Republican opponent in the 1940 election, Wendell L. Willkie, asked Roosevelt why he continued to keep assistant Harry Hopkins, he replied that

> I can understand that you wonder why I need that half man around me. But someday you may be sitting here where I am now as president of the United States. And when you are, you'll be looking through that door over there and knowing that practically everybody who walks through it wants something out of you. You'll learn what a lonely job this is, and you'll discover the need for somebody like Harry Hopkins who asks for nothing except to serve you.[23]

Although most members of the inner staff are chosen from the president's friends and former aides, presidents sometimes choose senior aides primarily on the basis of reputation, and close working relationships may follow. For example, President Nixon selected Henry Kissinger as his national security adviser after just one meeting with him. The selection was based on Kissinger's writings on foreign policy and international politics. Only later did Kissinger have a good working relationship with Nixon. Similarly, James Baker was far from a close confidant of President Reagan when he was selected to fill the position of chief of staff. Thus, while special knowledge or qualifications may become important in filling high-profile senior posts such as budget director or national security adviser, new presidents continue to select most senior aides on the basis of old ties.

Lower White House personnel, who fill more specialized roles, may be appointed on the basis of either connections or merit. Depending on the desires of the president, such staffers are selected in a systematic screening process similar to that used for other executive branch personnel. Potential staff who meet the criteria of agreement with the president's program and competence may be subjected to background checks (to prevent something embarrassing to the administration from surfacing later) before taking their positions. White House staff appointments do not require congressional confirmation.

Every recent administration has had a White House personnel office responsible for finding and screening potential appointees. The care with which such searches are undertaken, however, varies from one administration to another. Under Lyndon Johnson, for example, a computerized file was set up to keep records on possible appointees; whenever a position became available, Johnson's personnel staff could scan the computer banks and find people qualified for the job. Other presidents have employed less advanced methods. After President Nixon's election in 1968 his staff tried to find personnel by soliciting recommendations from everyone in *Who's Who in America* (which included such political notables as Casey Stengel and Elvis Presley; a letter also was sent to Nixon himself).[24]

What seems to be more common than computers and systematic searches is the BOGSAT method of appointing personnel: a bunch of guys sitting around a table saying, Who do you know? Frequently, White House staff selection appears to be based on connections; it is a matter of knowing a person who knows a person who knows the president. Like Franklin Roosevelt, many presidents have chosen a large part of their staff by drawing upon friends, colleagues, campaign workers, the "old boys' network," and party operatives to fill posts both in the White House and in the administration at large. While most administrations worked this way, the Johnson, Carter, and Reagan administrations, who were more systematic than most in their selection of executive personnel, avoided it to some degree.

Profiles of White House aides over the years are strikingly consistent—no doubt partly because of the way in which they are chosen. From 1948 through 1974 the staff was almost exclusively white men: 98 percent were white and 98 percent were male. Eighty-six percent had college educations. Of these, 57 percent had undertaken some advanced graduate work, particularly in law. Sixty-nine percent of the staffers were between the ages of thirty and fifty, and the average age has tended to decline over the years. The private sector has produced 60 percent of the White House staffers, with the predominant fields being law (16 percent), business (15 percent), journalism (13 percent), and education (11 percent). Nonelected government positions produced 29 percent of the staff, while 4 percent were former elected officials and 6 percent were former military men.[25]

Styles of Organization of the White House Office

No hard or fast rules govern the way presidents shape their staffs; the only variables are their preferences and work habits. At the same time certain patterns of organization have recurred over the years, leading scholars to discern two types of patterns: pyramidal and circular.

As the name suggests, pyramidal staffs are structured as a hierarchy with the president occupying the top position. Immediately under the president is usually a chief of staff who has a few key assistants who are close to the president; some may have direct access to the Oval Office. Arranged in order of importance below these close aides are the other assistants, increasing in number as their relative importance decreases.

This structure is designed to insure a clear chain of command and provide precise channels of communication for information going up and directives coming down. It permits specialization at the lower levels and control at the top. In theory, those higher up in the system are able to provide the president with more accurate information in a timely manner, while filtering out and eliminating unnecessary information. President Eisenhower argued that "a president who doesn't know how to decentralize will be weighted down with details and won't have time to deal with the big issues."[26] A pyramidal staff arrangement provides this decentralization.

Critics of the pyramidal staff have contended that the structure may distort information and problems. Highly complex problems may resist compression into the one-page memoranda preferred by presidents Eisenhower and Reagan; information and policy alternatives that the president should have may be lost or discarded at the lower staff levels.

A staff pyramid also may malfunction and isolate the president. By acting as a screen the staff may keep from the president not only unnecessary but also just unpleasant information. What staff member wants to be the bearer of bad news? Critics charge that pyramidal staffs can cause the president to lose contact with reality. Indeed, it may happen that the staff is controlling the president more than the president is controlling the staff.

In the circular or "spokes of the wheel" method of organizing the White House, the president also acts as chief of staff. Surrounded by a number of trusted advisers, all of whom have approximately equal access to the Oval Office, the president makes assignments, receives reports, and largely determines how presidential time is allotted among staffers. Essentially, the president sits in the middle of a ring of advisers who funnel information to and are in equal contact with the Oval Office, much like the hub of a wheel.

The circular approach to staff organization permits the president to obtain information from a variety of sources. Properly pursued, this approach reduces the possibility that dissenting voices are lost in the shuffle and never reach the president. Because not all details are worked out at the lower staff levels, the president can have more input in the specifics of the administration's policies, thereby ensuring that an important idea is not lost in the evolution of a brief policy memo. As some scholars have noted, activist presidents who want an exchange of ideas at the highest levels have tended to prefer this approach.

The circular staff arrangement may permit too much access to the president, however. Given the size of the modern White House staff, a president who does not have someone else to control the flow of people and paper to the Oval Office is at serious risk of being inundated and swept away. There is simply not enough of the president to go around. H. R. Haldeman once observed that "if everyone who wanted to see [the president] got in, nobody would get in because there wouldn't be room."[27] And as President Ford noted,

> because power in Washington is measured by how much access a person has to the president, almost everyone wanted more access than I had access to give. I wanted to have an "open" door, but it was very difficult; my working day grew longer and longer, and the demands on my time were hindering my effectiveness. Someone ... had to be responsible for scheduling appointments, coordinating the paper flow, following up on decisions I had made....[28]

Circular staffing arrangements also have been criticized as stimulating unhealthy friction between staffers, who may find themselves competing for the president's attention. Most (but not all) presidents have found such jealousies disruptive to peak staff performance. But, if internal bickering is not a factor, a circular staff could easily become excessively collegial and lose its critical perspective, thus developing what is referred to as "groupthink." [29]

Roosevelt and the Competitive Staff

Some presidential scholars have drawn a distinction between the circular model employed by Franklin Roosevelt and those of other presidents. The Rooseveltian model has been characterized as a "competitive" one in which members of the president's staff are set on conflicting assignments. Out of the competition between staffers to win the president's favor, the president can get a better array of options and data, more forcefully argued. Other presidents with circular staffs have used a "collegial" approach, intended to facilitate staff cooperation and to promote more harmony and efficiency.

Roosevelt surrounded himself with a small staff of about a half dozen administrative assistants, most of whom were simply "special assistants," or generalists, able to handle whatever problems emerged. Formal staff meetings were rare or nonexistent, as the president preferred informal gatherings with any assistant who needed to see him. There were no experts on particular policy areas, no special-interest liaisons, and no rigid lines of authority; aides moved across policy areas as the president saw fit.

The president served as his own chief of staff and handed out assignments himself on a seemingly random basis, often selecting the aide most readily available. He could be so capricious in his assignments because he had created a staff that could move readily from one problem to another. Roosevelt expected his aides to take on whatever assignment that he might give them, resulting in a very fluid staff structure.

Roosevelt also received all of the staff's reports personally. In his constant search for more information about problems and issues, Roosevelt tapped numerous sources, both within and outside of his immediate staff, for facts and advice. For Roosevelt, a separate chief of staff to sort out incoming information would have been an unwelcome obstruction. A master politician and manipulator, he wanted all the facts to come directly to him so that he personally could evaluate and use them.

Roosevelt's staff, which in most ways was a prototypical circular arrangement, was unique in the extent to which he turned it upon itself. Most presidents have disliked internal staff competition and infighting, but Roosevelt seemed to thrive upon it. Instead of trying to discourage intrastaff competition, he promoted it. Instead of worrying about stress and struggles within his staff, he encouraged them. In fact, Roosevelt often gave the same assignment to more than one assistant, thus setting them potentially in conflict. Yet he always maintained control of the competition; unlike most presidents he did not even feel the need to maintain a facade of internal staff harmony.

For Roosevelt, operating a staff by the principle of competition had several distinct advantages. The president reasoned that putting aides in competition would stimulate them to work faster, dig harder for needed information and critical insights, and devise more creative solutions to national problems. This was something Roosevelt was constantly seeking, particularly in his early years. He also was better able to evaluate his personnel and their ideas. And the conflict itself apparently appealed to Roosevelt; as Kennedy adviser Richard E. Neustadt has noted, he encouraged his staff to jostle and "evidently got a kick out of bruised egos." [30]

To an outsider, Roosevelt's staff operation seemed chaotic, strife-ridden, and often wasteful of time and resources. It appeared that too many people were duplicating efforts and there was no organization or planning. For Roosevelt, however, the open staff system provided what he wanted: a flow of ideas. For that, the lack of order was a fair trade-off. Then too the small size of the staff and Roosevelt's manipulative skills made it possible for him to retain sufficient control over the operation. His staff arrangement remains unique; no other president has been willing or able to operate with the somewhat acrimonious confusion in which Roosevelt thrived.

President Truman certainly was not willing to adopt the Rooseveltian style and set out to alter it soon after becoming president. While he maintained a basically open and circular staff, he took steps to provide more order and reduce the intrastaff competition that had been so dear to his predecessor. Assignments were more functional; overlap was reduced. Still, Truman preferred to remain at the center of the staff wheel.

Kennedy, Johnson, and the Collegial Staff

Two later Democratic presidents also operated circular staffs. Indeed, President Kennedy's staff is often cited as a prototype of the collegial staff system.

When he organized his White House staff, Kennedy made a conscious decision to return to the informal staffing arrangements once employed by Roosevelt. In this decision, which was encouraged by advisers such as Neustadt, he was reacting to the Eisenhower administration. Kennedy believed that Eisenhower's staff was too rigid in its structure and that it stifled creativity and debate. His staff was designed to avoid this rigidity.

Like Roosevelt, Kennedy created an open, circular staff structure in which he was accessible to all of his advisers equally. Because the president made assignments and received papers personally, the business of his government moved through him. There was no chief of staff to censor the flow of papers and advisers.

As an activist president, Kennedy thought that his circular staff would be more creative in dealing with problems and devising policy. The bureaucracies were too slow in their operation and too traditional in their thinking to suit him; he wanted more originality and faster action, and he set up an interactive staff to produce it.

The president's tendency toward an informal staff structure was no doubt reinforced by the number of crises that arose during his administration. In foreign affairs, particularly, Kennedy had to confront such problems as the Bay of Pigs fiasco, the Berlin crisis, and the Cuban missile crisis. Crisis management is necessarily improvised, and the frequency of the crises confronting Kennedy's administration strengthened the president's belief in fluid staff patterns. [31]

The Kennedy staff was very fluid in structure. On

paper there was more organization than had existed under Roosevelt, but in practice the dividing lines were not often observed. Like Roosevelt, Kennedy wanted a staff of generalists; he wanted every aide to be able to assume whatever duties were called for at a given moment. The staff was composed of equals, all of whom were free to interact with the president or one another.

The Kennedy staff was notable for its harmony. Most presidents have encountered jealousies among staffers, sometimes to the extent of disrupting staff performance, but an unusual degree of collegial spirit existed in the Kennedy White House, perhaps because the president's staff perceived itself to be on the cutting edge of the New Frontier, distinct from the rest of the Washington establishment. This camaraderie helped Kennedy's circular staff structure function effectively.

In the aftermath of Kennedy's assassination on November 22, 1963, Johnson tried to keep most of his predecessor's advisers around him, believing that he needed the expertise and the legitimacy that their presence would provide. At the same time, he began to bring in his own people gradually, often without dislodging the Kennedy staff. Thus, Johnson ran a dual staff for a time, overlapping former Kennedy staffers with his own personnel.

The circular staffing structures that Kennedy had employed appealed to the new president. A great admirer of Franklin Roosevelt, Johnson was a very active president, eager to create a Great Society of social programs to help the nation's poor and disadvantaged. In doing this, he wanted to emulate Roosevelt and perhaps overshadow Kennedy. He was eager for new ideas and programs and sought any pertinent facts aggressively, particularly in the early days of his administration before the Vietnam quagmire engulfed him.

Thus, the Johnson White House was very idiosyncratic and loosely structured to fit the whims of an energetic and mercurial president. It was so unstructured in fact that anyone who asked for its organization chart was told that there was no such thing. Aides declared that drawing up one would simply be a waste of time, as no one would follow it anyway.

Unlike the Kennedy staff, Johnson's aides were in constant competition for the president's ear. Preferring informal arrangements and one-on-one encounters, Johnson avoided large staff meetings. He particularly liked to meet with selected staffers in his bedroom, either first thing in the morning or last thing at night, and aides who were admitted to such meetings were viewed as very influential.

Although the structure of Johnson's staff was similar to Kennedy's, the atmosphere was quite different. A man with incredible energy, Johnson drove his staff mercilessly to keep up. The president's energy was legendary. He would work from seven o'clock in the morning until two in the afternoon, when he would stop for lunch, a short nap (on his doctor's orders; he already had had a heart attack), a shower, and a change of clothes. Then from four until nine o'clock or later he would resume working as furiously as ever. Aides were supposed to be available at any time, night or day; no excuses were acceptable (when Joseph Califano failed one day to answer a presidential phone call because he was in the bathroom, Johnson ordered him to put an extension in there). The pace and pressure under Johnson thus were such that he simply wore his staff down. The collegiality that had marked the Kennedy staff was much less present under Johnson.

Eisenhower, Nixon, and the Staff Pyramid

The Eisenhower staff was the first attempt at a more formal, hierarchical staff structure. An orderly person, Eisenhower was repelled by the chaos of the Roosevelt staff, even after it had been somewhat refined by Truman. His military experience had taught him the benefits of organization, and the result was a degree of differentiation and specialization previously unseen in the White House.

Eisenhower's staff was the traditional pyramid, with none of the fluid and shifting assignments that Roosevelt had used. Everyone had specific areas of responsibility and knew what they were. Eisenhower was more interested in good management than spontaneity; specialization was the name of the game. This arrangement allowed the president to know exactly where to go for information or action.

The desire for specific areas of responsibility among the staff naturally led to a bigger staff, which, for better organization, was divided into subunits. One example of this was the National Security Council staff. The first president to give much organization to the NSC, Eisenhower created a rather elaborate system of working groups to analyze particular problems and to produce studies and recommendations. The NSC operation was criticized by opponents as a useless paper mill, but it typified the organization and specialization that Eisenhower wanted of his staff.

Unlike Roosevelt, Eisenhower did not want to be involved in every detail of operation or policy; he believed that presidents were supposed to make big decisions and leave little ones to subordinates. His attitude is captured in his remarks to Defense Secretary Charles E. Wilson, who repeatedly came to him with minor problems early in the administration: "Charlie, you have to run Defense. We can't both run it. And I won't run it." [32]

To ensure that problems found their appropriate level, Eisenhower created a chain of command to control the paper flow through the staff. Problems and papers came up from the lower levels until they reached a point of decision (which in most cases was below the president), and then orders went back down. Eisenhower was thus relieved of the need to bother with most problems at all, while at the same time ensuring that they were being dealt with systematically.

At the top of the pyramid was the president, but because Eisenhower preferred to distance himself from everyday business, the most important operations figure was the chief of staff. From 1953 to 1958 that person was Sherman Adams, followed by Maj. Gen. Wilton B. (Jerry) Persons. Simply put, the chief of staff managed the operation of the staff, making sure that it ran smoothly and efficiently, and kept unimportant matters and people away from the president. Adams in particular acted as gatekeeper and arbiter for Eisenhower, restricting access to the Oval Office and forcing decisions, whenever possible, to be made somewhere else. "We must not bother the president with this" was his watchword. [33]

Adams's authority over the president's business and Eisenhower's distance from daily events, particularly in domestic affairs, led to the perception that the chief of staff, with his extensive power, was some sort of an "assistant president." Adams was seen as being so influential that a joke began to make the rounds: "Wouldn't it be awful if Eisenhower died and Nixon became president?

Unlike FDR and Truman, Eisenhower ran a structured and diversified staff. Sherman Adams became the gatekeeper to the president during Ike's first six years in office.

Yes, but what if Adams died and Eisenhower became president?" In fact, if Adams had so much authority as presidential gatekeeper, it was because the president wanted it that way.

Beneath Adams the Eisenhower staff was the prototypical hierarchy. At least at the top, however, it was not completely rigid in its organization. There were lines of command, but they were not irrevocable; Eisenhower's staff structure was meant to control staff interaction, not necessarily eliminate it. Senior staff had access to the president and participated in policy discussions whenever appropriate.

The hierarchic staff, abandoned after Eisenhower, was resurrected by Nixon in 1969. Having served as Eisenhower's vice president, Nixon knew the organizational merits of a more formal staff structure. It also well served his personal needs. A man who preferred to work alone, making decisions in solitude from the many briefing papers he received, Nixon used his staff to insulate himself from the rest of the world and provide the isolation he sought.

In the Nixon White House with its pyramidal structure, information and options were passed up the chain of command from specialists at the lower staff levels, and decisions and requests were returned down the ladder from the top. Much more information made its way to the top, however, than during the Eisenhower years. Unlike Eisenhower, who wanted one-page policy summaries and oral briefings, Nixon wanted detail and read extensively.

Nixon used the staff as a buffer even more than Eisenhower did. Senior staff members contended that no unreasonable restrictions were placed on the flow of traffic through the Oval Office, but complaints from outsiders about the difficulties encountered in seeing the president were numerous. Transportation Secretary John Volpe,

frustrated over lack of access to the president, once pulled a list of problems out of his pocket while greeting Nixon in a church reception line.

At its peak, the Nixon staff was a model of efficiency. Everyone knew their roles; everyone knew the chain of command. As one staffer noted, "The place had a structure, had a way of doing things, had a flow and a follow-up system that was beyond belief. Things happened." There was relentless pressure from the top to get work done quickly and thoroughly. The staffer who was late or sloppy in his assignments was immediately brought into line. Nixon aide John W. Dean remembered that

> I spent too much time preparing my answers to a few action memoranda, let the due dates slide by, and discovered the consequences. First a secretary in the staff secretary's office called my secretary, asking where the answer was, and when the explanation was found unsatisfactory, a very bitchy Larry Higby called to say, "What's the matter, Dean, can't you meet a deadline? Do you think you're somebody special?" When I explained I was working on the response, Higby snapped, "Work a little faster." Higby was chewed out by Haldeman when the paper did not flow as the chief of staff wanted, so he leaned on others.[34]

The man who ran this machine with a firm hand was chief of staff H. R. Haldeman. Haldeman performed many of the same functions that Sherman Adams had performed for Eisenhower, and in fact once acknowledged himself that he was more like Adams than any other past staffer. But where Eisenhower had placed Adams alone at the top of the pyramid, Nixon included more specialists at the lower levels and broadened the top, making his chief of staff first among equals instead of a majordomo. In reality, although Haldeman remained the major figure on the staff, two other members also had ready access to the president: John Ehrlichman, who was first counsel to the president and later domestic adviser, and Henry Kissinger, the national security adviser. Increasingly, Haldeman, Ehrlichman, and Kissinger were the filter through which the outside world, including cabinet secretaries, had to pass to see the president. Furthermore, because Nixon's distrust of the permanent bureaucracy led him to concentrate more authority within the White House, the influence wielded by the "Big Three" became formidable indeed.

To meet his desire for organization and concentration of authority over the government within the White House, Nixon devised a new plan for structuring his staff. In July 1973 he unveiled a supercabinet proposal, in which the various executive departments were grouped into three blocks, each of which was to report to a presidential counsellor who doubled as a department head. The counsellors in turn reported to Ehrlichman, who was to oversee the entire operation. The goal was greater efficiency and better organization. How well it might have worked will never be known. No sooner had it been introduced than the Watergate controversy began to overwhelm the Nixon administration. After the resignations of Haldeman and Ehrlichman in early 1974, the system was dismantled.

Because staff arrangements are a reflection of the president and the president's needs, the Nixon White House did not change greatly in structure with the replacement of Haldeman by Gen. Alexander M. Haig, Jr. Haig continued to sit atop the White House bureaucracy, controlling the flow of business to the president. Although he tried to coordinate the administration's domestic programs, the increasing disarray of the staff and the growing congressional hostility made his task difficult. His efforts to expand the circle of White House advisers was for naught when the embattled Nixon, always a private man, increasingly withdrew into himself as Watergate destroyed his presidency. By the end of his administration, Nixon was seeing few people besides Haig, Kissinger, and Press Secretary Ziegler.

Reacting to Watergate:
Ford and Carter

The pattern of staff organization used in the White House has reflected not only each president's personality, but also their desire to avoid the errors of their predecessors. Thus, Kennedy adopted a circular staff in part because of the perception of overcentralization on Eisenhower's staff, and Nixon returned to a centralized staff because of the disarray he perceived in Johnson's staff. Similarly, Gerald Ford and Jimmy Carter tried to incorporate more openness into their staffs in response to what they saw as the excessive authority of the "Prussian guards" under Nixon. Neither was completely successful.

President Ford inherited his staff from the departing Nixon. Desiring continuity, Ford kept many of the Nixon staffers for a time, particularly at the lower and middle levels of the White House bureaucracy; most higher-level staffers were replaced early in the Ford administration. He set out quickly, however, to modify Nixon's staff structure. Ford's desire to open the Nixon structure stemmed in part from the apparent excesses of the Watergate period and in part from his long congressional experience, which led him to prefer personal interaction.

Ford therefore changed the Nixon pyramid into a rectangle. Each of nine senior aides was given specific areas of responsibility, a small staff, and equal access (at least in theory) to the president. The chief of staff position was abolished. Donald Rumsfeld was put in charge of White House operations, the traditional chief of staff duty, but Ford insisted carefully that there was no real chief. Ford did not entirely abandon hierarchy, however. His staff design was supposed to delineate clearly staff responsibilities and thus maintain more order than a circular staff, while also providing more accessibility and more channels of communication than the traditional pyramid.

In practice, the staff rectangle failed to operate as Ford had hoped. Despite his preference for receiving information orally and having personal contact, the president found that his staff arrangements permitted too many people to have access to him and too many demands on his time. Eventually, Ford was forced to have someone control the flow of traffic to and from his office. He thus appointed Richard B. Cheney chief of staff, in fact if not in title. The rectangle had become a pyramid again.

President Carter came into office seeking to re-create the circular staff system used by his illustrious Democratic predecessors, Roosevelt and Kennedy. Carter wanted to serve as his own chief of staff, sitting in the middle of a circle of advisers who would keep him in touch with the events of his administration. Like the presidents he was emulating, Carter wanted innovation and valued new ideas, and he thought that a circular staff system would encourage them.

No doubt Carter thought that he could manage a circular staff, even a large one, because of his ability to handle facts and details. Like Ford, however, he soon found that there was not enough of him to go around. With no gatekeeper, too many people brought too many problems to his attention, and Carter was soon handling such trivial matters as the allocation of parking spaces in the White House garage. It was no wonder that he quickly was overwhelmed by the volume of demands on his time. Overall policy and long-range goals were lost as he tried to cope with the mass of visitors and papers that descended upon him.

In the end, Carter was forced to capitulate to the reality of the modern White House. In 1979, attempting to shake off the "great malaise," he reorganized his staff into a more pyramidal form. He appointed a chief of staff (originally Hamilton Jordan, who was Carter's closest aide, and later Jack H. Watson, Jr.) to control the president's business. Formal staff meetings replaced small informal gatherings. Although he never became so structured as Nixon or Eisenhower, Carter necessarily adopted a more systematic approach to his staff.

Reagan and the Triumvirate Staff

The most unusual staff arrangement of any president was that employed by President Reagan during his first term in office. Although it resembled the traditional pyramid structure in the concentration of power at the top, Reagan did not use a single chief of staff to guard the door to the Oval Office. Instead, the president divided his staff into separate units, each headed by a senior staff member who had direct access to him. The senior staff linked the president to the lower staff. One can visualize the staff as a set of columns supporting the president.

Initially, the Reagan staff was broken down into three divisions which addressed (1) policy development, (2) the political problems of promoting the president's programs, and (3) the actual operation of the White House. A fourth division was added later when William P. Clark arrived as national security adviser. This division of the staff by functions was unique in the history of the White House staff.

Policy development was handled by a staff supervised by presidential counsel Edwin Meese. Staff units under Meese included the Office of Policy Development, the Office of Planning and Evaluation, and initially the National Security Council. This portion of the White House staff was supposed to formulate policy options and proposals for the president to consider.

The task of organizing political support for President Reagan's programs and pushing them through Congress and into action was given to a staff unit headed by chief of staff James Baker. Baker supervised the White House liaison units such as those for Congress, the public, other government agencies, and political organizations, as well as the press secretary's office, the Communications Office, and the speechwriters.

Operation of the White House was supervised by the deputy chief of staff, Michael Deaver. Deaver's staff handled the support services, travel arrangements, and scheduling for the president. Deaver's influence was much greater than his title or nominal duties might indicate, however. An old confidant of the president, he was closely involved in many presidential decisions and was important to the smooth operation of the staff. Indeed, another staff member referred to Deaver as "the glue that holds this [staff] together."[35]

A few months into the Reagan administration, the triumvirate of Meese, Baker, and Deaver was joined by

William Clark, who replaced Richard Allen as national security adviser. Although Clark knew little about foreign affairs, he was an old friend of the president and so was included immediately in the inner circle. Clark envisioned himself as the honest broker in the foreign policy process and supported the consensus view of the foreign policy establishment.

Together, the foursome of Baker, Clark, Deaver, and Meese were the cornerstones of the Reagan staff. They operated as equal partners, working together to ensure coordination and to facilitate the transmission of information from below and directions from above. The president met with them regularly, and they in turn worked with their section of the White House staff. Responsibilities were assigned by mutual decision among them.

That the four-pillar staff functioned at all is perhaps remarkable. As Deaver once noted, the staff arrangement worked "in spite of the fact that it probably shouldn't have worked.... You see you are supposed to have a chief of staff, but in fact what you have are three or four different systems that are all working here." [36] Yet despite the potential for discord and infighting, always present in the White House bureaucracy, and some tension, the Reagan staff managed to operate relatively harmoniously and effectively. The impressive string of political successes rung up by President Reagan during his first term testifies to the efforts of his senior staff to make his unique staffing arrangement work.

Unique and effective as it seemed to be, the original Reagan staff plan did not survive into his second term. Each of the four key staffers who made it function had left the White House by early 1985. Meese moved from his position as counsel to the president to that of attorney general. Clark first became secretary of the interior and then went home to California. Deaver resigned his position to go into private business. And Baker, in a rather unusual move, swapped jobs with Donald T. Regan: he became secretary of the Treasury, while Regan took over as White House chief of staff.

By the beginning of Reagan's second term the pillar-and-platform structure that had characterized his White House staff had collapsed into the traditional pyramid. Essentially, new chief of staff Regan was replacing four top staffers. A successful businessman and powerful chief executive officer with little political experience, Regan preferred to operate the White House much like a business. Seeing himself as the White House CEO, he tried to draw all the staff's business through him and to have a hand in all aspects of the White House operations.

The staff Regan created was perhaps the most centralized of any ever found in the White House, equaling or exceeding that of Sherman Adams or H. R. Haldeman. He also was among the most visible of White House chiefs; in the aftermath of the 1985 Reykjavik summit, for example, Regan gave fifty-three media interviews. A man who was used to being prominent, he did not shrink from public view, nor from asserting the extent of his authority.

Unfortunately for Regan, his highly centralized staff failed to achieve the successes of the first Reagan term (although some of the reasons for that were beyond his control), and his high profile made him a natural target when the Iran-contra controversy erupted in late 1986. Having claimed to have control over all aspects of the White House, Regan became the focus of criticism when the staff went awry. He resigned under pressure in February 1987 after the Tower Commission's report blamed him

for failing to control his subordinates and to protect the president's interests.

The basic staff structure remained the same under Regan's successor, former U.S. senator Howard H. Baker, Jr. (R-Tenn). The staff pyramid was left in place, but the new chief was not seen as being as aloof and domineering as Regan. The structure remained the same because that was the way the president wanted it, which, of course, is the final determinant of how the White House Office is organized.

Criticism of the White House Staff

The steady growth of the White House Office over the past fifty years has given presidents more resources to handle problems and the personnel needed to deal with the increasing demands on their time and energy. Given the size of the government and the active role it plays in American society, the president could not hope to keep up with either the sprawling executive branch or a growing and diverse Congress without the assistance of a large White House staff, which has become a permanent fixture of the presidential establishment.

Despite this, or perhaps because of it, the enlarged White House has been subjected to serious criticism by a number of scholars, all related to its increased size and prominence. Some of this criticism has been echoed by White House insiders as well.

One major fault pointed out by critics is that the White House staff simply has grown too large to be supervised and managed adequately. Instead of being an efficient personal staff, the White House Office is a small bureaucracy that is often unwieldly and inefficient. Complaints about the excessive size of the staff are not limited to scholars; recent White House chiefs of staff have agreed that it has grown too much and should be reduced as much as possible. [37] Despite this, none have had significant success at reducing the staff while in office themselves.

One problem arising from a swollen White House staff is that the larger the staff, the greater the possibility that needed information may be distorted or lost as it passes through different hands on its way to the president. This problem inevitably stems from the pyramidal organization needed to manage a large staff. It is complicated by staffers who try to shield the president from what they see as unnecessary or unpleasant information. Delays in implementation of presidential directives as the directives work their way back down the chain of command are also a problem. [38]

Members of an oversized staff who are underemployed and undersupervised may look for their own (generally unauthorized) projects to pursue and may wind up embarrassing the president. The Iran-contra affair was largely such a project and indicates the managerial problems that large staffs pose for the president.

Critics also have contended that the size of the White House staff has passed the point of diminishing returns for the president. The overly large staff can provide more information than a president with a limited supply of time and attention to devote to solving problems can hope to use. Thus, much of the staff is superfluous, if not actually counterproductive. Political scientist Aaron B. Wildavsky has argued that "after a while, the addition of new staff just multiplies [the president's] managerial problems without giving him valuable service in return. Forcing a president to 'count hands' all the time, by making him consider endless strings of alternatives, is a good way of rendering him useless."[39]

A second major criticism leveled at the modern White House is that the president's staff has entirely too much influence on policy. Presidential assistants have always had a political role, but their input into the policy-making process is a recent development. The Brownlow Commission report issued during Franklin Roosevelt's administration envisioned a staff of neutral aides who would provide the president with objective information and options; policy advocacy or formation was not part of the staff's role. For reasons put forth elsewhere in this chapter, over the years that ideal has been lost.

According to the critics, the modern White House staff now operates as a policy-making organism, often in unequal competition with the federal bureaucracy. Indeed, the staff frequently leaves the established departments with a secondary role in policy making. While the staff rarely dominates the bureaucracy to the extent it did in the Nixon administration, it still tends to be the primary actor in the policy-making process.

The problem with this, critics argue, is twofold. First, the staff has too narrow a focus: it tends to see everything through the limited perspective of the president's needs. Unlike the bureaucracy, the staff has no institutional memory and may easily overlook the problems of implementing a policy. The result may be policy that is idiosyncratic and lacks long-term perspectives on what is feasible and effective.[40] Second, there is something disturbing about major policy decisions in a constitutional democracy being made by the presidential staff, whose members are unelected and are responsible to no one except the president (if the president can supervise them) and one another.

A further criticism of the enlarged presidential staff is that the presence of so many special interests pleading for the president's attention is not in the president's best interests. Over the years liaison aides for different social groups have been added to the White House, and, although a few were dropped by the Reagan administration, the majority remain.

As the staff grows, it also increasingly isolates the president from the rest of the government. As a consequence, depending on the personality of the president, the large and influential staff may only reinforce the natural doubts that the president may have about the bureaucracy's loyalty and efficiency. In any event, the president is at serious risk of becoming a prisoner of the staff, dependent upon it alone for information and options and able to be no more effective and to make no better decisions than the staff's abilities will allow.

Notes

1. A good discussion of this problem is found in John Hart, *The Presidential Branch* (New York: Pergamon Press, 1987), 96-109. Unless noted otherwise, the figures on staff size used in this chapter are from Stephen J. Wayne, *The Legislative Presidency* (New York: Harper and Row, 1978), 220-221.

2. George Edwards and Stephen J. Wayne, *Presidential Leadership: Politics and Policy Making* (New York: St. Martin's Press, 1985), 181.
3. Edward H. Hobbs, "An Historical Review of Plans for Presidential Staffing," *Law and Contemporary Problems* 21 (August 1956): 666-675.
4. The President's Committee on Administrative Management, *Report of the Committee* (Washington, D.C.: Government Printing Office, 1937), 5.
5. The figures cited are taken from U.S. Congress, House, *Congressional Record*, daily ed., 92d Cong., 2d sess., June 20, 1972, H21512; and from Wayne, *The Legislative Presidency*, 220.
6. Stephen Hess, *Organizing the Presidency* (Washington, D.C.: Brookings, 1976), 74.
7. Quoted in Patrick Anderson, *The President's Men: White House Assistants of Franklin D. Roosevelt, Harry S Truman, Dwight D. Eisenhower, John F. Kennedy, and Lyndon B. Johnson* (Garden City, N.Y.: Doubleday, 1968), 152-153.
8. Hess, *Organizing the Presidency*, 88.
9. Ibid., 87.
10. Ibid., 118-119.
11. Dom Bonafede, "Dual Capacity Brings Power to Ronald Ziegler," *National Journal*, March 2, 1974, 325.
12. Quoted by Thomas E. Cronin in "The Swelling of the Presidency," *Saturday Review of the Society* 1 (August 1973): 33.
13. Dom Bonafede, "As Pollster to the President, Wirthlin Is Where the Action Is," *National Journal*, December 12, 1981, 2184-2188.
14. Dick Kirschten, "The White House Office: Where the Power Resides," *National Journal*, April 25, 1981, 678.
15. Thomas E. Cronin, "The Swelling of the Presidency: Can Anyone Reverse the Tide?" in *American Government: Readings and Cases*, 9th ed., ed. Peter Woll (Boston: Little, Brown, 1987), 336.
16. Hart, *The Presidential Branch*, 94.
17. Congressional staff figures are taken from *Guide to Congress*, 3d ed. (Washington, D.C.: Congressional Quarterly Inc., 1982), 583.
18. Cronin, "The Swelling of the Presidency," in Woll, *American Government*, 346-347.
19. Dan Rather and Gary Paul Gates, *The Palace Guard* (New York: Harper and Row, 1974), 240.
20. Dom Bonafede, "There's More to the Counsel's Job than Just Giving Legal Advice, *National Journal*, December 22, 1979, 2139.
21. Dom Bonafede, "President Still Seeks to Restore Staff Efficiency, Morale," *National Journal*, January 5, 1974, 1-6.
22. For more on the selection process for the executive branch, see John W. Macy, Bruce Adams, and J. Jackson Walter, *America's Unelected Government: Appointing the President's Team* (Cambridge, Mass.: Ballinger, 1983).
23. Anderson, *The President's Men*, 7.
24. More details of presidential appointment practices can be found in Matthew B. Coffey, "A Death at the White House: The Short Life of the New Patronage," *Public Administration Review* 34 (September 1974): 440-444; and in Macy, *America's Unelected Government*, especially chapters 2 and 3.
25. Figures are from Patricia S. Florestano, "The Characteristics of White House Staff Appointees from Truman to Nixon," *Presidential Studies Quarterly* 7 (Fall 1977): 186.
26. Quoted in Anderson, *The President's Men*, 135.
27. Rather and Gates, *The Palace Guard*, 239.
28. Quoted in Edwards and Wayne, *Presidential Leadership*, 203.
29. Ibid., 188.
30. Quoted in Wayne, *The Legislative Presidency*, 32.
31. Hess, *Organizing the Presidency*, 88.
32. Quoted in Richard T. Johnson, *Managing the White House: An Intimate Study of the Presidency* (New York: Harper and Row, 1974), 84.
33. Quoted in Anderson, *The President's Men*, 152.
34. Both quotations in this paragraph are from Wayne, *The Legislative Presidency*, 47.
35. Quoted in John H. Kessel, "The Structures of the Reagan

White House," *American Journal of Political Science* 28 (May 1984): 253.
36. Ibid., 251.
37. Samuel Kernell and Samuel L. Popkin, eds. *Chief of Staff: Twenty-five Years of Managing the Presidency* (Berkeley: University of California Press, 1986), 199.
38. Hess, *Organizing the Presidency*, 9.
39. Aaron B. Wildavsky, "Salvation by Staff: Reform of the Presidential Office," in *The Presidency*, ed. Aaron B. Wildavsky (Boston: Little, Brown, 1969), 697.
40. Hess, *Organizing the Presidency*, 9.

Selected Bibliography

Anderson, Patrick. *The President's Men: White House Assistants of Franklin D. Roosevelt, Harry S. Truman, Dwight D. Eisenhower, John F. Kennedy, and Lyndon B. Johnson.* Garden City, N.Y.: Doubleday, 1968.

Cronin, Thomas E. "The Swelling of the Presidency: Can Anyone Reverse the Tide." In *American Government: Readings and Cases*, ed. Peter Woll. 9th. ed. Boston: Little, Brown, 1987.

Cronin, Thomas E., and Sanford D. Greenberg. *The Presidential Advisory System.* New York: Harper and Row, 1969.

Hess, Stephen. *Organizing the Presidency.* Washington, D.C.: Brookings, 1976.

Johnson, Richard T. *Managing the White House: An Intimate Study of the Presidency.* New York: Harper and Row, 1974.

Kernell, Samuel, and Samuel L. Popkin, eds. *Chief of Staff: Twenty-five Years of Managing the Presidency.* Berkeley: University of California Press, 1986.

Koenig, Louis W. *The Invisible Presidency.* New York: Holt, Rinehart, and Winston, 1960.

Macy, John W., Bruce Adams, and J. Jackson Walter. *America's Unelected Government: Appointing the President's Team.* Cambridge, Mass.: Ballinger, 1983.

Patterson, Bradley H., Jr. *The Ring of Power: The White House Staff and Its Expanding Role in Government.* New York: Basic Books, 1988.

Redford, Emmette S., and Richard T. McCulley. *White House Operations: The Johnson Presidency.* Austin: University of Texas Press, 1986.

Wayne, Stephen J. *The Legislative Presidency.* New York: Harper and Row, 1978.

Wildavsky, Aaron B. "Salvation by Staff: Reform of the Presidential Office." In *The Presidency*, ed. Aaron B. Wildavsky. Boston: Little, Brown, 1969.

Executive Office of the President: Supporting Organizations

Beyond the president's inner circle of White House Office aides lies an outer circle of presidential advisers who head the supporting organizations of the presidency. These organizations, together with the White House Office, form the Executive Office of the President (EOP). Most of these offices are housed adjacent to the White House in both the new and old Executive Office buildings.

While EOP organizations perform services directly for the president, their staff members may or may not have daily access to the Oval Office. The heads of EOP organizations, like the president's closest White House advisers, are appointed by the president. Unlike the president's personal staff, however, the top positions in the EOP are subject to Senate approval.

Only recent presidents have enjoyed the increased management and control that the EOP provides. Based on the recommendations of the Brownlow Committee on Administrative Management, and with congressional authorization, President Franklin D. Roosevelt established the Executive Office of the President in 1939 to help him manage the burgeoning bureaucracy resulting from his "New Deal" programs. At that time the EOP consisted of five units, the most important of which were the Bureau of the Budget and the White House Office. As federal programs proliferated and the ensuing bureaucracy grew even larger, the EOP became the more specialized and complex organization needed to coordinate federal activities.

Styles and Methods of Appointment

The composition and organization of the EOP have changed many times since its inception. Over the last fifty years, forty-six different boards, offices, and councils have been established within the EOP. Congress created some of these, but many others were created by executive order. During Reagan's second term (1985-1989) the EOP consisted of nine units: White House Office, Office of Management and Budget, National Security Council, Office of

By W. Craig Bledsoe, Margaret C. Thompson, and Harrison Donnelly

Policy Development, Council of Economic Advisers, Office of the U.S. Trade Representative, Office of Science and Technology Policy, Council on Environmental Quality, and Office of Administration. Some of these organizations are so large that they may be considered small bureaucracies themselves. *(See Figure 1.)*

Even though the components of the EOP have changed from one administration to the next, the functions of the EOP have continued to fall into several general categories. According to presidential scholar Richard M. Pious, four functions traditionally have been carried out by EOP organizations. First, organizations such as the Office of Economic Opportunity (1964-1975) gained autonomous "presidential status" but really performed departmental functions. Second, offices such as those for consumer affairs (1971-1973), science and technology (1962-1973), and drug abuse policy (1976-1978) represented the interests of various constituencies. Third, EOP units such as the National Security Council (1947 to present) and the Council of Economic Advisers (1946 to present) develop policy. And finally, offices such as the Office of Management and Budget (1970 to present) perform management functions.[1]

The organization and structure of EOP have changed considerably over the years, but this change has not occurred systematically. Most presidents have altered the composition of EOP based upon their needs and problems, resulting in its rather piecemeal development. Recent presidents have attempted, nevertheless, to centralize and streamline the operations of EOP to make it more responsive to their programs and objectives.

Appointment Process

While most federal jobs are filled by appointment procedures designed to ensure that selections are made on the basis of qualifications and without political influence, the president is responsible for appointing staff to certain federal positions. The legal authority for making such appointments is derived from two sources: the Constitution and the various statutes that created the federal agencies requiring presidential appointments. Article II of the Constitution empowers the president to make many federal appointments with "the advice and consent of the Senate." While there occasionally has been some dispute over which executive officers require confirmation by the Senate, it generally is recognized that the very top positions in the supporting organizations of the EOP are subject to such review. In fact, Congress has absolute power to make any officer of the EOP subject to Senate confirmation.

No consistent legal principle clearly defines, however, which middle-level jobs in the EOP are appointed by the president and confirmed by the Senate and which jobs are appointed by an office head. Some scholars have suggested that the rules of appointment stem from whatever presidential-legislative relations exist at the time a particular component of the EOP is created.[2] Thus, while the president is responsible for appointing staff to the top-level positions in the EOP, a presidential subordinate may appoint staff to many other positions, including high-level ones.

A president-elect must fill vacancies in the EOP during the period of transition (about seventy-five days) from the old to the new administration. Unfortunately, it is during this period that the new president is least prepared to make the best choices. According to presidential scholar Stephen Hess, just three weeks after his election John F. Kennedy reacted to the difficulty he had in finding qualified people by saying, "People, people, people! I don't know any people. I only know voters." [3]

Public relations considerations further complicate the EOP staffing procedure. A president's first appointments indicate the tone and style of the new administration. The kind of individuals the president has chosen to fill EOP positions and the policy direction the new administration appears to be taking will be of keen interest to both the media and the public. Political party activists and other supporters will wonder whether the initial presidential appointments to EOP will reflect the president's campaign goals.

The president also has the political problem of appointing people who agree with the administration's policy positions and who will be loyal to the administration and its objectives. According to the authors of *America's Unelected Government:*

> [The president] will want to build teams that can work together when they share jurisdiction over critical issues like the economy or national security. He will want to pick appointees who can command the respect of the career civil servants and of foreign governments. And, of course, he will want people whose ability to do their jobs effectively is beyond doubt.[4]

The president is not always successful in appointing qualified people, however. Pressures from congressional supporters will influence some appointments; in fact, the number of congressional recommendations for executive office vacancies is quite large. Frederic V. Malek, President Richard Nixon's personnel director, claimed that during his tenure the White House received five hundred letters each month from Congress requesting executive positions. Frank Moore, head of President Jimmy Carter's congressional liaison office, estimated that during Carter's first month in office the administration received over a thousand requests for jobs from legislators.

The demands of political party patronage will influence appointments as well. Shortly after Dwight D. Eisenhower's election to the presidency, Sen. Robert A. Taft of Ohio, the Republican leader in the Senate, led a delegation of Republicans to the president-elect's headquarters. They complained that Eisenhower and his staff were ignoring traditional patronage considerations and trying to depoliti-

cize the executive recruitment process. As a result of political party pressure, Eisenhower acquiesced and instructed his staff to make more staffing decisions on the basis of patronage.

Although the president may pay off political debts by filling some positions with appointees who may or may not be competent to fill them, other positions will be filled by people with whom the president has had little or no personal contact but who are eminently qualified to work in the EOP. As a result, some EOP officeholders feel a strong sense of loyalty to the president's programs, while others do not and may be publicly at odds with them.

Staffing of the EOP does not end with the close of the presidential transition period. Normal appointment intervals and the turnover that occurs during any presidential administration require presidents to continue to make major personnel decisions throughout their tenure in office. Often the factors and conditions that govern these in-term decisions are different from those that prevail during the transition period. Since most electoral debts have been paid off, presidential attention turns to finding people who will best help accomplish administration goals. Presidential appointment scholar G. Calvin Mackenzie found that in-term appointment decisions usually are based on two very practical questions: Will the quality and character of the executive appointment have a strong impact on the president's ability to control and direct the government? And will the appointee improve the president's relation with Congress?[5] In-term appointments therefore usually reflect presidential concerns in dealing with the bureaucracy and Congress, and they thus become a central part of an administration's political and administrative strategy.

Some presidents have struggled to remedy the initial and ongoing helter-skelter EOP staffing process, and make it more responsive to the administration's needs, by use of a transition appointments staff. But throughout their administrations presidents face a flood of personnel decisions that would benefit from some kind of centralized personnel management. Recent presidents have attempted to handle ongoing staffing problems by incorporating full-time personnel managers into their administrations.

The Changing Styles and Methods of EOP Appointments

Presidents, with their different needs and policy objectives, have used a variety of styles and methods for filling positions in the Executive Office of the President. While presidents have relied generally on the traditional methods of presidential appointments—such as appointing friends and colleagues—the expanded size of the modern EOP is making such methods increasingly impractical. Indeed, presidents have had to make innovations in the appointment process, including establishment of a staffing agency in the White House to locate talented administrators who also exhibit loyalty to the president's programs.

The Early Years

As the EOP began to expand in the early 1940s, President Franklin Roosevelt recognized the need for greater presidential control over the appointment process. When initially staffing the EOP, Roosevelt, like earlier presidents, relied on old friends and colleagues: those who had served in his New York gubernatorial administration, some

Figure 1 Executive Office of the President, Reagan Administration

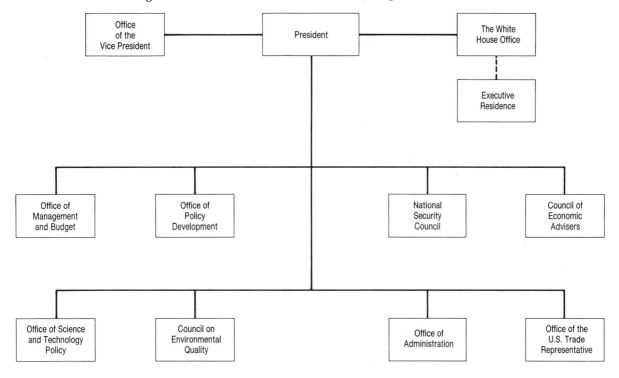

Source: U.S. Government Manual (Washington, D.C. : Government Printing Office, 1988), 88.

of his 1932 campaign workers, people from the "old boys' network," and Democratic party activists. His method of appointment lacked coordination and control. As one presidential scholar noted: "Roosevelt's staffing practices were primarily a haphazard blend of fortuity, friendship, obligation, and pressure, as were those of presidents who followed him. He was luckier than most and his network of acquaintances was larger than most." [6]

In 1939 Roosevelt designated a personnel manager to coordinate his EOP staffing procedure. Partisan politics played a significant role, however, in even this attempt at appointment coordination. As Roosevelt's administration evolved, it became obvious that the primary responsibility of the president's personnel manager was to serve as the presidential liaison to the Democratic National Committee and to certify potential appointees' Democratic credentials. Thus, by removing much of the control of the appointment process from the president and placing it squarely in the hands of the Democratic party leadership, the administration increased the Democratic party's influence over the process.

Presidents Harry S Truman and Dwight Eisenhower viewed the appointment of their White House staffs and the top positions in the supporting organizations of the EOP as an important way to control their presidencies, but they usually left mid- and lower-level appointments to the office heads. Truman took a more active role than Eisenhower, however, as he enjoyed dealing with people directly by calling them to the White House for personal interviews.

Because Truman assumed office upon the death of Roosevelt, he faced an EOP made up of Roosevelt loyalists. He was determined, however, that his appointees would be loyal to him and his administration's goals, and he wasted little time in actively replacing carryover officials who could not give their allegiance to him. Not sharing in Truman's enthusiasm for the day-to-day routine of dealing with possible appointees, Eisenhower decentralized the appointment process by allowing many heads of offices to make the initial recommendations for staff selection. The president, however, always reserved the right to make the final decision.

Eisenhower had little choice in delegating most of his appointment authority. The size of the ever-expanding EOP made his personal involvement in every personnel decision increasingly difficult. Thus, early in his first term Eisenhower created the position of special assistant for executive appointments. Although the special assistant, Charles F. Willis, Jr., was responsible for managing the appointment process for the administration's executive offices, he did not choose the president's appointees. Instead, he managed the paperwork and served as the president's liaison with the Republican National Committee and members of Congress who solicited appointments for their political allies. The special assistant and his staff then weeded through the various lists of nominees presented to the president and identified the strongest candidates with the fewest political drawbacks.

Eisenhower had two major criteria for selecting personnel to fill executive posts: loyalty and demonstrated success. Presiding over the first Republican administration in twenty years, he wanted a federal government bureaucracy that was responsive to his programs. In addition, according to Hess, "Eisenhower believed that a successful person, someone who had already proven that he could run something big, would be best able to tame a government department." [7]

The Kennedy Administration

Shortly after his election in 1960, President-elect Kennedy set up a loosely organized staff, known as "Talent Hunt," to sift through the possible appointees to his administration. Composed of some of his best campaign aides, Talent Hunt was designed to reward people who had helped Kennedy win the presidency by giving them jobs in his administration and to identify the most important jobs in the administration and the best-qualified persons to fill them. After the transition a more permanent staffing operation was established in the White House. Headed by Dan Fenn, Jr., this operation reached out beyond the traditional political channels and established a "contact network" as a source of potential appointees. By drawing on contacts at the Brookings Institution and other "think tanks," Fenn was able to make a list of several hundred national leaders in industry, labor, state government, academia, and other sectors. These "contacts" then either suggested potential appointees or served as references for appointees suggested by others.

The Kennedy administration used this list of contacts to circumvent normal political channels. Kennedy did not intend to depoliticize the appointment process, however. Rather, he wanted a personnel operation that would allow him to triumph in the political conflict among his administration, his political party, and Congress over executive office positions. According to presidential scholars John W. Macy, Bruce Adams, and J. Jackson Walter, "With an independent recruiting capability the president could often find better qualified candidates than those recommended to him by his party, by members of Congress, and by the leaders of interest groups." [8] Kennedy could also expect a higher degree of loyalty and responsiveness from his own nominees than from patronage appointees.

Kennedy's appointments to EOP generally reflected what presidential historian William Manchester has called his "generational chauvinism." Kennedy felt more comfortable with people with whom he had something in common. Among the factors he considered in his appointments to the EOP were age, military service, quality of education, and participation in his campaign for the presidency. As a result, the three original members of the Council of Economic Advisers were relatively young at forty-five, forty-four, and forty-two, very close to Kennedy's age of forty-three. Moreover, the educational backgrounds of Kennedy's appointees were impressive; fifteen Rhodes scholars served in his administration. And many of his top EOP appointees had been members of his campaign team since 1956. [9]

The Johnson Administration

When Lyndon B. Johnson suddenly became president in 1963 after Kennedy's assassination he moved very slowly in replacing Kennedy appointees with his own. To Johnson, the nation's need for stability was greater than his need for his own loyal appointees—a decision he later regretted. After six months, however, President Johnson found himself filling many EOP positions and taking a strong personal interest in appointment decisions. Johnson was even more concerned than Kennedy about outside influence on these decisions; to him, loyalty was essential. Political scientists Emmette S. Redford and Richard T. McCulley have noted that in making new appointments "Johnson was extremely cautious in selecting people to meet his qualifications for executive performance and especially careful to assure their loyalty to his objectives and to him personally. Even when responding to political influence in appointments, he normally sought assurance of loyalty." [10]

Like Kennedy, Johnson set up a systematized personnel office in the White House for help in making appointments, but unlike Kennedy, he relied on it much more frequently. Johnson eventually appointed John W. Macy as head of his personnel selection operation. While the selection of Macy was unusual, since he also served as chairman of the Civil Service Commission, it helped Johnson distance his appointments from political pressures. In fact, Johnson often used Macy's civil service position to dissuade potential job seekers and their patrons on the grounds that Macy insisted that all appointments be based on merit and thus he, Macy, had a well-qualified candidate of his own. This relieved President Johnson from having to rely excessively on appointments that appeared to fulfill some political obligation.

Macy introduced a more systematic approach to the presidential appointment process to replace the BOGSAT ("a bunch of guys sitting around a table") method of political recruitment used previously. The computer system he designed, known as the White House Executive Biographic Index, provided the president with quick and accurate information about a pool of potential appointees. By the end of the Johnson administration, almost thirty thousand names were in the index. When a position opened up, Macy sent Johnson names from the talent bank for his consideration. Johnson then chose the nominee and sent the name back to Macy, who had the nominee's background checked by the Federal Bureau of Investigation.

Curiously, Johnson's appointees to second-echelon slots tended to come up through the civil service, because he found it difficult to attract qualified outsiders to his administration. During President Johnson's first eighteen months in office, career civil servants filled almost half of the major appointments, and the political turmoil characterizing the last part of his administration prolonged the president's difficulty in attracting quality people from outside government. Even though Johnson looked for loyalty in his appointees, his inability to find many staffers beyond the confines of the civil service limited his staff's devotion to his programs. Former Kennedy staffer and presidential scholar Theodore C. Sorensen reported, "Lyndon Johnson complained privately that too many of his policy positions went by default to career civil servants who were willing, available, and technically competent but had no 'fire in their bellies.'" [11] They lacked the drive and devotion to administration programs that Johnson desired.

The Nixon Administration

Early in his administration, President Richard Nixon asserted that ability, not loyalty, would be the standard for appointment. Beyond his top White House aides and cabinet members, however, Nixon expressed little interest in personally choosing members of the EOP, and most of the time he delegated responsibility for making appointments to members of his White House staff. When he did express an interest, it was usually to approve or reject a candidate selected by his staff.

In the transition period and early stages of the Nixon administration the appointment process was slow and awkward; no systematic appointment procedure was in place. Macy, Adams, and Walter noted that because of this lack of control over the appointment process and Nixon's early lack of interest in staffing, "the management needs of the president were often a low-level consideration in appointment decisions, and far too many appointees were people who did not agree with the president on important substantive matters." [12] Nixon eventually recognized the need to tie personnel to his management needs, however, and his administration developed a more sophisticated staffing system.

By 1971 Nixon and his senior White House staff members had recognized the important relationship between loyalty and talent in selecting people to fill executive positions. Consequently, Nixon hired Frederic Malek to take over the personnel staffing operation. Based on his experience as a student of scientific management and a former manager in the Department of Health, Education, and Welfare, Malek implemented a personnel system that aggressively pursued Nixon's policies by appointing loyal and skilled executives. Under the direction of Malek the practice of achieving White House policy objectives by appointing officials who were loyal to the president soon became official White House procedure.

In the process of linking personnel to policy objectives, Malek created the White House Personnel Operation (WHPO) to bring professional executive practices to the EOP appointee search procedure. WHPO was composed largely of private sector "headhunters." Following models established by the Kennedy and Johnson administrations, WHPO rated potential appointees and recommended those who expressed loyalty to Nixon's objectives. Primarily, Nixon wanted to exert control over almost all noncareer appointments in the federal government.

By developing the largest and most systematic evaluation system ever found in the executive branch, the Nixon administration effectively tied its management objectives to its appointments. Following Malek's departure in 1972 to direct the Office of Management and Budget, however, the Nixon personnel operation took on a life of its own. WHPO tried to push its influence beyond the scope of its original conception, and some of its members attempted to influence the appointment of civil service assignments, generating a damaging controversy in the press and in Congress.

The question of loyalty continued to be the most important consideration in choosing personnel for the EOP throughout Nixon's tenure in office. During his first term the White House produced the *Federal Personnel Manual*, which advised the appointment of only those persons who held the same partisan beliefs as the administration. As a guideline for appointments the *Manual* argued that policy control depended on political control of appointees:

> The record is quite replete with instances of the failures of the program, policy, and management goals because of sabotage by employees of the Executive Branch who engage in frustration of those efforts because of their political persuasion and their loyalty to the majority party of

Congress rather than the Executive that supervises them. [13]

Moreover, according to G. Calvin Mackenzie,

> Eventually, perhaps inevitably, the territorial aggressiveness of the postelection WHPO began to get out of control. Political criteria were applied to appointments to competitive positions in the civil service. A variety of ingenious ways to circumvent the merit system were developed and employed.... Subsequent investigations by congressional committees, journalists, and grand juries uncovered abundant evidence of agency, departmental, and White House efforts to subvert civil service merit hiring procedures for political purposes. [14]

The Ford Administration

Because of the political situation that triggered his rise to the presidency, Gerald R. Ford moved into the White House with little planning for staffing his Executive Office. From the beginning, however, Ford played an active role in the appointment process. He initially appointed a four-member transition team composed of some of his closest friends and colleagues: Donald Rumsfeld, Rogers C. B. Morton, William W. Scranton, and John O. Marsh, Jr. In the aftermath of Watergate, and faced with a possibly brief tenure in the White House, the administration and its transition team had to go to extra lengths to attract talented and loyal personnel from outside government. Ford's participation in the appointment process, however, facilitated the recruitment of appointees.

While Ford tried to follow the recommendations of his transition team by replacing all Nixon appointees, he did not succeed as quickly as he would have liked. Early in his administration the EOP largely was made up of both Nixon and Ford appointees. This resulted in a lack of staff loyalty to Ford's programs and objectives, and Ford thus began appointing those with whom he felt comfortable; his early appointments reflected his reliance on old friends and colleagues.

According to presidential scholar Edward D. Feigenbaum, the appointments made by Ford during his administration originated from four groups: the "old boys' network," including colleagues from the House of Representatives and some of Ford's congressional aides; the Grand Rapids crowd, or those from his Michigan past; the New York set, or colleagues of Vice President Nelson A. Rockefeller, a former New York governor (they were appointed primarily to the Domestic Council); and the "New Wave" group, who were primarily young and energetic and were appointed to highly responsible positions. [15]

The Carter Administration

When Jimmy Carter became president in 1976, he already had a personnel selection system in place. In the summer before the national election and a possible transition to the presidency, he had set up a small staff in Atlanta, known as the Policy Planning Office (PPO). Under the direction of Jack H. Watson, Jr., this group identified important positions in the new administration and people qualified to fill them. After the election the PPO became known as Talent Inventory Program (TIP) and was firmly established in the White House. Like similar programs before it, TIP provided a comprehensive inventory of potential candidates for the EOP and other positions.

The good intentions of TIP were upset, however, by

Vicissitudes of the ...

Since its creation by Franklin D. Roosevelt in 1939, the Executive Office of the President (EOP) has been a constantly changing, fluid entity. The strength and composition of a particular EOP office in the final analysis have depended on its relationship to the president. Some chief executives have preferred a formal organization; others have opted for informality. Some have relied on a small inner circle of advisers; others have drawn on a larger pool of talent. The distinction between a White House office or advisory body and an EOP office often has been blurred. Moreover, some offices were created first in the EOP and then transferred to the White House, or vice versa.

As presidential scholar Stephen Hess has noted, EOP offices frequently experience conflicting pulls between their mandate to serve the institution of the presidency as "objective" advisers and their loyalty toward a particular president and administration policies. At times Congress has tried to impose its view on the kind of advice a president needs by creating offices that an administration might not want. (Presidents, however, always can ignore such statutory advisers.)

President Franklin Roosevelt relied on an informal coterie of close White House advisers, as well as a large group of perhaps more than a hundred outside advisory bodies. At the same time, he established many new offices within the executive branch (primarily interdepartmental), the proliferation of which led to chaos. To address this problem the Committee on Administrative Management, which was convened in 1936, recommended changes in the White House staff and the creation of the Executive Office of the President. When the office finally came into being in 1939, the Bureau of the Budget (the predecessor of the Office of Management and Budget) and the National Resources Committee (renamed the National Resources Planning Board or NRPB) were added to it. The NRPB consisted of three part-time advisers who were responsible for planning long-range public works, assisting state and local governments, and informing the president of economic trends. The board was not very effective, however, and Congress abolished it in 1943. Another agency transferred to EOP in 1939 was the Office of Government Reports (a public information clearinghouse that became part of the Office of War Information in 1942). Roosevelt also established the Office of War Mobilization in 1939 as part of the Executive Office. The Committee for Congested Production Areas (1943-1944) and the War Refugee Board (1944-1945) were added later.[1]

During the presidency of Harry S Truman the Council of Economic Advisers (CEA), the National Security Council, and the Office of Defense Mobilization, among others, were added to EOP. The mission of the latter was to direct and coordinate federal agency activities during the Korean War. "Possibly no other legal act of either the Congress or the President ever came so close to the actual creation of an Assistant President," wrote John R. Steelman and H. Dewayne Kreager of the office's wide-ranging powers.[2] In 1951 the Office of Director for Mutual Security was established to provide military, economic, and technical aid to other nations. In 1953 its functions were transferred to the Foreign Operations Administration.

Eisenhower's EOP staff, like his cabinet, was composed primarily of business leaders, not politicians, and pragmatic "doers," rather than strictly conservative theoreticians. In contrast to Roosevelt's informal and some-

political infighting within the Carter administration. While Watson intended to make personnel selection a nonpolitical undertaking, the Georgia politicians who had managed Carter's campaign wanted some political control of the process. Macy, Adams, and Walter reported that as a result "no central coordinating mechanism emerged to manage the appointment process, and much of the work done by TIP was simply disregarded." Even though a personnel organization eventually emerged in the White House, "its ability to control the appointment process was undermined by a confused mandate."[16]

The confusion surrounding appointments arose from two conflicting concerns. Like most presidents, Carter wanted a responsive administration, staffed by appointees who were not only qualified but also loyal and free of conflicts of interest. At the same time, however, Carter came into office committed to a cabinet administration in which departments would run their own show, including selection of their own personnel. While these concerns little affected the selection of EOP members, they fostered in the Carter administration a conflict and ensuing paralysis that frustrated the filling of many EOP appointments. Many of the positions in Carter's executive branch went unfilled until the spring of his first year in office.

At first, Carter took an active interest in the appointment process. As time went on, however, he lost his enthusiasm for filling executive positions, and the task of filling most of the major vacancies became one of the primary responsibilities of Hamilton Jordan. One of Carter's top assistants from his home state of Georgia, Jordan was fiercely loyal to Carter. And in seeking similar loyalty in Carter appointees, Jordan made the appointment process a decidedly political affair. This set up a power struggle between Jordan and Watson over the control of appointments, which Jordan eventually won because of his close relationship to President Carter.

Carter's appointment process throughout his administration largely reflected the conflict of styles exhibited by Watson and Jordan. Major appointments were made either by department and agency heads or by Carter's staff through the "old boys' network." Consequently, there was little consistency in their quality and character.

One of Carter's most important EOP appointments indicates the problems the Carter administration faced in staffing. In nominating Bert Lance, a Carter supporter from Georgia, for director of the Office of Management and Budget, Carter's staff either failed to identify or ignored important information. Carter demanded a rather rigorous

... Executive Office of the President

what haphazard methods of seeking advice, Eisenhower—drawing on his military background—established an ordered chain of command and was not averse to delegating authority. He relied heavily on the National Security Council and CEA and was the first president to appoint a special assistant for national security affairs. During Eisenhower's tenure the directors of the Bureau of the Budget and Defense Mobilization, as well as the mutual security administrator, regularly attended the weekly cabinet meetings.

The White House EOP complex expanded considerably under President John F. Kennedy, with establishment of the Office of the Special Representative for Trade Negotiations, the Office of the Food for Peace Program, and others. Lyndon B. Johnson's "Great Society" programs resulted in a further expansion of EOP, including addition of the Office of Consumer Affairs and the Office of Economic Opportunity.

Richard Nixon also established a number of EOP offices during his presidency. Among them were the cabinet-level Council for Urban Affairs (precursor of the Domestic Council), the Office of Intergovernmental Relations, the Council on Environmental Quality, the Council for Rural Affairs, the Council on International Economic Policy, the Special Action Office for Drug Abuse Prevention, and the Office of Telecommunications Policy, which dealt with highly technical questions. At the same time Nixon abolished a number of offices, including the Space Council and Office of Economic Opportunity. He shifted the advisory functions of the Office of Science and Technology to the National Science Foundation and transferred the duties of the Office of Emergency Prepared-

ness to other agencies.

During his brief tenure in the White House, President Gerald R. Ford did little restructuring in the EOP except to replace Nixon's Special Action Office for Drug Abuse Prevention with the Office of Drug Abuse Policy. Most of Ford's organizational changes took place within the White House Office, which he reorganized to insure an open administration and accessibility to the president.

President Jimmy Carter reduced the White House office staff by 28 percent and the total EOP staff by 15 percent. His Reorganization Plan 1, which was implemented in April 1978, eliminated seven of the seventeen units in the Executive Office: the Office of Drug Abuse Policy, the Office of Telecommunications Policy, the Council on International Economic Policy, the Federal Property Council, the Energy Resources Council, the Economic Opportunity Council, and the Domestic Council (the latter, however, was reorganized). Congressional criticism of the plan focused primarily on the elimination of the Office of Drug Abuse Policy. Critics complained that the office had been created by Congress less than a year before and had not been given time to prove itself.

President Ronald Reagan further streamlined the Executive Office, particularly where its functions were related to support for cabinet councils, which he reduced in number during his second term.

1. Stephen Hess, *Organizing the Presidency* (Washington, D.C.: Brookings, 1976), 38.
2. John R. Steelman and H. Dewayne Kreager, "The Executive Office as Administrative Coordinator," *Law and Contemporary Problems* 21 (Autumn 1956): 704.

security and conflict-of-interest check on each appointee, but the system broke down in the case of Lance. Facing political pressures for appointment, the administration overlooked evidence that Lance may have been involved in questionable banking practices and campaign conduct. After several press revelations to this effect, Lance was forced to resign in September 1977.

The Reagan Administration

Ronald Reagan, like Carter, set up a presidential staffing organization during the 1980 presidential campaign that was carried over into the new administration. Headed by E. Pendleton James, a professional headhunter who had worked in the Nixon administration, this organization attempted to increase the president's control over his administration by tying policy objectives to executive appointments. Appointees not only had to have the qualifications and talent necessary to carry through on policies, but they also had to agree with Reagan's objectives. Reagan's chief advisers believed that only then could the administration be confident that the president's programs would be implemented.

Unlike the Carter administration, the Reagan adminis-

tration showed consistency in its appointments, and the appointment procedure worked well under James. While there was much internal debate over various nominees, almost always agreement was reached on the criteria for appointment and the objectives to be sought in potential appointees. The Reagan administration's stated criteria for appointment to the EOP were fairly straightforward: "Support for Reagan's objectives, integrity, competence, teamwork, toughness, and a commitment to change." [17]

During the transition period and the first year of his administration, Reagan consistently displayed an active interest in the appointment process. Reportedly, he made all the important staffing decisions. This helped reduce congressional influence on administration appointments because congressional leaders did not attempt to exert as much influence on Reagan as they might have if they believed his staff was making the final decisions.

Political party influence over the appointment process also declined during the Reagan administration. In the past, political parties had served as clearinghouses for patronage requests and had put pressure on the White House to make certain appointments for political reasons. During the Reagan administration, however, potential appointees went directly to the president and his staff to apply for

EOP jobs. This situation relieved some of the pressure on the president to appoint candidates who may not have been his choice, but it also created something of a logistical problem. It placed a tremendous burden on Reagan's personnel staff at a time when the staff was not in the best position to handle it, during the transition and the early stages of the new administration.

Further complicating the selection procedure for Reagan (and future presidents) were the increasingly rigorous ethical and conflict-of-interest considerations mandated by Congress after the Watergate scandals. This increased scrutiny not only delayed the appointment process by requiring much more complicated investigation and disclosure procedures, but it also made recruiting much more difficult by raising the stakes for public employment. Potential EOP officeholders had to endure a thorough and considerable background check. And in many cases they had to give up control of their financial holdings by putting them into some form of financial trust to avoid potential conflicts of interest. Such measures caused many to think more than once about leaving a lucrative private endeavor to serve the federal government.

Office of Management and Budget

The history of the Office of Management and Budget (OMB), previously known as the Bureau of the Budget (BOB), is inextricably linked to the development of the president's Executive Office, which was established in 1939. The budget office, created in 1921, was one of several offices to be reconstituted in the EOP where it joined the National Security Council and Domestic Policy Council as one of the three primary Executive Office advisory organizations. Indeed, the budget office has considered itself "first among equals" in the Executive Office, according to many observers.

The Office of Management and Budget, as it has been known since 1970, has far-reaching influence over not only how much the federal government spends but also how it spends and how the states disburse what they are allocated. The office is the final arbiter of the budgets that the cabinet departments and other agencies propose to send to the president and Congress for authorization and appropriation. It is a principal broker in distributing the taxpayers' dollars.

As OMB has described its own role:

> The actions of OMB touch the lives of all Americans. Nowhere are those actions more directly and broadly felt in society than in OMB's preparation of the budget.... The budget is essentially a resource allocation plan for the vast amount of federal funds and staff involved in activities that range from agriculture to zoology and cover locations that range from a lone fire lookout tower in Idaho to a housing project in the heart of New York City, from research in the Antarctic to a Peace Corps office in Ecuador, from salaries for all government employees to school lunch subsidies, and from the operating budget of the Supreme Court to funds for the launch of a spacecraft.[18]

Throughout its long existence the president's budget office has been a steadfast accountant of federal expenditures. It also has played a major role in fashioning government policy by virtue of its recommendations, its director's access to the president, and periodic self-reappraisals of its own functional efficacy and organization.

Shifts in the office's influence on presidential—and subsequent congressional—decisions have been caused largely by each director's relations with the president and Congress, each director's perception of the role of the budget office, and, more indirectly, changes in overall relations between the executive branch and Capitol Hill. But OMB is the president's right-hand adviser on what federal spending and revenue should be. The president, in close consultation with the budget office, approves or modifies the proposals made by OMB. Thus, it is the president's budget that is sent to Congress, which then deals with the spending and revenue program as it sees fit.

Projections for the vast spending of the federal bureaucracy (amounting to three-quarters of a trillion dollars, or about 20 percent of the nation's gross national product) are contained in several volumes produced by a rather small budget office staff (numbering 533 in 1987). These volumes are compiled from submissions by federal agencies on a timetable that allows little latitude for further extensive revision by those agencies. What the administration proposes to spend in the forthcoming fiscal year, beginning October 1, is presented by the president in a January message to Congress. This major document is supplemented by a thick appendix that details the presidential plans (and frequently through its expenditure breakdowns gives a sharp insight into an agency's overall goals), by a less technical hundred-page "Budget in Brief," and by other analytical documents on special topics. Congress then decides item by item, through the relevant authorization and appropriation committees and subcommittees and finally on the floor, which parts of the president's program it will accept, modify, or reject. The budget office plays a central role throughout the process.

Since 1974 the president's budget office has had something of an analytical counterpoint on Capitol Hill. In enacting the Congressional Budget and Impoundment Control Act (PL 93-344), Congress established a Congressional Budget Office to oversee deadlines on clearing appropriations bills and to make its own recommendations on government spending. Another check on the federal government's expenditures is the General Accounting Office (GAO), which was established in 1921 by the same act that created the Bureau of the Budget. But while GAO's initial mandate and activities essentially have remained unchanged (a congressional arm for overseeing and auditing federal spending), the executive branch budget office has expanded its role, increasingly injecting itself into areas that some critics have viewed as being beyond the bounds of its initial mandate of providing objective accounting and analysis. The budget office's history provides much evidence of the push and pull between a perception of its role as a nonpartisan "factual" adviser and its role as a premier executive office with an obligation to promote the office of the presidency, if not always the policies of a particular president.

Origins and Development of the Budget Office

Before 1921 no system existed in the executive branch for unified consideration or control of fiscal policy. The secretary of the Treasury did no more than compile the estimates of the various departments before forwarding them to Congress for approval. No coordination, analysis, or recommendation was attempted, and it became increasingly apparent that the procedure was inadequate.

In 1911 President William Howard Taft appointed a Commission on Economy and Efficiency to review the budget process. The panel recommended creation of a central office, but this measure was not enacted for several years, largely owing to the involvement of Taft's successor, Woodrow Wilson, in World War I and its aftermath. The next president, Warren G. Harding, refocused attention on the idea, however, and in 1921 Congress enacted the Budget and Accounting Act, thereby ending the right of federal departments and agencies to decide for themselves what appropriations levels to seek. The act established the Bureau of the Budget to serve as a central clearinghouse for the president's budget requests; the office, however, initially was placed in the Department of the Treasury. The bill authorized BOB "to assemble, correlate, revise, reduce or increase the requests for appropriations of the several departments or establishments." The bureau also was authorized to develop "plans for the organization, coordination and management of the Executive Branch of the Government with a view to efficient and economical services." The act further required the new office, at the request of any congressional committee having jurisdiction over revenue or appropriations, to provide that panel with the assistance or information it requested.

Budget Circular 49, approved by President Harding on December 19, 1921, called for all agency proposals for appropriations to be submitted to the president before they were sent to Congress. The proposals were to be reviewed for their relationship to "the president's financial program" and were to be forwarded to Capitol Hill only if the president approved them.

Early Directors of BOB

Much depended on the personality and capabilities of the first budget director, as well as his relationship with the president. Gen. Charles G. Dawes, a former chief of supply procurement for the U.S. Army in France and later vice president (1925-1929) under Calvin Coolidge, was selected by President Harding for the post. Hard working and enthusiastic, Dawes established a close working relationship with the president, who allowed him frequent access to cabinet officials. Although Dawes set out to develop long-range tasks, his major emphasis was on efficiency and economy in government agency programs, including his own bureau's operations.

Dawes believed, moreover, that Treasury was not the place for BOB because it should be independent of any agency influence and answerable solely to the president. He was a strict constructionist, however, concerning his organization's role as policy maker, firmly believing that BOB should be impartial and nonpolitical. According to the 1945 budget bureau *Staff Orientation Manual,* "Dawes had not prepared the bureau for the assumption of functions more typical of a general administrative staff agency. The broader aspects of administrative management, outside the province of economical conduct of business transactions, had not received the attention they deserved." [19]

The three succeeding bureau directors, including Franklin D. Roosevelt's first appointment, Lewis W. Douglas, had similar views about BOB's role. As a result, the agency's staff remained relatively small given its broad

statutory mandate, and its effectiveness was curtailed. Douglas disagreed with Roosevelt's burgeoning New Deal projects and their hefty expenditures, and he resigned in 1934. He was succeeded by a Treasury Department staffer, Daniel Bell, who served as acting BOB director for the next five years. Although relations between Bell and the president were not close, a number of changes effected during the period enhanced the bureau's standing.

An Expanded Role and New Home

In 1935 President Roosevelt broadened the budget office's clearinghouse function to include other legislation as well as appropriations requests, saying that he had been "quite horrified—not once but a dozen times—by reading in the paper that some department or agency was after this, that or the other without my knowledge." [20] According to political scientist Richard E. Neustadt, Roosevelt's actions were not merely designed to extend the budget process. "On the contrary ... this was Roosevelt's creation, intended to protect not just his budget, but his prerogatives, his freedom of action, and his choice of policies in an era of fast-growing government and of determined presidential leadership." [21]

In 1939 Roosevelt heeded the recommendations of his Committee on Administrative Management—chaired by Louis Brownlow and appointed to study the organization of the executive branch—by issuing the first reorganization plan in the nation's history. Approved by Congress, it created the Executive Office of the President, of which BOB was a major part. A second reorganization plan established divisions of the Executive Office and gave more power to BOB to improve and coordinate statistical services. *(See box, Presidential Reorganization Authority, p. 72.)*

The budget office expanded considerably under the direction of Harold Smith, who served as its director from 1939 to 1946, the longest tenure of any budget director. Growing from a staff of forty to more than six hundred in 1944, BOB retained its position as the central budget review agency and increased its powers in the areas of legislative clearance and administrative management. While before it had been empowered to send departmental legislative requests to the president—and, with presidential approval, to Congress—only if they had fiscal implications, BOB was given oversight authority during Smith's tenure for all proposed legislation, executive orders and proclamations, and recommendations for reorganization plans. According to presidential scholar Stephen Hess, under Smith BOB attracted competent young professionals who recommended far-reaching management changes in federal departments.[22]

During World War II the budget office played a central role in managing the defense and war effort. According to Roger Jones, a former BOB official, "There was rapid acceleration of attention to the Budget Bureau's role as an organization and management planner for the President and as a sorter out of fiscal priorities and possibilities." [23]

Smith was succeeded by James E. Webb, a little-known bureaucrat from Texas, who proved to be an effective manager. "While Harold Smith was responsible for creating the modern BOB, James Webb was instrumental in redirecting bureau staff work into the program development process," wrote Larry Berman in his history of OMB. "Many observers viewed the Webb period as the golden age of the Bureau of the Budget." [24] Under Webb's direction the bureau assumed responsibility for drafting complex legislation such as the 1946 Employment Act (which created the Council of Economic Advisers) and the Taft-Hartley Labor-Management Relations Act of 1947. BOB's relations with Congress also expanded; congressional committees increasingly requested the bureau's opinion on pending legislation.

Hiatus and Reorganization

Because of BOB's added responsibilities it soon became apparent that a restructuring was needed to bring more efficiency and coordination to the budget office's operations. Although postponed by Webb's resignation in 1948, a major overhaul of BOB was carried out in 1952. Budgetary, fiscal analysis, and administrative management were divided along functional lines, and five operating divisions were established to work directly with government agencies on program, budgetary, economic, and management issues.

Although streamlined, the bureau during the first years of Dwight D. Eisenhower's two-term presidency became less central to policy making. Two of the BOB directors were bankers and two were accountants; none had experience in public administration. The president, wrote Berman, viewed the budget office primarily as "his agent for obtaining control of spending trends." [25] Yet Eisenhower's initial appointment as budget director, Joseph M. Dodge (who served from January 1953 until April 1954), was the first to hold cabinet rank. Later, in 1958, when the president named deputy director Maurice Stans to head the office, a senior budget official said it was "like opening up all the curtains in the building and letting the sun shine in. There was confidence, there was leadership, everything turned around...." [26]

Despite that assessment, others expressed the view that BOB had lost some initiative, flexibility, and creativity. Outside pressure for reform was growing as well. In 1957 the President's Advisory Committee on Government Organization, chaired by Nelson A. Rockefeller, proposed an overhaul of BOB that would establish an Office of Administration reporting directly to the president. The recommendation was opposed by Stans, who suggested instead reorganizing and upgrading the bureau into an Office of Executive Management. In 1959, while these proposals were pending, the budget office initiated its own internal review of operations.

In 1960 President-elect John F. Kennedy asked the Brookings Institution (a private research organization) to study the role of the Bureau of the Budget. The Brookings report recommended that the BOB director possess "sensitivity to political and administrative as well as financial and organizational matters." [27] In fact, the political emphasis dominated during Kennedy's three years in office. BOB directors David E. Bell and Kermit Gordon were program oriented and served as close personal advisers to the president. But in doing so, oversight of the day-to-day management of the office fell by the wayside, and the bureau's operations suffered.

The Great Society and the Bureau

Questions about BOB's role, organization, purpose, and efficiency deepened during the presidency of Lyndon B. Johnson with the advent of his complex and financially burdensome "Great Society" programs. The numerous task forces established advocated new welfare and other proposals with little attention paid to their cost or how they would work together. As a result, the focus of the budget office shifted from its primary institutional mandate as budget overseer to that of coordinator of interagency activities.

The problem BOB confronted by the end of the Johnson presidency in 1969 is reflected in the figures. In 1949 the bureau employed 534 employees to oversee federal expenditures of $40 billion. By 1969, 503 staffers had to contend with a budget of $193 billion, involving scores of innovative programs, conflicting agency priorities, and uncoordinated activities.

Dissatisfaction with the bureau's performance was apparent both within and outside the office. A task force established in 1965 by Budget Director Charles L. Schultze concluded that BOB needed to "develop a clear definition of its role and of its organization and staff requirements under the pressure of new federal programs and responsibilities." [28] According to an internal staff survey, the bureau's prestige was at an all-time low because of too much attention to detail, personnel problems, lack of internal management (the director spent too much time advising the president and too little time attending to the agency's organization), a rapidly growing work load, lack of feedback on what was wanted, and inadequate skills for dealing with current problems. A number of outside studies also were highly critical of BOB's management of the Great Society programs.

From BOB to OMB

Like Kennedy, President-elect Richard Nixon established a task force to study government organization. The panel gave top priority to revising the structure of the Executive Office and White House staff and to renewing the president's expired authority to make organizational changes. Congress granted the authority in March 1969, and in April Nixon established an advisory council, headed by industrialist Roy L. Ash, to study the issues confronting the establishment of more effective executive branch operations. The Ash panel recommended creation of an Office of Executive Management and a Domestic Policy Council. The primary responsibility of the Office of Executive Management (which would include a substantially revised budget bureau) was to manage programs, while the Domestic Policy Council would make forecasts, analyze alternative policies, and suggest program revisions. (See "Office of Policy Development," p. 39, in this chapter.)

After renaming the Office of Executive Management the Office of Management and Budget (and dropping "Policy" from the Domestic Policy Council), Nixon sent Reorganization Plan 2 to Congress on March 12, 1970. It was accompanied by a message:

> The Domestic Council will be primarily concerned with what we do; the Office of Management and Budget will be primarily concerned with how we do it, and how well we do it.... The creation of the Office of Management and Budget represents far more than a mere change of name for the Bureau of the Budget. It represents a basic change in concept and emphasis, reflecting the broader management needs of the Office of the President. [29]

The House Subcommittee on Executive and Legislative Reorganization approved a resolution of disapproval. Some top staffers at BOB also opposed the reorganization, but the House of Representatives approved the measure on

May 13, 1970 (after strenuous Ash committee lobbying), and the Senate followed suit on May 16. On July 1, 1970, by means of Executive Order 11541, the Bureau of the Budget was officially redesignated the Office of Management and Budget.

This redesignation did not downgrade the budgeting function of the office; rather, it amplified it. The budget office's existing responsibilities were expanded, and greater emphasis was placed on organization and management systems, development of executive talent and a broader career staff, better dissemination of information, and appropriate use of modern techniques and equipment. All these changes were intended to enhance the capability of the executive branch to coordinate, evaluate, and improve the efficiency of government programs. Thus in one major new role, OMB was to help implement major legislation, such as bills to preserve the environment, under which several agencies would share responsibility for action.

Another major new task assigned OMB was coordination of the complex system of federal grants. This often involved more than one federal agency as well as agencies and government entities at the state and local levels.

Finally, OMB was asked to evaluate the cost-effectiveness of particular programs and the relative priority of the needs they were designed to meet.

Some observers have speculated that OMB was established to strengthen the budget planners' hand in questioning the expenditure requests of the Department of Defense. This task had fallen into disarray as Pentagon budgets skyrocketed and became almost uncontrollable.

George P. Shultz, OMB director from 1970 to 1972, established himself as a principal adviser in domestic affairs. Under his leadership career officers were replaced by noncareer officers who served as assistant directors and dealt with policy decisions. The career officers then retained responsibility for day-to-day OMB operations.

During the Watergate crisis, when the president was under seige and his domestic policy adviser, John D. Ehrlichman, and several others on the White House staff were under investigation, OMB assumed de facto responsibility for day-to-day management of the government. Yet according to observers, OMB, even with its expanded role, did not fare well under the Nixon presidency. "The Office of Management and Budget was a major casualty of the Nixon presidency, in part for what it did, but also for what it appeared to be doing," wrote Berman. "By responding to the partisan needs of the president, OMB depleted valuable credibility with its other clients—leading many observers to maintain that OMB could not serve the long-range needs of the presidency." [30]

Controversies over the Role and Directors of OMB

Partly in reaction to what was perceived as OMB's partisan role, Congress enacted legislation in 1973 that required Senate approval of the office's director and deputy director. James Lynn, who served under Nixon's vice president and successor, Gerald R. Ford, was the first head of OMB to be subject to confirmation. He did much to repair the agency's "overly politicized" image.

Thomas Bertram Lance was appointed OMB director by President Jimmy Carter, who succeeded Ford in 1977. Lance followed Lynn's philosophy of reestablishing the agency's image as an objective assistant to the presidency, rather than a partisan political adviser. He was one of Carter's closest confidants, however. Lance resigned after less than a year in office when faced with accusations of unethical banking practices during his years as a Georgia bank president. He was succeeded by James T. McIntyre, Jr., who was serving as deputy director of OMB.

During President Ronald Reagan's first term in office (1981-1985), OMB found itself the center of political attention with Reagan's appointment of David A. Stockman, a two-term Republican representative from Michigan, to the director's post. Reagan selected Stockman to lead his revolutionary campaign to cut both government spending and taxes after Stockman caught the presidential candidate's eye in 1980 while playing the role of independent candidate John B. Anderson in a practice debate. Stockman began his career in Washington in 1970 as a legislative assistant to Anderson.

Reagan was particularly impressed with Stockman's knowledge of economics. And Stockman's November 1980 "manifesto" on how the new Republican administration could avoid an "economic Dunkirk" seemed to seal his fate as Reagan's chief economic adviser. In fact, Stockman has been credited with being the main architect of the massive 1981 tax and budget cuts that he and others in the administration said would lower inflation, spur economic growth, and eventually eliminate the deficit.

Instead, the economy began to sour, and in the December 1981 issue of the *Atlantic Monthly* Stockman conceded that the tax cutting went too far and defense spending should have been restrained. He revealed other doubts as well about the administration's economic policy, saying, "None of us really understands what's going on with all these numbers."

Publication of the article, it was thought, would mean the end of Stockman's time in office. He offered his resignation, but instead of accepting it, Reagan took Stockman to the "woodshed" for a verbal beating. Afterward, Stockman's impact was primarily in behind-the-scenes negotiations on the budget. During the following three years he was credited with using his knowledge of the minutiae of the federal budget to help steer through Congress several deficit-reduction measures that cut spending and raised taxes.

Nonetheless, during his latter days in office Stockman's growing exclusion from the inner circle in the administration cost him influence on Capitol Hill, according to members of Congress. Frustrated by his inability to bring down the deficit, Stockman resigned in July 1985.

"He was an extraordinarily talented and capable person," said House Budget Committee Democrat Thomas J. Downey (N.Y.), who often disagreed with Stockman on policy. "He had a tenacity and ability to frame the issues politically. Those qualities will be missed." [31] Stockman was succeeded by James C. Miller III, then chairman of the Federal Trade Commission and former administrator of OMB's Office of Information and Regulatory Affairs.

Organization and Functions of OMB

The organization and functions of the president's budget agency have changed often through the years. The scope of its purview has reflected the growth of the economy and federal budget, each president's political inclinations and perception of what the office should do, changing relations within the executive branch and with Congress, and the office's own perception of its mission. Internal organizational realignments usually have accompanied such changes.

Organization of OMB

OMB is headed by a director who is assisted by a deputy director. Both are appointed by the president and confirmed by the Senate.

The office, which had 533 employees in 1987, is broken down into budget and management divisions, as well as an administrative and support staff. The budget staff is grouped into program areas: national security and international affairs; human resources, veterans, and labor; economics and government; and natural resources, energy, and science. These staff members are responsible for preparing agency funding requests, supervising spending authorized by Congress, and formulating economic and financial analyses and forecasts. Special studies groups within the division conduct in-depth reviews of selected programs. The work of the budget analysts is compiled by the Budget Review Division, which looks at the programs in light of overall federal spending. The division also is responsible for developing better management techniques for formulating and presenting the budget.

The management staff—subdivided into a management improvement and evaluation division, an intergovernmental affairs division, and a financial management division—oversees government procurement and management. In doing this, the staff evaluates the efficiency of programs and proposes methods for improving interagency coordination (state and local as well as federal). The Office of Federal Procurement Policy develops and monitors government-wide purchasing policies.

Functions of OMB

In 1970 OMB was designated "the President's principal arm for the exercise of his managerial functions." This responsibility grew in 1974 with enactment of the Congressional Budget and Impoundment Control Act; it added oversight of congressional budget reporting deadlines to the office's work load, among other tasks. The same year, Congress established a forty-person Office of Federal Procurement within OMB to handle procurement and contracting policy development. In 1980 the Office of Information and Regulatory Affairs (OIRA) was created in OMB to coordinate the administration's efforts to cut down on federal regulations and paperwork.

By 1987 OMB's responsibilities included:
~ advising the president on the nation's fiscal and economic policies
~ preparing the budget and formulating the government's fiscal program
~ supervising execution of the executive branch budget
~ reviewing the organizational structures and management procedures of the executive branch
~ evaluating the performance of federal programs
~ encouraging interagency and intergovernmental cooperation and coordination
~ coordinating and clearing with the president departmental recommendations for proposed legislation to be sent to Congress and for presidential action on bills passed by Congress
~ assisting the relevant departments and the White House in the consideration, clearance, and preparation of executive orders and proclamations

~ keeping the president advised of activities proposed, actually initiated, and completed by federal agencies, and coordinating interagency activities to ensure that funds appropriated by Congress were spent with the least possible overlap.[32]

By far the most important function of the Office of Management and Budget is its central role in the federal budget process. The administration's budget proposes specific levels of new spending authority for appropriations, as well as outlays (amounts to be spent for the fiscal year) for all government agencies and functions. The budget presents as well a detailed account of the administration's program.

Controversial New Role: OIRA and Regulation

President Reagan entered office in 1981 determined to cut down on the number of federal regulations and amount of paperwork that the private sector must contend with in doing business. The 1980 Paperwork Reduction Act (PL 96-511) established the Office of Information and Regulatory Affairs as a principal unit of OMB. Its task is to oversee and review the actions of all major regulatory agencies to determine whether they meet administrative guidelines for studying the costs and benefits of proposed and existing regulations.

All of Reagan's top economic advisers favored regulatory reform and deregulation wherever it seemed possible, and plans for the attack were developed before Reagan was inaugurated. Incoming OMB director Stockman called for an "orchestrated series of unilateral administrative actions to defer, revise, or rescind existing and pending regulations where clear legal authority exists." [33]

On February 17, 1981, Reagan issued Executive Order 12291, which required executive branch agencies to prepare a regulatory impact analysis for all new and existing major regulations. OMB's regulatory office was authorized to issue criteria for deciding when a regulation was needed and to order an agency to perform a regulatory impact analysis that would assess the potential benefits, costs, and net benefits of a regulation.

A second executive order (12498), issued in January 1985, required agencies to give OMB their agendas for each year, including activities such as studies that might lead to regulation. The order gave OMB authority to determine whether agency plans met administration objectives and guidelines.

The zeal with which the Office of Information and Regulatory Affairs assumed its role, however, came under attack by outside experts, regulators, and members of Congress. Congressional critics of the expanded OMB function argued that the office had become a regulatory czar and that department and other federal agency personnel—not the budget office staff—should have final authority over rules needed to implement laws passed by Congress. According to a May 1986 report by the Senate Environment and Public Works Committee, "OMB's ability to . . . substantively influence agency regulations and to delay their promulgation is inappropriate encroachment upon congressional legislative authority and upon agency independence and expertise. . . ." [34]

In February 1986 that position was upheld by a federal district court in Washington, D.C. The court ruled (*Environmental Defense Fund* v. *Thomas*) that OMB's ability to delay or force changes in agency regulations was "incompatible with the will of Congress and cannot be sustained as a valid exercise of the president's Article II powers" (Article II of the Constitution delineates the president's powers as chief executive).[35]

The result of congressional ire over OMB's new regulatory authority was a 1986 attempt to eliminate funding for the OIRA. Although that effort failed and a compromise authorized the office through 1989, the authorizing bill required that future administrators of OIRA be presidential appointees, subject to Senate confirmation. The bill also restricted OMB's regulatory oversight functions to reviewing requests for information contained in proposed rules or regulations.

In addition to OMB's regulatory authority, which was a source of contention during the Reagan administration, Congress scrutinized the entire structure of the federal government's budgetary procedures. In June 1986 the Senate Governmental Affairs Committee approved a sweeping bill that would create within OMB an Office of Financial Management, two deputy director positions, and an executive deputy director position. Although the bill died that year and was not reintroduced in 1987, its introduction and testimony on the legislation indicated that, as stated by Governmental Affairs Chairman William V. Roth, Jr. (R-Del.), "We're dissatisfied with the 'M' [in OMB]." [36]

Indeed, over its long history the president's budget office has assumed a variety of functions and responsibilities so vast that it has not been difficult to find some critics of aspects of its work. Yet the overall consensus has appeared to be that OMB is dedicated to performing its functions well and that, although some internal restructuring might be needed, the agency has a secure place in the Executive Office structure.

National Security Council

In the decades following World War II the Executive Office of the President assumed an increasingly important role in all aspects of the management of foreign and defense policy. A key vehicle used by most presidents in seeking to expand their authority in these areas has been the National Security Council (NSC).

Formally, the NSC is composed of the president, the vice president, and the secretaries of state and defense, with the director of central intelligence and the chairman of the Joint Chiefs of Staff serving as advisers. It is the highest-level advisory body to the president on military and diplomatic issues.

The National Security Council was established in 1947 to help the president coordinate the actions of government agencies into a single cohesive policy for dealing with other nations. Many members of Congress also saw the new panel as another institutional check on President Harry S Truman's power in the areas of foreign affairs and defense. The council has acted as a true decision-making body on only a few important occasions. In 1956, for example, members of the NSC helped formulate President Dwight D. Eisenhower's response to the Soviet invasion of Hungary.

Instead, the prime significance of the NSC has stemmed from the development of its staff into an apparatus used by presidents to implement their personal visions of U.S. foreign policy. The NSC staff is made up of policy experts who analyze foreign policy issues and make recommendations to the president. They are distinct from the formal members of the council. Presidents have turned to the NSC because it is subject to little effective control from Congress and is without the independent institutional loyalties frequently evident in the State, Defense, and other departments.

The role of the NSC has varied greatly over the years, usually depending on the personal influence of the president's national security adviser, who heads the NSC staff. When the national security adviser has been a relatively weak figure within the government, the NSC staff has been merely a bureaucratic shell with little power. At other times, however, it has been the dominant institutional force in the setting of foreign policy; this occurred under President Richard Nixon's national security adviser, Henry A. Kissinger.

During the Reagan administration NSC staffers played key roles in carrying out secret plans to sell arms to Iran and to divert the proceeds to guerrillas fighting the leftist government of Nicaragua. The so-called Iran-contra affair was a major political embarrassment for President Ronald Reagan during his second term.

Since Kissinger's term as national security adviser, considerable debate has raged over how much independent authority the NSC staff should exercise. Many experts in the organization of foreign policy argue that the NSC staff should be limited to managing the flow of information and policy options from the departments to the president. But some former national security advisers argue that their office and the NSC staff in general should have considerable authority to define the president's overall policy and to control the departments to ensure that this policy is carried out.

Origins and Development of NSC

The NSC represents the first institutional attempt in U.S. history to foster coordination and cooperation among the organizations contributing to a U.S. national security policy. Before the end of World War II the president was essentially the only person able to impose harmony on the often opposing positions and actions of the State and War departments and other agencies.

The conflicts and lack of coordination among the military services and civilian agencies during World War II convinced many government officials that a fundamental reorganization of the national security structure was needed. This realization led in 1947 to passage of the National Security Act, landmark legislation that created the Defense Department out of the old War (Army) and Navy departments. The act also established the Central Intelligence Agency (CIA).

Passage of the National Security Act was marked by bitter debate in Congress and in the services over the creation of a single military command system. But the law's provisions establishing the NSC as a permanent agency for policy coordination enjoyed broad support. According to the act, the purpose of the NSC was to "advise the president with respect to the integration of domestic, foreign, and military policies relating to the national security...." [37]

The role played by the NSC in the decades that followed was generally the product of the attitudes of succeeding presidents toward it. As a 1978 Congressional Research Service study of the NSC observed, "The NSC was a malleable organization, to be used as each President saw fit. Thus, its use, internal substructure and ultimate effect would be directly dependent on the style and wishes of the President." [38]

In its early years under President Truman, the NSC was not a major factor in the formulation of foreign and defense policy. Truman viewed the council as only an advisory body and rarely attended its meetings. President Eisenhower, by contrast, carried out a major expansion and institutionalization of the NSC. Perhaps most important, he appointed an assistant to the president for national security affairs—a position not mentioned in the 1947 act—to head the council staff. He frequently attended NSC meetings, moreover, and relied on its advice during times of international crisis.

Eisenhower's heavy reliance on the NSC led to complaints from the Senate Government Operations Committee and others that the council had become "overinstitutionalized." President John F. Kennedy came into office thus determined to rely more on a small group of personal advisers than on the NSC bureaucracy. Although Kennedy worked closely with his national security adviser, McGeorge Bundy, he ordered a substantial reduction in the staff size and responsibilities of the NSC. President Lyndon B. Johnson followed a pattern similar to Kennedy's. Although the NSC system as a whole was not a major factor in determining policy, Walt W. Rostow, who became national security adviser in 1966, played an important role in encouraging Johnson to order a major escalation of the Vietnam War.

The role of the NSC underwent a radical change under Nixon and his national security adviser, Kissinger. The NSC staff tripled in size, to about fifty high-level professional experts, and it wielded unprecedented power within the Washington bureaucracy. Kissinger himself became the coarchitect of Nixon's key foreign policy moves, including the negotiated end to the Vietnam War, the opening to Communist China, and the onset of détente with the Soviet Union.

Kissinger enlarged the power of his office in two major ways. One was a shift from the strictly advisory role played by his predecessors to an active involvement in diplomatic negotiations. Beginning in 1969, for example, he engaged in secret diplomacy with the North Vietnamese, holding private talks with enemy leaders in Paris that eventually led to a peace settlement. Even more dramatic was his secret trip to China in 1971. At that point, Nixon and Kissinger were ready to end the decades-old hostility of the United States toward the Communist Chinese regime, but they were unwilling to reveal their intentions to the world. On a trip to Pakistan, Kissinger eluded the press and observers and flew unnoticed to Peking, where he met with Communist leaders. Upon returning to the West, Kissinger made an announcement that shook world power diplomacy: the potential alliance of the United States and China against the Soviet Union.

Kissinger also succeeded in completely overshadowing Nixon's secretary of state, William P. Rogers. He worked to exclude Rogers from key information and negotiations, resulting in a strong personal and institutional antagonism that has continued to affect relations between subsequent national security advisers and secretaries of state. In his memoirs, Kissinger revealed the bitter strains between the two men. Rogers was an "insensitive neophyte," Kissinger wrote, while acknowledging that Rogers viewed him as an "egotistical nitpicker." [39]

The conflict between the national security adviser and the secretary of state ended in 1973 when Kissinger assumed the latter post while retaining the former. Tensions continued at a relatively low level under the administration of Gerald R. Ford, who became president following Nixon's resignation in 1974. In November 1975 Kissinger relinquished his position as Ford's national security adviser to Lieut. Gen. Brent Scowcroft. Scowcroft viewed his responsibilities primarily in terms of coordinating and overseeing foreign policy actions; he did not attempt to challenge Kissinger's primacy in determining foreign policy.

President Jimmy Carter came into office proclaiming his intention to place more responsibility in the departments and agencies while reducing the policy-making role of the NSC. Almost from the start, however, there were sharp conflicts between National Security Adviser Zbigniew Brzezinski and Secretary of State Cyrus R. Vance. Not content with being a mere facilitator of the policy views of others, Brzezinski was determined to assert his own views, which centered around a policy of hard-line confrontation with the Soviet Union. Carter did not indicate whether he agreed with Brzezinski or with Vance, who stressed mutual cooperation and arms control agreements with the Soviets. As a result, the public and foreign governments frequently were left in confusion about which man truly reflected U.S. foreign policy. Finally, however, Vance resigned in protest against the unsuccessful 1980 attempt to conduct a military rescue of American hostages held in Iran, leaving Brzezinski with more influence over foreign policy during the last year of Carter's presidency.

Ronald Reagan assumed the presidency affirming cabinet government as his model. Although Reagan was somewhat more willing than his immediate predecessors to hold formal NSC meetings with the vice president and secretaries of state and defense, he de-emphasized the role of the NSC staff and dismantled much of the existing elaborate system of NSC staff committees that analyzed and formulated policy. He did not move to establish a formal NSC structure until 1982. At the same time, he designated the secretary of state as his principal foreign policy adviser.

During his first six years in office, Reagan had four national security advisers, who were viewed in Washington as relatively weak figures, lacking either strong foreign policy experience or close ties to the president. They were virtually unknown to the public. Behind the scenes, however, two of the advisers and their staffs were directing operations of pivotal importance to Reagan's presidency. Investigations of the Iran-contra affair revealed that Robert C. McFarlane and Vice Adm. John M. Poindexter masterminded the secret plan to sell arms to Iran in exchange for the release of American hostages held in Lebanon. Moreover, NSC staffer Lieut. Col. Oliver L. North, with Poindexter's approval, arranged for the allegedly illegal transfer of proceeds from the sales to Iran to the "contra" guerrillas in Nicaragua. In carrying out these activities, McFarlane, Poindexter, and North became involved in the operational side of foreign policy at a level far beyond that achieved by Kissinger even at his most active. In the wake of disclosures in late 1986 about the secret transactions, Reagan replaced Poindexter with Frank C. Carlucci, who moved to scale back the power of the NSC staff.

Organization and Functions of NSC

The organizational structure of the NSC over the years has been as fluid as the roles to which different presidents have assigned it. Other than the presence, since Eisenhower's presidency, of a national security adviser as head of the NSC staff, there has been little consistency in either the organization of the NSC staff hierarchy or in the large number of interagency working groups and oversight committees established within the NSC structure. Nor has the number of NSC employees remained constant. Reaching a total of three hundred or so under Kissinger, the number of employees at all levels within the NSC structure fell to perhaps a quarter of that under Brzezinski and rose again to 180 by the end of Reagan's first term.

One theme has been consistent over time, however: the high degree of independence of the NSC from outside control. Like other parts of the Executive Office of the President, the NSC is institutionally responsible only to the chief executive. Thus over the years, presidents have relied increasingly on the council's staff because of their confidence that it could be held accountable only to them. Presidents frequently have questioned the loyalty of staff members of the State and Defense departments, the CIA, and other agencies, who may have long-term institutional commitments that are at odds with the president's personal agenda. That concern usually does not apply to NSC staffers, however, as they are dependent on the president alone.

Presidents also have acted to strengthen the loyalty of NSC staffers to themselves alone. Originally, the staff was thought to be a nonpolitical group of experts, who, like many of the fiscal experts at the Office of Management and Budget, might hold their positions over the course of several administrations. Beginning with President Kennedy, however, new presidents have purged the ranks of the NSC upon taking office, substituting their own allies for those of the outgoing presidents.

The president selects a national security adviser without fear of congressional questioning or rejection. The position is not subject to Senate confirmation, which, according to a long-standing Washington tradition, means that the officeholder cannot be compelled to testify before Congress. It was not until 1980 that a national security adviser made his first formal appearance before a congressional committee, and subsequent appearances have been rare.

Another factor that increases the autonomy of the NSC is the relative lack of congressional controls over its budget. Although Congress sets the NSC's budget, council officials are able to exceed that limit by having staffers detailed, or lent, by other agencies. At the end of 1986 about half of the 180 NSC staff members were detailed from other agencies.

As the history of the council and its staff shows, views about how the NSC should function have changed many times over the years. Many foreign policy scholars argue that the NSC staff should not be a strong, independent force in decision making. According to this viewpoint, national security advisers and their staffs should be facilitators rather than policy makers, "honest brokers" who present the views of different departments to the president without prejudice and monitor the departments' actions to make sure presidential policies are being followed. National security advisers should not contest the secretary of state's role as chief foreign policy spokesperson for the administration, nor should they assume a direct role in international negotiations and the management of covert operations.[40]

Surprisingly, this view came to be held even by Kissinger, the foremost example of NSC power. "Though I did

not think so at the time, I have become convinced that a President should make the secretary of state his principal adviser and use the national security adviser primarily as a senior administrator and coordinator to make certain that each significant point of view is heard," wrote Kissinger in his memoirs. "If the security adviser becomes active in the development and articulation of policy he must inevitably diminish the Secretary of State and reduce his effectiveness."[41]

Other experts argue, however, that the NSC needs the authority to strive for unity and cohesiveness among the competing forces in an administration. Even some of those who were most critical of the NSC staff's moves into covert action in the Reagan administration complained that the council as an institution did not have the strength to insure agreement within the administration on key issues. Critics frequently found foreign policy disarray within the administration—for example, the continuing differences between the State and Defense departments over arms control negotiations with the Soviet Union—and some attributed this disarray to the weakness of the NSC. Past national security adviser Brzezinski thought that the system would work best if "the practical coordination and definition of the strategic direction would originate from [the president's assistant for national security affairs], who would then tightly coordinate and control the secretary of state, the secretary of defense, the chairman of the joint chiefs, and the director of central intelligence as a team, with them knowing that he was doing so on the president's behalf."[42]

Office of Policy Development

Established in 1977 as the Domestic Policy Staff, the Office of Policy Development (OPD, redesignated as such in 1981) supports the coordination and implementation of policy for the White House Domestic and Economic Policy councils. It is unique among Executive Office agencies in that *all* staff members (including nonprofessionals) are political appointees. Its history is therefore closely tied to that of the White House staff (its head serves as a special assistant to the president), and it has one client: the president.

Origins and Development of OPD

In 1970 President Richard Nixon established the first formalized office for domestic policy; his predecessors had relied on ad hoc arrangements for advice on domestic policy making. For example, with the growth of the presidency as an institution under Franklin D. Roosevelt, domestic planning was centralized in the White House. There was no organized staff structure, however. Instead, President Roosevelt—to ensure his control over policy making—established a web of overlapping responsibilities for his advisers.

President Harry S Truman depended on a small core of advisers headed by his special counsel, Clark M. Clifford. During the Truman presidency, however, as George Washington University political scientist Stephen J. Wayne observed, "policy initiative clearly rested with the individual department secretaries."[43]

The same kind of informal system was used by Dwight

D. Eisenhower, whose chief of staff, Sherman Adams, co-ordinated domestic policy. Under John F. Kennedy, policy planning was further centralized in the White House. Kennedy's top domestic aide, special counsel Theodore C. Sorensen, assumed an active role in the "New Frontier" legislation.

The seeds of an institutional domestic policy staff were planted during the presidency of Lyndon B. Johnson. His chief of White House staff, Joseph A. Califano, Jr., formed a cadre of aides who played a key role in drafting Johnson's Great Society domestic programs. The idea of establishing a formal domestic policy council to strengthen the president's capacities for fomulating policy arose as early as 1964, when White House staffer Richard Goodwin wrote Johnson: "I suggest the establishment of a Domestic Policy Planning [Council]. There is such a staff on foreign policy . . . yet the need is far more obvious in the field of domestic policy. . . . This would be a full-time council of experienced people—scholars, government people, etc. Its director would be on your staff. It could be attached to the Bureau of the Budget or operate independently and report directly to you." [44]

Nixon's Reorganization

It was not until Richard Nixon entered the White House that the idea caught hold. As a president-elect who wanted to streamline and formalize policy-making procedures, Nixon appointed an advisory panel on executive organization, chaired by industrialist Roy L. Ash, to propose solutions. The Ash panel recommended redesigning the Bureau of the Budget to form an Office of Management and Budget (OMB) and creating a Domestic Council. Acting on the panel's advice, Nixon sent Congress Reorganization Plan 2 in March 1970, proposing these changes. While OMB's function was conceived as primarily budgetary and managerial oversight, the Domestic Council was to serve in a broader policy-making capacity. *(See "Office of Management and Budget," p. 32, in this chapter.)*

Under the reorganization plan, the new Domestic Council would be composed of the president (who would act as chairman), the vice president, and the attorney general. It also would include the secretaries of the Treasury; Interior; Agriculture; Commerce; Labor; Health, Education, and Welfare; Housing and Urban Development; and Transportation. The president could designate others to serve on the council as the relevant issue arose. The staff of the council, located in the Executive Office, would be headed by an executive director who would act as an assistant to the president.

"The staff of the Domestic Council formalized the development over the last decade of a substantial policy group in the White House," observed political scientist Peri E. Arnold. "The Domestic Council staff would greatly increase the president's support system for developing policy proposals at the same time that it removed that system from the White House, thus appearing to fulfill the Nixon pledge for a lean White House." [45]

According to the president, the creation of a council had two assets. First, it placed those responsible for domestic policy making in the forefront of the effort. A second, more important asset was suggested by Nixon in his message transmitting the reorganization plan to Congress:

The Council will be supported by a staff. . . . Like the National Security Council staff, this staff will work in close coordination with the President's personal staff but will have its own institutional identity. By being established on a permanent, institutional basis, it will be designed to develop and employ the "institutional memory" so essential if continuity is to be maintained, and if experience is to play its proper role in the policy-making process. [46]

Some members of Congress were troubled by Nixon's concept of the proposed staff. During hearings on the reorganization plan—at which Ash and Dwight A. Ink, Jr., assistant director of management for the budget bureau, appeared—Rep. Chester E. Holifield (D-Calif.) queried the meaning of "institutional memory," noting that the staff would be "a political organization headed by a political appointee, none of whom have civil service tenure, and the director, of course, not being confirmed by the Senate." Ink admitted that would be the case, but he said the staff would be heterogeneous: "It is not expected that they have tenure," he declared. He then added that "institutional memory" should not be "interpreted as necessarily going from administration to administration," to which Holifield responded that it must be "a four-year institutional memory." [47]

The problem of relations with OMB also threatened congressional acceptance of the reorganization plan. The Domestic Council was charged with developing domestic policy; yet the budget director was not a statutory member. Moreover, the council was to have a large, expert staff, implying that the new OMB was in fact being demoted. The administration denied that was the case, but Budget Director Robert P. Mayo testified, "The Budget Bureau makes policy recommendations to the President. . . . This will continue as far as I know. . . ." [48] Another troubling point was the first section of the reorganization plan. It stated: "There are hereby transferred to the President . . . all functions vested by law . . . in the Bureau of the Budget or the Director of the Budget." This implied that the statutory functions of the bureau could be placed anywhere at the president's discretion.

Despite these misgivings and the fact that the head of the Domestic Council staff, like the new OMB director, was not subject to Senate confirmation (and therefore was not required to testify on Capitol Hill), Congress approved the plan.

Like OMB, the Domestic Council "never quite fulfilled the expectations of the Ash Council," wrote Arnold. "Far from becoming a mechanism for policy formulation, the Domestic Council became a large staff for presidential errands, admittedly increasing presidential reach, but providing little analytic or formulative capacity over policy." [49] During Nixon's tenure the cabinet-level council and its subcommittees met infrequently.

The president had described the Domestic Council as "a domestic counterpart to the National Security Council" (NSC), which was established in 1947. [50] Although the two agencies had been conceived as cabinet-level advisory groups, during the Nixon years both became White House offices whose heads—Henry A. Kissinger of the NSC and John D. Ehrlichman of the Domestic Council—were among the president's closest advisers. Ehrlichman and OMB Director George P. Shultz (the latter gained influence with Nixon as Watergate consumed the presidency and led to Ehrlichman's downfall) were the "czars" of domestic policy and agency budgets. "Traditionally, Cabinet officers . . . had the right of appeal to the President when negotiating their budgets; now this right was to be denied them," wrote presidential scholar Stephen Hess. "Shultz and Ehrlichman became the final arbiters." [51] Although the stated function of the council was coordination, under Ehrlichman its major activity was to overrule departmental agencies, who complained that they in fact had less access to the president than before. The staff under Ehrlichman was viewed as "high handed"; during the Watergate crisis, however, the council ceased to play much of a role in domestic policy making, while the role of OMB grew. [52]

During Nixon's tenure the Domestic Council staff became highly professional, according to political scientist John H. Kessel. [53] Of its twenty-one professional members, twelve had law degrees, seven had Ph.D. degrees, and two had degrees in business administration. Each of the six assistant directors covered a policy field (transportation and crime; energy, environment, and agriculture; and so forth). In addition, ad hoc working groups were formed to address specific policy areas. Such a group might consist of representatives of the Domestic Council and OMB staffs and assistant secretaries from each of the concerned departments.

Changes under Ford and Carter

President Gerald R. Ford gave his vice president, Nelson A. Rockefeller, control of the Domestic Council. Rockefeller then installed a longtime colleague, James M. Cannon, as associate director. The staff did not jell, however, largely because of their varied allegiances (some were holdovers from the Nixon presidency). Moreover, the austerity-minded president gave the council and its staff little to do.

In February 1977 President Jimmy Carter, in an effort to streamline White House operations, sought—and subsequently was granted—legislation to restore presidential reorganization authority, which had expired in 1973. He then submitted Reorganization Plan 1, which abolished the Domestic Council and reorganized it into the Domestic Policy Staff. Georgia lawyer Stuart E. Eizenstat, who headed the redesignated office, soon was described as "one of the most powerful men in Washington." [54] Under his purview the Domestic Policy Staff launched a host of varied and important legislative initiatives, among them a tax on oil windfall profits, hospital cost-control proposals, criminal code revisions, and a Social Security overhaul. The staff steadily gained influence as well, overseeing the framing of legislation and resolving interagency conflicts. "Often, it has the last word on the shape of an administration bill before it is sent to Capitol Hill," wrote reporter Larry Light in 1979. [55] Eizenstat did point out, however, that the staff did not initiate legislation. "Rather, we coordinate it," he said. [56]

The staff also served as a principal adviser to the president. "I give personal advice to the president himself, telling him what I think he should do," noted Eizenstat. [57] Carter's domestic adviser was a member, moreover, of the Economic Policy Group, composed of government officials concerned with fiscal policy. And during Eizenstat's tenure a close working relationship with OMB was developed.

The Domestic Policy Staff included twenty-seven professionals, generally young and highly educated, who won high praise from Congress. The total staff numbered eighty, however, even though President Carter sought a leaner White House and Executive Office. Under the director there were ten associate directors, each responsible for an "issues cluster" such as economics or government reorganization; the remainder of the staff worked in one of those clusters.

The staff played a central role in formulating the domestic legislative agenda and maintained close ties with White House lobbyists on Capitol Hill. Although the Domestic Policy Staff itself did not lobby, it briefed members of Congress on legislative issues. Much of its stature resulted from Eizenstat's personal influence with the president and Congress.

Organization and Functions of OPD in the 1980s

Soon after entering office in 1981 Ronald Reagan restructured the Domestic Policy Staff, renaming it the Office of Policy Development. At first, the House of Representatives refused to fund the office because the administration declined to send anyone to testify on its behalf. To explain that reasoning, White House counsel Fred F. Fielding wrote Rep. Edward R. Roybal (D-Calif.), chairman of the House Appropriations Subcommittee on the Treasury-Postal Service: "The President is not subject to questioning as to the manner in which he formulates executive policy." And, according to Fielding, the principle applied equally to senior members of the president's staff. [58] The Senate, however, restored the $3 million requested for the office, and the funds cleared Congress.

Reagan's Office of Policy Development proved to be a leaner version of its predecessor. Its staff was reduced (numbering forty-one in 1981), as were professional titles (under Carter, almost all professional staff members were associate or assistant directors). Reagan's first appointment as domestic policy adviser (assistant to the president for policy development) was Martin C. Anderson, an economist who made his name as a critic of welfare and urban renewal. During Anderson's tenure the policy development staff was organized around seven cabinet councils (commerce and trade, economic affairs, food and agriculture, human resources, legal policy, management and administration, and natural resources and the environment). A senior member of the policy development staff served as executive secretary to each, while a second member of the staff served as OPD's representative on the "staff secretariat."

The cabinet council system collapsed under its own weight, however, and in an April 11, 1985, statement Reagan announced the consolidation of the seven councils into a Domestic Policy Council and an Economic Policy Council. The former was composed of the attorney general (who served as chairman pro tempore); the secretaries of the Interior, Health and Human Services, Housing and Urban Development, Transportation, Energy, and Education; and the director of OMB. The heads of nonmember departments were invited to participate in the council's deliberations whenever matters affecting their organizations were on the agenda. The vice president and chief of staff served as ex officio members of both councils. [59] "Under Reagan, the White House domestic staff concept has come nearly full circle to the idea originally put forth by the Ash council: a White House support mechanism designed to facilitate discussion and decision making by the Cabinet itself," wrote reporter Dick Kirschten. [60]

By 1987 there had been four assistants to the president for policy development in the Reagan administration. Among the staff the turnover rate was high. The organization of the office (always extremely fluid) consisted then of a director, three assistant directors, and several special assistants. They served both the Domestic and Economic Policy councils. Total staff numbered thirty-nine—all political appointees.

The major functions of the OPD were threefold: (1) to provide the president with an early warning of important domestic issues likely to arise, (2) to produce an independent evaluation of policies, and (3) to oversee implementation and follow-up of initiatives in domestic legislation. Two major areas of OPD activity in 1986-1987 concerned drug abuse programs and welfare reform.[61]

Perhaps because of its political nature, the domestic policy staff—whatever its name—had not by 1987 evolved into a lasting, "institutional" center of power and influence. One reason might be that, as Kirschten observed, no administration had been willing to commit itself to a "permanent" staff with an "institutional memory."[62] In any event, the domestic policy staff continued to be overshadowed by the firmly entrenched budget office.

Council of Economic Advisers

Twenty-five years after Congress established the Bureau of the Budget (renamed the Office of Management and Budget—OMB—in 1970), another organization was authorized to help president handle the economy. The Council of Economic Advisers (CEA) was a central part of the 1946 Employment Act, which created a three-member committee to advise the president on wide-ranging issues confronting the nation's economic future. The president had therefore a source of ammunition for documenting problems and their solutions.

The position of the CEA in the Executive Office of the President (EOP) is unique. Unlike other presidential offices of its stature, the council acts independently, advising the president instead of rigidly adhering to administration policy pronouncements. Throughout its existence the CEA has viewed its mission as strictly professional—that of an adviser to the president to point out trends in the economy. Yet there is an unstated conflict in its role as an "objective observer" for the president: the council naturally wants to point out measures the president should take to adjust economic assumptions and actions in light of its own analyses. Because the president appoints—and the Senate confirms—all three members of the council, the CEA has become an important presidential policy-making tool.

According to professor of public administration Edward S. Flash, Jr., in an opinion shared by many observers, "The Council of Economic Advisers, originally characterized as a source of objective and politically neutral expertise, has instead emerged as an active and frequently influential font of knowledge and ideas, which often provides a foundation for the President's economic policy."[63]

This relationship has continued to characterize the status of the CEA within the Executive Office structure. Its small staff, supplemented by a large number of consultants, works closely with the White House, OMB, and congressional committees to advocate the administration's view of economic trends and policies, to identify the trouble spots and opportunities that lie ahead, and to suggest what the federal government might do to avoid or promote them.

Although slight fluctuations in staff size and some reorganization have occurred during the existence of the CEA, its functions and character "have remained remarkably consistent," noted Roger Porter in his 1983 study of the CEA.[64] Its members and staff have come primarily from academe, usually "on loan" for two to three years. Political party affiliation is of little importance in selection of staff, and institutional loyalty to the council is not strong. The CEA, noted Porter, is primarily an advocate, not a policy broker. "It has no 'constituency'; rather, it has a 'client,' the president."[65]

Origins and Development of the CEA

According to political scientist David Naveh, "The creation of the President's Council of Economic Advisers was a landmark in transforming the science of economics into a policy-making tool."[66] The CEA was an integral part of the 1946 Employment Act—post-World War II legislation that was born of the recognition that a laissez-faire economic policy would be inadequate for dealing with the transition from a wartime, high-production environment to a civilian economy. Transition aids and new economic goals were needed.[67] In general, the 1946 legislation was intended to provide employment opportunities for those returning to a civilian economy who were willing and able to work and to promote maximum employment, production, and purchasing power for the nation as a whole. At the same time the act emphasized the government's continued commitment to a free enterprise system.

To assist the administration in carrying out the mandate of the act, Congress, in a bipartisan effort, established the CEA. It was a unique undertaking: never before had an independent, professional council (instead of a single adviser) been established to provide the president with an objective overview of where the economy was headed. Moreover, the bill's requirement that the three members of the CEA be confirmed by the Senate also was unique at the time. The Capitol Hill initiative was viewed by many observers as an attempt to reassert congressional control over economic policy making, which had been conducted rather haphazardly during Franklin D. Roosevelt's presidency. Congress also established the Joint Committee on the Economic Report (later renamed the Joint Economic Committee), composed of House and Senate members, to prepare its own annual analysis of the economy and to critique the CEA findings.

Section 4 (a) of the Employment Act set out the qualifications for the three-member CEA panel, "each of whom shall be a person who, as a result of his training, experience and attainment, is exceptionally qualified to analyze and interpret economic developments, to appraise programs and activities of the Government . . . and to recommend national economic policy to promote employment, production and purchasing power under free competitive enterprise." Each council member was to receive $15,000, and the total council budget was not to exceed $345,000.

The CEA's initial mandate—which has changed little over the years—was fivefold:

1. To assist and advise the president in the preparation of the president's annual Economic Report to Congress in January and to submit an annual report to the president during the previous December.

2. To gather, analyze, and interpret information on economic developments and trends.

3. To assess federal government programs in light of how well they are satisfying the president's goals and those of the Employment Act.

4. To provide ongoing studies and advice to the president on the state of the economy.

5. To provide additional studies and reports to the president as requested or on its own initiative.

Early Years of the CEA

Like the other EOP offices, from the beginning the CEA and its stature have been highly dependent upon the chairman's (and the president's) perception of its mission. The relationship of the council members—particularly the chairman—to the president, as well as to Congress, also has been important. Perhaps the most decisive factor in the status of the council has been whether the CEA chairman has viewed his role as primarily that of an economic analyst or that of a major voice in economic policy making.[68]

President Harry S Truman did not propose creation of the CEA. It was first proposed by the House Committee on Executive Expenditures. Congress overwhelmingly passed the measure, and in signing the bill on February 20, 1946, the president hailed it as "a commitment to take any and all measures necessary for a healthy economy." [69] The act did not specify whether the "exceptionally qualified" members of the CEA should come from academe. The president therefore received hundreds of applications from people of varied backgrounds. Even congressional supporters of the legislation were divided about whether the council's members should have solid academic credentials or practical experience—in either government or business. The former attribute prevailed.

Truman nominated Edwin G. Nourse to serve as the first chairman of the CEA. Vice president of the Brookings Institution, Nourse was a highly regarded moderate conservative with a background in academics and agricultural policy. According to Erwin C. Hargrove and Samuel A. Morley in their oral history of the CEA, this appointment was seen as an "indication of [Truman's] desire to appoint a person of professional standing rather than partisan loyalty." [70] Truman named as vice chairman, however, an experienced government professional, Leon Keyserling, who was a firm advocate of Roosevelt's New Deal policies and a principal drafter of the 1946 Employment Act. The third CEA member, John D. Clark, also was a liberal.

Differences soon emerged in the members' interpretations of the CEA's mission. Nourse, for example, did not wholeheartedly embrace the administration's economic policies, and he was firmly convinced that the economic advisers should assume a "scientifically objective" view without injecting themselves into policy making. Perhaps because he hailed from academe, Nourse found it difficult to adapt to the quick decision making and policy formulation that were facts of life for anyone with influence in Washington (although several succeeding "academic" CEA chairmen adjusted to the atmosphere quite well). In any event, relations between Nourse and Truman were not close. Looking back on the situation some years later, Gerhard Colm, a CEA staff member during Nourse's term, observed that the president might have felt uncomfortable in dealing with the CEA chairman because Truman "did not feel equal to discussing economics with a man whom he respected as a great scholar and authority." [71] Nourse himself recognized the difficulties in his relations with the president:

After the lapse of a little more than a year, it can be said that there has been no single case when he [Truman] has called upon us in any specific situation for counsel in his study of any matter of national economic policy. While he has accepted the material which we have presented to him for use in the Economic Report and passed it on without material change . . . there is no clear evidence that at any juncture we had any tangible influence on the formation of policy. . . .[72]

In an article written in 1948, Nourse emphasized that the council's function was to assist the president in a strictly advisory manner.[73] But the chairman soon found himself outvoted on a controversial issue—whether CEA members should testify on Capitol Hill before the Joint Committee on the Economic Report. Nourse refused to appear on the grounds that doing so would jeopardize the CEA's tradition of confidentiality with the president and that the council's economic policy role was to advise, not advocate. (The Employment Act did not require CEA congressional testimony, nor did it mandate council accountability to the joint committee.)

Nourse thus viewed the CEA's role as somewhat like that of a top administrator in a large corporation—primarily advisory, with policy decisions and implementation left in the hands of professional executives.[74] During his tenure the CEA expanded its research capabilities, drawing on a coterie of outside specialists for consultation. Professionalism, not politics, was the trademark of Nourse's council.

With the 1948 presidential elections approaching, Keyserling and Clark expressed their wish to be helpful by testifying in behalf of the administration's economic programs. Truman encouraged such activity, and the two CEA members complied, thereby fueling dissension within the council's ranks. In 1948 a midyear CEA economic review contained a minority statement written by Chairman Nourse. A few months earlier the Hoover Commission on the Organization of the Executive Branch had recommended ending the ambiguity in relations between the CEA chairman and members by forming an Office of Economic Adviser with a single head. Although a version of this recommendation was to take effect later, no action was taken at the time.

Nourse resigned in November 1949 and was succeeded by Keyserling, who almost immediately set about redefining the CEA's philosophy and position. Although he played a more active role as chairman than Nourse, Keyserling condoned statements of disagreement by his colleagues. He was more interested than his predecessor in organization of the staff, and he encouraged outside contacts and informality. Keyserling also established a number of interagency committees chaired by council staff, thereby affording a greater role for the CEA in developing government programs. He continued, however, like Nourse, to hire staff analysts who were familiar with government bureaucracy and legislative procedures.

"Unlike Nourse, Keyserling perceived the CEA as trustee for the president's economic programs in Congress," wrote Hargrove and Morley. "He rejected Nourse's claims to objectivity and nonpartisanship, claiming instead that the Council was part of the administration and should act accordingly." [75] The result was a closer relationship with the president and White House staff. Keyserling contributed to drafts of presidential speeches, used the media to publicize the CEA's work, and was made a de facto member of the cabinet and National Security Council. Indeed, he viewed the CEA's role as equivalent to that of a cabinet office, which included appearances before Congress to explain and defend presidential economic proposals. Keyserling himself became increasingly active in Democratic party politics. Partly for this reason, he clashed with the Republican-controlled Joint Committee on the Economic Report, which issued a brittle critique of the CEA's Economic Report as overly political and paving a path to a controlled economy.

Nonetheless, according to presidential scholar Stephen Hess, the CEA under Keyserling

> became a serious contending force in the formulation of administration policy.... [F]reed of operating responsibility (with the exception of preparing the Economic Report) and located in close proximity to the President, the CEA had ample opportunity to develop and to expound its judgments within the higher reaches of the administration....
>
> Congress was wrong in its belief that it could direct the president to accept economic advice; the experience under Nourse graphically proved otherwise. But it was right in believing that the quantity and quality of economic advice might be force-fed. The presence of a group of professional economists in the White House resulted in additional sources of information and analysis, which the President absorbed, often through his personal staff, sometimes by osmosis.[76]

Changes under Eisenhower

By the time Dwight D. Eisenhower entered office, the CEA's existence was in jeopardy. The Republicans in Congress had taken issue with the council's role and activities under Keyserling. Thus, in considering a bill providing continuing appropriations for the council, Congress was uncertain whether to grant supplemental funding to continue the existing CEA or to pass new legislation restructuring it. Congress finally decided to provide monies for the rest of the fiscal year, but for only one economic adviser. Shortly after his inauguration, however, Eisenhower decided to continue the CEA, but in its previous form as a strictly professional, nonpolitical body whose primary mission was to provide factual advice. He asked his White House staff to seek out 'the best man in the country on the ups and downs of business." [77] On the advice of Gabriel Hauge, Eisenhower's assistant on economic matters, the president selected Arthur F. Burns, a highly respected economist, to assume the post. Burns, a "Democrat for Eisenhower," had impressive academic credentials as a professor of economics at Columbia University and the director of the National Bureau of Economic Research. He also was well known for his study of business cycles. "The CEA survived its crucial transition in administrations because of the increased stake of the President in the behavior of the economy, because the council members and their staff were congenial to the President, and because they provided the President with information that he considered immediately useful," concluded Hess.[78]

In August 1953, shortly after assuming office, Eisenhower issued Reorganization Plan 9, which effected far-reaching changes in the CEA's structure. Much of the rearrangement had been suggested by Burns. The major change of the brief reorganization order was to make the chairman—not the three-person council—the linchpin of CEA contacts with the president. The post of CEA vice chairman was eliminated. In a letter accompanying the reorganization plan, Eisenhower declared that its purpose was "to take the appropriate actions to reinvigorate and make more effective the operations of the CEA."

Burns, a newcomer to the Washington scene, soon made his mark on the CEA. Not only was he the preeminent member of the council as spokesman to the president, but as CEA chairman he also had the sole authority for employing staff, specialists, and consultants. Only three members of the staff had remained on board from the Keyserling era, and Burns set about filling the vacancies with a substantial number of academic economists. He felt more comfortable working with colleagues from academe, and he viewed their presence as "a means to depoliticize the CEA and establish its professional credibility." [79]

Like Nourse, Burns viewed his role as independent, but he was less objective. Hargrove and Morley observed that "if the Burns Council was determined to stay out of the political spotlight, it nevertheless took an active role in policy formation that extended beyond the scientific expertise and neutral competency that Edwin Nourse had sought during his tenure." [80] Adhering to the policies of the first CEA chairman, Burns refused to appear before the Joint Economic Committee in public hearings (a decision that severely strained his relations with Congress), yet he made numerous public appearances to defend the president's programs. "While Keyserling had encouraged policy considerations by the staff, Burns felt the staff's role was simply to advise him, providing him with whatever information he needed to make the necessary policy decisions," wrote Hargrove and Morley. "He wanted a completely objective support staff." [81] Burns controlled all staff contacts with administration agencies (the staff totaled thirty full-time and part-time professionals as well as consultants), and under his stewardship, the CEA no longer authored the annual reports it prepared.

During his tenure as council chairman, Burns developed close contact with the president, and he regularly advised the cabinet. In 1953 he was designated chairman of the new Advisory Board on Economic Growth and Stability, an economic subcabinet. Task forces and interagency groups abounded under Burns.

Burns resigned in December 1956 and was replaced by CEA member Raymond J. Saulnier, who, like his predecessor, viewed the council's mission as that of an objective adviser. Saulnier, however, was more inclined to delegate responsibility to his colleagues on the council. Although his relationship with the president was not as close as that enjoyed by Burns, the CEA chairman continued to attend all cabinet meetings, and he helped draft speeches and legislation. The council was in fact an active participant in policy making.

That role was spurred in part by Treasury Secretary Robert B. Anderson, who in 1957 suggested that he, Saulnier, Federal Reserve chairman William McChesney Martin, Jr., and presidential economic adviser Hauge consult regularly on economic issues and trends. The group, known as the "little four" or "financial committee," was a consultative, not policy-making, body. It was the precursor of President John F. Kennedy's Troika and Quadriad. (See following section, "The CEA in the 1960s.")

The CEA in the 1960s

The tendency to appoint academics to CEA positions intensified during President Kennedy's three years in office, beginning in 1961. Kennedy nominated Walter W. Heller, a well-respected economics professor from the University of Minnesota, to chair the council, and he selected professors James Tobin of Yale University and Kermit Gordon of Williams College as the remaining members. When the president approached Tobin with the offer of the position, the professor hesitated, remarking, "I'm afraid I am only an ivory tower economist." Kennedy responded, "That is the best kind. I am only an ivory tower president." [82] All three council members, however, had extensive Washington experience.

As before, staff vacancies were filled primarily by academicians. Most were young and lacking government experience, but they were eager to apply their knowledge to the many challenges of the New Frontier.[83] "They were, in short, 'action intellectuals,' " wrote Hess. "They knew the proper way to lecture the President, and a CEA memorandum reached Kennedy's desk on the average of once every third day. Before long, CEA members were taking on the sort of programmatic assignments that had been unknown to prior councils, such as developing legislative proposals regarding poverty and transportation." [84]

One of the president's close personal advisers, Heller was an active chairman, concerned more with policy than economic theory. According to Hargrove and Morley, "He saw nothing wrong with the CEA publicly advocating the policies it felt to be economically wise and educating the public in the 'New Economics' espoused by himself and his colleagues." [85] President Kennedy was a bit more conservative, but he encouraged Heller and his colleagues to expound their views in public congressional testimony, speeches, and articles.

As chairman of the CEA, Heller established the Quadriad—composed of the heads of the CEA, Federal Reserve Bank, OMB, and Treasury—which met regularly. (The Troika was composed of the heads of the CEA, OMB, and Treasury.) The CEA assumed an active role in wage-price stabilization policy in 1961 and began work on poverty programs. This role continued under President Lyndon B. Johnson (1963-1968), who wholeheartedly embraced the War on Poverty and continued the wage-price guideposts.

Heller resigned in November 1964 and was succeeded by Gardner Ackley, a professor of economics at the University of Michigan, who had served as a CEA member since 1962. Ackley made few policy changes. The council's staff remained small (sixteen professional economists), but the chairman retained full access to the president. Ackley was succeeded for a brief period by Arthur M. Okun (1968-1969), the youngest chairman in the council's history (he was thirty-nine), who had been responsible for the CEA's economic forecasts. Under both Ackley and Okun the CEA gained influence as the Vietnam War impinged on the economy and the president became increasingly preoccupied with the conflict, leaving much of domestic policy making to others.

The Nixon and Carter Eras

Shortly after his Republican victory in 1968 President-elect Richard Nixon announced that Paul W. McCracken, a member of the CEA under Eisenhower, would become its new chairman. Characterized as a "centrist," the new CEA chairman believed that fiscal policies (which determine the amount of taxing and spending) and monetary policies (which determine the amount of currency and credit in the country) were equally important in establishing the nation's long-term economic goals.

Although Nixon retained the Troika and Quadriad, the Troika worked more closely with the White House staff than with the president, while the Quadriad assumed a larger role in macroeconomic policy making. The CEA also participated in the cabinet's Council on Economic Policy as well as White House working groups on economic matters convened by John D. Ehrlichman, the president's domestic policy adviser. Although the council was represented in daily White House staff meetings, Nixon's establishment of the Domestic Council under Ehrlichman and reorganization of the Bureau of the Budget into the Office of Management and Budget cut into the CEA's influence on economic policy.

The major economic problem confronting the administration during Nixon's first term was inflation. McCracken was a principal force in the president's decision to impose wage and price controls in 1971. He served as chairman of the Executive Policy Committee of the Cost of Living Council (CLC), which was established to monitor the freeze. The policy committee was responsible for interpreting existing policies and recommending new ones to the CLC.

In January 1972 Herbert Stein, a council member and senior fellow at the Brookings Institution, became chairman of the CEA, serving until September 1974. Although Stein was "perhaps the most ardent free-marketer and opponent of economic controls within the Nixon administration," [86] by the time he assumed the CEA leadership he had come to believe in the necessity of wage and price controls. During his tenure the CEA continued to be represented on the CLC, the Council on Economic Policy, the Domestic Council, and the Council on International Economic Policy, but its influence diminished as that of Treasury Secretary John B. Connally and that of his successor, George P. Shultz, grew.

That situation was reversed with the accession of Nixon's vice president, Gerald R. Ford, to the presidency following Nixon's resignation in 1974. The new CEA chairman, Alan Greenspan, had in fact been recruited by Nixon. Unlike previous heads of the CEA, Greenspan came from the business community, where he was a consultant. He was a critic of government intervention in the economy and an advocate of reduced government spending to achieve a balanced budget. Greenspan's "sound reputation as a forecaster and his plans for restoring the CEA to an advisory role easily won him the support of the profession," wrote Hargrove and Morley. "Although he was perhaps the most conservative chairman in the council's history, even the more liberal past chairmen affirmed their respect for his abilities as an economist. He announced intentions to 'depoliticize' the CEA and avoid a public role." [87] According to Greenspan, he did this by assuming a low profile as CEA chairman, making few speeches, reducing congressional contacts, and cancelling monthly press briefings. And during his tenure the Troika and Quadriad all but faded from view.

President Jimmy Carter entered the White House in 1977 as unemployment was running at 6-7 percent, the budget deficit was rising, and inflation was pegged at 5-6 percent. Carter's new CEA chairman, Charles L. Schultze, came from the Brookings Institution; he also had served in the CEA and OMB. Much of Schultze's preinaugural package of programs to stimulate the economy (returning to full employment without inflation) was adopted by the Carter administration. "It is difficult to imagine a selection for the CEA chairmanship who could have won more respect or have been more in the mainstream of pragmatic, liberal approaches to economic policy," wrote Hargrove and Morley.[88] Schultze has been described as a liberal Democrat and a Keynesian economist who believed that government could actively influence the economy through fiscal policy to insure healthy expansion. But he also was known as a hard-headed skeptic when it came to assessing the value of government spending programs.

Congress adopted Schultze's plan to stimulate the economy quickly through tax refunds that would generate business and consumer confidence. Testifying before the House Budget Committee in January 1977, the CEA chairman noted, "This package has been designed to tread prudently between the twin risks of over- and under-stimulation."[89]

Regulatory reform was another concern of the president and his economic adviser. As chairman of both the CEA and the Regulatory Analysis Review Group, Schultze focused attention on the inflationary consequences of many proposed regulations and favored in some cases the use of taxation, rather than specific standard setting, as a cost-effective approach to compliance. Regulatory reform became even more of a major issue during Ronald Reagan's presidency, but primary responsibility for it was lodged in OMB. *(See "Office of Management and Budget," p. 32, in this chapter.)*

The CEA under Reagan

Reagan's first appointment to the CEA leadership, Murray Weidenbaum, reflected the president's view that one of the major tasks of his administration was to cut down on federal regulations. Weidenbaum, a former assistant secretary of the Treasury and head of the Center for the Study of American Business at Washington University in St. Louis, was a conservative who advocated a cost-benefit analysis approach to weeding out unnecessary government rules.

It soon became apparent, however, that Weidenbaum's talents would be better used in a position in which he had a decisive role in the mission to prune federal regulations—and that position had been created in the OMB's new Office of Information and Regulatory Affairs. Weidenbaum also had come under attack for his 1981 congressional testimony that played down the importance of deficits, appearing to contradict years of Republican rhetoric. Even though White House spokespersons later denied that the remarks reflected administration policy, stunned Senate Republicans denounced the CEA comments as "incredible," "disheartening," and "foolish."[90]

Weidenbaum was succeeded by Martin S. Feldstein, a professor at Harvard University and president of the National Bureau of Economic Research. Feldstein served as CEA chairman for almost two years (from October 1982 to July 1984), but, ironically, his outspoken calls for deficit reduction above all issues—including the need to increase defense spending—angered other administration officials.

Feldstein's replacement was an undersecretary of the Treasury, Beryl W. Sprinkel, who was confirmed in April 1985. Sprinkel, a former Chicago bank executive and economics professor, had close personal ties to Donald T. Regan, the president's chief of staff. Although Sprinkel had direct contacts with the president, Treasury Secretary James A. Baker III was the Reagan administration's chief economic spokesperson. Sprinkel's first economic forecast, envisioning strong economic growth, was attacked as excessively rosy by members of Congress when it was presented

to them in February 1986. Other economists appearing before the Joint Economic Committee were equally skeptical about the CEA's projected economic growth rate.

The controversy continued in 1987. In presenting the annual Economic Report to Congress, Sprinkel observed that "the U.S. economy demonstrates continued strength as it moves into the fifth year of the current economic expansion, but ... important sectoral and structural problems remain." Those problems, discussed in the report, included the large and persistent budget and trade deficits.[91]

Organization and Functions of the CEA

The activities of the president's Council of Economic Advisers include:

~ Briefing the president on overall economic policy objectives and what programs needed to be implemented.

~ Preparing an annual economic report to the president and an Economic Report of the President for submission to Congress in January.

~ Informing the president on a continuing basis of major policy issues, including international economic issues.

~ Chairing an interagency forecasting group that included the Treasury and OMB for developing economic projections.

~ Participating in the cabinet-level Council on Economic Policy to discuss the economic effects of tax reform, trade and balance-of-payments issues, international policy coordination, and budget reform. The CEA participated as well in the cabinet-level Domestic Policy Council and dealt with such issues as agricultural problems, regulatory and antitrust reforms, catastrophic health insurance, welfare reform, energy policy, transportation and communications regulation, and tax policy.

The CEA chairman also headed the economic policy committee of the twenty-five-nation Organization for Economic Cooperation and Development (OECD) and other OECD committees as well. Moreover, the CEA chairman was particularly active in U.S.-Japan meetings to discuss trade issues.

In 1986 the professional staff of the three-member council consisted of a special assistant, a senior statistician, twelve senior staff economists, two staff economists, four junior economists, and one research assistant. There were eleven support staff members.

Most CEA heads and staff members have been outspoken in their belief that the council's staff should remain small and transitory (most have tenured positions elsewhere). Indeed, the small size of the staff, and its transitory nature, have been considered advantages. The party affiliations of staff members remain of little importance.

The CEA has continued to avoid operational responsibility for programs, serving instead as an adviser to the president to forecast economic trends and provide analyses of issues. The CEA's position on administration economic policy making has always depended upon three factors: the quality of its advice, the chairman's perception of CEA's role, and the relation between the president and the council (particularly the chairman). But these factors have their nuances. "The CEA was created by Congress in 1946 to force presidents to accept economic advice in a particular form. Yet they have chosen to use or not use the CEA largely on the basis of whether they preferred working with an individual council chairman to receiving economic advice from other sources," wrote Hess.[92] According to former CEA chairman Arthur Okun,

> When the President's economists decide to go on public record, they cannot serve two masters. They cannot speak for both the President and for the [economics] profession. And they cannot speak for the Profession publicly and still maintain confidence and rapport internally with the President. The choice should be clear. It is far more important for society and for the Profession to have economists who maintain rapport with the President and thus have the greatest influence on the inside.[93]

Office of the U.S. Trade Representative

The Office of the Special Representative for Trade Negotiations was established in 1963 and redesignated the Office of the U.S. Trade Representative in 1980. The original office was created in response to a perception that a presidential spokesperson was needed to deal with the increasingly complex issues facing the nation in its economic contacts with foreign nations. Almost twenty-five years later that perception remained unaltered, but the circumstances were drastically reversed. In 1962 the government's trade philosophy—both in Congress and within the Kennedy administration—advocated opening the doors to international transactions and promoting free trade. By 1987, faced with spiraling balance-of-payments deficits—brought on primarily by imports from Japan and the other fast-growing economies of Singapore, South Korea, and Taiwan—the United States confronted a crisis situation. The Reagan administration U.S. trade representative, Clayton K. Yeutter, found himself in the eye of a cyclone, with a mandate to fend off congressional demands for retaliation, advance the administration's commitment to fair and free trade, and retain the good will of the major trading partners of the United States, while trying to persuade them to modify their own protectionist practices.

Origins and Development of the Trade Office

The removal of barriers to the free flow of international trade was a principal goal of American foreign policy for more than two decades following World War II.[94] With little variation, presidents Harry S Truman, Dwight D. Eisenhower, John F. Kennedy, and Lyndon B. Johnson held that a liberal trade policy, no less than foreign aid, was an essential means of establishing a more secure and prosperous world. Each was forced to do battle, however, with an array of protectionist interests whose pressures on Congress complemented a historic legislative view that tariffs were a domestic matter, not to be subordinated to foreign policy objectives.

By 1962 there were new and compelling reasons for the United States to champion the free flow of trade. Although exports and imports remained small in relation to a gross national product of more than $500 billion, they occupied an increasingly important role in an economy beset by a slow rate of growth. Moreover, despite its substantial and continuing surplus of exports over imports, the United States was experiencing severe deficits in its total international accounts because of heavy expenditures abroad for military and other purposes. Of the several alternatives for bringing the payments deficit under control, rapid expansion of exports was in many ways the most desirable.

Creation of the Trade Office

The expansion of exports depended, however, upon reversal of a new trend toward protectionism abroad, as evidenced in the common tariff wall constructed by the six-member European Community (EC or Common Market) in 1957. In 1962 the large economic stake of the United States in the freest possible access to world markets, as well as the overriding political interest of the United States in building a strong and interdependent free world, led Congress to authorize President Kennedy to take a new initiative in behalf of trade leberalization. Even though some U.S. industries were unable or unwilling to compete with the products of other nations, the Trade Expansion Act of 1962 reflected the majority view that freer trade was no longer a choice but a necessity for the United States.

In a special message sent to Capitol Hill on January 25, 1962, Kennedy asked Congress for unprecedented authority to negotiate with the Common Market for reciprocal tariff concessions. With the help of strong bipartisan support in the business community and concessions to potentially obstructive interests, Kennedy finally got substantially all that he wanted in the Trade Expansion Act of 1962 (PL 88-794). The act granted the president far-reaching tariff-cutting authority and provided safeguards against damage to American industry and agriculture. The act further authorized the formation of a cabinet-level Interagency Trade Organization and the establishment of the post of special representative for trade negotiations, who would act as the chief U.S. spokesperson in trade talks. On January 15, 1963, Kennedy appointed Christian A. Herter, secretary of state under Eisenhower, to the new post. According to a former trade negotiator, Herter "had supported the purposes of the bill from the outset and had the courage to resist any efforts of special interest groups to divert him from achieving them."[95] Herter was the chief U.S. negotiator for the "Kennedy Round" of tariff-cutting talks (1963-1967), undertaken under the auspices of the General Agreement on Tariffs and Trade (GATT, formed in 1947, had a membership of about one hundred nations in 1987).

1974 Trade Act

By the late 1960s and early 1970s competition for world markets was growing, the U.S. share of world trade was in persistent decline, and protectionist sentiment was on the rise. Like his predecessors, however, President Richard Nixon remained committed to free trade, although conflicts with the EC and Japan, in particular, over trade reciprocity and quotas were occurring more frequently. In late 1969 the president sent Congress legislation that would have permitted him to retain his tariff-cutting authority while increasing assistance to U.S. businesses harmed by imports. But the protectionist mood on Capitol Hill was strong, and by the end of 1970 the administration's bill had been altered severely by the House of Representatives. The measure never reached the president's desk.

In 1973 Nixon resubmitted proposals for new trade-negotiating authority, largely in response to growing trade deficits and as the major industrial nations were preparing for another series of trade negotiations (known as the Tokyo Round). In December 1974, after a year's delay, Congress passed the 1974 Trade Act (PL 93-618) which authorized U.S. participation in the tariff negotiations and established a cabinet-level special trade representative's office within the Executive Office of the President. The office was given the powers and responsibilities needed to coordinate trade policy.

Carter Reorganization

The Tokyo Round of negotiations on reducing nontariff barriers to trade was completed in 1979. Submitted by President Jimmy Carter that same year and quickly approved by Congress, the bill (PL 96-39) implementing the agreement consolidated and coordinated U.S. trade policy making.[96] Carter effected the consolidation and coordination by Executive Order 12188 in January 1980. Under this act, the U.S. trade representative was designated as the nation's chief trade negotiator and U.S. representative in the major international trade organizations. The act also transferred domestic oversight of most trade programs from the Treasury to the Department of Commerce, including responsiblitiy for determining whether countervailing tariffs or antidumping duties should be imposed against what were considered unfair trade practices or excessive foreign imports. Carter's final trade reorganization plan was close to House proposals but fell short of demands made by the Senate for a separate trade department.

Reagan's Trade Representatives

President Ronald Reagan continued his predecessors' commitment to free trade, despite the deepening trade deficit, mounting concern over the competitiveness of U.S. products abroad, and growing criticism about the restrictiveness of other nations' markets. All three issues applied primarily to Japan. Reagan's first trade representative, William E. Brock III, remained an advocate of free trade, As he noted in January 1983: "In recent years four out of five of the new U.S. jobs in manufacturing have been created by international trade. One out of every three acres planted by American farmers is producing crops for export internationally and the potential for growth is unlimited." [97] But Brock also summarized the ironies and difficult choices in the free protectionism versus trade debates. "Everyone is against protectionism in the abstract," he said in 1983. "That is easy. It is another matter to make the hard, courageous choices when it is your industry or your business that appears to be hurt by foreign competition." [98]

Brock was succeeded in June 1985 by Clayton Yeutter, who was head of the Chicago Mercantile Exchange when nominated. Yeutter had served as deputy special trade representative during the administration of Gerald R. Ford and as assistant secretary for agriculture under Nixon. In his confirmation hearings Yeutter said he was prepared to take a more aggressive approach to dealing with trade pressures. He pledged to step up enforcement of existing statutes, including provisions that protected U.S. business from foreign products sold in the United States at unfairly low prices. And he emphasized the need for international trade talks, identifying the biggest problem as that of convincing other nations to lower nontariff barriers, such as foreign government purchasing programs, that discriminated against U.S. exports. To set the agenda for trade

talks, Yeutter planned to consult actively with Congress and the business community. He also indicated that he was prepared to take a pragmatic approach to trade.[99]

Organization and Functions of the Trade Office

The trade office is headed by the U.S. trade representative (USTR), a cabinet-level official with the rank of ambassador, who is directly responsible to the president and Congress.[100] The representative is confirmed by the Senate and thus testifies before congressional committees. Of the three deputy representatives, who also have ambassadorial rank, two are located in Washington, D.C., and one is in Geneva, Switzerland (GATT headquarters).

The USTR is the president's chief adviser on international trade policy and is responsible for developing this policy and coordinating its implementation. The holder of this position also acts as the nation's chief negotiator for international trade agreements. The USTR also chairs the cabinet-level Trade Policy Committee and three interagency committees: the Trade Policy Review Group, the Trade Negotiations Committee, and the Trade Policy Staff Committee (which has forty-four subcommittees). The USTR serves as an ex officio member of the boards of directors of the Export-Inport Bank and the Overseas Private Investment Corporation and sits on the National Advisory Council for International Monetary and Financial Policy.

With the advice of the cabinet-level Economic Policy Council of which it is a member, the USTR office is responsible for policy guidance on issues related to international trade, including the expansion of U.S. exports; matters concerning GATT; overall U.S. trade policy on unfair trade practices, to the extent permitted by law; international trade issues involving energy; and direct investment matters, to the extent they are trade related.

As the principal trade negotiator for the United States, the U.S. trade representative is the chief U.S. representative at international negotiations. These include all activities of GATT; discussions, meetings, and negotiations within the Organization for Economic Cooperation and Development (OECD) on matters affecting trade and commodity issues; meetings of the United Nations Conference on Trade and Development (UNCTAD) and other multilateral institutions dealing with trade and commodity issues; and other bilateral and multilateral negotiations where trade, including East-West trade or commodities, is the primary issue.

The deputy USTR in Geneva is the U.S. representative to GATT and is responsible for negotiations on commerce and trade under UNCTAD. One of the deputy trade representatives located in Washington, D.C., oversees trade policy coordination and bilateral and multilateral negotiations outside GATT and UNCTAD. This official is also responsible for USTR's offices for trade policy and anslysis, trade policy coordination, and bilateral trade negotiations, as well as its region-specific offices (Canada/ Mexico, Japan/China, Latin America/Caribbean/Africa, Asia and the Pacific). The second deputy located in Washington is responsible for sectoral and external affairs and management, including industry and services, agriculture and commodities, congressional affairs, public affairs and private sector liaison, management, and computer operations. The chief textile negotiator, who also has ambassadorial rank, has primary responsibility for negotiating textile agreements and representing the government in matters related to textile trade.

Finally, the USTR office includes a general counsel and a counselor to the trade representative who provides advice on trade policy and represents the United States on the OECD trade committee. In 1987 the staff of the office of the U.S. Trade Representative numbered 146.

Outlook for the Trade Office in the Late 1980s

During Reagan's second term in office, trade policy became a central concern. One principal area of contention was U.S.-Japan trade relations. In May 1987, in response to what it perceived as unfair trading practices, particularly on the part of Japan, the House of Representatives passed comprehensive legislation designed to toughen U.S. actions against unfair trading practices abroad while improving U.S. competitiveness at home. Although Yeutter and others criticized the House bill, they shied away from threatening a presidential veto. In a March 16, 1987, speech to the National Grain and Feed Association, the trade representative cautioned against "get tough" actions that might provoke retaliation.[101] Three days earlier in an address to the Heritage Foundation, Yeutter had asserted that the administration had confronted unfair foreign trade practices "more aggressively than has any administration in history," was negotiating stronger international trade agreements that will provide more opportunities for American exporters to compete in foreign markets, and was striving "to improve the international economic climate for exports by cutting our own budget deficit."[102] Finally, in an April 7 address at the University of Chicago, Yeutter declared that the Uruguay Round of tariff negotiations, then underway, was "the most significant multilateral trade undertaking in 40 years. A successful conclusion of the Uruguay Round will strengthen GATT and create new rules in areas of critical importance to the United States, including trade in agriculture and services, intellectual property protection and investment."[103]

In August 1988 the Senate gave final approval to a sweeping revision of U.S. trade law, which Reagan subsequently signed. The bill for the first time defined trade policy comprehensively, reaching well beyond traditional remedies of tariffs and quotas to include such matters as currency imbalances and third world debt, patent law, and education. The legislation had received bipartisan support from its origins in 1985, when congressional anger over accelerating trade deficits and currency imbalances, and at administration reluctance to intervene, was at its height.

But for all its bipartisan support, the trade bill moved only fitfully through Congress. Although a similar bill was approved by both chambers in April 1988, President Reagan vetoed it primarily because the legislation included a controversial requirement that certain industries give workers sixty days notice of plant closings and mass layoffs. In June Democratic leaders reintroduced the bill without the plant closing requirement, which was introduced in separate legislation. Reagan signed both measures. "This [trade bill] is not going to solve all problems," said Democratic vice-presidential nominee and Senate Finance Committee chairman Lloyd Bentsen (D-Texas). "It's not going to turn the trade deficit around, but it's a plus."[104]

Office of Science and Technology Policy

Although it was formally established in 1976, the president's Office of Science and Technology Policy (OSTP) has had a longer history that began during World War II, when the government recognized that science and technology were vital to the nation's military capabilities.

According to the National Science and Technology Policy, Organizations, and Priorities Act of 1976 (PL 94-282), OSTP provides "a source of scientific and technological analysis and judgment for the president with respect to major policies, plans and programs of the federal government." Its mission became even more central to the government during the late 1970s and 1980s as scientific and technological breakthroughs in other parts of the world challenged America's leadership. The urgency of the situation was addressed in stark terms by the OSTP in its 1983-1984 biennial report:

> A quarter century ago, U.S. industry had few worries about competition. The United States dominated essentially all industrial technologies and had always been able to develop and introduce them at its own pace. Today we must use our technological resources much more aggressively.
>
> In the decades after World War II, the United States built the world's largest research and development capability, primarily through investment of Federal money.... Industry was strongly stimulated by and benefited from this Federal role. But the commercial market for technology has expanded tremendously in the past decade.... Non-Federal spending for research and development reached that of the Federal Government in 1978 and has been rising ever since.
>
> Today, Federal research and development [R & D] spending is about 46 percent of the national total. It is industry, not Government, that is pushing hardest at technological frontiers in many areas.[105]

Although OSTP has tried to encourage the government to participate in a wide range of R & D efforts, the science counselors in the Executive Office of the President (EOP), like the academicians who generally compose the Council of Economic Advisers, have found it often difficult to make their voices heard in the highly political and bureaucratic environment of the nation's capital.

Origins and Development of OSTP

During World War II a number of White House advisory panels were created, primarily to serve the war effort. In 1950 President Harry S Truman signed a bill establishing the National Science Foundation (NSF); a year later he appointed a Science Advisory Committee in the Office of Defense Mobilization. That panel was a forerunner of President Dwight D. Eisenhower's Presidential Science Advisory Committee (PSAC). According to Lee A. Dubridge, President Richard Nixon's science adviser, "PSAC and the science adviser were regarded as the capstone of the government's scientific advisory structure...." The president, said Dubridge, "found it very helpful to have an unbiased, broadly-based and distinguished scientific group helping him to unravel the many technical problems which he faced in defense, space, and various civilian enterprises." Under Eisenhower, concluded Dubridge, "PSAC developed some extraordinarily penetrating and far-reaching recommendations."[106]

The need to upgrade U.S. scientific efforts was perceived as even more urgent after the Soviet Union launched the *Sputnik I* satellite in 1957. Americans, who generally had prided their country for being in the forefront of scientific and technological know-how, were shocked that their major adversary appeared to be taking the lead in space efforts. In light of that concern PSAC recommended creation of the National Aeronautics and Space Administration (NASA).

According to James R. Killian, Jr., science adviser to Eisenhower and chairman of PSAC (after *Sputnik I,* he was given the title of special assistant to the president for science and technology), PSAC worked very closely with the president, the National Security Council, and the budget bureau. Most PSAC members were nonpartisan, with no political ambitions (sometimes they were criticized for being too conservative and unimaginative). "They were motivated primarily by a feeling of obligation to make their specialized learning and skills available to the government in time of need," said Killian.[107]

After John F. Kennedy's election to the presidency in 1960, the position of science adviser was further upgraded. Jerome B. Wiesner, Kennedy's science adviser and chairman of PSAC, found the president extremely receptive to science advice. Indeed, according to Wiesner's successor, Donald F. Hornig, the science adviser "became the White House contact point for the entire governmental science apparatus."[108]

Reorganization Plan 2, implemented in 1962, institutionalized the Office of Science and Technology (OST) in the Executive Office of the President, with its own budget and staff. Its director also served as an official special science adviser to the president, which gave the office more statutory responsibility. Wiesner and PSAC members were apprehensive that the move from the White House Office to EOP might downgrade their access to and influence with the president. Yet, under Kennedy OST took on greater responsibility for energy, environment, and natural resource policies, as well as other civilian technology concerns. At the same time the science office continued to be involved in arms control, defense, and space issues.

Wiesner's apprehensions were perhaps well founded, not so much because of the reorganization, but because President Lyndon B. Johnson, unlike Kennedy, was not particularly comfortable with scientists and academicians. Although OST grew during Johnson's presidency (the staff numbered about twenty professionals, and the office employed between two hundred and three hundred consultants), federal sponsorship of research and development was drastically reduced. Hornig, who served as director during that period, noted that his relationship to the president could be described as "friendly but arms-length." According to Hornig, Johnson "used the talents of PSAC, the OST staff, and the Science Adviser and was happy to hear from them, but one never had the feeling that he depended on them to shape his views."[109] The president's growing preoccupation with the Vietnam War made him even less accessible to his domestic advisers. OST had more contact with members of Congress—and in fact was required to appear before its committees—but it spent less time advising the president.

The science adviser's influence in the White House was further eroded with the accession of Richard Nixon to the presidency in 1969. Under Nixon, White House staff members placed themselves between the science adviser and the president; at the same time, PSAC began openly to criticize the president's policies. The result was Nixon's decision to abolish OST, PSAC, and the position of science adviser. According to one observer, Nixon's science adviser, Dubridge, "lacked toughness" and was unable to develop a close personal rapport with the president. His opposition to presidential policies, including the development of the supersonic transport (SST) aircraft, also distanced him from the White House.[110]

President Gerald R. Ford was more comfortable with and interested in science policy. In June 1975 he introduced legislation that established the Office of Science and Technology Policy (OSTP) within the Executive Office; it was enacted in 1976. The director was chief policy adviser to the president on science and technology for major national policies, programs, and issues. OSTP was authorized to examine the adequacy of federal programs, the utilization of new ideas and discoveries, and the coordination of government scientific activities. Ford was "receptive and interested" in science advice, commented the OSTP's first director, H. Guyford Stever.[111] Vice President Nelson A. Rockefeller further promoted the science advisory role; under the Ford administration, the government's R & D budget began to grow, and initiatives were undertaken in basic research.

The 1976 act had assigned OSTP the responsibility for producing a five-year outlook and annual reports to the president and Congress. But in 1977 these reporting responsibilities were transferred to the National Science Foundation (they were later assumed by the National Academy of Sciences), because of a general feeling that OSTP was overly taxed with reports to Congress and that its prime function was to serve as adviser to the president. (Subsequently, OSTP was asked to submit a biennial report.)

The position of OSTP under President Jimmy Carter was somewhat ambiguous. Frank Press (who served as presidential science adviser from 1977 until 1981 and who later became president of the National Academy of Sciences) maintained a low profile. He was well respected, however, by the president, the scientific community, government departments, and the Office of Management and Budget (OMB), which was important because OSTP had to work closely with OMB. Under the Carter presidency more emphasis was placed on the role of the science office in encouraging R & D, but according to presidential scholar James Everett Katz, OSTP's role under Carter was nevertheless "greatly diminished."[112] The staff was proscribed from taking policy initiatives, particularly in the areas of defense, natural resources, and energy. "The vision of a vigorous, politically significant science policy office was snuffed out, largely because the President's top advisers recognized that many areas of science and technology were politically sensitive and hence should be handled at the political level," wrote Katz.[113] Press reduced the office's already small staff by 30 percent.

Press was succeeded by G. A. Keyworth II, who served as President Ronald Reagan's first appointee to the post (Benjamin Huberman was acting science adviser from January to August 1981). On January 1, 1986, John P. McTague, incumbent deputy director, became acting science adviser and acting OSTP director until May of that year. Between May and October, Richard G. Johnson served as acting OSTP director, until William R. Graham was appointed science adviser and OSTP director.

Organization and Functions of OSTP

The director of OSTP, who is appointed by the president and confirmed by the Senate, also serves as the president's science adviser. In this capacity the director advises the president on how science and technology will affect, for example, the nation's economy, national security, foreign relations, health, energy, environment, and resources. The OSTP head also assists the president in coordinating the government's R & D programs and evaluates existing government science and technology efforts as a basis for recommending appropriate action. Finally, the director advises the president on science and technology considerations in the federal budget and works with OMB on the review and analysis of research and development items in the budgets of all federal agencies.[114]

The National Security Council seeks advice from the director on matters related to science and technology. Moreover, he or she works closely with the Council of Economic Advisers and the Council on Environmental Quality, as well as with other government agencies.

The two associate directors are nominated by the president as well, subject to Senate confirmation. Five assistant directors, appointed by the director, work on areas of current concern, and a small group of policy analysts deal with specialized policy fields. Finally, the executive director manages the OSTP office.

Most of OSTP's coordination tasks are carried out through special committees that address such topics as ocean pollution, radiation policy, solar-terrestrial research, supercomputers, federal laboratories, and food/agriculture/forestry research.

According to OSTP's 1983-1984 *Biennial Science and Technology Report to Congress*, "The U.S. science and technology enterprise still leads the world." [115] Prepared by OSTP with assistance from the National Science Foundation, the report estimated that total U.S. expenditures for research and development in 1983 and 1984 were $86.6 billion and $95.9 billion, respectively (more than the total spent by the United Kingdom, Japan, West Germany, and France); private industry contributed slightly more than 50 percent. "It is industry, not Government, that is pushing hardest at technological frontiers in many areas," noted the report.[116] During the Reagan administration OSTP emphasized basic research, instead of the applied research and development stressed during the late 1970s. Some of the subjects addressed by OSTP activities during the Reagan administration were a national aeronautics policy, agricultural research (including a new competitive awards program in plant science), Arctic research, health issues surrounding the use of the defoliant "Agent Orange" during the Vietnam War, biotechnology, basic research in defense and space policy, and the nation's scientific and technological competitiveness with the Soviet Union in national security matters. During the Reagan years OSTP also tackled emergency preparedness planning, energy policy issues (focusing on nuclear and electric), and international scientific cooperation (particularly between the United States and the People's Republic of China, Brazil, and Japan). Animal rights and the protection of human subjects in experimentation were subjects of OSTP policy statements and monitoring. OSTP sponsored, moreover, a report intended to be a framework for regulatory agencies in assessing cancer risks from chemicals and, with the cooperation of an informal policy group, the office took the lead in establishing an interagency research program to study the climatic effects of a nuclear war, known as the "nuclear winter" phenomenon.

Overall Position of OSTP

"The most effective science advisers were those with clear understanding of the government, and how to make it work," observed David Z. Robinson, who served on the science adviser's staff in the 1960s.

> Technical skill is available outside the government, and a science adviser can find technical help. The help needed to accomplish goals is harder to find. Successful advisers had long experience with government agencies. They knew how far to push things. . . . They knew how to form alliances, both with the agencies and with key parts of the Executive Office. . . . In summary, they were first-rate politicians.[117]

William G. Wells, Jr., former staff director of the House Subcommittee on Science, Resources, and Technology, agreed:

> There should be at least a general political rapport between a president and his science adviser. This is not to argue that the post of science adviser should be strictly a political appointment. . . . Yet, there is no escaping the reality that the White House is a political place, that the problems of the public sector are primarily political, and that a science advisory apparatus—especially the president's science adviser—must be able to function in an intensely political environment.[118]

Katz has noted the problems inherent in OSTP's umbrella function.[119] On many issues it serves as the lead agency, assembling and chairing interagency panels, often tapping outside resources for human resources, money, and administrative support. Yet the office's regular outreach program to draw in private sector experts entails a potential conflict in relying on private organizations to contribute to public policy work. OSTP has been spread even thinner by involvement in a growing "user" group—state and local governments—as well as coordination problems with other executive agencies. "The massive workloads combined with this high rate of dispersal of the tasks to various agencies and organizations have led to problems of coordination for the OSTP," wrote Katz. "It is difficult for the director and the second-rung assistant directors to know what is going on in each division and the information problem is magnified for those lower down in the hierarchy. In the past the lack of communication has led to inefficiency and overlapping responsibilities within OSTP." [120]

"The need for balance and diplomacy means that there is no simple recipe for a science adviser's effectiveness," concluded Katz. "Each science adviser must carve out his own niche within the flow of the dynamic and powerful forces surrounding the central position in the U.S. political system, or be swept away by them." [121]

Council On Environmental Quality

Like the Office of Science and Technology Policy (OSTP), where the director acts in a dual capacity as OSTP head and science adviser to the president, the chair of the Council on Environmental Quality (CEQ) also serves as director of the Office of Environmental Quality (OEQ), whose staff acts as backup for the council. The council was established by the National Environmental Policy Act of 1969 (PL 91-190). The three members of the council are appointed by the president, subject to Senate confirmation, and the president designates one member as chair. Although the chair interacts with the cabinet, cabinet rank does not accompany the position. The chair does serve, however, on the cabinet's Council on Natural Resources and Environment.

The 1970 Environmental Quality Improvement Act (PL 91-224) established the OEQ in the Executive Office of the President "to provide the professional and administrative staff for the Council." Although the council received permanent authorization, periodic reauthorization is required for the OEQ.[122]

In submitting its 719-page annual report on environmental policy for fiscal year 1984, the council noted that the initiatives undertaken marked

> another milestone in the development of a unified national environmental policy. That development has not been easy. For the past 15 years, numerous statutes dealing with environmental quality and natural resources have been enacted, with each new law designed to solve some specific pollution or resource problem, rather than to advance environmental quality as a whole. Thus, they provided little flexibility for resolving difficulties arising when the "solution" to one problem caused or exacerbated another. The task of blending these diverse laws into a more unified environmental policy, and of structuring the environmental agencies accordingly, is a difficult one.[123]

Because the oversight responsibility of the council and the office is extremely broad, they have been selective in choosing areas of study. These areas have depended in turn on the priorities of a varied constituency, which includes their own members and staff, Congress, the president, the American public, and the international community. Their relations with federal agencies, state and local governments, and private interests have made it even more difficult for the council and office to preside over the formulation of a unified national environmental policy.

Origins and Development of CEQ and OEQ

Both CEQ and OEQ were created in response to the nation's increasing concern about declining air and water quality and a general deterioration of the environment. The dramatic blowout of an oil well in the channel off the coast of Santa Barbara, California, in late January 1969, focused public attention on the seriousness of environmental problems. Miles of beaches were covered with oil, and thousands of fish and wildfowl were killed.

On June 3, 1969, four months after the Santa Barbara incident, President Richard Nixon established by executive order the cabinet-level Environmental Quality Council. Congress was not satisfied, however, calling the formation of the council a patchwork approach to environmental problems. In December 1969 Congress passed the National Environmental Policy Act (NEPA), which made environmental protection a matter of national policy. The act required all federal agencies to submit environmental impact statements for all proposed actions and created the

Council on Environmental Quality to replace the Environmental Quality Council. NEPA was denounced by many industry groups, but conservation organizations such as the Sierra Club hailed it as "an environmental Magna Carta." [124]

During its early days the Nixon administration was criticized widely for not displaying a strong commitment to environmental protection. In 1970, as the pressure for corrective action mounted, the president submitted to Congress a plan to consolidate the federal government's widespread environmental efforts into a single Environmental Protection Agency (EPA). There was little congressional opposition, and on December 2, 1970, the EPA was created by executive order as an independent agency within the executive branch. The Council on Environmental Quality continued to exist as an advisory and policy-making body. While EPA was charged with setting and enforcing pollution control standards, CEQ focused on broad environmental policies and coordination of the federal government's activities in that area.

Organization and Functions of CEQ and OEQ

For budget planning purposes CEQ and OEQ divided its responsibilities into three categories: analysis and development of environmental policy, interagency coordination of environmental quality programs, and acquisition and assessment of environmental data.[125]

The environmental policy analysis and development functions are a primary responsibility of the CEQ chair and the two council members, who provide the president with expert opinion and policy advice on environmental issues. The council chair participates in discussions of the Domestic Policy Council when matters concerning the environment arise, while the other members of the CEQ serve on two White House subcabinet working groups on environmental policy.

A primary function of the council is preparation of a lengthy annual Environmental Quality Report, which details how activities of the federal, state, and local governments, as well as private enterprise, are affecting the environment. This report is based on CEQ's own research, work with other federal agencies, the findings of the OEQ staff, and contract studies. The council also publishes reports on specific topics.

The second major responsibility of CEQ and OEQ—interagency coordination of environmental quality programs—includes the promulgation and implementation of regulations related to the National Environmental Policy Act, coordination of federal environmental programs, and participation in the review process conducted by the Office of Management and Budget (OMB) for proposed legislation related to environmental quality. A principal effort of CEQ and OEQ in the mid-1980s was participation in an interagency task force on acid rain, chaired by a council member. The CEQ has coordinated other studies as well. Prominent among them was a study of hazardous waste cleanup, carried out with other groups such as EPA, the National Institute for Environmental Health Sciences, the National Science Foundation, and the congressional Office of Technology Assessment. CEQ members also regularly testify before Congress on the administration's environmental policies.

The role of CEQ and OEQ in the acquisition and

assessment of environmental data has been directed toward coordinating an interagency effort to update information about environmental data sources. For example, the council's chair joined the EPA administrator in heading an Interagency Toxic Substances Data Committee. In 1985 a management fund was established to support OEQ participation in interagency environmental policy studies by allowing it to enlist outside expertise.

One of CEQ's major functions has been monitoring federal compliance with provisions of the NEPA. This act required CEQ to prepare detailed statements (environmental impact statements) on proposed legislation and other major federal actions that would significantly affect the quality of the human environment. CEQ revised the guidelines for its purview in 1971 and 1973, but they were advisory, not binding. As CEQ chairman and OEQ director A. Alan Hill testified on April 9, 1987, "By the mid-1970s significant problems had become associated with the NEPA process. As the number of court cases increased, so too, the number of pages in [environmental impact statements] doubled and tripled, and complaints about the paperwork and delay associated with the process were frequently heard." [126] In 1977, in response to this problem, President Jimmy Carter issued Executive Order 11991, which provided CEQ with the legal authority to issue regulations to federal agencies for implementing the procedural provisions of the NEPA. The order also established a referral process to CEQ for any conflicts among agencies about NEPA implementation. The executive order directed that the regulations "be designed to make the environmental impact statement more useful to decisionmakers and the public," thereby reducing the paperwork involved and turning the attention to the "real environmental issues and alternatives." After soliciting reviews and comments, CEQ issued the NEPA regulations in November 1978; they became effective for all federal agencies in 1979.

With the accession of Ronald Reagan to the presidency in 1981 the NEPA regulations were reviewed and approved by his newly created Task Force on Regulatory Reform, chaired by Vice President George Bush. CEQ later amended the regulations, however, to deal with cases of incomplete or inadequate information on environmental impact. The new rules, which went into effect in May 1986, required federal agencies to point out in the statements that accompanied and documented their material any inadequacy in or lack of information.

The CEQ is also active in international environmental conferences and in the resolution of issues that go beyond national boundaries. For example, in 1981 the CEQ chair headed the Global Issues Working Group, which was established at President Reagan's request. Composed of senior policy representatives from eighteen major federal agencies, the group was convened to coordinate the administration's policies on international issues dealing with environmental protection, population, and the utilization and protection of natural resources. In 1986 and 1987 the council participated in the World Commission on Environment and Development, an independent group which had its origins in a United Nations General Assembly resolution calling for preparation of an "environmental perspective to the year 2000 and beyond." The commission examined a wide range of topics, including air, water, and ocean pollution; hazardous and nuclear waste; deforestation and soil erosion; human shelter; land tenure; and industrial and environmental controls.

Other CEQ and OEQ projects undertaken during the

Reagan administration included studies of depletion of the ozone layer and related issues of climatic change stemming from the "greenhouse effect"; participation in an international conference on the assessment processes for environmental impacts held in Nairobi, Kenya, in June 1987; and participation in bilateral environmental agreements with the Soviet Union and Japan.[127]

Considering its broad responsibilities, the Office of Environmental Quality had a small staff of ten in 1987, a few of whom were detailed temporarily to the OEQ from various federal agencies. Nonetheless, its mission was almost overwhelming, as the office itself noted in its 1984 annual report:

> The scope of the tasks defined under current environmental and natural resources policies is massive; the federal government is charged with managing the whole economy as it impacts upon environmental or natural resource questions, which increasingly means almost every activity by almost everyone in society.... [The CEQ report] describes an active search for ways to address environmental quality and resource conservation problems in new and innovative ways. Clearly, these efforts are important. However, it is also important to note that this administration along with the vast majority of all Americans continues to support the environmental agenda. Possibly no other national goal retains such strong public support from such a broad base of the population. In a very real sense, all Americans are now environmentalists. The disagreements that have arisen and are likely to continue to arise concern the selection of policies viewed as best able to advance environmental objectives. All answers are not yet available. [128]

Office of Administration

As the scope and activities of the Executive Office of the President (EOP) expanded over the years following its establishment in 1939, it became apparent that the support functions of all EOP offices needed to be centralized in a single agency. Reorganization Plan 1 of 1977 (implemented by Executive Order 12028, issued on December 12, 1977) established the Office of Administration within EOP. The director of the office, who was appointed by and is directly responsible to the president, has the task of "ensuring that the Office of Administration provides units within the Executive Office of the President common administrative support and services" (Section 2, Executive Order 12028).

The office provides administrative support services to all EOP offices in the White House. These services include personnel management; financial management; data processing; library services, record-keeping, and information services; and office services and operations, including mail handling (except for presidential mail), messenger service, printing and duplication, graphics, word processing, procurement, and supply.

In 1987 the Office of Administration consisted of 165 full-time and 35 temporary and part-time employees. These employees were divided into five sections: personnel, financial, library and informational services, automated systems, and administrative operations. The two printing plants of the office prepare the Budget Message and other documents for distribution. (For large print quantities, the type is set by the Office of Administration and sent to the Government Printing Office, which either prints and binds the publication itself or seeks an outside printer and binder.) For all EOP offices the Administration Office maintains accounts, recruits employees (with the exception of the Office of Policy Development and White House staff, all of whom are political appointees), and maintains official records, including those of the White House. In 1987 the Office of Administration provided support services for the 1,495 men and women who served in the Executive Office. It also provided services to the Commission on the Bicentennial of the Constitution (not officially part of the EOP). Three libraries (not open to the general public) come under its oversight as well: a general reference library located in the New Executive Office Building and reference and law libraries in the Old Executive Office Building.

Since its inception the Office of Administration has developed a sophisticated computer system, which responds to the ever-growing and increasingly complex needs of the White House and the EOP.

Notes

1. Richard M. Pious, *The American Presidency* (New York: Basic Books, 1979), 253.
2. John W. Macy, Bruce Adams, and J. Jackson Walter, *America's Unelected Government: Appointing the President's Team* (Cambridge, Mass.: Ballinger, 1983), 4.
3. Stephen Hess, *Organizing the Presidency* (Washington, D.C.: Brookings, 1976), 14.
4. Macy, Adams, and Walter, *America's Unelected Government,* 7.
5. G. Calvin Mackenzie, *The Politics of Presidential Appointments* (New York: Free Press, 1981), 8-9.
6. Hess, *Organizing the Presidency,* 29.
7. Ibid., 62.
8. Macy, Adams, and Walter, *America's Unelected Government,* 30.
9. Hess, *Organizing the Presidency,* 79-80.
10. Emmette S. Redford and Richard T. McCulley, *White House Operations: The Johnson Presidency* (Austin: University of Texas Press, 1986), 137.
11. Theodore C. Sorensen, *Watchmen in the Night* (Cambridge, Mass.: MIT Press, 1973), 36.
12. Macy, Adams, and Walter, *America's Unelected Government,* 33.
13. Quote found in Stephen J. Wayne, *The Legislative Presidency* (New York: Harper and Row, 1978), 187.
14. Mackenzie, *The Politics of Presidential Appointments,* 54-55.
15. Edward D. Feigenbaum, "Staffing, Organization, and Decision-making in the Ford and Carter White Houses," *Presidential Studies Quarterly* 10 (Summer 1980): 366-367.
16. Macy, Adams, and Walter, *America's Unelected Government,* 37.
17. Ibid., 49.
18. Office of Management and Budget, "The Work of the Office of Management and Budget," mimeographed (Washington, D.C.: OMB, 1987).
19. Bureau of the Budget, *Staff Orientation Manual* (Washington, D.C.: Government Printing Office, 1945), 38.
20. Quoted in *Congress and the Nation, 1969-1972* (Washington, D.C.: Congressional Quarterly Inc., 1973), 3:73.
21. Richard E. Neustadt, "Presidency and Legislation: The Growth of Central Clearance," *American Political Science Review* 48 (September 1954): 641-671.
22. For a discussion of this period, see the chapter on Franklin D. Roosevelt in Hess, *Organizing the Presidency.*
23. Quoted in Larry Berman, *The Office of Management and Budget and the Presidency, 1921-1979* (Princeton, N.J.: Princeton University Press, 1979), 28.
24. Ibid., 42.
25. Ibid., 52.
26. Ibid., 55.
27. Brookings Institution, *Study of the 1960-61 Presidential Transition: The White House and the Executive Office of the President* (Washington, D.C.: Brookings, 1960), 33.
28. "Task Force Report on Intergovernmental Program Coordination: The Bureau of the Budget During the Administration of Lyndon Baines Johnson," mimeographed (Washington, D.C.: U.S. Executive Office of the President, Bureau of the Budget, November 14, 1968).
29. *Presidential Documents,* March 16, 1970 (Washington, D.C.: Government Printing Office, 1970), 355-357.
30. Berman, *The Office of Management and Budget and the Presidency,* 125.
31. *Congressional Quarterly Weekly Report,* July 13, 1985, 1356.
32. See Office of Management and Budget, "The Work of the Office of Management and Budget," 5.
33. *Federal Regulatory Directory, 1983-84* (Washington, D.C.: Congressional Quarterly Inc., 1983), 66.
34. Julie Rovner, "OMB's Activities Draw Fire in Congress, Courts," *Congressional Quarterly Weekly Report,* June 14, 1986, 1341.
35. See *Congressional Quarterly Weekly Report,* June 14, 1986, 1340.
36. Quoted in Dave Kaplan, "Senate Committee Approves OMB Overhaul," *Congressional Quarterly Weekly Report,* June 28, 1986, 1488.
37. From Title I, "Coordination for National Security," of the National Security Act, PL 80-253. See *Congress and the Nation, 1945-1964* (Washington, D.C.: Congressional Quarterly Inc., 1965), 1:247.
38. From Mark M. Lowenthal, "The National Security Council: Organizational History," Congressional Research Service, Washington, D.C., June 27, 1978.
39. From Henry A. Kissinger, *White House Years* (Boston: Little, Brown, 1979), 31.
40. For a description of this "conventional wisdom" on the NSC, see I. M. Destler, "National Security Management: What Presidents Have Wrought," *Political Science Quarterly* 95 (Winter 1980): 81.
41. Kissinger, *White House Years,* 30.
42. From Allen Weinstein and Michael R. Beschloss, "The Best National Security System: An Interview with Zbigniew Brzezinski," *Washington Quarterly* (Winter 1982): 74.
43. Larry Light, "White House Domestic Policy Staff Plays an Important Role in Formulating Legislation," *Congressional Quarterly Weekly Report,* October 6, 1979, 2202.
44. Quoted in Peri E. Arnold, *Making the Managerial Presidency: Comprehensive Reorganization Planning 1905-1980* (Princeton, N.J.: Princeton University Press, 1986), 285.
45. Ibid., 284-285.
46. *Public Papers of the Presidents of the United States, Richard Nixon, 1970* (Washington, D.C.: Government Printing Office, 1971), 257.
47. House Committee on Government Organization, *Hearings, Reorganization Plan No. 2 of 1970,* 91st Cong., 2d Sess., 1970, 55-56.
48. Ibid., 23.
49. Arnold, *Making the Managerial Presidency,* 298.
50. Quoted in Hess, *Organizing the Presidency,* 131.
51. Ibid., 132.
52. Dick Kirschten, "Policy Development Office: A Scaled-down Operation," *National Journal,* April 25, 1981, 684.
53. John H. Kessel, *The Domestic Presidency: Decision-Making in the White House* (Boston, Mass.: Duxbury Press, 1975), 29.
54. Light, "White House Domestic Policy Staff," 2199.
55. Ibid., 2199.
56. Ibid., 2200.
57. Ibid.
58. *Congressional Quarterly Almanac: 1981* (Washington, D.C.: Congressional Quarterly Inc., 1982), 356. The letter was dated July 8, 1981.

59. Text of announcement in *Congressional Quarterly Weekly Report,* April 20, 1985, 757.
60. Kirschten, "Policy Development Office," 684.
61. The organization and functions of the OPD were provided by special assistant Michael Driggs in a May 19, 1987, interview.
62. Kirschten, "Policy Development Office," 684.
63. Edward S. Flash, Jr., "The Broadening Scope of the President's Economic Advisers," *The George Washington Law Review* 35, no. 2 (December 1966): 286.
64. Roger Porter, "Economic Advice to the President from Eisenhower to Reagan," *Political Science Quarterly* (Fall 1983): 404.
65. Ibid., 405.
66. David Naveh, "The Political Role of Academic Advisers: The Case of the U.S. President's Council of Economic Advisers, 1946-76," *Presidential Studies Quarterly* 11 (Fall 1981): 492.
67. The origins and politics of the act have been well documented by Stephen K. Bailey in *Congress Makes a Law* (New York: Columbia University Press, 1950).
68. For a good discussion of this issue, see E. Ray Canterbury, *The President's Council of Economic Advisers* (New York: Exposition Press, 1961).
69. Edwin G. Nourse and Bertram M. Gross, "The Role of the Council of Economic Advisers," *American Political Science Review* (April 1948).
70. Erwin C. Hargrove and Samuel A. Morley, eds., *The President and the Council of Economic Advisers: Interviews with CEA Chairmen* (Boulder, Colo.: Westview Press, 1984), 47.
71. Gerhard Colm, "The Executive Office and Fiscal and Economic Policy," *Law and Contemporary Problems* 21 (Autumn 1956): 716.
72. Edwin G. Nourse, *Economics in the Public Service* (New York: Harcourt Brace, 1953), 380.
73. Nourse and Gross, "The Role of the Council of Economic Advisers."
74. Edwin G. Nourse, "The Employment Act and the Economic Future," *Vital Speeches XII* (January 1, 1946).
75. Hargrove and Morley, *The President and the Council of Economic Advisers,* 50.
76. Hess, *Organizing the Presidency,* 55.
77. Hugh S. Norton, *The Council of Economic Advisers: Three Periods of Influence* (Columbia, S.C.: Bureau of Business and Economic Research, 1973), 23.
78. Hess, *Organizing the Presidency,* 75.
79. Naveh, "The Political Role of Academic Advisers," 497.
80. Hargrove and Morley, *The President and the Council of Economic Advisers,* 91.
81. Ibid., 90.
82. Arthur M. Schlesinger, Jr., *A Thousand Days: John F. Kennedy in the White House* (Boston: Houghton Mifflin, 1965), 137.
83. Edward S. Flash, Jr., *Economic Advice and Presidential Leadership* (New York: Columbia University Press, 1965), 209.
84. Hess, *Organizing the Presidency,* 90.
85. Hargrove and Morley, *The President and the Council of Economic Advisers,* 163.
86. Ibid., 359.
87. Ibid., 409.
88. Ibid., 459.
89. *Congress and the Nation, 1977-1980* (Washington, D.C.: Congressional Quarterly Inc., 1981), 5:233.
90. *Congressional Quarterly Almanac: 1981* (Washington, D.C.: Congressional Quarterly Inc., 1982), 270.
91. Council of Economic Advisers, *Economic Report of the President* (Washington, D.C.: Government Printing Office, January 1987).
92. Hess, *Organizing the Presidency,* 167.
93. Quoted in Naveh, "The Political Role of Academic Advisers," 501.
94. For a general history of U.S. trade policy, see *Trade: U.S. Policy Since 1945* (Washington, D.C.: Congressional Quarterly Inc., 1984).
95. John W. Evans, *The Kennedy Round in American Trade Policy: The Twilight of the GATT?* (Cambridge, Mass.: Harvard University Press, 1971), 156.
96. See, among other sources, *Congress and the Nation, 1977-1980,* 5:273.
97. *Trade,* 2.
98. Clyde M. Farnsworth, "William Brock: Our Man for Trade," *New York Times Magazine,* November 13, 1983.
99. *Congressional Quarterly Weekly Report,* June 29, 1985, 1303.
100. Information on the organization and functions of the USTR was supplied by interviews with staff members and a mimeographed article produced by the office.
101. *Congressional Quarterly Weekly Report,* March 28, 1987, 555.
102. Office of the U.S. Trade Representative, mimeographed copy of an address by Clayton K. Yeutter to the Heritage Foundation, Washington, D.C., March 13, 1987.
103. A mimeographed copy of the April 7, 1987, address by Clayton K. Yeutter to the Graduate School of Business, University of Chicago, was provided by the Office of the U.S. Trade Representative.
104. Elizabeth Wehr, "Senate Clears Trade Bill by Lopsided Vote," *Congressional Quarterly Weekly Report,* August 6, 1988, 2215.
105. Office of Science and Technology Policy (in cooperation with the National Science Foundation), *Biennial Science and Technology Report to the Congress: 1983-1984* (Washington, D.C.: Government Printing Office, 1985), 4. This report summarizes OSTP's wide-ranging activities. See also a mimeographed fact sheet by OSTP, available from that office.
106. Lee A. Dubridge, "Science Advice to the President: Important and Difficult," in *Science Advice to the President,* ed. George Bugliarello and A. George Schillinger, a special issue of *Technology and Society* (New York: Pergamon Press, 1980), 2:11. These volumes provide invaluable articles by former presidential science advisers, observers, and legislative experts on the evolution of the science advisory role.
107. James R. Killian, Jr., "The Origins and Uses of a Scientific Presence in the White House," in *Science Advice,* 31.
108. Donald F. Hornig, "The President's Need for Science Advice: Past and Future," in *Science Advice,* 42.
109. Ibid., 47.
110. William G. Wells, Jr., "Science Advice and the Presidency," in *Science Advice,* 214. Wells served as staff director of the House Subcommittee on Science, Resources, and Technology at the time.
111. H. Guyford Stever, "Science Advice—Out of and Back to the White House," in *Science Advice,* 74.
112. James Everett Katz, "Organizational Structure and Advisory Effectiveness," in *Science Advice,* 230.
113. Ibid.
114. For greater detail, see Office of Science and Technology Policy, *Biennial Science and Technology Report.*
115. Ibid., 3.
116. Ibid., 4.
117. David Z. Robinson, "Politics in the Science Advising Process," in *Science Advice,* 163.
118. Wells, "Science Advice and the Presidency," 214.
119. Katz, "Organizational Structure." Katz himself noted, "Conventional wisdom dictates that the science advisor's usefulness is predicated entirely on his personal rapport with the president" (p. 243).
120. Ibid., 233.
121. Ibid., 243.
122. To learn the full relevant statutory authority at the time, see Executive Office of the President, Council on Environmental Quality, *Regulations for Implementing the Procedural Provisions of the National Environmental Policy Act* (Washington, D.C.: Government Printing Office, November 1978), reprint 43FR 55978-56007.
123. Executive Office of the President, Council on Environmental Quality, *Environmental Quality,* Fifteenth Annual Report (Washington, D.C.: Government Printing Office, 1985), 1.

124. For background, see *Federal Regulatory Directory, 1983-84,* 113.
125. A succinct summary of the council's activities was given by CEQ chairman A. Alan Hill in a statement before the House Merchant Marine and Fisheries Subcommittee on Fisheries and Wildlife, Conservation and the Environment, April 9, 1987.
126. Ibid., 8.
127. For summaries of CEQ and OEQ activities, see the annual reports of the Council on Environmental Quality, particularly the eleventh and fifteenth reports (Washington, D.C.: Government Printing Office, 1981). Other reports of particular interest are: *Report of an Expert Meeting on Research Needs and Opportunities at Federally-supervised Hazardous Waste Site Clean-ups* (Washington, D.C.: Executive Office of the President, Council on Environmental Quality, October 20, 1986); *Report on Long-term Environmental Research and Development* (Washington, D.C.: Executive Office of the President, Council on Environmental Quality, Office of Environmental Quality, March 1985).
128. Council on Environmental Quality, Fifteenth Annual Report, 6, 8.

Selected Bibliography

Arnold, Peri E. *Making the Managerial Presidency: Comprehensive Reorganization Planning 1905-1980.* Princeton, N.J.: Princeton University Press, 1986.

Bailey, Stephen. *Congress Makes a Law.* New York: Columbia University Press, 1950.

Berman, Larry. *The Office of Management and Budget and the Presidency, 1921-1979.* Princeton, N.J.: Princeton University Press, 1979.

Bugliarello, George, and A. George Schillinger, eds. *Science Advice to the President,* a special issue of *Technology in Society,* Vol. 2, Nos. 1 and 2. New York: Pergamon Press, 1980.

Feigenbaum, Edward D. "Staffing, Organization, and Decision-making in the Ford and Carter White Houses." *Presidential Studies Quarterly* 10 (Summer 1980): 364-377.

Hargrove, Erwin C., and Samuel A. Morley, eds. *The President and the Council of Economic Advisers: Interviews with CEA Chairmen.* Boulder, Colo.: Westview Press, 1984.

Hess, Stephen. *Organizing the Presidency.* Washington, D.C.: Brookings, 1976.

King, Anthony. *Both Ends of the Avenue: The Presidency, the Executive Branch, and Congress in the 1980s.* Washington, D.C.: American Enterprise Institute, 1983.

Light, Larry. "White House Domestic Policy Staff Plays an Important Role in Formulating Legislation." *Congressional Quarterly Weekly Report,* October 6, 1979, 2199-2204.

Macy, John W., Bruce Adams, and J. Jackson Walter. *America's Unelected Government: Appointing the President's Team.* Cambridge, Mass.: Ballinger, 1983.

Mosher, Frederick C. *A Tale of Two Agencies: A Comparative Analysis of the General Accounting Office and the Office of Management and Budget.* Baton Rouge: Louisiana State University Press, 1984.

Naveh, David. "The Political Role of Academic Advisers: The Case of the U.S. President's Council of Economic Advisers, 1946-76." *Presidential Studies Quarterly* 11 (Fall 1981).

Pious, Richard M. *The American Presidency.* New York: Basic Books, 1979.

Redford, Emmette S., and Richard T. McCulley. *White House Operations: The Johnson Presidency.* Austin: University of Texas Press, 1986.

Sorensen, Theodore C. *Watchmen in the Night.* Cambridge, Mass.: MIT Press, 1973.

Trade: U.S. Policy Since 1945. Washington, D.C.: Congressional Quarterly Inc., 1984.

Wayne, Stephen. *The Legislative Presidency.* New York: Harper and Row, 1978.

Cabinet

The cabinet is one of the most unusual institutions of the presidency. Although not specifically mentioned in the Constitution or specifically provided for in statutory law, the cabinet has become an institutionalized part of the presidency. The country's first president, George Washington, initiated the practice of meeting with the secretaries of state, Treasury, and war as well as his attorney general, to seek their advice on domestic and foreign policy. The modern presidential cabinet consists of the president, vice president, heads of the fourteen executive departments, and any other officials the president might wish to invite, such as the head of the Office of Management and Budget and the ambassador to the United Nations. While some presidents have attempted to use their cabinets regularly, recognizing that a presidency that effectively utilizes its cabinet is still considered ideal, presidential cabinets have for the most part been the stepchildren of the presidency. In fact, because cabinet members usually become advocates of their departments, they contribute little to presidential decision making unless the decisions involve matters that concern their respective bailiwicks. As a result, most presidents have viewed their cabinets as more of a burden than a help.

Origin and Development of the Cabinet

The idea of some kind of advisory council for the president was discussed at the Constitutional Convention. Gouverneur Morris and Charles Cotesworth Pinckney, the first delegates to use the term "cabinet" at the convention, proposed creation of a council of state, composed of the executive department heads, to advise the president. This proposal failed to win adoption, but advocates of a cabinet kept the idea alive throughout most of the convention. Indeed, less than two weeks before finalization of the Constitution, Benjamin Franklin continued to insist that a council of state "would not only be a check on a bad president but be a relief to a good one." [1]

The cabinet concept eventually failed to win enough support among the convention's delegates, however. The majority of the Founders apparently feared that the presidency might become too overburdened with unnecessary advisory councils. Alexander Hamilton explained the Founders' concerns in the *Federalist* No. 70: "A council to a magistrate, who is himself responsible for what he does, are generally nothing better than a clog upon his good intentions; are often the instruments and accomplices of his bad, and are almost always a cloak to his faults." [2] Consequently, when the Committee on Style finished drafting the Constitution, all that remained of the idea was the authorization that the president "require the Opinion, in writing, of the principal Officer in each of the executive Departments, upon any Subject relating to the duties of their respective Offices" (Article II, section 2).

Having no constitutional or statutory mandate for the institution of a cabinet, presidents have relied on the constitutional mandate that allows them to seek the advice of their principal executive branch officers. Under the Articles of Confederation, several executive departments already existed. Thus, in reality Washington's first cabinet merely evolved out of an already established executive pattern that began in the early 1780s. President Washington understood that the constitutional language about the responsibility of the departments was ambiguous. His biographer, James Thomas Flexner, has written: "Whether what was defined as 'the heads of the great departments' were to be under the jurisdiction of the president was not stated: the president was merely empowered to require their opinions relating to their duties." [3] When Washington was inaugurated in 1789, he consulted with Alexander Hamilton, James Madison, and others on the powers and duties of the presidency and permanently settled the matter by instituting the foundation of the modern cabinet. Early in his administration, Washington took the view that department heads should be assistants to the president and not to Congress.

Seeking both administrative and advisory help in his new administration, Washington asked Congress to create three executive departments to oversee, respectively, foreign affairs, military affairs, and fiscal concerns. During the months before the executive branch was firmly in place, Washington relied on the services of those who had served in the same areas under the Articles of Confederation. John Jay continued temporarily as secretary of foreign affairs, Henry Knox remained at the secretary of war post, and the old Treasury Board continued to manage fiscal concerns.

By W. Craig Bledsoe

For more than two months Congress debated the proper establishment of these three executive departments. Primarily concerned with the relationship of each department to Congress and believing that not all departments should be alike in these relationships, most members of Congress preferred that the departments concerned with foreign affairs and war be primarily under the control of the executive. The Treasury, however, had some legislative purposes and thus should fall more under the control of Congress. The statutes setting up these departments reflected these preferences. On July 27, 1789, Congress established the Department of Foreign Affairs. The secretary of foreign affairs was given the responsibility of performing duties assigned by the president. Two months later Congress changed the name to the Department of State. Similarly, the statutory language setting up the War Department placed it squarely under the control of the president. Unlike the Departments of State and War, the Treasury Department was not designated by Congress as an "executive department." Instead, the secretary of the Treasury was directed to report fiscal matters directly to Congress. Part of the rationale for this special status was the constitutional requirement that revenue bills originate in the House of Representatives.

Alexander Hamilton did much to increase the prestige and independence of the cabinet. Early in his administration Washington asked Hamilton to head the Treasury, and there is some evidence that the secretary contributed greatly to the drafting of the Treasury Act. Hamilton, who had served as Washington's chief adviser during the organization of the new government, virtually assumed the role of prime minister after his confirmation as secretary of the Treasury on September 11, 1789. In addition to his abilities and his special relationship with Washington, Hamilton's ascension to a position of such unofficial prominence was assisted by the relative statutory importance of the Treasury Department. He assumed an office that Congress had intended as an extension of its own authority and made it a stronghold of executive power. According to presidential scholar R. Gordon Hoxie, "With his admiration of the British model and his high regard for Washington, Hamilton conceived of executive power as generated through a cabinet of department heads, administered by a judicious executive head. In such a system, by the sheer vent of his energies and genius, Hamilton came to be Washington's dominant adviser." [4]

Washington's use of the cabinet soon resulted in an institution that the Framers of the Constitution had failed to include. The president eventually appointed Henry Knox as secretary of war (September 12, 1789) and Thomas Jefferson, who had been serving as minister to France, as secretary of state (March 22, 1790). In addition, Edmund Randolph was named attorney general, although there was no Department of Justice until 1870.

Washington initially believed that the Senate would fill the role of an advisory council, but that hope faded in August 1790 when Washington, accompanied by Knox, went to the Senate floor to get advice on an Indian treaty. The senators made it clear that they were uncomfortable meeting with the president and that they would not serve in the capacity of an advisory council. As a result, Washington gradually began to rely on the advice of his department heads, the attorney general, Vice President John Adams, and Chief Justice John Jay.

At first Washington consulted with each individually, both in person and in writing. Later, in 1791, when he was

Library of Congress

Although the Treasury secretary was not part of the original cabinet, Alexander Hamilton made the department a stronghold of executive power and became Washington's dominant adviser.

preparing to leave the capital for a few days, he authorized his vice president, the chief justice, and the secretaries of Treasury, state, and war to meet and discuss government matters during his absence. In the following year the president conferred frequently with his department heads and attorney general, omitting the vice president and the chief justice. These meetings occurred even more often during the undeclared naval war with France. By 1793 James Madison was applying the term "cabinet" to these conferences. The name stuck, and the cabinet became a permanent addition to the executive branch.

Like many presidents after him, Washington had hoped that his advisers would consult with one another and work together harmoniously. Early cabinet meetings, however, were marred by a growing rift between Jefferson and Hamilton, who detested each other and differed on a number of important policy positions. Although Washington tried to get them to work together, they quarreled continuously. Jefferson finally resigned in the summer of 1793. Less than two years later Hamilton retired from government service to return to his lucrative law practice, yet Washington continued to write him for advice during his remaining two years in office. In fact, the president apparently abandoned his hopes of his cabinet serving as an advisory board.

When Washington replaced Jefferson and Hamilton in his cabinet, he chose men of cooler heads but lesser talents, and evidently he did not value their advice as much as that from his first cabinet. Flexner wrote: "Unlike their predecessors they were not consulted concerning executive decisions; they were limited to the routines of their departments." [5] This disillusionment and uncertainty surrounding the proper role of the cabinet has afflicted almost every administration since Washington's.

President John Adams, who retained all of Washington's cabinet members, was even more disillusioned with his cabinet than his predecessor. Early in his administration important differences of opinion developed between Adams and his department heads. Indeed, his cabinet members were more loyal to Hamilton than to him. And because the president was often away from the capital, cabinet members began to advise each other and to seek Hamilton's advice. In the final year of his administration Adams removed two cabinet members. Yet during his administration the formal cabinet remained the president's principal official advisory unit.

The role of the cabinet under Washington and Adams

thus established a pattern of ambiguity that has endured throughout the history of the presidency. According to R. Gordon Hoxie,

The twelve Federalist years had established the joint consultation between the president and the department heads as a body, but it was clear that the president was bound neither to consult nor to accept the advice received. Nor was the cabinet an administrative body. The business of government was carried out throughout the executive departments.[6]

Nineteenth-Century Cabinets

The first part of the nineteenth century witnessed a gradual decline in the importance of the cabinet. Few cabinets got along all that well, and few presidents relied on their cabinets as advisory groups. Because the selection of cabinet members became more and more dictated by political and geographic considerations, presidents increasingly appointed cabinet members whom they did not know personally or necessarily trust. Indeed, many times presidents had to struggle to maintain control over their cabinets. If because of a lack of interest in using the cabinet a president declined to prepare an agenda for a cabinet meeting, the secretaries would take the initiative.

Appointments to earlier cabinets were based primarily on the appointee's abilities. Beginning with President James Madison's administration (1809-1817), however, political and geographic factors often took precedence over ability or loyalty. For example, the Senate strongly opposed Madison's selection of Albert Gallatin, Jefferson's secretary of the Treasury, to succeed Madison as secretary of state. Instead, several senators forced the president to appoint Robert Smith, the brother of an influential senator, to the position. For the first time the president was no longer in complete control of the cabinet selection process.

Because of these pressures, as well as his own personality, Andrew Jackson (1829-1837) was the first president to largely ignore his collective cabinet. During his first two years in office, he did not even meet with his cabinet, and he convened it only sixteen times during his entire eight years as president. Jackson preferred the intimacy of his "kitchen cabinet," a group of close personal advisers (many of whom were newspapermen who kept him in touch with public opinion), over the formality of his official cabinet. Throughout his administration, he steadfastly refused to use his formal cabinet to help him make final decisions. As he explained: "I have accustomed myself to receive with respect the opinions of others, but always take the responsibility for deciding for myself."[7]

Abraham Lincoln (1861-1865) appointed strong political leaders, many of them his political antagonists, to his cabinet. In fact, some of his cabinet members believed themselves superior to Lincoln. This resulted not only in several overly ambitious cabinet members but also in some rather bitter relationships between cabinet members and the president. Cabinet officers during the Lincoln administration were known for their intrigues. Secretary of State William H. Seward, for example, considered himself Lincoln's prime minister. Salmon P. Chase, secretary of the Treasury, schemed with a few members of the Senate to remove Seward and increase his own influence. Lincoln's strong leadership, however, allowed him to retain control of his cabinet and use it for his own ends. Indeed, as the story goes, when seeking advice on one critical decision, Lincoln

polled his entire cabinet, only to be overwhelmingly outvoted. He then proclaimed: "Seven nays and one aye, the ayes have it." The critical decisions, such as the Emancipation Proclamation, were his alone, although he usually sought cabinet endorsement. Hoxie wrote: "Just as he was the strongest nineteenth-century president, he had the strongest cabinet members, who worked strenuously in their respective departments, although as a body they were subordinated to him."[8]

During the latter part of the nineteenth century an attempt was made to move responsibility for the cabinet from the White House to Congress, thereby giving Congress considerable access to information on the executive branch. Chief among the members of Congress introducing legislation to accomplish this goal was George Hunt Pendleton (D-Ohio), who in 1864 proposed a bill that would allow secretaries of executive departments to occupy seats on the House floor. Supported strongly by others in Congress (including future president James A. Garfield), the bill came up for debate in 1865 and several times thereafter. The proposal was never voted into law.

Twentieth-Century Cabinets

Early in the twentieth century the cabinet grew in size but continued to play only a modest role as an advisory body. As the federal government became more complex and the power of the presidency began to expand, the size of the cabinet expanded as well. In 1913, during Woodrow Wilson's administration (1913-1921), the cabinet swelled to ten members. President Wilson, however, rarely met with his cabinet. Even during World War I Wilson did not consult with his cabinet about the 1915 sinking of the *Lusitania* or his 1917 call for Congress to declare war. Instead, he relied for advice on his Council of National Defense, which was created in 1916 and composed of the secretaries of war, navy, interior, agriculture, commerce, and labor. As one department secretary complained, "Nothing talked of at Cabinet that would interest a nation, a family, or a child. No talk of the war."[9]

Under Franklin D. Roosevelt (1933-1945) cabinet meetings continued to be more of a forum for discussion than a decision-making body. Roosevelt even downplayed the importance of the cabinet. During cabinet meetings he customarily went around the table and asked each cabinet member what was on his or her mind. His secretary of the interior, Harold L. Ickes, summarized Roosevelt's attitude: "The cold fact is that on important matters we are seldom called upon for advice. We never discuss exhaustively any policy of government or question of political strategy.... Our cabinet meetings are pleasant affairs, but we only skim the surface of routine affairs."[10] In addition, Roosevelt often interceded in the activities of his cabinet members. According to Hoxie,

Roosevelt constantly interposed in the executive departments both in domestic and foreign policy. He became, in essence, his own secretary of state, war, and navy. Secretary of State Cordell Hull and Secretary of War [Henry L.] Stimson both voiced their unhappiness. So did Roosevelt's new vice-president, Harry S Truman, who was neither consulted nor informed of what was going on.[11]

President Truman (1945-1953) boasted that he had "revived the cabinet system," believing that it should be similar to a board of directors. Indeed, Truman called for a

Truman called for a strong, active cabinet, yet not once did he convene his cabinet to discuss the North Korean invasion of South Korea.

strong, active cabinet: "The cabinet is not merely a collection of executives administering different governmental functions. It is a body whose combined judgment the president uses to formulate the fundamental policies of the administration." [12] Unlike Roosevelt, Truman actually asked his cabinet to vote on some major issues. Toward the end of his administration, however, he backed away from the board of directors approach. For example, when North Korea attacked South Korea in 1950 Truman never once convened his cabinet to discuss the matter. He relied instead on an informal group—consisting of the secretaries of defense and state, the Joint Chiefs of Staff, and some of his closest aides—to advise him on the entry of the United States into the war. Throughout his administration Truman reserved the most difficult decisions for himself. Presidential scholar Stephen Hess has written: "Over the years he [Truman] drew back from the board of directors concept; powers delegated could be powers lost, and Truman, while modest about himself as president, was zealous in protecting those prerogatives that he felt were inherent in the presidency." [13]

Dwight D. Eisenhower (1953-1961) took his cabinet more seriously than any other twentieth-century president. He established a cabinet secretariat (one of the cabinet secretaries set the agenda and served as liaison with the president), and he charged his cabinet with both advising him on major issues and seeing that every decision was carried out.

Eisenhower expanded cabinet meetings to include not only department secretaries but also important aides such as the U.S. ambassador to the United Nations, the budget director, the White House chief of staff, as well as the national security affairs assistant and other top White House advisers. Vice presidents have served on cabinets since Franklin Roosevelt's first administration, but Eisenhower was the first president to effectively use his vice president in the cabinet. He made the vice president chairman of several cabinet committees and his acting chairman of the cabinet if he was unable to attend a meeting. Eisenhower's cabinet, which usually numbered around twenty or more, held regularly scheduled, weekly meetings which often lasted three or more hours.

Although Eisenhower accepted responsibility for final

decisions, he attempted to make the cabinet more than just a body of advisers by including wide-ranging, important issues on the cabinet agenda. According to noted presidential scholar Thomas E. Cronin,

> [Eisenhower] did, within certain limits, encourage his cabinet members to take an independent line of their own and argue it out within the cabinet session. Eisenhower fully appreciated the limits of a cabinet system but seemed motivated to use the cabinet sessions both as a means to keep himself informed and as a way to prevent the personality conflicts, throat-cutting, and end-running that had characterized the history of past administrations. [14]

In his relationship with his cabinet, John F. Kennedy (1961-1963) did not follow the example set by President Eisenhower. Although he spent time with his department heads individually, President Kennedy held cabinet meetings as seldom as possible. Historian Arthur M. Schlesinger, Jr., has quoted Kennedy as saying, "Cabinet meetings are simply useless. Why should the Postmaster General sit here and listen to a discussion of the problems of Laos?" [15] Because he believed that few subjects warranted discussion by the entire cabinet, Kennedy preferred to spend his time with the aides and secretaries most concerned with a specific issue. Eisenhower was highly tolerant of meetings because of his long military experience, but Kennedy wanted to avoid them. Hess wrote: "Kennedy was too restless to sit for long periods, too impatient with long-winded speakers, and too mentally agile to accept repetitious, circuitous Cabinet-NSC discussions as a tolerable method for receiving information." [16]

Although Lyndon B. Johnson (1963-1969) used his cabinet much more than Kennedy, cabinet meetings were mostly for show and contained little in the way of substantive discussion. Johnson, in fact, used cabinet meetings to create the impression of consensus within his administration. According to Johnson's press secretary George Reedy, "Cabinet meetings were held with considerable regularity, with fully predetermined agendas and fully prewritten statements. In general, they consisted of briefings by cabinet members followed by a later release of the statements to the press. It was regarded by all participants except the president as a painful experience." [17] Johnson thus gave little credit to the cabinet as a consultative body, keeping many of his cabinet officers at a distance. His use of his cabinet to dispense information and to promote the appearance that a substantive debate was taking place led one of his cabinet officers to complain: "Cabinet meetings under L.B.J. were really perfunctory. They served two purposes: to let Dean Rusk brief us on the state of foreign affairs and let the president give us some occasional new political or personnel marching orders." [18]

Prior to his election in 1968 Richard Nixon (1969-1974) seemed to be calling for a powerful cabinet in his administration: "I don't want a government of yes-men. . . . [I want] a cabinet made up of the ablest men in America, leaders in their own right and not merely by virtue of appointment . . . men who will command the public's respect and the president's attention by the power of their intellect and the force of their ideas." [19] After his election Nixon took the unprecedented step of introducing his soon-to-be appointed cabinet on national television.

Despite his announced intention to use a cabinet system, President Nixon held few cabinet meetings and relegated the cabinet to a position of lesser importance than that of most of his White House staff. At one point Secretary of the Interior Walter J. Hickel, complaining that he had had only two or three private meetings with the president, advised Nixon: "Permit me to suggest that you consider meeting, on an individual and conversational basis, with members of your cabinet. Perhaps through such conversations we can gain greater insight into the problems confronting us all, into solutions of these problems." [20] Because of his disdain for his original cabinet, Nixon had a totally new one in place five years later. Only the Watergate revelations forced him to promise to deal regularly and openly with his cabinet, but his eventual resignation prevented him from making good on that promise.

Both Gerald R. Ford (1974-1977) and Jimmy Carter (1977-1981) pledged to use their cabinets as decision-making bodies. Although both held regular cabinet meetings at the beginning of their administrations, only President Ford came close to making his cabinet a meaningful advisory group. Convinced that Watergate resulted from Nixon's carelessness in allowing his personal aides to gain too much power at the expense of his cabinet, Ford restored the cabinet secretariat established by Eisenhower but abandoned by subsequent presidents. Like Eisenhower, he asked a cabinet secretary to draw up formal agendas for

cabinet meetings, which often were used to gauge the views of his department heads on different issues. Hoxie noted: "More than any other president in the period from 1916 to 1981, he [Ford] restored the cabinet as a deliberative, meaningful advisory and administrative body." [21]

Jimmy Carter, in contrast, failed to achieve his goal of revitalizing the cabinet. Early in his administration President Carter made this promise: "There will never be an instance while I am in office where the members of the White House staff dominate or act in a superior position to the members of the cabinet." [22] In fact, regular use of his cabinet became less of a concern as his administration elapsed, resulting in fewer and fewer cabinet meetings. Carter met with his cabinet weekly during the first year of his administration; biweekly during the second year; monthly during the third year; and only sporadically during his last year in office.[23] Early on, the Carter White House became embroiled in a controversy over the cabinet's status. Aide Jack Watson advocated a strong cabinet, but close Carter adviser Hamilton Jordan preferred that major decisions be made by high-level White House staffers. Jordan finally won, and Carter's cabinet lost any hope of achieving much prominence in presidential decision making.

Similarly, Ronald Reagan (1981-1989) met less frequently with his cabinet as his term in office progressed. His administration was much more successful, however, in utilizing the cabinet as an advisory group. Reagan divided the cabinet into seven councils, each of which addressed a specific substantive area: economic affairs, commerce and trade, food and agriculture, human resources, natural resources, legal policy, and management and administration. Under this system, cabinet members could concentrate on matters germane only to them and not to the cabinet as a whole. Indeed, in some respects this system restored the advisory function that the cabinet enjoyed during the Eisenhower administration.

Role and Function of the Cabinet

Most presidents have come to expect little from their cabinets except the opportunity to exchange information. At best, the cabinet may serve as a source of advice for the president, but this use of the cabinet has been rare. Even when presidents, such as Nixon and Carter, emphasized the importance of their cabinets early in their administrations, commitment to a strong cabinet soon diminished. As administrations mature, daily administrative matters and domestic and international crises often take more and more of a president's time. Moreover, presidential programs and goals become fixed, and cabinet secretaries, as heads of their departments, may find themselves competing for scarce resources. Cabinet meetings thus become less frequent, less enthusiastic, and less cordial, as well as a burden for both the department secretary and the president. Indeed, some department secretaries see cabinet meetings as nothing more than opportunities for their peers to take potshots at their departments' programs. Seeking to protect their administrative turf and hoping to avoid excessive and detrimental departmental sniping, many secretaries intentionally exercise restraint in cabinet meetings. Jesse H. Jones, Franklin Roosevelt's secretary of commerce, de-

Nixon fired Interior Secretary Walter J. Hickel, who, it turned out, was an outspoken opponent of some of the Nixon administration's programs.

Nixon Project, National Archives

clared: "My principal reason for not having a great deal to say at cabinet meetings was that there was no one at the table who could be of help to me except the president, and when I needed to consult him, I did not choose a cabinet meeting to do so." [24]

Cabinets as Advisers

Although many presidents have intentionally avoided placing their cabinets in an advisory role, such a role is still considered the ideal one for the presidential cabinet. In 1940 the leading British scholar on the presidency, Harold J. Laski, offered this description of what a good cabinet should do for an American president:

> A good cabinet ought to be a place where the large outlines of policy can be hammered out in common, where the essential strategy is decided upon, where the president knows that he will hear, both in affirmation and in doubt, even in negation, most of what can be said about the direction he proposes to follow. [25]

No American presidential cabinet has lived up to Laski's model, however, and some presidents—Jackson, Wilson, and Kennedy, for example—have even gone to great lengths to avoid taking advice from their cabinets. Only Eisenhower came close to the model suggested by Laski, and even his cabinet procedures came up lacking.

Historical experience suggests that cabinets can serve presidents as an advisory group in one of three ways. First, in the cabinet meetings of some past presidents, department heads discussed issues and problems informally, primarily to exchange information. This custom was generally followed by Roosevelt, Truman, Kennedy, Johnson, and Nixon. Second, the Eisenhower cabinet regularly considered specific issues, using papers authored by cabinet members and circulated prior to meetings. Both the president and the cabinet were aided by agendas, concise records, and a small secretariat. And third, under both Eisenhower and Truman the National Security Council provided summit discussions of issue papers that earlier had been subjected to a thorough interdepartmental review, with dissidents identified and alternative language proposed. No president has ever utilized a cabinet in this manner, however. [26]

Why then do most presidents avoid using their cabinets as advisory groups? Primarily, presidents are rarely willing to delegate the decision-making power needed to make the cabinet an effective advisory board. Many presidents feel that doing so might challenge their power. Moreover, a strong, institutionalized cabinet with its own staff might put the president at a disadvantage in the control of resources and information. Few presidents want to feel that they are not in control of the flow of information in the White House. According to presidential scholar Richard M. Pious, "A collective cabinet with its own staff could become a competitor for 'The Executive Power' and come to function as a 'council of state'—the system rejected at the Constitutional Convention." [27] Consequently, presidents have tended to downgrade the importance of their cabinets.

The presidential reluctance to use cabinets as advisory groups also stems from situations in which presidents are forced to choose cabinet appointees who may be weak or who may not represent the goals of their administrations. Schlesinger has contended that "genuinely strong presidents are not afraid to surround themselves with genuinely strong men [in the cabinet]." [28] Past presidents, however, have rarely had more than one or two notable departmental secretaries at one time. Most of the time cabinet selections are influenced heavily by political considerations. Hess has written:

> Historically, presidents have selected their cabinets on the basis of traditions, trade-offs, and obligations.... Once the obligations were fitted into the appropriate slots, balances had to be made.... The end result was often that a new president found himself surrounded with some people of less than inspiring ability, personalities that were incompatible, and even some cabinet members of questionable loyalty. [29]

Because past presidents seldom have been closely associated with their cabinet officers, they have tended to rely on their White House staffs for advice. Since the establishment of the Executive Office of the President and the White House staff in 1939, the White House staff has acted as a threat to the cabinet's role as a policy-making institution. With their closer proximity to the Oval Office, White House staffers have more access to the president than the cabinet. Moreover, these staffers often are longtime personal friends of the president, and they exhibit loyalty not necessarily found among members of the cabinet. Both Presidents Nixon and Carter reduced the influence of their cabinets in favor of the personal loyalties of certain members of their staffs. Indeed, both presidents asked their cabinets to resign en masse to allow them to appoint new "loyal" cabinet members and to rely more closely on their personal staffs. Specifically, cabinet advice gave way to Nixon's reliance on his trusted aide John Ehrlichman and Carter's close connections with aide Hamilton Jordan and press secretary Jody Powell. Writing about this tendency for presidents to rely on advice from their staffs rather than their cabinets, British author Godfrey Hodgson noted:

> The cabinet has been losing ground to the White House staff for a long time now.... Where successive presidents ... have all come to rely more and more on their own staff and less and less on their cabinet members, where, moreover, two such different presidents as Richard Nixon and Jimmy Carter have both turned to their staff for help after an initial, apparently sincere effort to reverse the trend and give more authority to cabinet members, it is tempting to come to the conclusion that the decline of the cabinet is inevitable. [30]

The result is that the stronger and more assertive presidents attempt to be, the less likely they are to use their cabinets as vital advisory bodies. Thus, to protect their powers and to guard against a vigorous cabinet system that may be more of a threat than a help, presidents may use cabinet meetings more as devices for generating enthusiasm or displaying cabinet unity than as devices for a thorough discussion of problems facing the nation. Most presidents want advice when they ask for it, but they also want to reserve the right to either disregard it or not even seek it. A strong cabinet system that imposes advice upon them is then something to be resisted.

Inner Cabinet

Although presidents may shun their collective cabinets as sources of information for decision-making purposes, individual cabinet members may serve as important sources of experience and advice. According to political scientist Frank Kessler, "Seasoned political veterans in the cabinet can provide a president one thing that the most dedicated and informed White House staffer often cannot, and that is a sense of perspective gained from years of experience and political savvy." [31]

Certain cabinet members, by virtue of either their close relationship with the president or the department they head, find themselves with greater access to the president and often the opportunity to influence the administration's policy. In fact, every cabinet usually has one or two members who have dominant personalities and who form close relationships with the president. In the Truman administration, for example, Secretary of State Dean Acheson and George C. Marshall, who served at different times as secretary of state and secretary of defense, overshadowed the rest of the cabinet. With his strong and outspoken foreign policy positions, Secretary of State John Foster Dulles dominated the Eisenhower cabinet. As defense secretary during the cold war and the Vietnam war, Robert S. McNamara enjoyed close ties with both Presidents Kennedy and Johnson. Most of these cabinet members also had a significant influence on presidential decision making based upon their personal friendships with the president. Acheson's friendship with Truman, for example, allowed him to greatly influence the president. These were, however, personal relationships based upon intimate friendships and confidences; they were never transferred to colleagues or successors.

Access to the president is often determined by the amount of importance that the president places on a particular department. Because departments of defense and state receive much attention from presidents, their secretaries usually have a more cordial relationship with their presidents based on the frequency of their contacts. On occasion some departments, and thus their secretaries, might actually increase in importance in the eyes of the president. For example, the Department of Health, Education and Welfare (HEW) took on more significance as the number and size of social programs increased during the 1960s. John W. Gardner, secretary of HEW, gained status within the cabinet as he began the significant task of managing the Johnson administration's major education and health programs. Usually, however, presidents devote most of their time and attention to national security and foreign policy matters. Consequently, some staff members, particularly heads of agencies such as the Central Intelligence Agency (CIA), may have more access to the president than most cabinet members.

Composition of the Inner Cabinet

Not all cabinet members are treated equally. Cronin has suggested that contemporary presidential cabinets can be divided into inner and outer cabinets.[32] Based on extensive interviews with White House aides and cabinet officers about their views of the departments and their access to the president, Cronin found that the inner cabinet generally includes the secretaries of state, defense, and Treasury, and the attorney general (a body analogous to President Washington's first cabinet). Because of the importance of their departments to the making of public policy, these cabinet members have been the most successful in influencing presidential decisions in a broad range of policy areas. The departments that deal almost exclusively with domestic policy and commerce form the outer cabinet. Their secretaries usually are more concerned with advocacy for their constituent groups than with advising the president on policy issues.

Because presidents usually are very selective in filling appointments to inner cabinet positions, the views of these cabinet members are likely to mirror those of their chief executive. In addition, these appointees are often Washington veterans such as John Foster Dulles, Cyrus R. Vance (Carter's secretary of state), and George P. Shultz (Reagan's secretary of state). Significant responsibility and visibility accompany these cabinet positions, and the officials holding them are usually in contact with the president on a daily basis. In addition to the top four cabinet positions, the inner cabinet frequently includes White House aides who have a close counseling relationship with the president.

The inner cabinet is generally divided into two subgroups, the first of which Cronin labeled the national security cabinet. This group is composed of the two cabinet members responsible for national security policy, the secretaries of state and defense. During the French crisis of 1793 President Washington met with his cabinet almost every day. Similarly, recent presidents have met at least weekly with their national security cabinets and have maintained telephone contact with them daily. One Johnson aide believed that President Johnson trusted just two of his cabinet members, Secretary of State Dean Rusk and Secretary of Defense Robert McNamara. Likewise, Secretary of State Cyrus Vance and Secretary of Defense Harold Brown were probably Carter's closest cabinet counselors.[33]

In addition to the national security cabinet, presidents rely heavily on the legal and economic counsel that they receive from their attorneys general and secretaries of the Treasury—the second inner cabinet subgroup. In recent years the Justice Department has been headed by close friends—or relatives—of the president. John Kennedy, for example, appointed his brother Robert, and Richard Nixon appointed his law partner and trusted friend John N. Mitchell. Jimmy Carter named his close friend Griffin B. Bell, and Ronald Reagan, during his second term in office, appointed one of his longtime California advisers and friends, Edwin Meese III. Because the attorney general usually serves as the president's attorney, the head of the Justice Department has a special responsibility that brings about close, personal contact with the president.

The secretary of the Treasury has been an important presidential adviser since the days of the Washington administration when Alexander Hamilton first occupied the office. Although the formal responsibility of the Treasury Department may have been somewhat diminished with its loss of the Bureau of the Budget and the creation of the Council of Economic Advisers as an independent presidential advisory board, the secretary of the Treasury continues to play a significant role in domestic monetary and fiscal matters, as well as international commerce and currency. The latter area brings the Treasury secretary into the inner cabinet of foreign policy counselors. Cronin has suggested that the importance of the Treasury secretary as a member of the inner circle is to some degree a function of the intelligence and personality of the secretary. President Eisenhower said of his Treasury secretary George M. Humphrey: "In cabinet meetings, I always wait for George Humphrey to speak. I sit back and listen to the others talk while he doesn't say anything. But I know that when he speaks, he will say just what I was thinking." [34]

One curious feature of the inner cabinet is that its members tend to be more noticeably interchangeable than the members of the outer cabinet. Henry L. Stimson, for example, served as William Howard Taft's secretary of war,

Herbert C. Hoover's secretary of state, and Franklin Roosevelt's secretary of war. Dean Acheson was undersecretary of the Treasury under Roosevelt and secretary of state under Truman. Eisenhower's attorney general William P. Rogers later became Nixon's first secretary of state. Elliot L. Richardson served as undersecretary of state, secretary of health, education and welfare, defense secretary, and attorney general. George Shultz, another versatile cabinet member, served as Nixon's secretary of the Treasury and later as Reagan's secretary of state. When Kennedy was trying to attract McNamara to the cabinet, he reportedly offered him his choice of either the defense post or the Treasury post. There has been some movement between the inner and outer cabinets, but most position shifts have remained in the inner cabinet.

Although outsiders are brought into the inner cabinet by all presidents, why is there so much movement within that cabinet? Why are presidents reluctant to go beyond those few cabinet members who served in an earlier inner cabinet? Cronin has suggested simply that presidents look for appointees with whom they feel comfortable for these positions.

> This interchangeability may result from the broad-ranging interests of the inner-cabinet positions, from the counseling style and relationships that develop in the course of an inner-cabinet secretary's tenure, or from the already close personal friendship that has often existed with the president. It may be easier for inner-cabinet than for outer-cabinet secretaries to maintain the presidential perspective; presidents certainly try to choose men they know and respect for these intimate positions.[35]

Cabinets as Advocates: The Outer Cabinet

The outer cabinet deals with more highly organized and specialized clientele than the inner cabinet. While inner cabinet members are selected more on the basis of personal friendships and loyalty, outer cabinet members are selected more on the basis of geographical, ethnic, or political representation. And because they have fewer loyalties to the president, they often adopt an advocacy position for their departments.

The secretaries of interior, agriculture, commerce, labor, health and human services, housing and urban development, transportation, energy, education, and veterans affairs form the outer cabinet. Because their interests are so specialized, these secretaries are under extreme pressure from their clientele groups and political parties to serve specific interests. According to Cronin, "Whereas three of the four inner cabinet departments preside over policies that usually, though often imprudently, are perceived to be largely nonpartisan or bipartisan—national security, foreign policy, and the economy—the domestic departments almost always are subject to intense crossfire between partisan and domestic interest groups."[36]

Department secretaries are torn between loyalty to their presidents and loyalty to the departments they represent. Almost all secretaries go through what political scientist Richard P. Nathan has called "the ritualistic courting and mating process with the bureaucracy."[37] Because most outer cabinet members have only limited loyalty to the president, they usually are "captured" by the permanent bureaucracies. In fact, it is often in the best interest of secretaries to "go native" by adopting the concerns of the

departments they administer, thereby gaining the confidence of the career bureaucrats who work daily to further the pursuits of the department. Political scientist Hugh Heclo wrote: "Fighting your counterparts in other departments creates confidence and support beneath you. . . . Less politically effective executives may be personally admired by civil servants but have little to offer in return for bureaucratic support."[38] Not surprisingly, the tendency of cabinet secretaries to assume an advocacy role for their respective departments increases over the term of an administration. As they see their influence with the president diminishing, department secretaries try to build their political base of support within their own bureaucracies by forging good will with their bureaucrats.

Cabinet members who adopt an advocacy position contrary to their president's may find life in Washington difficult. The history of the presidency is full of examples of department secretaries who were "fired" by their presidents for not publicly supporting the president's programs. Truman fired Henry Wallace, his secretary of commerce, for criticizing his foreign policy, and Eisenhower fired Secretary of Labor Martin P. Durkin. In appointing Durkin, former head of the AFL Plumbers and Pipe Fitters Union, Eisenhower was seeking to broaden the perspective of his cabinet. Durkin apparently proved to be more of a spokesperson for labor than Eisenhower had expected. Later, Nixon fired Secretary of the Interior Walter J. Hickel, who, it turned out, was an outspoken opponent of some of the Nixon administration's programs. In fact, few cabinet members stay the length of a president's administration. In recent years the average tenure of a cabinet member has been forty months. In the first five years of his administration Nixon replaced his entire cabinet with a total of thirty appointments, making the average tenure of a cabinet member in the Nixon administration about eighteen months. Over a single year and a half period Nixon had five attorneys general.[39]

Relations between presidents and their cabinet members—sometimes even members of the inner cabinet—deteriorate rapidly after the inauguration. For example, scarcely one and a half years after being sworn into office, Secretary of State Alexander M. Haig, Jr., left the Reagan administration when he failed to gain the confidence of the president and his aides. More often than not, however, friction develops between presidents and their cabinet members because cabinet secretaries adopt the view of the bureaucracies and constituencies they represent, whether that view represents that of the president. Further complicating the problem, department secretaries—who have the political power and skill needed to achieve their leadership positions in their own right—are usually not afraid to stand up to the president on policy positions they believe are correct.

As a cabinet secretary assumes a larger advocacy role, the relationship between president and cabinet member becomes more strained. Cabinet meetings become increasingly confrontational, and the cabinet becomes less useful to the president as an effective advisory body. If cabinet secretaries carefully build their bases of support, they can effectively frustrate a president's policy-making initiatives. Franklin Roosevelt often complained about the difficulty he had in dealing with the bureaucracies:

> The Treasury is so large and so far-flung and ingrained in its practices that I find it almost impossible to get the action and results that I want even with Henry [Morgenthau] there. But, Treasury is nothing compared with the

Cabinet Holdovers

When President-elect Herbert C. Hoover sent his list of cabinet nominations to the Senate for approval in 1929, he failed to mention that his predecessor's controversial Treasury secretary, Andrew W. Mellon, would be staying on the job. "He wanted to minimize the fight" by shielding Mellon from a confirmation battle, said Senate historian Richard A. Baker. Mellon had already been confirmed once when President Warren G. Harding tapped him for the Treasury post in 1921. And he had held the job throughout Calvin Coolidge's 1923-1929 presidency as well.

Hoover's decision to keep Mellon on drew howls of protest from liberal and progressive lawmakers who opposed Mellon's economic policies. But the president-elect had ample precedent for his move.

From the time of John Adams's presidency, cabinet members appointed by one administration had been passed to the next without having to wait for Senate approval. In fact, holdovers were quite common. John Adams retained five members of George Washington's cabinet. Between then and 1929, 110 cabinet appointees served in consecutive administrations. The majority of those, however, were retained between terms of the same president. From Washington's time to the present, only 42 appointees have been held over from one administration to the next when there was a clear change of power.

In 1989 George Bush followed in Hoover's footsteps. Three of his cabinet appointments—Treasury Secretary Nicholas F. Brady, Education Secretary Lauro F. Cavazos, and Attorney General Dick Thornburgh—were holdovers from the Reagan administration. None had to be reconfirmed.

In the years between Hoover and Bush, many presidents have retained their closest advisers from one term to the next. When a president died in office, his successor often kept the cabinet team intact. In fact, when Lyndon B. Johnson was elected in his own right in 1964, he held onto eight cabinet members originally appointed by John F. Kennedy.

The Bush cabinet, however, marks the first time since Hoover took over from Coolidge that a completely new administration has retained department heads named by a former president. In part, that is because it is the first time since 1929 that there has been a "friendly takeover" at the White House, with the incoming president belonging to the same party as his predecessor. "Obviously when a new party comes in, they'll want new cabinet members," Baker said.

Bush was on firm legal ground when he asserted that his holdovers did not need to be reconfirmed. "Nowhere in the Constitution is there a specific termination date" for cabinet secretaries, a Senate legal adviser explained. "They are appointed for an indefinite period of time, and unless they are dismissed by the president [or resign], they are not subject to reconfirmation."

Cavazos and Thornburgh submitted letters of resignation in compliance with President Reagan's efforts to clear the way for Bush. But Reagan did not accept those letters once Bush made his choices public. Brady was writing his letter when Bush asked him to stay on the job November 15. He never finished it.

Source: Excerpted from Macon Morehouse, "Cabinet Holdovers Need No Senate Approval," *Congressional Quarterly Weekly Report*, November 26, 1988, 3390.

State Department. You should go through the experience of trying to get any changes in thinking, policy, and action of the career diplomats and then you'd know what a real problem was.[40]

Close presidential advisers usually view outer cabinet members as more of a burden than a help to presidential decision making. Over the years, many high-level White House staffers have performed cabinet-level roles for the president. Some actually found themselves attending presidential cabinet meetings. Eisenhower, for example, designated aide Sherman Adams to serve as an ex officio member of his cabinet. Other presidents have simply trusted and confided in their close aides more than their cabinets. For example, for his important decisions, Kennedy preferred the advice of aides Theodore C. Sorensen and McGeorge Bundy over that of his cabinet members. Such White House advisers believe that they have the president's best interests in mind. In their view, most outer cabinet members neglect the president's interests for those of their own clientele. One close Carter aide explained: "Nobody expects Ray Marshall at Labor to be a spokesman for anything other than big labor. You just have to live with this...."[41] The White House does not view advocacy as anything positive.

Advocacy alienates outer cabinet members even more than they already are. For example, in response to pressure from western Republicans, Richard Nixon appointed Walter Hickel, a former governor of Alaska, to head the Department of the Interior, instead of his first choice, Rogers C. B. Morton from Maryland. At first feared by environmentalists, Hickel turned out to be an opponent of big oil's plans to route the Alaskan pipeline through some northern wilderness lands. Hickel's opposition to the Nixon administration's programs and his tendency to be outspoken quickly got him into hot water with the president, who then considered Hickel an adversary. Hickel explained:

Initially I considered it a compliment because, to me, an adversary in an organization is a valuable asset. It was only after the president had used the term many times and with a disapproving inflection that I realized he considered an adversary an enemy. I could not understand why he would consider me an enemy.

As I sensed that the conversation was about to end, I asked, "Mr. President, do you want me to leave the administration?"

He jumped from his chair, very hurried and agitated. He said, "That's one option we hadn't considered." He called in Ehrlichman and said: "John, I want you to handle this. Wally asked whether he should leave. That's one option we hadn't considered." [42]

A week later Hickel was fired. Although extreme, Hickel's case is typical of what most outer cabinet members face when they consider their relationships with their presidents.

In reality, presidents rarely fire cabinet members; cabinet members usually anticipate presidential dissatisfaction and resign. Hickel's case was an exception, as he forced Nixon to ask him to leave. Cabinet members sometimes become so disenchanted with presidential programs and policies that they decide to leave on their own accord. For example, after becoming increasingly concerned about the direction of U.S. foreign policy during the late 1970s, Secretary of State Cyrus Vance finally decided to part company with the Carter administration over the attempted Iranian hostage rescue mission. Although he disagreed privately with many of Carter's foreign policy decisions during his tenure, Vance did not make his concerns public until three weeks after his resignation.

Cabinet Alternatives

Has the presidential cabinet outlived its usefulness? Presidents continue to seek the advice of their inner cabinets, but rarely in the history of the presidency have collective cabinet meetings been meaningful. Many scholars believe that as long as presidents are subject to political pressures to appoint certain cabinet members who are not personally loyal to them and as long as cabinet secretaries are captured by the interests of their departments, the collective cabinet will remain useless as an advisory group.

This is not to say, however, that presidents and presidential scholars have ignored alternatives to the present cabinet system. Many, in fact, have sought ways to utilize individual cabinet members. Most presidents have used task forces composed of several cabinet or subcabinet members and White House aides to help them study specific problems. President Kennedy, for example, used many such task forces to study national security problems, chaired invariably by his brother, Attorney General Robert F. Kennedy. Kennedy required these study groups to produce both majority and minority reports.

Although task forces produce some meaningful and innovative policy analysis, they have had some problems. Typical of the Kennedy task forces was the executive committee he created to handle the Cuban missile crisis in 1962. It was composed of the president, Vice President Lyndon Johnson, Secretary of State Dean Rusk, Secretary of Defense Robert McNamara, Secretary of the Treasury C. Douglas Dillon, Attorney General Robert Kennedy, Special Foreign Affairs Assistant McGeorge Bundy, Chairman of the Joint Chiefs of Staff Gen. Maxwell Taylor, White House aide Theodore Sorensen, CIA Director John McCone, and Paul Nitze, George W. Ball, and Llewellyn Thompson, all from outside the executive branch. Kennedy ordered the task force to put any other duties they might have aside. The system worked well for the missile crisis, but would it have worked if there had been anything else pressing the administration for attention? According to Frank Kessler, "Presidential task forces and White House staff-created options provided a certain creative chaos to the Kennedy system for gathering foreign policy ideas. The arrangements proved useful in moving from crisis to crisis but left much to be desired in heading off crises before they reached the flash point. Long-range policy making suffered. . . ." [43]

Some scholars such as Stephen Hess have maintained that the cabinet should be strengthened and made more collegial. Hess has argued for a presidency in which responsibility is shared by the president and the cabinet:

Effective presidential leadership in the immediate future is likely to result only from creating more nearly collegial administrations in which presidents rely on the cabinet officers as the principal sources of advice and hold them personally accountable—in the British sense of "the doctrine of ministerial responsibility"—for the operations of the different segments of government. [44]

Benjamin V. Cohen, one of Franklin Roosevelt's chief advisers during the 1930s, suggested a similar idea in a 1974 lecture at the University of California. Cohen called for creation of an executive council composed of five to eight distinguished citizens appointed by the president. The council would have staff, access to information, and the power to monitor and coordinate government activities. The president would be obliged to consult with this group before acting on critical decisions. [45]

President Nixon apparently considered introducing a "supercabinet" in his second term. In his 1971 State of the Union address he proposed merging the eight existing domestic departments into four new superagencies: resources, human resources, economic affairs, and community development. Although Congress proved uncooperative and refused to approve his plan, Nixon proceeded to name four cabinet members (the secretaries of Treasury, agriculture, HEW, and HUD) as presidential counselors. As White House aides as well as cabinet members, they assumed functional responsibility over the areas served by the proposed superagencies. Nixon's efforts in this area were soon sidetracked, however, as he became engulfed in the Watergate scandal.

Some presidents have formed cabinet councils in an attempt to integrate the advice of department secretaries and White House advisers on important policy decisions. Organized on the basis of broad policy areas, such councils function much like Eisenhower's full cabinet; they deliberate policy recommendations, develop administration positions, and coordinate presidential decisions. Nominally in charge of each council, the president usually designates one of the department heads as chair. Because the White House provides staff support, the councils are able to act fairly independently.

Both Presidents Ford and Reagan, who tended to delegate much of their authority, used cabinet councils. Reagan usually designated one of his cabinet members or White House aides to chair a council in its initial stages of discussion. During the final sessions the president presided. Patterned after the National Security Council, Reagan's cabinet councils were designed to make cabinet members part of the presidential decision-making process by centralizing policy discussions. During the first eighteen months of the Reagan administration, the councils considered approximately two hundred issues. There appeared to be some danger, however, that the councils would do just the opposite of what they were intended to do. Critics have argued that instead of decentralizing the presidential advisory system, cabinet councils actually centralize decision making in the White House or in an even smaller group similar to the inner cabinet.

Notes

1. See Richard F. Fenno, Jr., *The President's Cabinet* (New York: Vintage Books, 1959), 12.
2. Alexander Hamilton, John Jay, and James Madison, *The Federalist*, Intro. by Edward Gaylord Bourne (New York: Tudor, 1937), ii, 57.
3. James Thomas Flexner, *Washington: The Indispensable Man* (Boston: Little, Brown, 1974), 220.
4. R. Gordon Hoxie, "Cabinet," in *Encyclopedia of American Political History: Studies of the Principal Movements and Ideas*, 3 vols., ed. Jack P. Greene (New York: Scribner's, 1984), 1:149.
5. Flexner, *Washington: The Indispensable Man*, 326.
6. Hoxie, "Cabinet," 152.
7. Quoted in Emmet John Hughes, *The Living Presidency: The Resources and Dilemmas of the American Presidential Office* (Baltimore, Md.: Penguin, 1973), 147.
8. Hoxie, "Cabinet," 156.
9. Quoted in Fenno, *The President's Cabinet*, 123.
10. Quoted in ibid., 125.
11. Hoxie, "Cabinet," 158-159.
12. Quoted in Thomas E. Cronin, *The State of the Presidency*, 2d ed. (Boston: Little, Brown, 1980), 263.
13. Stephen Hess, *Organizing the Presidency* (Washington, D.C.: Brookings, 1976), 46.
14. Cronin, *The State of the Presidency*, 271.
15. Arthur M. Schlesinger, Jr., *A Thousand Days* (New York: Fawcett, 1967), 632.
16. Hess, *Organizing the Presidency*, 84.
17. George Reedy, *The Twilight of the Presidency* (New York: New American Library, 1970), 74.
18. Quoted in Cronin, *The State of the Presidency*, 266.
19. Excerpted from a radio address dated September 19, 1968, in Robert Hirschfield, ed., *Power of the Modern Presidency*, 2d ed. (Chicago: Aldine, 1973), 165-166.
20. *New York Times*, May 7, 1970, C18.
21. Hoxie, "Cabinet," 161.
22. Quoted in Edward D. Feigenbaum, "Staffing, Organization, and Decision-Making in the Ford and Carter White Houses," *Presidential Studies Quarterly* 10 (Summer 1980): 371.
23. George C. Edwards III and Stephen J. Wayne, *Presidential Leadership* (New York: St. Martin's Press, 1985), 173.
24. Quoted in Robert J. Sickels, *Presidential Transactions* (Englewood Cliffs, N.J.: Prentice-Hall, 1974), 31.
25. Harold J. Laski, *The American Presidency: An Interpretation* (New York: Harper, 1940), 257-258.
26. Bradley H. Patterson, Jr., *The President's Cabinet: Issues and Questions* (Washington, D.C.: American Society for Public Administration, 1976), 113.
27. Richard M. Pious, *The American Presidency* (New York: Basic Books, 1979), 241.
28. Arthur M. Schlesinger, Jr., "Presidential War," *New York Times Magazine*, January 7, 1973, 28.
29. Hess, *Organizing the Presidency*, 180.
30. Godfrey Hodgson, *All Things to All Men: The False Promise of the Modern American Presidency* (New York: Simon and Schuster, 1980), 109-112.
31. Frank Kessler, *The Dilemmas of Presidential Leadership: Of Caretakers and Kings* (Englewood Cliffs, N.J.: Prentice-Hall, 1982), 92.
32. Cronin, *The State of the Presidency*, 276-293.
33. Ibid., 278.
34. Quoted in ibid., 280.
35. Ibid., 282.
36. Ibid., 283.
37. Richard P. Nathan, *The Plot That Failed* (New York: Wiley, 1975), 40.
38. Hugh Heclo, *A Government of Strangers* (Washington, D.C.: Brookings, 1977), 196.
39. Pious, *The American Presidency*, 238.
40. Quoted in Kessler, *The Dilemmas of Presidential Leadership*, 93.
41. Quoted in Cronin, *The State of the Presidency*, 283.
42. Walter J. Hickel, *Who Owns America?* (Englewood Cliffs, N.J.: Prentice-Hall, 1971), 259.
43. Kessler, *The Dilemmas of Presidential Leadership*, 106.
44. Hess, *Organizing the Presidency*, 154.
45. Benjamin V. Cohen, "Presidential Responsibility and American Democracy," Royer Lecture, University of California, Berkeley, May 23, 1974; quoted in Cronin, *The State of the Presidency*, 361-362.

Selected Bibliography

Cronin, Thomas E. *The State of the Presidency*. Boston: Little, Brown, 1975.

Edwards, George C., III, and Stephen J. Wayne. *Presidential Leadership*. New York: St. Martin's Press, 1985.

Feigenbaum, Edward D. "Staffing, Organization, and Decision-Making in the Ford and Carter White Houses." *Presidential Studies Quarterly* 10 (Summer 1980): 364-377.

Fenno, Richard F., Jr. *The President's Cabinet*. New York: Vintage, 1959.

Flexner, James Thomas. *Washington: The Indispensable Man*. Boston: Little, Brown, 1974.

Hamilton, Alexander, John Jay, and James Madison. *The Federalist*. Intro. by Edward Gaylord Bourne. New York: Tudor, 1937.

Heclo, Hugh. *A Government of Strangers*. Washington, D.C.: Brookings, 1977.

Hess, Stephen. *Organizing the Presidency*. Washington, D.C.: Brookings, 1976.

Hickel, Walter J. *Who Owns America?* Englewood Cliffs, N.J.: Prentice-Hall, 1971.

Hirschfield, Robert, ed. *Power of the Modern Presidency*, 2d ed. Chicago: Aldine, 1973.

Hodgson, Godfrey. *All Things to All Men: The False Promise of the Modern American Presidency*. New York: Simon and Schuster, 1980.

Hoxie, R. Gordon. "Cabinet." In *Encyclopedia of American Political History: Studies of the Principal Movements and Ideas*, Vol. 1, ed. Jack P. Greene. New York: Scribner's, 1984.

Hughes, Emmet John. *The Living Presidency: The Resources and Dilemmas of the American Presidential Office*. Baltimore, Md.: Penguin, 1973.

Kessler, Frank. *The Dilemmas of Presidential Leadership: Of Caretakers and Kings*. Englewood Cliffs, N.J.: Prentice-Hall, 1982.

Laski, Harold J. *The American Presidency: An Interpretation*. New York: Harper, 1940.

Nathan, Richard P. *The Plot That Failed*. New York: Wiley, 1975.

Patterson, Bradley H., Jr. *The President's Cabinet: Issues and Questions*. Washington, D.C.: American Society for Public Administration, 1976.

Pious, Richard M. *The American Presidency*. New York: Basic Books, 1979.

Reedy, George. *The Twilight of the Presidency*. New York: New American Library, 1970.

Schlesinger, Arthur M., Jr. *A Thousand Days*. New York: Fawcett, 1967.

_____. "Presidential War." *New York Times Magazine*. January 7, 1973, 28.

Sickels, Robert J. *Presidential Transactions*. Englewood Cliffs, N.J.: Prentice-Hall, 1974.

Executive Departments

Executive departments are the largest units of the federal executive branch. Each department covers broad areas of responsibility. As of 1989, there were fourteen cabinet departments: Agriculture, Commerce, Defense, Education, Energy, Health and Human Services, Housing and Urban Development, Interior, Justice, Labor, State, Transportation, Treasury, and Veterans Affairs.

Styles and Methods of Appointment

Selection of the department secretaries, who also serve as members of the cabinet, is a crucial presidential decision because the cabinet is the most prominent feature of the president's team. Although the number of appointments each president makes is small when compared to the size of the departments themselves, appointments to the cabinet and subcabinet (the more than one thousand deputy secretaries, undersecretaries, assistant secretaries, and deputy assistant secretaries who staff the departments) indicate both the policy direction and credibility of a new administration. *(See Table 1.)* Consequently, most new presidents face intense public scrutiny of their cabinet appointments. In fact, after the 1980 election the public interest was so great that in the two and a half months' between the election and Ronald Reagan's inauguration the *New York Times* printed one hundred articles and editorials on the new administration's cabinet appointments. Twenty-one of these articles appeared on the front page.[1]

Beyond their symbolic importance, however, cabinet appointments provide presidents with their best early opportunity to show their leadership. Moreover, the first step toward a successful administration is in all likelihood the wise and prudent selection of a new cabinet.

The cabinet secretary's job is by any standard a difficult one. The relationship that secretaries maintain with the president and their individual departments has an important bearing on the success of an administration. Presidential scholar Richard M. Pious has pointed out that department secretaries "must manage their departments and set priorities; represent constituencies to the president and the president to constituencies; help make administration policy and propose new policy initiatives; offer advice to the president."[2]

Ideally, cabinet appointees should be able to demonstrate that they are uniquely qualified to head one of the major departments of the federal government, and presidents should be able to make appointments to cabinet positions based upon the administrative qualifications of the nominee. In practice, however, presidents rarely make appointments based solely on administrative ability. Instead, they consider such factors as personal loyalty, political party loyalty, ideological compatibility, acceptability to Congress, geographic representation, constituent group representation, reputation, expertise, and prior government experience.

Different presidents use different strategies for filling cabinet positions. Although no president has ever adhered to a single appointment strategy, political scientist Nelson W. Polsby found that most recent presidents have used at least one of three major approaches.[3] First, some presidents base appointments on constituent concerns. They enter into coalitions with certain clientele groups by finding appointees who already have strong connections or political associations with groups served by the department. While such an arrangement may serve the department and certain constituent groups well in some respects, it also may prove to be divisive to the function of the department as a whole because very few departmental secretaries will be acceptable to all clientele groups. For example, conservationists might welcome a particular secretary of the interior, while miners might find the appointee to be completely unsympathetic to their concerns.

Second, for some presidents expertise in the subject area served by the department is the primary criterion for appointment. In practice, however, secretaries appointed on the basis of their technical mastery of the substantive concerns of the departments are concerned primarily with the performance and impact of their departments, and they are often oblivious to the political goals of the president's administration.

A third approach used by presidents is the appointment of generalists to cabinet positions. Such secretaries are not connected to the constituent groups served by the department, nor do they have expertise in the substantive interests of the department. They are sought instead for their loyalty to the president. Thus in theory, appointees are able to focus on implementing the president's programs

By W. Craig Bledsoe and Margaret C. Thompson

Table 1 Number of Employees and Political
Appointments in Cabinet Departments, 1989

Department	Total number of employees	Schedule C appts.	Total number of appts.[a]
Agriculture	124,706	226	308
Commerce	44,347	107	190
Defense	1,057,842[b]	119	248
Education	4,602	125	348
Energy	17,316	68	108
Health and Human Services	125,331	79	152
Housing and Urban Development	13,436	91	135
Interior	77,994	54	111
Justice	75,605	59	281
Labor	18,480	72	107
State	26,272	162	1,053
Transportation	63,386	73	136
Treasury	164,541	43	93
Veterans Affairs	246,529	9	190
Total	2,060,387	1,287	3,460

Sources: Office of Personnel Management; Center for Excellence in Government.

a. Includes noncareer employees in the Senior Executive Service and public law positions, such as State Department Foreign Service officers.

b. Total civilian employees.

and not on a narrow set of policies advocated by constituents or the department. Polsby contends, however, that the generalist's loyalty to the president can become pathological. For example, departmental officers not obligated by the charter of the department or ties to clientele groups would be much more likely to oblige a president who asks them to do things that are illegal or immoral to further the president's political cause.

After electoral debts have been paid off with the initial cabinet selections and the media attention has begun to fade, presidents often turn to appointees who will help them accomplish their objectives. Competence and loyalty become the most important criteria for selection. Presidents need competent and loyal cabinet officers to help them deal with the federal bureaucracy and with Congress. According to presidential appointments scholar G. Calvin Mackenzie, "It is characteristic of in-term selection decisions to reflect the president's concerns in dealing with the executive establishment and with Congress.... In-term personnel selections ... often become a central part of an administration's political and administrative strategies for accomplishing its policy objectives."[4]

While the criteria that presidents use in filling cabinet positions often call for certain selections, the appointment process itself can impose additional restrictions on their ability to choose the best possible cabinet. Unlike some presidential appointments, cabinet appointments must be submitted to the Senate for majority confirmation. Some nominees, however, are unwilling to submit to the scrutiny that accompanies the Senate confirmation procedure. And this procedure can be quite long and demanding. After a particularly exhausting confirmation hearing in the summer of 1975, Gov. Stanley K. Hathaway of Wyoming, Presi-

dent Gerald R. Ford's appointee for secretary of the interior, suffered a nervous breakdown. Although this type of confirmation hearing is hardly the rule, it indicates the potential hazards of a tough Senate confirmation procedure.

Other nominees may not be willing to make the financial sacrifice necessary to enter public service. In their study of the presidential appointment process, John W. Macy, Bruce Adams, and J. Jackson Walter found that almost all executives in the private sector are better paid than those holding positions at similar levels of responsibility in the public sector.[5] Consequently, presidential appointees recruited from the private sector usually take a cut in salary to work for the federal government. It is conceivable that a cabinet appointee might give up a $300,000 annual salary for a cabinet post that pays $99,000 a year. Similarly, the rigors of financial disclosure are a disincentive to some nominees. Some conflict-of-interest regulations, such as those imposed on President Jimmy Carter's appointees, contain very precise demands. From his nominees Carter required full financial disclosure of their net worth, a promise not to return to Washington to lobby for pay for at least one year after leaving federal employment, and a commitment to shed all financial holdings that might be affected by a later official decision.

Those who decide to accept the challenges of the confirmation process and the terms of presidential appointment now face higher standards for appointment to public office, as well as the increased expectations of the American public. Thus, cabinet officers must have the management skills necessary to administer a large public bureaucracy, as well as some knowledge of the subject area under the purview of their departments. The personal lives of appointees are subject to higher standards as well. Former Texas senator John Tower, President George Bush's nominee for secretary of defense in 1989, saw his nomination defeated on the Senate floor following allegations of drunkenness and other improprieties.

How well do cabinet officers meet these public demands? A 1967 Brookings Institution study analyzed the background, tenure, and later occupations of those in high executive positions, including cabinet posts, from 1933 through April 1965. It found that most high federal officeholders had high levels of education and substantial federal administrative experience; generally they were well prepared for their positions. But the study also suggested that with their short tenure, top executives rarely had enough time to learn the issues and personalities of the job.[6]

A comparable study conducted by the National Academy of Public Administration (NAPA) in 1987 found that political executives of the past twenty years were very similar to those in the Brookings Institution study. Using data on federal political executives for the period 1964-1984, the NAPA study reported very little difference in these appointees and those holding office fifty years ago. Executive-level appointees remain predominantly elites. They are mostly white, middle-aged males with degrees from prestigious universities. While the number of women and members of racial minorities in cabinet positions has increased in recent years, their proportions in no way reflect their representation in the general population.[7]

The NAPA survey also pointed out a few significant changes in the characteristics of executive appointees. For example, career public servants increasingly are filling executive-level appointments. As a result, fewer people are being recruited (or are willing to be recruited) from business, professional, and academic careers, and more appointees are coming from public service "professions" such as state and local governments, congressional staffs, and other noncareer and career federal appointments. The NAPA study found as well that more appointees are going into private business after leaving the federal government. Apparently, executive appointees are benefitting from their federal offices. Nearly half of the NAPA survey respondents believed that their public service had increased their earning power.[8]

In general, presidents replace cabinet members frequently, leading the critics to argue that cabinet members are not in their positions long enough to learn all the important aspects of their jobs. How long does a typical cabinet member stay in office? The 1967 Brookings study found that cabinet secretaries remained in office a median of 3.3 years, while the more recent NAPA study found that the length of tenure of cabinet secretaries had dropped significantly, to a median of 1.9 years. The authors of the Brookings study argued, however, that length of tenure in a particular office is not as important as length of tenure in the federal government. The NAPA survey discovered that cabinet secretaries have a median of four years of general federal experience, indicating that many have come from public service with several years of experience.

Nominees to cabinet or subcabinet and undersecretary positions often view their appointment as a ticket to a later position in private business. In the NAPA twenty-year survey almost 93 percent of those questioned decided to leave public service for the private sector, a much higher percentage than that for appointees leaving the private sector for the public sector. The Department of Defense has suffered the most from this public service drain. Two-thirds of its top political appointees later found their way into business positions.

Some presidents have come into office determined to control the staffing of the over one thousand high-level department positions directly below those of the department secretaries. In seeking to accomplish their programs and goals, presidents want the loyalty of these high-ranking department executives. The Reagan administration, for example, sought to keep the appointment of these subcabinet officials squarely within the control of the White House, allowing little counsel from the department secretaries. Richard Nixon and Jimmy Carter, in contrast, invited their department secretaries to make their own senior departmental appointments. Both presidents wanted their cabinets to be independent of the White House. Later, however, these administrations spent a great deal of energy trying to bring this decision-making power under their control to maintain some degree of loyalty to administration objectives.

Recent Presidential Appointments

No president is ever really free to make the cabinet or subcabinet appointment of choice. Political parties, special-interest groups, members of Congress, and constituent concerns all play a role in the selection process. Their role is not constant, however; sometimes one factor has been more important than others, and at other times presidents have ignored some or all of these factors. A look at recent cabinet selection decisions may illustrate more adequately how presidents select cabinet appointees.

Franklin D. Roosevelt

In the general staffing of his administration Roosevelt usually relied on five sources: friends and colleagues from his younger years, participants in his New York gubernatorial administration, his 1932 presidential campaigners, the "old boys' network" (or people-who-knew-people-who-knew-Roosevelt), and the rank and file of the Democratic party.[9] As a result, his selection of nominees for cabinet positions outwardly showed no underlying purpose or consistency. For example, apparently Frances Perkins was appointed secretary of labor because Roosevelt wanted a woman in his cabinet. He appointed Harold L. Ickes, a nominal Republican, as secretary of the interior, Henry A. Wallace, a noted agricultural economist and also a nominal Republican, as secretary of agriculture, and Daniel C. Roper, an old friend who was not well known in public life, as secretary of commerce.

Presidential scholar Stephen Hess contends that in reality Roosevelt had two principles that dictated his cabinet appointment strategy. First, early in his administration Roosevelt sought to appoint only cabinet members who would not overshadow him or threaten him politically. The only appointee of any real national prominence was Secretary of State Cordell Hull. As World War II approached, however, Roosevelt appointed cabinet members, such as Henry L. Stimson and Frank Knox, who had more of a national stature. This early strategy of appointing relative unknowns to the cabinet was designed to make sure that the public perceived the administration to be distinctively Rooseveltian.

Second, Roosevelt embarked on a deliberate strategy of appointing opposites to his cabinet; he revelled in the give and take of opposing opinions. For example, by appointing both fiscal conservatives, such as Secretary of the Treasury William H. Woodin, and fiscal liberals, such as Secretary of Commerce Harry L. Hopkins, to the cabinet, Roosevelt was able to play each side against the other and hear both sides of an issue. He once told Frances Perkins, "A little rivalry is stimulating. . . . It keeps everybody going to prove he is a better fellow than the next man. It keeps them honest too."[10]

Similarly, Roosevelt insisted on being involved in the appointments to lower-level cabinet positions, and he succeeded in appointing superior-quality subcabinet members. These young intellectuals and academics, who had little experience in politics but shared Roosevelt's ideological beliefs, included such qualified undersecretaries and subcabinet members as Dean G. Acheson, Jerome Frank, and

Frances Perkins was FDR's secretary of labor, the first woman ever appointed to the cabinet.

Presidential Reorganization Authority

For several decades presidents had the authority to reorganize the executive branch by shifting duties from one department to another, shifting responsibilities from one agency within a department to another, and creating new departments and agencies. The Reorganization Act of 1949 permitted presidents to make a wide range of organizational changes. The act provided that presidents did not have to seek congressional approval for organizational changes, but it did permit Congress to veto them. If either house of Congress passed a resolution disapproving the restructuring within sixty days of the presidential order, it took place automatically.

Before the Reorganization Act of 1949, twentieth-century executive reorganization was carried out with the specific approval of Congress. The first general authority to reorganize, the Overman Act of 1918, gave the president power to coordinate and consolidate government agencies to make them more efficient during World War I, but this authority lasted only through the end of the war. President Franklin D. Roosevelt received limited reorganization authority through the Reorganization Act of 1939. Under the provisions of this act, which expired on January 20, 1941, Roosevelt submitted five reorganization plans, none of which were blocked by Congress.

The Reorganization Act of 1949 grew out of recommendations made by the first Hoover Commission and gave presidents much greater latitude than earlier legislation. It eliminated exemptions for specific agencies and for the first time permitted presidents to create cabinet-level departments. Nevertheless, Congress continued to exercise influence over reorganization by occasionally using their legislative veto to block presidential plans. Because authority for reorganization expired periodically and had to be extended, it was not unusual for Congress to allow temporary lapses in executive reorganization authority.

In 1983 these longstanding reorganization procedures were dealt a blow by the Supreme Court. In *Immigration and Naturalization Service v. Chadha*, the Court declared that legislative vetoes such as the one used by Congress to pass judgment on presidential reorganization plans, were unconstitutional. Since the Reorganization Act's legislative veto provision was invalid, Congress refused to renew the act, which had expired in 1981. Consequently, reorganizations of the government can now be achieved only through laws passed by both houses of Congress and signed by the president.

James Landis. Although Roosevelt's cabinet secretaries may not have approved of this selection process, they nevertheless yielded to the president's selections.

Harry S Truman

Upon Roosevelt's death in 1945, Harry Truman at first encouraged his inherited cabinet to remain in the new administration. Within three months, however, he had replaced six of Roosevelt's ten department heads, as he found that he did not enjoy the conflicting policy advice offered by Roosevelt's diverse cabinet. Truman thus quickly began to replace Roosevelt's appointees with personal acquaintances and others whom he felt were qualified as well as personally loyal to him.

Because he wanted to have his own team in place in 1945, the president gladly accepted the resignations of Roosevelt loyalists. Their replacement by appointees loyal to Truman's programs and goals became a major task of his administration.

To show his keen interest in the selection of his new cabinet, Truman invited nominees to the White House to inform them personally of their nomination. For Truman, loyalty and experience in government were the two major criteria for appointment to his cabinet. Thus, in an attempt to justify the nomination of Lewis B. Schwellenbach (a former senator from Washington) as secretary of labor, Truman argued that he and Schwellenbach "saw right down the same alley on policy." [11] As for the criterion of experience in government, four of Truman's first six cabinet appointments were former members of Congress. He also chose more members of his administration from the ranks of the federal government than did any of his successors. Truman believed that success in government could be transferred to the political arena of the presidential cabinet. He wrote:

> I consider political experience absolutely necessary, because a man who understands politics understands free government. Our government is by the consent of the people, and you have to convince a majority of the people that what you are trying to do is right and in their interest. If you are not a politician, you cannot do it. [12]

For the most part Truman chose highly qualified, experienced cabinet appointees, especially in areas dealing with foreign affairs. His most celebrated cabinet appointments included Secretaries of State George C. Marshall and Dean Acheson, Secretaries of Defense James V. Forrestal and Robert A. Lovett, and Secretary of War Robert P. Patterson. Although some Truman appointments were members of America's governing elite, who went to the most prestigious schools and belonged to the American upper class, the president generally appointed those with whom he had the most in common and knew the best—government employees.

Dwight D. Eisenhower

As the first Republican president in twenty years, Dwight Eisenhower had to look beyond the Democratic-controlled federal government for cabinet appointees. And unlike Truman, he was not involved personally in most of these decisions. Even though Republican leaders were extremely interested in the new administration's choices for these positions, Eisenhower did not seek their advice in selecting his cabinet. The job of filling new government positions, including those of the cabinet, went to two friends, Herbert Brownell, Jr., a New York attorney, and Gen. Lucius Clay, chairman of the board of Continental Can Company. While Brownell and Clay made the initial selections for the cabinet, the choice of a subcabinet was left to the cabinet secretaries themselves.

Eisenhower strongly disliked the role that patronage played in the appointment process. Expressing the "profound hope" that he would not have to become too involved in the distribution of federal patronage, Eisenhower wrote in his diary: "Having been fairly successful in late years learning to keep a rigid check on my temper, I do not want to encounter complete defeat at this late date."[13]

With his distaste for patronage and a management style that sought to delegate as much administrative responsibility as possible, Eisenhower found himself with a cabinet made up almost entirely of strangers and Republican party unknowns. Only two of Eisenhower's ten initial choices, Attorney General Brownell and Postmaster General Arthur E. Summerfield, had played a major role in his presidential campaign.

The lack of conservative Republican party notables particularly offended party leaders. Although Eisenhower had appointed primarily Republicans to his cabinet, most were from the moderate faction of the party. When Sen. Robert A. Taft (R-Ohio), the Republican leader in the Senate, took exception to being excluded from the cabinet selection process, Eisenhower agreed to allow members of Congress to advise the departments in their selection of subcabinet-level appointees. Known as the "Commodore Agreement," this compromise did not entirely please congressional leaders. It succeeded in making Eisenhower aware, however, of the importance of political considerations in making cabinet selections.

The *New Republic* described Eisenhower's first cabinet as "eight millionaires and one plumber." The millionaires not only had money, but they also were successful in their professions. According to Stephen Hess, "Eisenhower believed that a successful person, someone who had already proven that he could run something big, would be best able to tame a government department."[14] Only three members of his cabinet did not have backgrounds in management. Secretary of State John Foster Dulles and Brownell were attorneys. Secretary of Labor Martin P. Durkin was the most notable exception. The nomination of Durkin, head of the AFL Plumbers and Pipe Fitters Union and an Adlai Stevenson supporter, surprised many observers. Apparently, Eisenhower wanted to appease the unions and broaden the perspective of the cabinet. Out of harmony with the rest of the Eisenhower administration, Durkin resigned within the first year.

John F. Kennedy

John Kennedy was elected to the presidency in 1960 by one of the narrowest margins in history. This factor, probably more than any other, dictated the selection of the Kennedy cabinet. Although Kennedy expressed a desire to choose men and women of superior quality, he was restricted by a number of political factors. Kennedy viewed the appointment of department secretaries primarily as an opportunity to consolidate various political factions and to enlarge his popular base of support. Consequently, he appointed representatives of both political parties, all sections of the country, a variety of religious backgrounds, and a wide range of professions as his first ten cabinet members. They included a corporation president, Robert S. McNamara, as secretary of defense, and a Republican who had contributed heavily to Richard Nixon's campaign, C. Douglas Dillon, as secretary of the Treasury.

Like his predecessors, President Kennedy wanted to make the federal government responsive to his programs and direction. He therefore sought cabinet members who would support his agenda and carry out his directives. After eight years of Republican control of the bureaucracy, Kennedy expressed the real fear that the departments had developed a life of their own. As G. Calvin Mackenzie noted, Kennedy did not want his department heads to be "simply the instruments or mouthpieces of the organizations they were appointed to lead."[15] He wanted a cabinet on whom he could rely to pursue his goals vigorously in the departments; otherwise, his task as president would be much more difficult.

From this perspective then it was not surprising that Kennedy appointed his younger brother, Robert, as his attorney general. While Robert F. Kennedy had limited judicial experience, he was close to the president and could be counted on to carry out the president's program in the Department of Justice.

Some of Kennedy's other appointments, however, were surprising. Both McNamara and Secretary of State Dean Rusk were unknown to Kennedy. They were the products of an informal network of talent hunters that produced much of Kennedy's cabinet and personal staff. To screen candidates personally for his cabinet, Kennedy called upon friends and acquaintances across the country to help him assess the qualifications or abilities of potential appointees. He then interviewed candidates himself, and he made the final decisions on appointments. This informal network and Kennedy's personal interest helped him recruit quality individuals from the U.S. business, professional, and university communities.

Robert McNamara, president of Ford Motor Company and a nonpolitical Republican, impressed Kennedy from the beginning. McNamara's management abilities meant that Kennedy would not have to worry about the day-to-day business of the Defense Department. Dean Rusk, an assistant secretary of state during the Truman administration, understood the folkways of the State Department. Kennedy expected this to be helpful in accomplishing his goal of moving the primary responsibility for foreign policy decision making from the National Security Council to the State Department. Rusk proved not to be assertive enough, however, in pushing for Kennedy's goals of diplomacy. Hess wrote: "In constructing a national security triumvirate of Rusk-McNamara-Bundy [McGeorge Bundy was Kennedy's national security adviser], the President put the most diffident in the post that required the most assertive."[16]

Early in his administration Kennedy also focused his attention on appointments to secondary cabinet positions, primarily in the State Department. Kennedy's lower-level appointments in the State Department, many of whom were named before he nominated the secretary, were more qualified than Rusk to be head of the department. They included Adlai E. Stevenson, W. Averell Harriman, and Chester Bowles. Although Kennedy apparently was attempting to spread talent and diversity throughout the State Department, he soon found the task of naming subcabinet appointees wearisome. Thus, he eventually gave McNamara an almost free hand in naming his top subordinates in the Pentagon. As a result, most of McNamara's appointees remained in the Defense Department for the duration of his tenure. In contrast, top-level State Department personnel left the department on average after about fourteen months.

Lyndon B. Johnson

Feeling the need to maintain stability in the government, Lyndon Johnson made no changes in the Kennedy cabinet until thirteen months after President Kennedy's assassination. After the 1964 election, however, Johnson decided to put his own stamp on the administration. Thus, during his term in office, fifteen of the twenty-five men who served in his cabinet he selected himself; the others he inherited from John Kennedy.

Even though Johnson relied heavily on a personnel staff to help him make his cabinet decisions, he participated in almost every step of the selection process. In fact, probably no other recent president has maintained the continuing interest that Johnson exhibited in the selection of all of his executive personnel. While he usually followed his personnel staff's recommendations, he always reserved the final decision for himself.

Johnson applied to his cabinet selections very explicit criteria, which included not only intelligence and ability but also some important political considerations. For example, because he wished to increase the number of minorities in the federal government, in 1965 Johnson appointed Robert C. Weaver, the first black cabinet member, as secretary of housing and urban development (HUD).

Johnson also considered loyalty to be of prime importance. At first he appeared to pay little attention to political party affiliation. He boasted, for example, that he was unaware that John W. Gardner was a Republican until shortly before he announced Gardner's nomination as secretary of health, education and welfare (HEW). Loyalty to his programs soon became very important, however. As Johnson's presidency matured and friction developed between some of his advisers and the remaining Kennedy staffers, it became increasingly clear that he needed to have his own team in place in the cabinet. According to journalist David Halberstam, Johnson, when discussing loyalty among his cabinet members, said: "If you ask those boys in the cabinet to run through a buzz saw for their president, Bob McNamara would be the first to go through it. And I don't have to worry about Rusk either. Rusk's all right. I never have to worry about those two fellows quitting on me." [17]

Nevertheless, Johnson soon began to confuse loyalty with blind allegiance to his Vietnam policies. G. Calvin Mackenzie observed that this made it increasingly difficult for Johnson to find people for all of his executive positions.

"The more criticism the war engendered, the more concerned Johnson became that his appointees support his war policies. The effect of his concern was to narrow the range of people from which executive selections were made." [18] Johnson thus began to turn increasingly to people who already held major positions in his administration, and his cabinet was a good example of Johnson's bias toward appointing those who already had experience in government. Of the fifteen cabinet members he appointed, only four came from outside government. The others were internal promotions, such as Wilbur J. Cohen's appointment as Johnson's last HEW secretary; Cohen had spent most of his career at the Social Security Administration. The Johnson cabinet thus tended to well represent the clientele of the agencies, but it also did not have much political independence from the president.

Richard Nixon

Soon after his election in 1968 Nixon turned over direction of the effort to select a cabinet to his law partner John N. Mitchell and a Wall Street banker named Peter M. Flanigan. On December 11, 1968, after a "crash program" of selection lasting five weeks, Nixon went before a national television audience to introduce twelve men of "extra dimension" who were to form his first cabinet.

In choosing a cabinet that proved more diverse than the Eisenhower counterpart, Nixon relied on some of the traditional sources of recruitment: personal friends (John Mitchell as attorney general, Robert H. Finch as secretary of HEW, and William P. Rogers as secretary of state); Republican governors (Walter J. Hickel as secretary of the interior, George W. Romney as secretary of housing and urban development, and John A. Volpe as secretary of transportation); academics (Clifford M. Hardin as secretary of agriculture and George P. Shultz as secretary of labor); members of Congress (Melvin R. Laird [R-Wis.] as secretary of defense); and business people (Winton M. Blount as postmaster general, David M. Kennedy as secretary of the Treasury, and Maurice H. Stans as secretary of commerce). And he followed the traditional patterns of constituency representation: he chose a westerner for Interior, a banker for Treasury, and a midwesterner with an agricultural background for Agriculture. Even though Nixon appointed a number of millionaires, they were generally self-made wealthy men who had meager beginnings.

In many ways Nixon chose an nontraditional cabinet, and he made a number of noticeable omissions. For example, traditionally presidents have appointed at least one member of the defeated party; there were no Democrats on Nixon's cabinet. Nixon ignored other prominent groups as well by not including any labor union members, blacks, Jews, or women. And because Republicans had gained little top-level federal experience over the last eight years, Nixon's cabinet was somewhat short on Washington executive experience. According to Mackenzie, "The selection process [for Nixon's cabinet] seems to have been guided by little more than the desire to follow convention, to pay off some personal and electoral debts, and to surround the new President with people who seemed to share his political outlook." [19] Historian Arthur M. Schlesinger, Jr., publicly criticized Nixon's cabinet appointments for a lack of independence, asking, "Who in President Nixon's cabinet will talk back to him?" [20]

Early in 1969 President Nixon told his cabinet that

LBJ appointed Robert C. Weaver, the first black cabinet member, as secretary of HUD.

Library of Congress

they would have the primary responsibility for filling subcabinet positions. Specifying that the selection process should be based on ability first and loyalty second, Nixon thus delegated to his cabinet the authority for determining the responsiveness of the federal government to his programs. Mackenzie wrote: "Nixon recognized almost immediately that in granting this discretion he had made an error in judgment. As he left the cabinet room after the meeting, he is reported to have said to an aide, 'I just made a big mistake.' " [21]

After Nixon delegated subcabinet appointment power to his department heads, the White House personnel staff found it difficult to exert much control over these appointments. The White House therefore spent a great deal of time trying to reconfirm its right to approve nominations made by department heads.

By 1970 Nixon had realized that he needed to install in the White House a selection process that would ensure that high-level departmental appointees were loyal enough and bold enough to carry out his programs. As a result, Frederic V. Malek, deputy undersecretary of HEW, was put in charge of studying the White House personnel operation. When Malek recommended that the centralization of all personnel decisions be placed in a new White House Personnel Operation (WHPO), Nixon agreed and asked him to run the operation.

By centralizing the appointment procedure in the WHPO, the Nixon White House hoped to protect the president's nominations from outside influences, thereby making it easier to limit appointments to those well in line with Nixon's policies. For all its good intentions, however, the WHPO was not entirely successful. Nixon continued to remain aloof from the nominating process. He even often refrained from meeting his subcabinet nominees when they joined the administration. This overall lack of interest, as well as the lack of presidential control over the selection process, made it difficult for the Nixon administration to instill loyalty to Nixon's policies and goals in its cabinet officers.

Gerald R. Ford

After Nixon's resignation Gerald Ford came into office facing many of the same problems that Johnson confronted after Kennedy's assassination. Primarily, he faced the need to place his own mark on the federal government. Ford entered the presidency with Nixon's cabinet and not much preparation for his new job. Thus, several months passed before his administration began to take shape. When he finally found himself in a position to make changes, he encountered many potential nominees who were hesitant to take executive positions in his administration because of the possible short tenure in office.

Ford sought geographical balance and group representation in all of his appointments by nominating women, minorities, and young people to his administration. Because of the Watergate scandal, which had forced Nixon's resignation, Ford asked his personnel staff to be particularly sensitive to political considerations; he sought nominees who shared his political beliefs and reflected his administration's goals. He was, however, less strenuous about political compatibility than many of his predecessors, and he thus appointed several cabinet members who were not responsive to Republican party demands: Secretary of Transportation William T. Coleman, Jr.; Secretary of Housing and Urban Development Carla A. Hills; Secretary

Gail S. Rebhan   Wide World Photos

Although Carter's goal for his cabinet was to choose new faces, he ended up with Washington insiders. Cyrus Vance, left, held the post of secretary of state; Zbigniew Brzezinski, right, headed the National Security Council.

of Labor John T. Dunlop; Secretary of Health, Education and Welfare F. David Mathews; and Attorney General Edward H. Levi. Most were not Republicans, and many represented minorities.

Jimmy Carter

Even though Jimmy Carter won the 1976 election by a slim margin, his cabinet selections did not reflect any obligations that he might have had to the groups that helped put him over the top. He came into office believing that he owed little to anyone, except blacks, and promising that his administration would appoint new leaders to key posts based on merit and well-balanced geographical representation. In an oft-quoted comment, Carter's closest adviser, Hamilton Jordan, stated during the transition period: "If, after the inauguration, you find a Cy Vance as Secretary of State and Zbigniew Brzezinski as head of national security, then I would say we failed. And I'd quit. But that's not going to happen. You're going to see new faces, new ideas. The government is going to be run by people you have never heard of." [22]

Promises of this kind set up many unfulfilled expectations. Initial cabinet and other executive position selections did little to satisfy either traditional Democratic party supporters or those hoping for new leadership. Democratic legislators expressed dismay when their suggestions were not heeded. Minority groups and women, who felt they had contributed significantly to Carter's election, were disappointed in his selections.

And in an unprecedented move the National Democratic Committee adopted a resolution criticizing the Carter administration for failing to confer with Democratic state officials in making federal appointments. Carter in fact was attempting to take firm control of the nomination process, and in doing so he sacrificed many traditional Democratic ties. Mackenzie wrote: "By failing to recognize some legitimate political claims and by promising a good deal more than it could deliver, the Carter administration failed to capitalize fully on the political opportunities the selection process provides, especially in the initial stages of a new administration." [23]

No president had started as early as Carter in finding personnel for his administration. In the summer of 1976, even before the election, Carter established a Policy Planning Office (PPO). Headed by Jack H. Watson, Jr., the PPO was charged with finding qualified nominees and giving the new administration a head start on the selection process during the transition. The early start in appointing executives to the new administration did little to speed up the cabinet selection process, however. Carter took longer in selecting his cabinet than had any of his postwar predecessors. Although all cabinet members were sworn in within a week of the inauguration, many subcabinet positions remained unfilled for several months. The deliberateness of the selection process and the exceptional security and conflict-of-interest checks contributed to the uncommon slowness of the appointment process.

Carter insisted on direct participation in the selection of his department heads, and he preferred to pick all appointees in a specific department before moving on to another. Because he was concerned about compatibility among his top advisers, Carter tried to ascertain the quality and compatibility of potential nominees by holding joint meetings with candidates in the same policy area. So many candidates were involved in these meetings that it was difficult to keep them out of the public eye. This had the advantage, however, of giving Carter feedback from observers who might have an interest in the nomination.

Carter compiled a list of potential cabinet nominees by soliciting suggestions countrywide from experts in foreign policy, domestic affairs, defense, economics, education, and other areas covered by cabinet appointments. He then turned his list of names over to Hamilton Jordan, who undertook a thorough analysis of each candidate. Before making his final decision, Carter talked to the individuals being considered.

This firm control of nominations occurred only at the department head level, however. Initially, President Carter invited his department secretaries to make their own senior departmental appointments, as he wanted to establish an independent cabinet. But this freedom of selection set up a power struggle between Jordan, who retained overall responsibility for personnel selection, and the department heads. According to presidential scholar R. Gordon Hoxie, "During the first year a warfare erupted between departmental personnel and White House staff over control of the turf and the action. The staff rationale was that *their* coordination, their orchestration, was required in all matters." [24] Eventually, because of his closeness to the president, Jordan and the White House staff won, and the process of selecting subcabinet personnel became concentrated in the White House.

Ronald Reagan

Following Carter's example, Ronald Reagan started the process of selecting cabinet members and other executive personnel well before the transition period ever began. E. Pendleton James, a professional executive recruiter, headed the overall personnel selection process. James believed it important that the president exercise his appointment power in a manner that would insure his control over his administration. Thus, the president had to appoint not only people who were loyal to him and shared in his objectives, but also those who were committed to implementing them.

Unlike the Carter administration, however, the Reagan administration initially succeeded in keeping the appointment process firmly within the White House under the control of James. Reagan supported the process and ac-

tively participated in it. During the transition, Reagan made the final decisions on all important appointments, especially cabinet selections. This made it difficult for the departments and agencies—and even for members of Congress—to exert much influence on the selection process in general.

Like Carter, Reagan required an excessive amount of time to get his administration fully in place. Ironically then, the two presidents who started the earliest to select executive appointees took the longest to fully staff their administrations. As in the Carter administration, post-Watergate-mandated security checks and conflict-of-interest disclosures contributed to the delay in the Reagan appointments. The diminished role that political parties played in Reagan's appointment process slowed the process as well. By the Reagan presidency, political parties no longer served as clearinghouses for political appointments. Instead, applications went directly to the White House, generating something of an administrative logjam. Appointment experts Macy, Adams, and Walter noted that "this creates an enormous and politically delicate logistical problem at a time when a new administration is unlikely to be well equipped to handle it." [25]

Another problem facing the Reagan administration was the growing conflict between differing ideologies and political philosophies. Senate confirmation hearings thus became even more difficult. For example, Reagan appointee Warren Richardson, nominated for assistant secretary of health and human services, withdrew his name from consideration when members of the Senate Labor and Human Resources Committee objected to his conservative political views. In another incident, Sen. Jesse Helms (R-N.C.) and a group of other conservative senators effectively delayed the nomination of twenty-nine State Department appointees before receiving assurances from Secretary of State George P. Shultz that six conservative employees of the State Department would not be fired. Faced with this kind of ideological tightrope, Reagan had difficulty finding acceptable cabinet appointees.

Reagan's initial cabinet nevertheless reflected many traditional political considerations. It was a combination of political cronies and strangers and well-known politicians and obscure state officials. Political scientist Ross K. Baker divided members of Reagan's cabinet into "mailmen" (management-oriented moderates) and "Grail seekers" (conservative advocates). The mailmen in Reagan's first cabinet were Treasury Secretary Donald T. Regan, Secretary of Housing and Urban Development Samuel R. Pierce, Jr., Secretary of Commerce Malcolm Baldrige, Secretary of Labor Raymond J. Donovan, and Secretary of Transportation Drew Lewis. His Grail seekers included Secretary of the Interior James G. Watt, Secretary of Energy James B. Edwards, and Secretary of Agriculture John R. Block.[26] More than anything else, Reagan's cabinet represented his electoral constituencies. Groups that did not support Reagan (liberals, environmentalists, and liberal labor unions) were not represented in his cabinet, while groups that helped give him his electoral majority (farmers, developers, and big business) were well represented.

Department of Agriculture

The U.S. Department of Agriculture (USDA) was established in 1862 and elevated to cabinet status in 1889. In

1987 it employed more than one hundred thousand people, with about ten thousand of them in Washington, D.C.

USDA assists the nation's farmers through a variety of programs, among them, subsidies, credit, and rural development (through loans for improved water systems, recreation areas, electrification, telephone service, and housing). USDA also oversees the nation's food quality through inspections of processing plants, and it establishes quality standards for every major agricultural commodity. It provides nutrition education programs as well. USDA's research facilities are investigating animal production, plant and animal diseases, pest controls, crop production, marketing and the use of agricultural products, food safety, and forestry. Moreover, the department supports environmental protection through its energy, soil, water, and forest resource conservation programs. Other responsibilities of the department include administering school lunch, food stamp, food-for-the-needy, and overseas distribution programs; managing the nation's 188 million acres of national forests and parklands; and helping developing nations improve food production.

Despite the importance of USDA, in 1971 President Richard Nixon proposed abolishing the department, and in 1977 President Jimmy Carter suggested transferring a number of USDA's functions to other agencies. Neither happened.

From Small Beginnings . . .

The idea of establishing an agricultural agency in the federal government surfaced in 1776, when farmers made up 90 percent of the nation's population, and virtually all exports were farm products. President George Washington recommended creating such an agency in 1796, but it was not until 1839 that Congress appropriated $1,000 for collecting agricultural statistics, conducting agricultural investigations, and distributing seeds. These functions were assigned at first to the Patent Office because Henry L. Ellsworth, commissioner of patents, had initiated the seed distribution idea.

The pressure to establish a federal agricultural agency mounted, led by the U.S. Agricultural Society, which was organized in 1852. The society found an ally in the Republican party, which pledged in 1860 to enact agrarian reforms. The law authorizing the department in 1862 instructed it "to acquire and to diffuse . . . useful information on subjects connected with agriculture in the most general and comprehensive sense of the word." In carrying out this mandate, the commissioner of agriculture was to conduct experiments, collect statistics, and "procure, propagate, and distribute among the people new and valuable seeds and plants."

The first commissioner of the department was Isaac Newton, a Pennsylvania dairy farmer and personal friend of President Abraham Lincoln. He had a staff of four clerks and a gardener as well as an annual budget of about $50,000. In his 1862 annual report the commissioner proposed a research and information program that was to become the basis of the department's activities over the next several years. The agency published statistical and research reports and dispatched scientists overseas to study other nations' agricultural practices.

Newton's successor, Norman J. Coleman, became the first secretary of agriculture in 1889, although he served in that capacity for only three weeks. A lawyer and lieutenant governor of Missouri, Coleman was active in state, regional, and national agricultural organizations. He played a key role in the passage of the 1887 Hatch Agricultural Experiment Stations Act, which authorized the establishment of such stations, under the direction of the land-grant colleges, in each state and territory.

Coleman's successor, Jeremiah M. Rusk, who was appointed by incoming President Benjamin Harrison, reorganized the department and inaugurated publication of farmers' bulletins. He created USDA's first assistant secretary post—to oversee the department's scientific work—and he named Edwin Williams to head the office.

Expansion of Functions

A new era for the department began in 1897 with the appointment of James ("Tama Jim") Wilson as secretary. Wilson, who served sixteen years—twice as long as any secretary before or since—had been director of the Iowa state agricultural experiment station and had served three terms in the House of Representatives. During his tenure the department became known as one of the great agricultural research institutions of the world. Wilson established new bureaus which operated autonomously under the leadership of well-known aggressive scientists. The Forest Service was established in 1905, as oversight of the national forests was transferred from the Department of the Interior to USDA. USDA was given additional regulatory authority as well, including responsibility for administering the 1906 Meat Inspection and Food and Drugs acts (the latter was transferred to the Food and Drug Administration in 1940). By 1912 the number of employees (13,858) and the department's budget were nearly seven times what they had been in 1897.

Under the leadership of David F. Houston (1913-1920), the department focused its efforts increasingly on the farmers' social and economic plight. Houston also made significant organizational changes, centralizing the department and establishing the Office of Markets and the Office of Information. Passage of the Smith-Lever Agricultural Extension Act in 1914 allowed the department and land-grant colleges, under formal cooperative agreements, to carry research directly to farmers. This arrangement resulted in creation of the Cooperative Extension Service, which served as a model for similar programs abroad.

In 1916 the department became active in establishing standards and grades for grain and cotton. Subsequently, standards were established for other products. The 1921 Packers and Stockyards Act barred unfair, deceptive, discriminatory, and monopolistic practices in livestock, poultry, and meat marketing.

The World War I years were accompanied by a surge in farm production and speculation. At the same time, farmers confronted declining prices for their products and high mortgage indebtedness. By the 1920s agriculture was swept into the general economic decline that was to culminate in the Great Depression. To help farmers meet market needs, the Bureau of Agricultural Economics was established in 1922 to foster statistical and economic research. During the depression Congress responded to the farmers' plight by passing a number of significant laws, among them the 1933 Agricultural Adjustment Act (AAA), which provided for production adjustment to be achieved principally through direct USDA payments to farmers. The Farm Credit Act, passed the same year, consolidated all farm credit programs under the Farm Credit Administration. The Soil Conservation Service was established in 1935, as were the Resettlement Administration (which later became the Farm Security Administration and Farmers Home Administration) and the Rural Electrification Administration. In 1936 the Supreme Court declared the AAA unconstitutional; it was replaced by Soil Conservation and Domestic Allotment Act.

In addition to assisting farmers during the depression, USDA joined the welfare agencies in aiding the poor in rural and urban areas through programs designed to distribute surpluses to the needy.

Postwar Farm Policy

Responding to overseas food needs following World War II, USDA urged U.S. farmers to expand their productive capacity. By the time the Korean War ended in 1953, however, the policy of emphasizing capacity production had resulted in surpluses and falling farm prices. Faced with that problem, President Dwight D. Eisenhower's secretary of agriculture, Ezra Taft Benson, chose to institute programs to expand markets rather than establish high price supports. A Soil Bank Program was put into place nevertheless, whereby farmers were paid to take farmland out of cultivation. The Rural Development Program was inaugurated in 1955 to help low-income farmers. That program was greatly expanded under Benson's successor, Orville L. Freeman (1961-1969). Passage of the Food Stamp Program, and expansion of the school lunch, school milk, and other food donation programs during this period, not only provided food aid to low-income families, but also reduced farm surpluses to more manageable levels. At the same time, "Food for Peace" activities were increased. More than 100 million people in 115 counries received U.S. food surpluses.

Clifford M. Hardin took over as USDA secretary in 1969 and was succeeded by Earl L. Butz in 1971. Butz, a controversial appointee, was forced to resign in 1976.

Fifty years after the federal government first paid farmers to plow under crops and slaughter surplus livestock, the Reagan administration launched a drive to end many depression-era farm programs and eliminate the assumption that the federal government is directly responsible for farmers' well-being. Reagan's first USDA secretary, John R. Block (an Illinois farmer), and others—including portions of the farm community—argued that earlier programs had in fact destabilized American agriculture and had to be changed radically.

During his tenure Block was alternately praised and criticized as a well-intentioned but often ineffectual director of the president's free-market philosophy for agriculture. Block came into office hoping to free farmers from relying so heavily on government programs, yet the crisis in agriculture—high interest rates and declining agricultural exports caused by the strength of the dollar—only deepened each year he was in office, despite unprecedented tax expenditures for price supports and income subsidies. Although Block lasted longer than all but three of Reagan's original cabinet officials, his influence on Capitol Hill waned considerably; he resigned in February 1986.

To replace Block, Reagan chose longtime associate Richard E. Lyng, an agriculture consultant and lobbyist and a former California seed company executive with wide experience in government. He was known to be Reagan's original choice for the cabinet post following the 1980 election, but congressional pressure then led Reagan to pick Block because he was a "working farmer" from the midwestern state of Illinois. Lyng then took the number-two job in the department. He remained in that position through Reagan's first term, overseeing day-to-day operations and often acting as point man on Capitol Hill for the administration's more controversial farm policies.

Organization

USDA has been reorganized a number of times in response to an emphasis on different problems and the gradual addition of functions. The only major organizational change made after the 1930s was the 1953 move to increase the number of assistant secretaries from one to five. In 1988 USDA was headed by a secretary, deputy secretary, two undersecretaries (one for international affairs and commodity programs, and the other for small community and rural development), and seven assistant secretaries (administration, economics, food and consumer services, governmental and public affairs, marketing and inspection services, natural resources and environment, and science and education). The offices of budget and program analysis, the general counsel, the judicial officer, and the inspector general report directly to the secretary.

Department of Commerce

Between 1850 and 1900 the nation's rapid economic growth fueled demands for business representation at the highest levels of government. The Panic of 1893 and the ensuing depression led the newly formed National Association of Manufacturers to lobby strenuously for formation of a department of commerce and industry that would include the Department of Labor (which had been established as a noncabinet-rank department in 1888). Congress responded by authorizing a U.S. industrial commission to study commercial problems.

In 1901, in his first state-of-the-union message, President Theodore Roosevelt proposed a combined department of commerce and labor. Labor representatives argued that workers needed a separate department, but business interests were willing to compromise. In the end the latter prevailed, and the Department of Commerce and Labor came into being in 1903. The new department was one of the largest and most complicated in the federal government; within five months its employees numbered 10,125. Its responsibilities included foreign and domestic commerce; mining, manufacturing, shipping, and fishery industries; labor interests; and transportation.

As the nation's manufactured exports continued to expand and workers moved from farms to industry, pressures built up on both sides to separate labor and commerce into independent departments. As a result a March 4, 1913, law gave labor cabinet status and the Department of Commerce was born.

Expansion of the Department

President William Howard Taft signed the bill on his last day in office. His Democratic successor, Woodrow Wilson, appointed the first commerce secretary, William C. Redfield, a manufacturing executive and politician. Despite the constraints of a $60,000 budget and elimination of funding for collecting domestic statistics, Redfield established a cadre of bilingual commercial attachés with business experience, opened branch offices in eight cities, and sent specialists overseas to study foreign markets.

Commerce came into the limelight during Herbert Hoover's tenure as its secretary (1921-1928). Hoover was determined to make Commerce the most powerful department in the government. His primary interest was to expand trade, and, indeed, by 1925 U.S. exports had increased by one-third over the figure recorded in 1913. During Hoover's stewardship, Commerce acquired a Building and Housing Division (1922), the Bureau of Mines and the Patent Office (both were transferred from Interior in 1925), an Aeronautics Division (1926; it was the forerunner of the Federal Aviation Administration), and a Radio Division (1927; it later became part of the Federal Communications Commission).

Keenly interested in revitalizing the department's statistical functions, Hoover instituted in 1921 a program of balance-of-payments reporting, publishing the data in the first *Survey of Current Business*. The department also developed safety codes for industry and transportation (including assistance in developing traffic signals and air and road safety standards, as well as expansion of its previous responsibility for safe ocean travel). In tandem with its increased responsibilities was the growth in the department's budget, from $860,000 in 1920 to more than $38 million in 1928.

Hoover left Commerce in 1928 to become president at the beginning of the Great Depression. The national income declined drastically, and U.S. exports fell below their 1913 levels. Franklin D. Roosevelt, who defeated Hoover in the 1932 election, slashed Commerce's budget and reduced its activities. There was even some thought of abolishing the department.

World War II and the years that followed ushered in a new role for Commerce. The National Bureau of Standards gained importance in its efforts to insure interchangeability of weapons parts, while the Civil Aeronautics Administration significantly expanded its pilot training programs. The Bureau of Public Roads and the Maritime Administration were moved to Commerce in 1949 and 1950, respectively. Until the Department of Transportation was established in 1967, Commerce was the principal overseer of transportation programs.

Although Commerce has remained an important source of economic information, its responsibilities in international economics have been taken over increasingly by special presidential advisers, the Treasury, and the Office of the U.S. Trade Representative.

Organization and Functions

In the Department of Commerce the general counsel, inspector general, Office of Business Liaison, and Office of Public Affairs report directly to the secretary and the deputy secretary. Four undersecretaries are responsible for oceans and atmosphere, international trade, economic affairs, and travel and tourism. The department has assistant secretaries for congressional and intergovernmental affairs, administration, patents and trademarks, communications and information, and economic development. A number of key offices are administered by directors. Commerce has offices in major U.S. cities and more than one hundred posts overseas. The department is organized according to the following functions.

Trade

The International Trade Administration (ITA) is the agency most closely associated with the department's mandate "to foster, promote and develop the commerce and industry of the United States." Congress authorized establishment of ITA in 1980 to help deal with soaring U.S. merchandise trade deficits. ITA helps formulate foreign trade and economic policies, works with the U.S. Trade Representative and other agencies, and administers legislation to counter unfair foreign trade practices.

The Bureau of Export Administration, established in 1987, formulates U.S. policy for the control of high-technology exports and monitors such exports. This program is designed to prevent the loss of commodities and technologies that would harm the nation's security and advance the military capabilities of adversaries. ITA originally had jurisdiction over this function.

The National Tourism Policy Act of 1981 replaced the U.S. Travel Service, established in 1961 to address a $1.2 billion balance-of-payments deficit in tourism, with the U.S. Travel and Tourism Administration (USTTA).

Economics

Created by President John F. Kennedy in 1961 to coordinate the formulation of economic policy, the Office of Economic Affairs provides foreign and domestic economic data, analyses, and forecasts, based on information provided by its two bureaus, Economic Analysis and Census. The Constitution stipulates that censuses are to be taken, but it was not until 1902 that Congress enacted legislation making the Census Bureau a permanent organization.

The Office of Productivity, Technology and Innovation was established in 1962 to spur U.S. competitiveness abroad by fostering government and private partnerships to stimulate the spread of innovative technologies.

The department's National Technical Information Service (NTIS) serves as a clearinghouse for scientific, technical, and engineering information and analysis. It is self-supporting through its sales of information products and services.

Sciences

In 1970 Congress authorized establishment of the National Oceanic and Atmospheric Administration (NOAA) in response to the presidentially commissioned report "Our Nation and the Sea," which called for bringing several existing agencies into a unified program. In 1987 NOAA employed thirteen thousand people and was the largest agency in Commerce. It predicts the weather, charts the seas and the skies, protects ocean resources, and collects data on the oceans, atmosphere, space, and sun.

The National Bureau of Standards was created in 1901, when the United States was the only major commercial nation without a standards laboratory. The new bureau—first located in Treasury and transferred to Commerce and Labor in 1903—was charged with custody, comparison, and, when needed, establishment of standards.

In 1978 an executive order merged the Office of Telecommunications in the Executive Office with the Office of Telecommunications in Commerce. The product of this merger was the National Telecommunications and Information Administration. Its mandate is to develop policies on the advancement and use of new technologies in common carrier, telephone, broadcast, and satellite communications systems.

The Patent Office, one of the oldest federal agencies, was authorized by Article I, section 8, of the Constitution. In 1802 a full-time Patent Office was established in the State Department; the office was transferred to Commerce in 1925. The Patent Office began registering trademarks in 1870. In 1975, one year after the one millionth trademark was registered, the office's name was changed officially to the Patent and Trademark Office.

Development

Authorized in 1965, the Economic Development Administration (EDA) works to generate and preserve private sector jobs in economically depressed areas by utilizing public works funds, business loans, loan guarantees, technical assistance, long-range economic planning, and economic research.

The Minority Business Development Agency was created in 1969 to promote minority businesses by generating private capital—and, later, by providing federal contracts and grants.

The Office of Business Liaison (1981) is a central source of information for people interested in doing business overseas or with the federal government.

Department of Defense

"The role of a Defense Secretary is to rein in the disparate interests in the defense establishment and shape a military program to suit the overall goals of himself and his administration," wrote Richard A. Stubbing, a defense analyst at the Office of Management and Budget for twenty years. "Given his limited time and political resources, the task is enormous, in some ways impossible, but the performance of the Defense Secretary is vitally important to the overall effectiveness and efficiency of the defense program." [27]

The Department of Defense (DOD) officially became part of the cabinet only in 1949, but in terms of human resources and money it is the largest of the fourteen departments that make up the cabinet. Providing the umbrella for the army, navy, Marine Corps, and air force, DOD is composed of about 2.2 million men and women on active duty. Of these, some 525,000—including about 72,000 on ships at sea—serve outside the United States. They are backed, in case of emergency, by the 1.7 million members of the reserve components. In addition, about 1.2 million civilian employees work for the Defense Department. The Reagan administration's defense budget request for fiscal year 1989 totaled $328.3 billion.

Creation of the National Military Establishment

Before the twentieth century there was little need for a centralized defense establishment; the army fought on land and the navy fought at sea. The acquisition of overseas territories and the growing U.S. role in international affairs, however, led many observers to conclude that a more coordinated national security system was needed—an observation that proved to be all the more true with the advent of air power in the period between World Wars I and II. The Air Corps, as the air force was then called, lobbied for equality with the other branches; although it was nominally a part of the army, it in fact operated independently.

Between 1921 and 1945 at least fifty bills aimed at unifying the armed forces were introduced in Congress. But the major argument for unification also acted as the stumbling block to an interservice agreement. The army's Air Corps sought separate status—a goal that was practicable only within a framework that provided some degree of unified direction at the top. To the navy, however, the logic of separate services for land, sea, and air represented the potential loss of naval aviation to the air force and the Marine Corps to the army.

Despite the navy's opposition, Congress passed the National Security Act of 1947 (PL 80-253) on July 25. This act provided "a comprehensive program for the future security of the United States" and gave the three services "authoritative coordination and unified direction under civilian control" without merging them. The law thus created a national military establishment, to be headed by the secretary of defense and to consist of the Departments of the Army, Navy, and Air Force. The secretary was designated "the principal assistant to the President in all matters relating to the national security." At the same time, however, the three service departments were to be "administered as individual executive departments by their respective Secretaries," who retained the right to present "to the President or to the Director of the Budget ... any report or recommendations relating to his department which he may deem necessary." The secretary of defense was not allowed to establish a military staff and was restricted to three civilian assistants. The Joint Chiefs of Staff (JCS), including a chief of staff, were given statutory authority as "the principal military advisers to the President and the Secretary of Defense," with authority to prepare strategic plans, "establish unified commands," and "review major material and personnel requirements of the military forces."

President Harry S Truman signed the law on July 26, 1947, and immediately named Navy Secretary James V. Forrestal as the first secretary of defense.

1949 Amendments

Concern over the high cost of national defense—not its adequacy—was the major factor that persuaded Congress to amend the National Security Act in 1949. The report of the Hoover Commission on Organization of the Executive Branch had recommended (1) giving the secretary of defense complete statutory authority over the three services, (2) eliminating the three military departments and demoting the service secretaries to undersecretaries of defense, and (3) appointing a chairman of the JCS responsible to the secretary. Truman essentially adopted the proposals and sent them to Congress.

As enacted, the National Security Act Amendments of 1949 converted the national military establishment into an executive cabinet-level Department of Defense. The amended act incorporated the military departments of the three services and stipulated that each was to be "separately administered" by a secretary under the "direction, authority, and control" of the secretary of defense. The secretary was barred, however, from acting to transfer, abolish, or consolidate any of the services' combatant functions. Moreover, nothing was to "prevent a Secretary of a military department or a member of the Joint Chiefs of Staff from presenting to the Congress, on his own initiative, . . . any recommendations relating to the Department of Defense that he may deem proper."

The law also provided for a deputy secretary of defense, three assistant secretaries, and a nonvoting chairman of the Joint Chiefs of Staff (to replace the chief of staff to the president), who was to rank first but hold no command. Finally, provision was made for adding comptrollers to the Defense Department and the three military departments and for instituting uniform accounting and budgetary procedures.

Dwight D. Eisenhower assumed the presidency committed to the same general foreign policy and security objectives as his predecessor, yet he pledged to bring about a sharp reduction in defense spending and a reorganization of DOD. For civilian leadership in the Pentagon, Eisenhower turned to the business world, selecting Charles E. Wilson, president of General Motors Corporation, as defense secretary. The deputy secretary and secretaries of the army, navy, and air force also came from the business community.

Like World War II, the Korean War pointed out the organizational shortcomings of the military complex. President Eisenhower thus asked a group of prominent citizens to propose changes in the Defense Department, and their recommendations were embodied in a reorganization plan that the president submitted to Congress. Although there were some objections from legislators, the plan was adopted, providing for six additional assistant secretary positions and giving the secretary the power to select the director of the joint staff of the Joint Chiefs of Staff.

Between 1953 and 1957 Eisenhower and Wilson were largely successful in holding down attempts to increase defense spending to levels unacceptable to them. But in the aftermath of the 1958 Soviet launch of the first unmanned satellite, *Sputnik I*, the administration found itself under attack from Republicans as well as Democrats, who called for major changes in the defense program. These changes included a reorganization of the Defense Department to speed decision making in the development of new weapons systems and to curtail waste and duplication of effort by the three services.

The administration reluctantly agreed to go along with some of the proposed changes. The Department of Defense Reorganization Act of 1958 authorized the secretary to consolidate common supply and service functions and to assign responsibility for the development and operation of new weapons systems. It also authorized the secretary to transfer, reassign, abolish, or consolidate existing combatant functions of the three services, subject to congressional veto. The act established the position of director of defense research and engineering as the principal adviser to the secretary for all scientific and technological matters. An administration proposal to appropriate all defense funds to the secretary—rather than to the military departments—to "remove all doubts" about the secretary's authority was dropped because of strong Republican as well as Democratic criticism.

McNamara, Laird, and Brown

Within six months of taking office, President John F. Kennedy had increased his predecessor's defense requests for fiscal year 1962 by almost $6 billion, initiating a sharp acceleration of strategic programs and a major expansion of conventional forces. In moving to a higher level of defense spending, however, the president and Defense Secretary Robert S. McNamara did not abandon all considerations of cost. On the contrary, McNamara continued and strengthened the policy of cutting back, terminating, or postponing programs of marginal or dubious effectiveness.

McNamara, president of the Ford Motor Company when Kennedy nominated him as secretary, quickly gained a reputation as a highly intelligent and forceful "boss" of the Pentagon. The new secretary asserted the full authority of his office under the 1958 reorganization act, achieving a greater degree of centralization and control over the services than had ever existed. In the field of management, he introduced a planning-programming-budgeting process that attempted to tie together, in terms of national objectives, the requirements and projected activities of all elements of the military establishment.

Richard Nixon's choice of Melvin R. Laird as secretary of defense was considered widely to be an astute one. Laird, an eight-term Republican representative from Wisconsin (1953-1969), was the first member of Congress to serve as DOD secretary. A professional politician who had served on committees dealing with defense, Laird had a reputation as a "mover and shaker" in Congress. He recognized his relative lack of managerial experience, however, and he chose David Packard, a highly successful industrialist, as his deputy to run the day-to-day business of the department. The two established a close working relationship.

Laird believed strongly in the power of appointments for both civilian and military posts; he personally selected the three service secretaries and met separately with them each week. He also held weekly meetings with his assistant secretaries. Despite major budget and force cutbacks and an end to the draft, Laird was popular among military personnel, and he developed a close rapport with Gen. Earle G. Wheeler, chairman of the Joint Chiefs of Staff.

Laird left Defense in 1973 to assume the position of presidential assistant for domestic affairs, which had been vacated by John D. Ehrlichman in the wake of the Watergate scandal. He was replaced in January 1973 by Elliot L. Richardson, who was reassigned the following May to Justice as attorney general. Richardson's tenure as defense secretary was the briefest in the twenty-six-year history of the office.

Nixon's third selection as DOD secretary was James R. Schlesinger, who had just been named director of the Central Intelligence Agency in January. Although Schlesinger was viewed as an intellectual, his approach to defense issues was pragmatic, and, unlike McNamara, whose emphasis on cost-effectiveness Schlesinger had criticized, he was willing to negotiate. Nonetheless, management suffered during Schlesinger's tenure; he did not get along well with President Gerald R. Ford, who fired the secretary in 1975 over policy disagreements.

In contrast to the musical chairs of the Nixon administration, Harold Brown's tenure as defense secretary lasted throughout the administration of Jimmy Carter. A physicist and former McNamara protege, Brown was secretary of the air force from 1965 to 1969 before becoming president of the California Institute of Technology. Brown brought with him a thorough knowledge of defense programs and a sterling reputation. He was, above all, a scientist and administrator, not a politician. As secretary, he utilized a more centralized management style than that favored by Laird or Schlesinger, and he took a more active role in making budget and program decisions.

During his first year in office Brown ordered a comprehensive review of DOD's organization. As a result, fewer people reported directly to the secretary, and a number of headquarters activities were consolidated. A General Accounting Office report concluded that no substantial economies had been effected, however. "Defense recently completed a Harold Brown ordered economy movement that resulted in almost no economy and even less movement," commented the *Washington Post* on October 7, 1978.[28]

One of Brown's major difficulties in asserting his role as secretary was Carter's personal involvement in defense issues, even small ones. Brown was unwilling to challenge the president and generally was overshadowed by him.

Buildup under Reagan

Caspar W. Weinberger was Ronald Reagan's choice as secretary of defense when the Republican administration entered office in 1981. A longtime friend of the president, Weinberger had a distinguished career in public service and private business. When he was nominated to be DOD secretary, however, opponents criticized Weinberger's lack of background in defense policy and feared that he would manage the Pentagon's budget too tightly. But he quickly established himself as a relentless advocate of a rapid military buildup.

After Reagan's first few years in office, Congress became less willing to back the defense buildup at the pace sought by the president and Weinberger. There was a growing sense that Pentagon funds were utilized poorly. Weinberger was hesitant to override the budget requests of the services and gave them a relatively free hand in setting military priorities and making program decisions. The secretary's "hands-off" approach and his inattention to management resulted therefore in strained relations with Congress, not helped by the increasingly perfunctory character of the secretary's dealings with Capitol Hill. Defense committees asked him for advice on where to find budget cuts, but Weinberger insisted that his requests were the minimum required for the nation's safety. Hardliners applauded his tenacity, but many congressional defense specialists contended that by refusing to bargain, he dealt himself out of the process.

Citing personal reasons, Weinberger resigned in November 1987. He was replaced by his longtime associate Frank C. Carlucci, who had established a reputation as a shrewd operator of the machinery of government.

Organization and Functions

DOD is structured around four principal elements: the office of the secretary, the military departments, the Joint Chiefs of Staff, and the unified and specified commands. The secretary's line of command is direct to both the staff and fighting forces. Nonetheless, "the responsibilities of the job [of DOD secretary] are not matched by corresponding powers," wrote John G. Kester, former special assistant to Defense Secretary Harold Brown. "The Secretary is an official whose position is impinged upon from many directions, and who often must feel that he is sitting on top of a centrifuge. Without a lot of pulling at the center, the Defense Department tends to fly off in all directions." [29]

The office of the secretary includes the offices of the deputy secretary, executive secretary, assistant to the secretary, undersecretary for acquisition, undersecretary for policy, comptroller, general counsel, inspector general, and directors of defense research and engineering, operational testing and evaluation, and program analysis and evaluation. Three deputy undersecretaries oversee policy, trade security policy, and planning and resources. In addition, in 1987 there were nine assistant secretaries: command, control, communications, and intelligence; health affairs; legislative affairs; force management and personnel; international security affairs; international security policy; public affairs; reserve affairs; and intelligence oversight.

Reporting to the office of the secretary are the following agencies: communications, mapping, legal services, contract audit, security assistance, national security, investigative service, logistics, advanced research projects, and intelligence. In January 1984, under Reagan's directive, the Strategic Defense Initiative Organization was established as a Defense agency reporting directly to the secretary of defense.

The Joint Chiefs of Staff—consisting of the chairman; chief of staff, U.S. Army; chief of naval operations; chief of staff, U.S. Air Force; and commandant of the Marine Corps—constitute the immediate military staff of the defense secretary. Other members of the JCS are the senior military officers of their respective services, the National Security Council (NSC), and the secretary of defense. The JCS is served by the joint staff, which is composed of not more than four hundred officers selected in approximately equal numbers from the army, navy (including the Marine Corps), and air force.

Each military department is organized separately under its own secretary, who is responsible to the secretary of defense. In addition, there are a number of unified and specified commands. A "unified command" is a force under a single commander that is engaged in a broad, continuing mission, assisted by assigned personnel from two or more services. The unified commands are the European, Atlantic, Central, Pacific, Southern, Transportation, Special Operations, and Space. A "specified command" is similar but normally represents only one service. In 1988 there were three such commands: Strategic Air Command, Military Airlift Command, and Forces Command.

Outside the functional organization structure is the Armed Forces Policy Council (AFPC), which advises the secretary of defense on matters of broad policy relating to the armed forces and such other matters as the secretary, who serves as its chair, may direct. Members of the council are the deputy secretary of defense, the secretaries of the military departments, the JCS chairman, the undersecretaries of defense, the chief of naval operations, and the army chief of staff, the air force chief of staff, and the commandant of the Marine Corps.

Department of Education

President Jimmy Carter entered office in 1977 with one much-publicized legislative priority in the area of education. During the 1976 presidential election campaign, he had vowed to establish a cabinet-level department to oversee education. In return, he received the endorsement of the 1.7 million members of the National Education Association, the first campaign endorsement given in the organization's history. Congress passed legislation creating the Department of Education in 1979.

Predecessors of the Department

Unlike many other countries for whom a centralized educational system was a vital component of nation building, the United States traditionally has avoided a strong federal role in education. It was not until 1867 that President Andrew Johnson called for the creation of an education department "for the purpose of collecting such statistics and facts as shall show the condition and progress of education in the several States and Territories, and of diffusing such information respecting the organization and management of schools and school systems, and methods of teaching. . . ." The new department had a staff of four: Commissioner of Education Henry Barnard and three clerks. Their total annual salary was $7,800.

The first Department of Education was downgraded quickly to the status of a bureau in the Interior Department. For the next seventy years it limped along as a small recordkeeping office, collecting information on the modest federal education efforts. Proposals for a separate department surfaced periodically, but they went nowhere. In 1939 the renamed Office of Education was transferred to the Federal Security Agency, which became the Department of Health, Education and Welfare (HEW) in 1953.

With the tremendous expansion of federal education programs in the postwar period, arguments for a separate department grew more persuasive. During the 1960s several studies recommended establishment of a separate department, as well as related reorganization proposals. In 1972 Congress established within HEW an Education Division, headed by an assistant secretary for education. It included the existing Office of Education.

Controversy over Its Creation

One of the main arguments for a separate education department was the confusing and contradictory structure of the existing federal educational administration. In 1978 the hundreds of existing federal educational programs were located in more than forty different agencies.

Lumping all these programs in one department, however, proved to be very difficult politically. For every program going into the department, some other department would have to lose power and money. Agencies and interest groups fought against giving up long, established relationships for an uncertain future in the Education Department. The bill creating the new department also was opposed by a coalition of labor and civil rights groups, who feared that their influence would be reduced in a department dominated by professional educators. The strongest supporters of the new department were those in elementary and secondary education. Higher education organizations were basically neutral on the question.

At first it appeared that the bill would clear Congress easily despite some bitter struggles among administration officials, interest groups, and members of Congress over exactly what should be in the new department. But, faced with dilatory tactics, House leaders decided to shelve the bill in 1978. Opposition was vigorous when the legislation came before Congress again in 1979, but effective lobbying by the agency's supporters—including President Carter—and the addition of some safeguards against federal domination provided the margin needed for creation of the department. Congress completed action on the bill on September 27, and Carter signed it on October 17. Some 152 federal education-related programs were consolidated in the new agency, which at its creation was the fifth largest department handling the eighth largest budget.

Shirley M. Hufstedler, the first secretary of education, took office on December 6. A member of the U.S. Court of Appeals for the Ninth Circuit since 1969, Hufstedler brought no professional education credentials to her new job other than her experience as a member of the boards of trustees of three California institutions of higher education. That lack of experience caused some concern in the education community. Defenders of Carter's appointment argued, however, that Hufstedler's lack of experience and close connection with one or another of the sectors of the education community was a virtue. They said she would bring a fresh perspective to the deep-seated problems of the nation's public education system.

The new department formally opened its doors on May 7, 1980. By 1987 its budget totaled $19.5 billion, and its staff numbered 4,500. The department is constrained in its authority, however, by the long-standing tradition in the United States that education be primarily a state and local function. Congress restated that commitment to decentralized control when it declared in the act that created the department that "the establishment of the Department of Education shall not . . . diminish the responsibility for education which is reserved to the states and the local school systems and other instrumentalities of the state." It is they who make policies on such matters as the length of the school day and year, textbook selection, teacher certification, high school graduation requirements, grading scales, and other instructional and administrative policies.

The Department of Education distributes most of its program funds directly to the states as formula grants. The amounts are based on the number of students in various special categories, and the states then distribute the money to local districts under Education-approved plans.

The existence of the department was precarious during its first years. Ronald Reagan, riding a wave of voter dissatisfaction with what was seen as widespread federal intervention into local affairs, promised during the 1980 election campaign to dismantle the young agency and reduce Washington's role in education programs. His selection of Terrel H. Bell as secretary of education was viewed, however, as an indication that the president would abandon, or at least scale back, his campaign pledge to abolish the department. Bell had been U.S. commissioner of education from 1974 to 1976 and Utah commissioner of higher education since 1976. Education groups were pleased by the selection of a fellow educator with long experience. Bell had supported creating the department, and he stated during his confirmation hearings that he did not want to see a return to the days when education was a low-status unit of the massive Department of Health, Education and Welfare.

After 1981 Reagan made little progress in his efforts to reduce spending and restructure federal involvement in education. Although in 1982 he proposed abolishing Education, Congress ignored the suggestion, and the proposal gradually faded from view.

Bell fought within the administration to moderate proposals to curb education spending, and as a result, he was criticized frequently by conservatives. He resigned as secretary at the end of 1984 and was succeeded in February 1985 by William J. Bennett, former chairman of the National Endowment for the Humanities. When Bennett resigned in 1988, Reagan named Lauro F. Cavazos to the post, making him the nation's first Hispanic cabinet member. When George Bush became president in 1989, he retained Cavazos as secretary.

Organization and Functions

The Department of Education is headed by a secretary who serves as the president's chief adviser on education and supervises the department's staff. The secretary also performs certain functions related to four federally aided corporations: American Printing House for the Blind in Lexington, Kentucky; Gallaudet University (for assisting the deaf) in Washington, D.C.; Howard University in Washington, D.C.; and National Technical Institute for the Deaf (part of Rochester Institute of Technology in New York State). The secretary is assisted by an undersecretary, general counsel, inspector general, three deputy undersecretaries, and eight assistant secretaries.

The deputy undersecretaries are in charge of the Office of Management; Office of Planning, Budget, and Evaluation; and Office of Intergovernmental and Interagency Affairs, which serves as the liaison between the department and its ten regional offices, state and local governments, and other federal agencies.

The Office of Elementary and Secondary Education provides state and local education agencies with the financial assistance needed to help improve preschool, elementary, and secondary education—both public and private. Its largest program, authorized under Title I of the 1965 Elementary and Secondary Education Act, is aimed at disadvantaged children. The office also administers funds provided by the Indian Education Act. It oversees voluntary and court-ordered school desegregation programs, provides assistance to school districts affected by federal activities that overburden local tax sources (impact aid), and helps districts struck by natural disasters.

The Office of Special Education and Rehabilitative Services assists in the education of handicapped children and in the rehabilitation of disabled adults. Many of the numerous children whose native languages are not English are aided by the Office of Bilingual Education and Minority Languages Affairs. Under programs administered by the office, children are instructed in their own languages as they are taught English.

The Office of Postsecondary Education supports financially needy young people who want to go to college or a vocational training school after high school. The office also supports programs for institutional development, student services, housing and facilities, veterans' affairs, cooperative education, international education, graduate education, historically black colleges, foreign language and area studies, innovative teaching methods and practices, and other subjects related to the improvement of postsecondary education.

The Office of Vocational and Adult Education helps states and communities provide specialized vocational education to young people and adults so that they can acquire marketable skills, or so that they can obtain a high school diploma or its equivalent.

Research and demonstration projects designed to improve education at all grade levels—preschool through graduate school—are funded by the Office of Educational Research and Improvement. The office also deals with libraries, museums, and educational programming by the media.

The Center for Statistics gathers, evaluates, and then disseminates information on the characteristics of U.S. education, while the Office for Civil Rights is responsible for seeing that educational institutions comply with four federal statutes that prohibit discrimination in programs and activities receiving federal financial assistance from the department.

Department of Energy

The 1973-1974 Arab oil embargo brought with it dramatic evidence that the U.S. government needed to formulate a more coherent and comprehensive energy policy to centralize its energy-related programs, which then were scattered among various federal agencies. The initial federal response to this need was creation in 1974 of the Energy Research and Development Administration (ERDA) and the Federal Energy Administration (FEA) to administer federal policy for energy planning and regulation. It soon was recognized, however, that additional steps were needed. Thus, on August 4, 1977, President Jimmy Carter signed into law a bill (PL 95-91) that created a cabinet-level Department of Energy (DOE). The new department came into existence on October 1, 1977.

The first new cabinet department since creation of the Department of Transportation in 1966, DOE assumed the powers and functions of FEA, ERDA, the Federal Power Commission (FPC), and the four regional power commissions. DOE also absorbed energy-related programs formerly administered by the Departments of the Interior, Defense, Commerce, and Housing and Urban Development, and the Interstate Commerce Commission. The department assumed as well the role of consultant to the Department of Transportation and the Rural Electrification Administration.

The first secretary of energy was James R. Schlesinger, President Carter's chief energy adviser during the early months of the administration. Although Schlesinger had a long record of government service, he drew vigorous criticism for his lack of administrative skill in putting the new department into working order; he resigned in mid-1979. Carter replaced him with Charles W. Duncan, Jr., deputy secretary of defense since 1977, who won high marks for his management of the new department.

DOE initially employed almost twenty thousand people—transferees from the existing energy programs in other departments and agencies. Its fiscal year 1978 budget was $10.6 billion.

Response to the Energy Crisis

President Richard Nixon was the first president to suggest that the federal agencies dealing with energy be reorganized and consolidated. In 1971 he proposed creation of a Department of Natural Resources, based upon the

Department of the Interior, but including such energy-related programs as those run by the Atomic Energy Commission. Congress greeted Nixon's proposal with yawns, and it progressed no further than the hearing stage. In 1973 Nixon resubmitted his proposal. Once again, it went nowhere on Capitol Hill. As the energy crisis became a fact of life, however, Congress responded in 1974 to Nixon administration requests to create FEA and ERDA.

One of President Gerald R. Ford's final official actions was submittal of a plan to Congress for reorganizing the energy bureaucracy into a Department of Energy. Congress had requested such a plan when it passed legislation in 1976 extending the life of the FEA. Ford's plan was in many respects similar to that proposed by Carter a few months later. "Nowhere is the need for reorganization and consolidation greater than in energy policy," Carter said in a March 1, 1977, message to Congress unveiling his reorganization plan. "All but two of the executive branch's Cabinet departments now have some responsibility for energy policy, but no agency . . . has the broad authority needed to deal with our energy problems in a comprehensive way."

The bill that finally reached Carter's desk for his signature differed in only one major respect from his original proposal. Carter and Congress disagreed over who in the new energy structure should have the power to set prices for natural gas, oil, and electricity. Carter would have given this power to the secretary, but the sentiment of the majority in both chambers of Congress was opposed on the ground that it was unwise to give such power to a single person who served at the pleasure of the president. To shield such sensitive and far-reaching economic decisions from political pressure, Congress included in the DOE legislation language that created an independent Federal Energy Regulatory Commission (FERC) that would set energy prices. If the president found that a national emergency required quick action on such matters, however, the secretary could circumvent the commission on the question of oil prices.

Declining Interest in Energy

During Ronald Reagan's administration, Congress all but forgot the national energy problems that it had spent the previous decade trying to solve. Indeed, by 1985 the stormy political debates over the energy policy of the 1970s had lost their thunder. With no crisis to raise an alarm, members of Congress who were still concerned about the adequacy of the nation's long-term fuel supplies could generate little political momentum for challenging Reagan's determination to scale back federal control over U.S. energy markets.

During the 1980 presidential campaign, Reagan had contended that federal actions had caused, rather than alleviated, the nation's energy problems. Declaring that "America must get to work producing more energy," he pledged to keep the government from interfering with marketplace supply-and-demand incentives that would encourage domestic fuel development. Reagan also vowed to abolish DOE; conservatives viewed the department as an unneeded instrument for federal meddling in energy matters. Congress refused to comply, but Reagan's first-term energy secretaries—former South Carolina governor James B. Edwards (an oral surgeon) and Donald P. Hodel (former deputy secretary of the interior)—de-emphasized the department's programs to promote conservation, encourage

solar and other alternative technologies, and develop new ways to burn fossil fuels.

Edwards had little experience in dealing with energy issues. As South Carolina's governor, however, he had been an unabashed advocate of developing nuclear power. Environmental groups were dismayed by his strong backing of the commercial reprocessing of spent nuclear fuel into fresh fuel, plutonium, and liquid wastes. As energy secretary, Edwards continued to back nuclear research and development as offering the best long-term solution to U.S. energy needs.

In selecting Hodel to replace Edwards, the administration ignored environmental groups' criticism of Hodel's close ties to Interior Secretary James G. Watt and his record of supporting nuclear power. Hodel was able, however, to improve the morale of DOE employees by playing down talk of abolishing the department. He also won praise from some members of Congress, even Democrats who opposed his policies. While Edwards and Hodel gave DOE a low profile, Watt, as chairman of Reagan's cabinet Council on Natural Resources and the Environment, took the lead in shaping the administration's agenda for easing federal regulatory restraints on the U.S. energy industry.

In January 1985 Reagan nominated John S. Herrington, then an assistant to the president for personnel, to replace Hodel, who was nominated to be secretary of the interior after the controversial Watt was forced to resign. The announcement came amid new rumors that Reagan would seek to abolish DOE and merge its functions into the Interior Department. But Herrington played down this possibility in an appearance before the Senate Energy and Natural Resources Committee, saying, "The president has nominated me to be a full-time secretary of energy, not a caretaker." The Senate confirmed both nominations in February. The idea of a merger then faded, and as of 1988 the two departments retained their separate identities. In 1989 President George Bush appointed as secretary James D. Watkins, a former nuclear submarine skipper and chief of naval operations. It was hoped that Watkins's expertise in nuclear energy would lead to solutions for the nation's problem-plagued weapons reactor complex.

Organization and Functions

DOE is responsible for the long-term, high-risk research and development of energy technology, the marketing of federal power, energy conservation, a nuclear weapons program, energy regulatory programs, and a central energy data collection and analysis program.

The department is organized around five broad groups of activities. The largest includes programs dealing with energy research, development, and demonstration activities. The next largest is the department's defense program—nuclear weapons development, production, and surveillance activities. The remaining three major programs are under the purview of DOE's Economic Regulatory Administration, which oversees most price, supply, and allocation activities; the Federal Energy Regulatory Commission, which controls the prices and the interstate transmission of natural gas, oil, and electricity; and the Energy Information Administration, which collects and analyzes energy data.

The secretary and deputy secretary are responsible for the overall planning, direction, and control of DOE activities. The undersecretary has the primary responsibility for developing the department's policies on energy conservation and renewable energy technology.

The assistant secretary for defense programs manages and directs DOE's programs for nuclear weapons research, development, testing, production, and surveillance. In addition, the office is responsible for the Nuclear Materials Production Program and the Defense Waste and Transportation Management Program.

The assistant secretary for nuclear energy is responsible for the administration of advanced technology programs and projects for nuclear fission power generation and fuel technology; the evaluation of alternative reactor fuel cycle concepts, including nonproliferation considerations; the development of space nuclear generator systems; the development of naval nuclear propulsion plants and reactor cores; uranium enrichment activities; and remedial actions and nuclear waste technology. Much of the nuclear energy effort is directed toward technology and engineering development programs.

The assistant secretary for international affairs and energy emergencies develops and directs international energy policy and coordinates energy emergency preparedness planning operations (excluding nuclear incidents and accidents). The deputy assistant secretary for international affairs develops and implements international energy policy; monitors world energy markets and trade, price/supply trends, and technological developments; and assesses energy supply vulnerability and the international implications of U.S. contingency plans.

The Office of Conservation and Renewable Energy, headed by an assistant secretary, formulates and directs programs for long-term, high-risk research and development on renewable and conservation technologies. The office also has responsibility for administering statutorily mandated, conservation-oriented assistance programs which operate through state and local governments.

The Nuclear Waste Policy Act of 1982 established within DOE an Office of Civilian Radioactive Waste Management to focus on research and development leading to the siting, construction, and operation of geologic repositories for the disposal of civilian and defense high-level radioactive wastes and spent nuclear fuel.

The director of energy research advises the secretary on DOE physical research programs, the department's overall energy research and development programs, and university-based education and training activities.

The mission of the Office of Fossil Energy, headed by an assistant secretary, is to develop technologies designed to increase domestic production of oil and gas and to permit the United States to shift from less abundant fuels to more abundant coal.

Other offices in DOE are: Management and Administration; General Counsel; Inspector General; Board of Contract Appeals; Minority Economic Impact; Small and Disadvantaged Business Utilization; Congressional, Intergovernmental and Public Affairs; and Environment, Safety and Health. Finally, DOE has an extensive network of field organizations.

Department of Health and Human Services

The Department of Health and Human Services (HHS) was established in 1979 as the successor to the Department of Health, Education and Welfare (HEW). The second largest federal agency (after defense), HHS is the cabinet department most involved with U.S. citizens. In fact, in one way or another—whether it is mailing out Social Security checks or making health services more widely available—HHS touches the lives of more Americans than any other federal agency. Its budget is second only to that of the Defense Department; President Ronald Reagan requested $273.3 billion in new budget authority for HHS in fiscal year 1989 ($81.9 billion of which is for Social Security), compared with $328.3 billion for defense.

Product of Reorganization

HEW evolved in a series of presidential reorganization plans and laws that became effective between 1939 and 1953. In 1939 President Franklin D. Roosevelt sent Congress his first presidential reorganization plan, creating a new federal office, the Federal Security Agency (FSA), to be headed by an administrator. The plan transferred a number of existing agencies to FSA, among them the Public Health Service (PHS) from Treasury, the Social Security Board (established in 1935 as an independent agency), and the Office of Education from Interior. A 1940 reorganization plan transferred additional units to FSA; among them, the most important was the Food and Drug Administration (FDA) from Agriculture. The 1943 Barden-LaFolette Act authorized an expanded federal-state vocational rehabilitation program, which led to the creation of a separate office of vocational rehabilitation in FSA.

A 1946 reorganization plan transferred the Children's Bureau to FSA (from Labor) and the Office of Vital Statistics to PHS (from the Census Bureau in Commerce). The Social Security Board was abolished and its functions handed over to the FSA administrator, who subsequently created a Social Security Administration (SSA) to oversee the program. In 1948 management of the Federal Credit Union Act of 1934 was shifted from the Federal Deposit Insurance Corporation to FSA, where a bureau of federal credit unions was established. One year later the Bureau of Employment Security (responsible for unemployment compensation) was transferred from Labor to FSA.

On March 12, 1953, President Dwight D. Eisenhower submitted to Congress a reorganization plan that transformed FSA into a cabinet-level Department of Health, Education and Welfare. There was little opposition in either party to the substance of the plan, which took effect April 11. Republicans and many southern Democrats, who had opposed similar efforts by President Harry S Truman in 1949-1950, supported Eisenhower's initiative, as did the American Medical Association, which also had criticized the Truman proposals. Objections to the earlier plans had stemmed largely from fears that creation of a new department would enhance the power of Oscar R. Ewing, then FSA administrator and a staunch advocate of compulsory national health insurance. Ewing was expected to be the president's choice as secretary, and in that capacity he was expected to help the Truman administration put across its national health insurance proposals. Republicans also had resisted the earlier plans on the grounds that they would submerge education and health matters in a welfare-oriented agency and subject decisions on health matters to "nonprofessional" bureaucratic control.

Later in 1953 those fears were obviated by several factors. First, Oveta Culp Hobby, a strong opponent of national health insurance, was to be the new secretary rather than Ewing. Second, the 1953 plan did not vest all departmental powers directly in the new secretary; it left the functions of the PHS and Office of Education the responsibility of those two agencies, which were to be subordinate units of the new department operating under the secretary's general supervision (the existing setup under FSA). Finally, the plan provided for the creation of a new post of special assistant to the secretary for health and medical affairs. The special assistant, to be appointed by the president, was to be a person of wide nongovernmental experience in that field (but not necessarily a physician). The plan also gave the new secretary the power to administer Social Security and welfare programs (as it had been vested in the FSA administrator since 1946), but it provided for the presidential appointment of a commissioner of Social Security, subject to Senate confirmation, to carry out whatever duties in connection with those programs that might be assigned by the secretary.

Expansion of Responsibilities

During the next few years the responsibilities of HEW increased significantly. In 1954 far-reaching changes were made in the Old Age and Survivors Insurance (OASI) program, greatly extending coverage. In 1956 OASI was changed to OASDI to include disability insurance. Also that year, Congress authorized the PHS to create a National Library of Medicine (its initial stock consisted of the existing Armed Forces Medical Library), which subsequently became one of the world's largest specialized libraries.

The department's purview continued to expand under presidents John F. Kennedy and Lyndon B. Johnson. One of the most enduring legacies of the Johnson administration was the wide range of innovative social programs initiated under the banner of the "Great Society." Certainly the most dramatic development was enactment of the Medicare program in 1965 to provide hospital insurance for the elderly, financed through the Social Security system. Also in 1965 a Medicaid program of aid to the poor for medical expenses was enacted. Existing programs were broadened, including community mental health and retardation as well as aid to education for doctors, nurses, and other health specialists. Social Security was revised, with retirement benefits raised and eligibility requirements eased.

Despite Richard Nixon's desire to shift power and funding from the federal government to the states and localities, entitlement programs—among them, Social Security—continued to grow.

President Jimmy Carter's first HEW secretary, Joseph A. Califano, Jr., wasted little time in pushing forward internal reorganization at HEW in an attempt to manage more effectively one of the government's largest bureaucracies, a task that had stymied many before him. Califano made changes in both the policies and procedures of his department. In March 1977 he announced a restructuring of the bureaucracy that he said was expected to save $2 billion a year in the long run. He consolidated administration of the Medicare and Medicaid programs in a new Health Care Financing Administration (HCFA). In July he announced a reorganization of the department's regional offices, and in September he pledged a thorough review of the department's voluminous regulations—six thousand pages in thir-

teen volumes. The overhaul was labeled "Operation Common Sense."

A much more dramatic reorganization occurred in 1979 when Congress voted to consolidate the education functions of HEW and several other cabinet departments in a separate Department of Education, with the remaining HEW responsibilities vested in the renamed Department of Health and Human Services.

Organization and Functions

HHS has nine offices: Inspector General, General Counsel, Civil Rights, Consumer Affairs, Management and Budget, Legislation, Personnel Administration, Public Affairs, and Planning and Evaluation. The latter five are headed by assistant secretaries. The Office of Consumer Affairs is located within HHS but reports directly to the president. The department has five operating divisions.

Office of Human Development Services

The Office of Human Development Services (HDS) oversees programs for the elderly, children and youth, families, Native Americans, rural dwellers, the handicapped, and public assistance recipients.

Within HDS, the administration on aging is designated the principal office for carrying out the provisions of the 1965 Older Americans Act. It advises the secretary and other federal departments on the characteristics and needs of older people and develops programs designed to promote their welfare. The administration for children, youth, and families manages the adoption opportunities program and discretionary grant programs providing Head Start preschool services and runaway youth facilities. The office also manages provisions of the Child Abuse Prevention and Treatment Act. The administration for Native Americans develops policies and legislation and administers grant programs designed to enhance the social and economic development of American Indians, Native Alaskans, and Native Hawaiians; it also serves as a departmental liaison with other federal agencies on issues concerning Native Americans. The administration on developmental disabilities helps states increase the provision of quality services to people with developmental disabilities through a grants program, development of standards and guidelines, technical assistance, and policy initiation.

Public Health Service

The PHS had its origin in a July 16, 1798, act which authorized a Marine Hospital Service for the care of American merchant sailors. Subsequent legislation vastly broadened the scope of its activities, and it was renamed the Public Health Service in 1912. The Public Health Service Act of July 1944 consolidated and revised substantially all existing legislation related to PHS. The service's basic responsibilities have been expanded many times since then.

PHS now administers grants to states for health services, financial assistance to educational institutions for the health professions, and national health surveys; grants to state and local agencies for comprehensive health planning; health services for American Indians and Native Alaskans; and funds for research in improving the delivery of health services. The PHS National Center for Health Services Research and Health Care Technology Assessment plans, develops, and administers a program of health services research, evaluation, research training, and related grant- and contract-supported research on the financing, organization, quality, and utilization of health services.

Within PHS, the Alcohol, Drug Abuse, and Mental Health Administration oversees the National Institute on Alcohol Abuse and Alcoholism, the National Institute on Drug Abuse, and the National Institute of Mental Health. Established by the HEW secretary in 1973, the Centers for Disease Control (CDC), based in Atlanta, Georgia, administers national programs for the prevention and control of communicable and vector-borne diseases and other preventable conditions.

The National Center for Health Statistics collects, analyzes, and disseminates health statistics, and conducts basic and applied research on health data systems and statistical methodology. The activities of the Agency for Toxic Substances and Disease Registry, established in 1983, are designed to protect both public health and worker safety and health from exposure to and the adverse effects of hazardous waste sites and hazardous substances released in fires, explosions, or transportation accidents.

The Food and Drug Administration was first established in the Agriculture Department in 1931, although similar law enforcement functions had been in existence under different organizational titles since 1907, when the 1906 Food and Drug Act became effective. The activities of FDA are directed toward protecting the health of the nation from impure and unsafe foods, drugs, and cosmetics, as well as other potential hazards. Within FDA are centers for drugs and biologics, food safety and applied nutrition, veterinary medicine, and radiological health.

The Health Resources and Service Administration develops health care and maintenance systems that are adequately financed, comprehensive, interrelated, and responsive to the public's needs. It is composed of bureaus of health care delivery and assistance, health professions, resources development, and the Indian health service.

The mission of the National Institutes of Health (NIH) is to improve the health of the American people by conducting and supporting biomedical research into the causes, prevention, and cure of diseases; supporting research training and the development of research resources; and communicating biomedical information.

Health Care Financing Administration

The HCFA was established by an internal HEW reorganization in 1977, which placed under one administration oversight of the Medicare and Medicaid programs and related federal medical care quality control staffs.

Social Security Administration

The SSA administers the national program of contributory social insurance whereby employees, employers, and the self-employed pay contributions that are pooled in special trust funds. When earnings stop or are reduced because the worker retires, dies, or becomes disabled, monthly cash benefits are paid to replace partially the earnings the family has lost. Part of the contributions go into a separate hospital insurance trust fund for Medicare. SSA also administers certain aspects of the black lung benefits provisions of the 1969 Coal Mine Health and Safety Act.

The principal SSA programs are OASDI (Old Age and Survivors Disability Insurance) and the supplemental security income (SSI) program for the aged, blind, and disabled (funds for SSI come out of general revenues rather than a special trust fund). Within SSA are ten regional offices, six program service centers, and more than thirteen hundred local offices.

Family Support Administration

The Family Support Administration (FSA) advises the HHS secretary on programs to assist children and families, especially low-income families. It recommends actions and strategies designed to improve coordination of family support programs among HHS programs, other federal agencies, state and local governments, and private sector organizations.

Department of Housing and Urban Development

After four years of lobbying by presidents John F. Kennedy and Lyndon B. Johnson, Congress elevated the federal government's role in housing to cabinet-level importance in 1965 by establishing the Department of Housing and Urban Development (HUD). This move was viewed as a response to the urgent problems arising from a situation in which more than 70 percent of the U.S. population lived in the cities and suburbs—and that percentage was growing rapidly. Programs intended to deal with the problems of urban and suburban living—housing shortages, pollution, lack of mass transit, urban renewal, inadequate roads— were in disarray, scattered among federal, state, and local governments. The results of this disarray were often illogical: a new public housing project or hospital might be located far from public transportation, while slums might be replaced by parking lots or new high-rent dwellings.

HUD is principally responsible for some 115 federal housing and urban development programs affecting the development and preservation of communities and the provision of equal housing opportunities. These programs include Federal Housing Administration (FHA) mortgage insurance programs that help families become homeowners and facilitate the construction and rehabilitation of rental units; rental assistance programs for lower-income families who otherwise are unable to afford decent housing; the Government National Mortgage Association (GNMA) mortgage-backed securities that help insure an adequate supply of mortgage credit; programs to combat housing discrimination and promote fair housing; assistance to community and neighborhood development and preservation; and programs that protect the home buyer in the marketplace.

When Ronald Reagan took office in 1981, about one of every three poor families who were renting lived in subsidized housing. HUD programs supported more than 3 million rental units—or about 11 percent of all the occupied apartments in the country. Of these, about 1.2 million units were public housing; the rest were under various federally subsidized housing programs.

Establishment of HUD was one of two major housing bills that became law in 1965. The first bill, which passed Congress on August 10, authorized rent supplements for poor persons unable to pay for decent housing from their own incomes. The bill establishing HUD soon followed and was signed into law on September 9. Accompanying legislation, passed between 1965 and 1968, gave the department additional, and controversial, responsibilities: administering rent supplements to help the poor who could not afford decent housing, a model cities program intended to pump extra federal funds into needy cities, and a program to promote home ownership by the poor.

Creation of HUD

The idea of establishing a department of housing was controversial from the time of its initial proposal by Kennedy in 1961. He promised to make House and Home Finance Agency (HHFA) Director Robert C. Weaver, a black, secretary of the new department. In the Senate, however, a leadership head count found almost solid southern Democratic and Republican opposition, ensuring defeat. Using his reorganization authority, Kennedy then submitted a plan to create a housing and urban development department, but the House disapproved the resolution to put the plan into effect.

On March 2, 1965, in his "Message on the Cities," Lyndon Johnson called for a department of housing and urban development "to give greater force and effectiveness to our effort in the cities." The president's proposal had rough sledding, however: on Senate and House roll calls, a majority of Republicans and southern Democrats voted against the bill, which nonetheless passed the House on June 16 by a 217-184 vote. The Senate concurred on August 11, with much less contention.

As signed by the president on September 9, 1965, the HUD bill (PL 89-174) basically upgraded the existing HHFA to cabinet-level status. The HHFA then consisted of the Office of the Administrator and five operating units: the Federal Housing Administration, the Public Housing Administration, and the Federal National Mortgage Association—all three of which had specific authorization in law—as well as the Community Facilities Administration and the Urban Renewal Administration—both of which were created administratively within the HHFA.

The new department was not given authority to administer all federal programs related to cities and urban problems. One section of the bill, however, required a study of the functions of other agencies to determine if any should be transferred to HUD. The bill did not attempt to define an urban area or to limit the size of communities that could benefit from a HUD program. Both small towns and villages as well as large cities were thus within the department's scope.

HUD became the eleventh cabinet-level department at midnight on November 8, under provisions of the bill ordering it created no later than sixty days after the president approved the legislation. Johnson, however, postponed HUD's actual establishment until a special study group completed a report on the government's role in solving urban problems. On January 13, 1966, he appointed HHFA Director Weaver as HUD secretary.

Development of HUD's Programs

The young department was thrust immediately into the fray of administering several major controversial and extremely complex housing laws. Rent supplements and the model cities program, as well as a program to promote home ownership by the poor, immediately came under HUD's purview. By the time Johnson left office in 1969, these programs were reasonably well established and were expected to survive. Even after the precariously close votes on enactment of the basic authorization, however, Congress threatened several times to deny implementing funds.

By the late 1970s the federal government was providing a wide range of housing assistance, including direct mortgage and rent subsidies and government-insured mortgages, loans, secondary market programs, and programs designed to help special-risk homeowners and renters. In addition to HUD, the Veterans Administration and the Department of Agriculture's Farmers Home Administration participated in these programs.

During the presidency of Jimmy Carter, attention turned to revising community development programs intended to improve the nation's cities and counties. In 1977 the administration introduced a new urban development program—Urban Development Action Grants (UDAG)—which was an immediate success among the nation's cities. Aimed at urban areas with the most severe problems, UDAG used federal funds to spur private investment. But a year later, Congress decided to take away some of HUD's authority to regulate community development projects. HUD Secretary Patricia Harris had wanted to require cities to spend 75 percent of federal community development funds for projects benefiting low- and moderate-income persons. After strenuous objection from House Banking Committee members, however, HUD retreated from the proposal and required instead that at least 51 percent of the block grant funds (federal money given to state and local governments to fund a group—or "block"— of programs) be set aside for low- and middle-income projects. In addition, the final legislation allowed the House and Senate banking committees to review all proposed regulations and delay their effective date for ninety days.

By 1980 the fights over allocating community development funds had subsided. The Reagan administration, however, proposed a fundamental shift in federal housing and urban policies in the early 1980s. Blight, housing shortages, and economic decline, Reagan said, represented the failure of past federal social programs. He consistently sought to reduce the federal role in solving urban problems, while increasing incentives for a larger role by the private sector. Although the president persuaded Congress to accept substantial reductions in federal housing programs, lawmakers resisted his attempts to eliminate or sharply curtail community development and other projects.

Reagan continued his effort to cut the housing budget in 1988, proposing a $13.8 billion reduction in HUD's budget, which would kill urban development action grants, rental development grants, economic development assistance grants, and loans for redevelopment and rehabilitation assistance. Early in the year the administration was the subject of congressional criticism when it came to light that HUD Secretary Samuel R. Pierce, Jr., had not testified before any of the agency's three oversight committees for almost three years.

Organization and Functions

The HUD secretary is assisted by an undersecretary and two deputy undersecretaries (intergovernmental relations and field coordination). The office of the secretary also contains five staff offices with department-wide responsibility in specialized functional areas: Indian and Alaskan Native programs, small and disadvantaged business utilization, labor relations, international affairs, administrative and judicial proceedings, and contract appeals.

In addition to the general counsel and inspector general offices, there are eight assistant secretaries, who are responsible for public affairs, legislation and congressional relations, administration, community planning and development, fair housing and equal opportunity, housing-federal housing, public and Indian housing, and policy development and research. HUD also maintains numerous regional and field offices.

The GNMA, a government corporation within the department, administers support programs for government-sponsored mortgages through its mortgage-backed securities programs. The latter are designed to increase liquidity in the secondary mortgage market and attract new sources of financing for residential loans.

Department of the Interior

As the nation's principal conservation agency, the U.S. Department of the Interior is responsible for more than 549 million acres of public lands, or about 28 percent of the total U.S. land area. The Department of Agriculture oversees the nation's forests.

During the nation's early years, functions that would be carried out by an "interior," "home," or "internal affairs" department were apportioned by Congress among other agencies. To streamline these activities, proposals to establish a home office were made as early as 1789, but to no avail.

Shortly before the War of 1812 a House committee appointed to study the operations and organization of the Patent Office revived the idea of setting up a separate home department. And in 1816, after the war, a cabinet report recommended that a new home department be established to supervise territorial governments, construction of federal highways and canals, and the Post Office, Patent Office, and Indian Office. President James Madison endorsed the report, and a bill was introduced in the Senate in 1817, but again no action was taken.

Interest in creating a home department lagged during the next decade. Various efforts to establish one were made between 1827 and 1849, but none proved successful until 1848 and the administration of James K. Polk. In December of that year Secretary of the Treasury Robert J. Walker sent Congress a proposal to create a Department of the Interior. Before becoming Treasury secretary, Walker had served in the Senate (D-Miss.) and chaired its Committee on Public Lands. During the 1830s he had advocated selling public lands solely to settlers to discourage land speculation. That policy served as the basis of his plan to establish a new executive department.

By the late 1840s the Treasury Department had become burdened by increasing fiscal duties, and Walker did not wish to become involved in managing the vast domain acquired from the Louisiana Purchase of 1803, the Mexican War of 1846-1848, and the 1848 treaty with Great Britain by which the United States acquired the Oregon Territory. The nation's expansion, he argued, had made the responsibilities of the Treasury greater than it could handle.

Congressional Struggle over Interior

On February 12, 1849, the House Ways and Means Committee reported out a bill to establish a Department of the Interior. Samuel F. Vinton, an Ohio Whig and chairman of the committee, was a key figure in securing enactment of the legislation. The House passed the bill three days later with only minimal debate. The Senate Finance Committee reported out the bill on March 3, the last day of the Thirtieth Congress. That night, in a dramatic session, the full Senate chamber approved the measure by a margin of only six votes, 31-25.

"The bill to establish the Home Department has become law, having passed the Senate after a long, arduous and rather stormy debate; and a new and valuable Department has thus been added to the Government," noted the Washington, D.C., *Daily National Intelligencer* on March 5, 1849.

Almost one hundred years later, Harold L. Ickes, a longtime secretary of the interior (1933-1946) and one of the most famous of its chiefs, speculated that the long delay in establishing the department resulted primarily from "States' rights and the ever occurring problem of expenditures in government."

Congress transferred to the new Interior Department the General Land Office from the Treasury Department, the Patent Office from the State Department, and the Bureau of Indian Affairs and Pension Office from the War Department. Other responsibilities assigned to the department included supervision of the commissioner of public buildings, the Board of Inspectors, the Warden of the Penitentiary of the District of Columbia, and the Census of the United States, as well as the accounts of marshals and other officers of the U.S. courts and the accounts of lead and other kinds of mines in the United States.

Evolution of the Department's Policy

For a long time Interior's policy mirrored the more general public sentiment that natural resources were the limitless foundation on which a powerful nation could be built. As a result, public policy on their exploitation was extremely permissive.

Gradually, however, Americans realized that their natural resources were not inexhaustible. The environmental movement of the 1960s and 1970s resulted in the establishment of a Council on Environmental Quality and the Environmental Protection Agency, which share responsibility for overseeing natural resources with Interior. The Energy Department, created in 1977 in response to growing awareness of the need to conserve fuel resources, also plays a role in establishing environmental policy.

Throughout most of the 1960s environmentalists found an ally in Interior Secretary Stewart L. Udall, a former representative (D-Ariz.), who was appointed to the position by President John F. Kennedy. Udall had been a well-known supporter of conservation, reclamation, and national park improvement during his tenure in the House. As interior secretary, he added significantly to the department's role in water planning, outdoor recreation, and national parks programs.

The federal government's philosophy underwent an abrupt turnaround with Richard Nixon's selection of Walter J. Hickel to succeed Udall. Hickel's nomination became controversial after conservation groups questioned his dedication to natural preservation and others criticized his ties with oil companies. At a December 1968 news conference he stated that he was opposed to "conservation for conservation's sake" and that the high national standards for clean water "might even hinder industrial development."

Hickel was criticized for his opposition, as governor of Alaska, to plans to create a foreign trade subzone for oil at Machiasport, Maine, which would result in cheaper fuel for New England. Another complaint concerned his opposition, as governor, to an Interior Department freeze on the status of Alaskan public lands until Congress settled pending claims to the land by Native Alaskans.

Despite the controversy the Senate confirmed Hickel's nomination. The Alaskan claims, giving natives 40 million acres of land and $962.5 million, were cleared in 1971, but Hickel's ideology and outspokenness led to his downfall; the president fired him in November 1970.

The environmental movement waned during the early 1970s, but President Jimmy Carter's appointment of conservationist Idaho governor Cecil D. Andrus as interior secretary brought praise from environmentalists and criticism from mining, logging, and other development interests. While Interior was headed by Andrus (1977-1981), major legislation was enacted to control strip mining, protect millions of acres of wilderness in Alaska, and clean up chemical contamination.

Although conservationists generally found an ally in the interior secretary, President Ronald Reagan's first appointee to the post, James G. Watt, aroused considerable controversy when he attempted to instigate broad changes in the department's programs and personnel. Although he was generally considered an able administrator, Watt's rhetoric was occasionally abrasive. Moreover, his philosophy of emphasizing private use of resources in the public domain and of returning to the states more control over government lands did not sit well with environmentalists.

Initially, Reagan stood by his secretary, but Watt was forced to resign in October 1983. He was succeeded by William P. Clark, who took over temporarily and was followed in 1985 by Donald P. Hodel, who had been secretary of energy and previously had served as undersecretary of interior under Watt.

Organization and Functions

The Interior Department consists of some thirty major bureaus and offices. The secretary is responsible for meshing departmental activities with the assistance of an undersecretary and five assistant secretaries (fish and wildlife and parks, Indian affairs, land and minerals management, territorial and international affairs, and water and science). An assistant secretary for policy, budget, and administration serves as principal policy adviser to the secretary. The department is divided into functional offices, which are responsible for a wide variety of managerial, regulatory, promotional, planning, and research activities.

The Bureau of Mines is primarily a research and statistics-gathering agency. It also frequently produces special studies on subjects of particular national interest, such as the effects of potential economic, technological, or legal developments on resource availability.

The U.S. Geological Survey (USGS) was established in 1879 to provide a permanent federal agency to conduct the systematic and scientific "classification of the public lands, and examination of the geological structure, mineral resources, and products of the national domain." USGS is the federal government's largest earth science research agency, the nation's largest civilian mapmaking agency, the primary source of data on the nation's surface water and groundwater resources, and the employer of the largest number of professional earth scientists.

The Bureau of Indian Affairs (BIA) is the federal agency with primary responsibility for working with Indian tribal governments and the village communities of Native Alaskans. Other federal agencies may deal with Indians or Native Alaskans as members of an ethnic group or simply as individuals, but the BIA is distinctive in that it deals with them as governments in a government-to-government relationship. For one of its principal programs, BIA administers and manages some 52 million acres of land held in trust by the United States for Indians.

The mandate of the U.S. Fish and Wildlife Service is to conserve, protect, and enhance fish, wildlife, and their habitats. Its primary focus is on migratory birds, endangered species, freshwater and anadromous fisheries, and certain marine mammals. Headquartered in Washington, D.C., the service has seven regional offices and numerous field units, including national wildlife refuges, national fish hatcheries, research laboratories, and a nationwide network of law enforcement agents.

Established in 1946, the Bureau of Land Management oversees about 300 million acres of public lands, located primarily in the West and in Alaska and comprising about one-eighth of the total U.S. land area. Day-to-day management of these lands and related resources is decentralized into twelve state offices.

The 1977 Surface Mining Control and Reclamation Act established the Office of Surface Mining to collect funds from coal companies and provide disbursements for reclamation of coal lands mined before August 1977. The office also establishes and enforces standards and regulations ensuring that current and future mining will be environmentally sound.

The Bureau of Reclamation was chartered in 1902 to reclaim the arid lands of the western United States for farming by providing a secure, year-round supply of water for irrigation. Among its most notable projects were the Grand Coulee Dam on the Columbia River and Hoover Dam on the Colorado River. In addition to irrigation, the bureau's responsibilities include hydroelectric power generation, municipal and industrial water supplies, river regulation and flood control, outdoor recreation, enhancement of fish and wildlife habitats, and research.

The Minerals Management Service, created in 1982, is responsible for establishing an effective means of collecting revenues generated from mineral leases offshore (including the outer continental shelf) and on federal and Indian lands. It is also charged with the orderly development of offshore energy and mineral resources while safeguarding the environment. These funds, the largest federal source of revenue outside the Treasury Department, are distributed in turn to Indian tribes and the appropriate states, the Land and Water Conservation Fund, the Historic Preservation Fund, and the U.S. Treasury.

The National Park Service, established in 1916, administers the National Park System, which comprises more than 330 parks, monuments, historic sites, battlefields, seashores and lakeshores, and recreation areas. The service also directs programs that assist states, other federal agencies, local governments, and individuals in the protection of historical, natural, architectural, engineering, and archeological resources that lie outside the National Park System. It maintains the National Register of Historic Places and a registry of natural sites.

The office of the assistant secretary for territorial and international affairs is responsible for coordinating federal policy in the territories of American Samoa, Guam, the Virgin Islands, the Commonwealth of the Northern Mariana Islands, and the Trust Territory of the Pacific. The office also oversees and coordinates various international activities of the Interior Department.

Department of Justice

The U.S. attorney general was one of the first positions to be established, with cabinet rank, in the federal government. The Judiciary Act of September 24, 1789, made the attorney general the chief legal officer of the federal government. At the time, the nation's top law officer was assisted by one clerk. The Department of Justice itself was established in 1870, with the attorney general as its head. Through its thousands of lawyers, investigators, and agents, the department investigates violations of federal law (ranging from income tax evasion to criminal syndicates), supervises the custody of those accused or convicted of federal crimes, oversees legal and illegal aliens, and directs U.S. domestic security when the nation is threatened by foreign or internal subversion. Moreover, Justice polices narcotics trafficking; helps state and local governments increase their numbers of police departments, courts, and correctional institutions (through federal aid); advises the president and other government agencies on legal matters; and drafts legislation. The Justice Department also conducts all suits in the Supreme Court to which the U.S. government is a party. The attorney general supervises and directs these activities, as well as those of the U.S. attorneys and U.S. marshals in the nation's ninety-four judicial districts.

Despite its staggering number of lawyers (the department employs about five thousand attorneys), Justice is one of the smallest cabinet departments. Writer Richard Harris has noted that "the federal government has only a small fraction of the manpower that is required to combat crime nationally," largely because the Constitution gives the policing power to the states. Nonetheless, Harris observed, "Limited as the federal role is . . . it can be critically significant. . . . [I]t provides a model for every lesser jurisdiction, and the federal government's overall approach . . . will probably determine whether or not the nation's traditional freedoms are preserved." [30]

Evolution of the Department in the 1950s and 1960s

Before the 1960s the department's mission was perceived as primarily one of prosecuting violations of the Internal Revenue Code, instituting some antitrust suits, and keeping watch over "subversives" and "public enemies." In the 1960s, however, Justice became intimately involved with major domestic issues—racial violence, mass demonstrations, riots, draft resistance to the Vietnam War, and rising crime rates, among others. To cope with its

increased responsibilities the department created a number of new divisions, and by 1970 Justice had 208 units.

Crime as a national political issue became the most emotionally charged, and perhaps the most crucial, of all domestic concerns in the 1968 elections. President Lyndon B. Johnson's attorney general, Ramsey Clark, was keenly interested in civil rights, but it was his approach to crime that brought him the greatest criticism and made him an issue in the 1968 presidential campaign. An uncompromising opponent of efforts to maintain order at the expense of due process, Clark became a natural target of those who advocated a "get tough" policy on crime. "If we are going to restore order and respect for law in this country, there's one place we're going to begin; we're going to have a new attorney general of the United States of America," stated Richard Nixon on accepting the Republican presidential nomination.

Nixon's "War on Crime" and Watergate

Crime was increasing at a frightening pace when Nixon was sworn in for his first term in 1969, elected on a tough "law and order" platform. But five years and billions of dollars later, with stringent new federal anticrime laws in place, the crime rate was still climbing. Late in 1974, plain-spoken attorney general William B. Saxbe declared the war on crime a "dismal failure." But even before Nixon left office in 1974, national opinion polls showed that the public's attention had shifted away from concern with street crime to economic problems, the energy crisis, and Watergate.

Climbing even more swiftly than the crime rate during the Nixon/Ford years was the amount of federal dollars spent on law enforcement. In fiscal year 1971 the Justice Department had its first billion dollar budget. In fiscal year 1975 its budget hit $2 billion. Justice spending levelled off just above the $2 billion mark in fiscal year 1976.

It was a peculiar twist on the "law and order" theme of the Nixon administration: the crimes that drew national attention in its last years were those committed by or charged against some of its highest officials, including the president himself. Among the Nixon administration officials accused of crimes during this period was Attorney General John N. Mitchell. Mitchell was convicted in early 1975 of conspiracy and obstruction of justice for his participation in the effort to cover up White House involvement in the Watergate break-in at Democratic National Headquarters in June 1972. The attorney general, who was also Nixon's campaign manager, was aloof, blunt, and a product of Wall Street. Unlike Clark, Mitchell stated that he believed Justice "was an institution for law enforcement, not social improvement." [31]

In 1972 Mitchell was replaced by Richard G. Kleindienst, who pleaded guilty in May 1974 to charges that he did not testify fully before the Senate Judiciary Committee when it was investigating charges that political pressure had figured in the settlement of the government's case against the International Telephone and Telegraph Corporation. After Kleindienst was forced to leave office in 1973, Secretary of Defense Elliott L. Richardson took over. He resigned on October 10, 1973, however, rather than obey the president's order to fire special Watergate prosecutor Archibald Cox. Nixon then selected William Saxbe as attorney general.

Justice under Ford, Carter, and Reagan

With the accession of Gerald R. Ford to the presidency, the tone of the administration's anticrime effort changed markedly. Emphasizing that law enforcement should focus more upon the needs of the victims of crime than upon the criminal, Ford asked Congress to authorize financial aid for the victims of crime, to approve a revised criminal code, to provide mandatory minimum sentencing for certain crimes, to provide for more consistency in sentences, and to enact a mild control on gun ownership.

Crime was not a top priority in the White House or on Capitol Hill from 1977 to 1980. Access to justice, rather than a war on crime, was the theme of the Carter administration's law enforcement program. That emphasis was explicable in light of the fact that the top two law enforcement officials in the administration—Attorney General Griffin B. Bell and Federal Bureau of Investigation Director William Webster—had served a total of more than twenty years on the federal bench before moving to the executive branch posts. In the Justice Department, Bell set up a new entity, the Office for Improvements in the Administration of Justice. Out of that office came proposals to expand the powers of federal magistrates—a measure that was passed in 1979.

For the most part, crime was mentioned little during Ronald Reagan's first years in office, even though the nation appeared more concerned about this issue than it had been during Carter's administration. The Federal Bureau of Investigation (FBI) nevertheless became a billion dollar operation for the first time in fiscal year 1984, spending more than the entire federal court system, whose funding rose from $631 million in fiscal year 1981 to $977.9 million in fiscal year 1985.

William French Smith, once Reagan's personal lawyer, served as attorney general throughout Reagan's first term, but he resigned in January 1984 to return to his law practice. Reagan then announced the nomination of White House counselor Edwin Meese III, one of his closest advisers, to succeed Smith. Questions about Meese's personal finances, however, led to a prolonged investigation that delayed Senate confirmation until 1985. As attorney general, Meese was criticized for his failure to conduct a thorough investigation of the Iran arms sales and contra aid scandal when it became public in November 1986. He also was probed for connections with individuals tied to a New York defense contractor, the Bronx-based Wedtech Corporation, which was the subject of federal investigations of fraud and bribery of public officials. In 1987 independent counsel James C. McKay was appointed to investigate Meese's personal finances, his involvement with Wedtech, and several other instances of alleged wrongdoing. After a fourteen-month investigation, McKay concluded in an 814-page report made public July 18, 1988, that although he would not indict Meese for criminal wrongdoing, the attorney general had "probably violated" the law. Before the report's release, Meese had announced on July 5 that he intended to resign in August. He left Justice on August 12, and Reagan appointed Dick Thornburgh to replace him.

Organization and Functions

The office of the attorney general provides overall policy and program direction for the offices, divisions, bureaus, and boards of the department. The office represents the United States in legal matters generally; it also makes recommendations to the president about appointments to federal judicial positions.

The attorney general is assisted by a deputy attorney general and associate attorney general, who are the principal agents for managing the department. In addition to offices, the department consists of seven divisions: offices and services, antitrust, civil, civil rights, criminal, land and natural resources, and tax—all of which are headed by assistant attorneys general.

Divisions

In the *Offices and Services Division,* the Solicitor General's Office supervises and conducts government litigation in the Supreme Court. Such litigation comprises about two-thirds of all cases decided by the Court each year. The Solicitor General, often called the "tenth justice" of the Court, determines for which cases the government will seek Supreme Court review as well as the position the government will take in the Court. Another function of the office is to decide which cases, of those lost before the lower courts, the United States should appeal.

The assistant attorney general in charge of the Office of Legal Counsel drafts the formal opinions of the attorney general and provides his or her own written opinion and informal advice in response to requests. The staff frequently prepares and delivers testimony to Congress on a variety of legal issues, particularly constitutional matters such as legislative vetoes, executive privilege, and the power of the president to enter into executive agreements.

Established in early 1981, the Office of Legal Policy is a strategic legal "think tank," which serves as the attorney general's principal policy development staff. The Office of Intelligence Policy and Review provides legal advice and recommendations on national security matters. It reviews executive orders, directives, and procedures related to the intelligence community and approves certain intelligence-gathering activities.

The Office of the Pardon Attorney receives and reviews all petitions for executive clemency, initiates the necessary investigations, and recommends to the president which form of executive clemency—including pardon, commutation of sentence, remission of fine, and reprieve—it finds appropriate.

The assistant attorney general in charge of the Office of Legislative Affairs is responsible for liaison between the department and Congress.

The Community Relations Service (CRS), created by Title X of the Civil Rights Act of 1964, falls under the general authority of the attorney general and is headed by a director, who is appointed by the president with the advice and consent of the Senate. The CRS helps resolve disputes through its field staff of mediators and conciliators, who work out of ten regional offices. It also is charged with integration into the United States of the almost 180,000 Cubans and Haitians who have entered the country since 1980 without documentation or imminent prospects of returning to their homelands.

Under the direction of the assistant attorney general for administration, the Justice Management Division assists senior management officials with matters related to basic department policy for selected management operations and provides direct administrative services to offices, boards, and divisions of the department.

The Office of Professional Responsibility, which reports directly to the attorney general, oversees investigations of allegations of criminal or ethical misconduct by employees of the department.

The Office of Liaison Services represents the department in dealings with other governments and with nongovernmental organizations—both foreign and domestic—interested in the justice field.

Under the supervision of the deputy attorney general, the Executive Office for United States Attorneys provides the ninety-four offices of U.S. attorneys with general executive assistance and nonlitigative oversight, and it publishes the *United States Attorneys' Manual* and the *United States Attorneys' Bulletin.*

U.S. trustees insure compliance with the federal bankruptcy laws and supervise the administration of cases and trustees in cases filed under Title I of the 1978 Bankruptcy Code. Formerly established as a pilot program with limited jurisdiction, the U.S. trustee program—under the Bankruptcy Judges, United States Trustees, and Family Farmer Bankruptcy Act of 1986—is a permanent, nationwide system for the administration of bankruptcy cases.

U.S. marshals serve as executive officers of the federal courts and agents of the Department of Justice. They and their staffs are located in each of the ninety-four federal judicial districts encompassing the fifty states, Guam, Puerto Rico, the Virgin Islands, and the Northern Mariana Islands. The director of the service provides overall supervision.

As a law enforcement agency, the *Antitrust Division* prosecutes criminal and civil antitrust cases, primarily under the Sherman and Clayton Antitrust acts. The division also appears as a competition advocate before congressional committees and federal regulatory agencies.

The *Civil Division* is known as the "government's lawyer." This is sometimes a complicated role, because in every case there are two clients: the agency concerned and the people of the United States. The division's clients include more than a hundred federal agencies and commissions, individual federal employees acting in their official capacities, and, in some instances, members of Congress and the federal judiciary. The division's litigation is organized into six areas: commercial litigation, federal programs, torts, appellate staff, immigration litigation, and consumer litigation.

Established in 1957, the *Civil Rights Division* enforces the nation's laws and executive orders related to civil rights. The division works primarily on litigation and connected matters. Except for criminal law enforcement work, where cases normally are tried before a jury, suits filed by the division are in equity, usually before a single judge and seeking injunctive relief.

The assistant attorney general in charge of the *Criminal Division* formulates criminal law enforcement policies and enforces and generally supervises all federal criminal laws except those specifically assigned to the other divisions. This division—by far the most active of the principal Justice divisions—also supervises certain civil litigation related to federal law enforcement activities (such as federal liquor, narcotics, counterfeiting, gambling, firearms, customs, agriculture, and immigration laws). It supervises as well litigation resulting from petitions for writs of habeas corpus by members of the armed forces, actions brought by or on behalf of federal prisoners, alleged investigative misconduct, and legal actions related to national security issues.

The *Land and Natural Resources Division* represents the United States in litigation involving public lands and natural resources, environmental quality, Indian lands and claims, and wildlife resources. The fastest growing area of its responsibility involves civil and criminal enforcement of environmental statutes.

In all courts except the U.S. Tax Court, the *Tax Division* represents the United States and its officers in civil and criminal litigation involving federal, state, and local taxes. The Internal Revenue Service (IRS) is the division's principal client. For IRS, the division collects federal revenues by instituting many types of actions at the request of IRS and defends tax refund and other suits brought by taxpayers.

Bureaus

Established in 1908, the Federal Bureau of Investigation is the principal investigative arm of the department. It is charged with gathering and reporting facts, locating witnesses, and compiling evidence in cases involving federal jurisdiction.

The Federal Bureau of Prisons is responsible for the care and custody of persons convicted of federal crimes and sentenced by the courts to incarceration in a federal penal institution. The bureau operates a nationwide system of maximum, medium, and minimum security prisons and community program offices.

The International Criminal Police Organization–United States National Central Bureau (INTERPOL-USNCB) was created to promote mutual assistance between all law enforcement authorities in the prevention and suppression of international crime. Established in 1923 and reorganized in 1946, INTERPOL has grown from an organization composed of a few European countries to a worldwide consortium of 142 member countries. In 1977 Justice and Treasury officials were given dual authority in administering INTERPOL-USNCB.

The Immigration and Naturalization Service, established in 1891, has four major areas of responsibility: (1) aliens entering the United States (controlling entry into the country, facilitating the entry of qualified persons, and denying admission to illegal aliens); (2) aliens within the United States (providing immigration benefits, maintaining information on alien status, and deporting illegal aliens); (3) naturalization and citizenship; and (4) aliens who enter illegally or whose authorized stay in the United States has expired (apprehending and removing such individuals).

The Drug Enforcement Administration (DEA) is the lead federal agency in enforcing the laws and regulations governing narcotics and controlled substances. Created in 1973, DEA concentrates on high-level narcotics smuggling and distribution organizations in the United States and abroad, working closely with such agencies as the Customs Service, the Internal Revenue Service, and the Coast Guard.

The Justice Assistance Act of 1984 restructured the criminal justice research and statistics units of the department and established a program of financial and technical assistance to state and local governments. The act also established the Office of Justice Programs, headed by an assistant attorney general, to coordinate the activities of some existing offices (such as statistics and juvenile justice and delinquency prevention) and to oversee a new program designed to locate and recover missing children.

Boards

Seven boards are associated with the Justice Department. They are the Executive Office for Immigration Review, Board of Immigration Appeals, Office of the Chief Immigration Judge, Office of the Immigration Judge, Office of the Chief Administrative Hearing Officer, United States Parole Commission, and Foreign Claims Settlement Commission of the United States.

Department of Labor

On March 4, 1913, President William Howard Taft signed a bill that established a cabinet-level department "to foster, promote, and develop the welfare of the wage earners of the United States, to improve their working conditions, and to advance their opportunities for profitable employment." Although the beginnings of the Department of Labor were rather small and somewhat inauspicious, the department was enforcing more than 140 laws by the 1980s. They deal with wide-ranging and significant areas of workers' well-being, including unemployment insurance and workers' compensation, minimum wages and overtime pay, occupational health and safety, antidiscrimination in employment, protection of pension rights, job training, and strengthening free collective bargaining. The department compiles statistics on prices, employment, and other appropriate subjects and strives to solve the job market problems of minorities, youth, older workers, women, and disadvantaged and disabled groups.

Background

As labor unions grew in strength, pressures increased after the Civil War to create a federal office that represented workers. This effort was led by William Sylvis, a well-known labor leader, who contended that existing federal departments were closely tied to wealthy businesses, and there was no federal agency that had as its "sole object the care and protection of labor." Sylvis and others lobbied President Andrew Johnson to support a secretary of labor, with cabinet status, to be selected from labor's ranks. According to labor historian Jonathan Grossman, more than one hundred bills and resolutions to create a labor department were introduced in Congress between 1864 and 1900.[32]

In 1884 Congress passed and President Chester A. Arthur signed a bill that established a Bureau of Labor in the Interior Department. The bureau was to gather information pertaining to workers and devise a "means of promoting their material, social, intellectual, and moral prosperity."

It took some time for Arthur to name the first commissioner of labor. The unions had expected that he would appoint Terence Powderly, leader of the Knights of Labor union, but the president apparently found Powderly too radical. Instead, he appointed Carroll D. Wright of the Massachusetts Bureau of Labor Statistics. Under Wright's leadership the new bureau flourished.

Arthur's successor, Grover Cleveland, pressed for enlarging the bureau and empowering it to investigate and arbitrate labor disputes. The Knights of Labor lobbied for creation of a cabinet-level department and succeeded in

having a bill introduced in 1888. The legislation was watered down, however; the bill that emerged, with little debate, established an independent Department of Labor, without cabinet status. Cleveland signed the legislation on March 21 and chose Wright to head the new agency.

Over the next few years the department gained in stature as the most important federal statistics-gathering agency and as author of significant reports on such subjects as labor legislation, compulsory insurance, housing, railroad labor, and the status of women in the work force. In 1895, it began publishing the *Bulletin of Labor* (today called the *Monthly Labor Review*).

Merger, then Independence

On becoming president after William McKinley's assassination, Theodore Roosevelt suggested appointing a secretary of commerce and industries, with cabinet status. "It should be his province to deal with commerce in its broadest sense, including among many other things whatever concerns labor and all matters affecting the great business corporations. . . ." Legislation reflecting this view was introduced in the Fifty-seventh Congress. It was opposed vigorously by Democrats, who argued that mutual distrust between business and labor would paralyze the department and that the powers of the existing independent Department of Labor would in fact be weakened. But Republicans, who were in the majority, responded that the two groups had mutual interests and that a new department would be more efficient in obtaining and synthesizing economic information scattered through existing departments. Their position predominated; legislation creating the new department, its name changed to the Department of Commerce and Labor, was signed into law in February 1903.

Democrats won control of the House in 1910, and fifteen union members were elected to Congress. Rep. William Sulzer (D-N.Y.) introduced a Department of Labor bill in 1912; it cleared both chambers and was signed into law on March 4, 1913. Although President Taft opposed the bill, a veto was fruitless: President-elect Woodrow Wilson had already selected William B. Wilson, a trade unionist and member of the House (D-Pa.), to be his secretary of labor.

During its early years the fledgling department faced rough going: businesses distrusted it, and conservative members of Congress slashed at its funds and functions. For many years Labor was the smallest and least influential cabinet department. But under President Franklin D. Roosevelt's labor secretary, Frances Perkins (the first woman named to the cabinet), the department's authority and stature grew considerably. Thereafter, other functions and responsibilities were added to the department's purview with the passage of significant labor relations legislation and Supreme Court decisions upholding these acts and workers' rights in general.

From the viewpoint of organized labor, the administration of Lyndon B. Johnson produced one of the most fruitful legislative periods in American history with the enactment of Johnson's "Great Society" programs. Congress also cleared an administration measure for far-reaching extension of minimum wage coverage and increases in the pay floor. Business interests and their allies emerged victorious, however, over both the labor unions and the administration when Congress refused to enact laws expanding unemployment compensation and lifting restrictions on construction site picketing by striking unions. Overseeing labor's interests during these years was secretary W. Willard Wirtz, who had served under the administration of John F. Kennedy and remained through the Johnson presidency. He figured in several critical labor-management confrontations.

Labor interests did not fare so well under Richard Nixon's presidency, when the administration was bent on cutting back on domestic social programs. Jimmy Carter's administration began optimistically enough—labor interests had hoped to take advantage of a labor-supported president and Congress—but those hopes quickly faded. Although Congress enacted traditional labor legislation measures such as an increase in the minimum wage, it rejected or qualified a number of items on labor's agenda. This happened despite the efforts of Carter's labor secretary, F. Ray Marshall, whose nomination had broad appeal to key elements of Carter's coalition: unions, civil rights groups, and the South. Marshall brought with him a distinguished career in economics—his work focused on employment problems of blacks and rural human resource and poverty issues.

Labor Secretaries in the 1980s

The influence of organized labor declined during the Reagan presidency. Moreover, the voice of labor's representative in the cabinet was weakened when Reagan's first labor secretary, Raymond J. Donovan, resigned his post March 15, 1985. Donovan was the last member of Reagan's original cabinet to win Senate approval because his confirmation was held up by the Senate Labor and Human Resources Committee. It was investigating charges, made by a Federal Bureau of Investigation informer, that Donovan and Schiavone Construction Company, a New Jersey firm Donovan had worked for since 1958, had provided illegal payoffs to corrupt union officials to maintain "labor peace." Other informants said the company had close ties with organized crime. Although the Senate did confirm the appointment, with only Democrats dissenting, a special prosecutor was appointed in December 1981 to investigate the charges, and in October 1984 a grand jury named Donovan in a 137-count indictment. Donovan pleaded not guilty, but he asked for a leave of absence. He resigned after a New York Supreme Court judge refused to dismiss larceny and fraud charges against him. On May 25, 1987, he was acquitted.

Reagan's choice of U.S. Trade Representative William E. Brock III to succeed Donovan drew praise from organized labor. "While we have not always agreed [with Brock], he has earned our respect," said AFL-CIO President Lane Kirkland.[33] Throughout Donovan's tenure, Labor's budget cuts and allegedly lax enforcement of labor laws had come under steady criticism from union officials, most of whom opposed Reagan's reelection in 1984.

Brock resigned in November 1987, and Reagan named Ann Dore McLaughlin to succeed him. McLaughlin, whose specialty was public affairs, had not worked in the Labor Department but had held ranking posts in Treasury and Interior. She was handily confirmed on December 11, 1987. McLaughlin had three goals: (1) ensure enforcement of the existing labor statutes; (2) use changes in the work force—largely the growing proportion of women—as an opportunity to galvanize labor and management to solve problems such as child care; and (3) along with the Education and Commerce departments, move quickly to develop retraining and education for workers in the fast-changing economy.

Organization and Functions

The secretary of labor is assisted by a deputy secretary and deputy undersecretaries for international affairs and for labor management relations and cooperative programs. The department has four assistant secretaries in charge of congressional affairs, public and intergovernmental affairs, administration and management, and policy. The secretary's office includes the Women's Bureau, an inspector general, a solicitor, the Benefits Review Board, the Employees' Compensation Appeals Board, the Office of Administrative Law Judges, and the Wage Appeals Board.

In addition to the commissioner of labor statistics, there are seven assistant secretaries responsible for the following areas: occupational safety and health, employment and training, labor management standards, mine safety and health, pension and welfare benefit programs, veterans' employment and training services, and employment standards.

The department's functions that most affect the lives of American workers include those administered by the Employment and Training Office, which is responsible for employment services, work experience, work training, and unemployment insurance. This office operates a Job Training Partnership Program, in which more than a million people (more than 40 percent are youths) participate. It also runs summer youth programs and a program to assist dislocated workers (primarily those affected by plant closings), and it oversees an employment and training program for Native Americans. The Job Corps provides a wide range of training, educational, and support services for disadvantaged youths aged sixteen to twenty-one. The Senior Community Service Employment Program helps older Americans obtain employment. The office administers as well apprenticeship programs and claims for unemployment benefits.

The Labor-Management Office assists collective bargaining negotiators, protects veterans' reemployment rights, oversees labor organizations through the Labor Management Reporting and Disclosure Act, and aids employees and unions in meeting problems caused by technological change.

The Employment Standards Office deals with minimum wage and overtime standards through its wage and hour division and attempts to achieve nondiscrimination in employment by federal contractors through the Office of Federal Contract Compliance Programs. Federal workers' compensation programs also are under the purview of this office.

Worker safety and health concerns are the responsibility of the Occupational Safety and Health Administration, which formulates safety and health standards for the workplace, and the Mine Safety and Health Administration, which operates in all types of mines.

The Bureau of Labor Statistics is the principal fact-finding agency for data on labor requirements, labor force, employment, unemployment, hours of work, wages and employee compensation, productivity, technological developments, and general economic trends. It publishes the *Monthly Labor Review, Consumer Price Index, Employ-*

ment and Earnings, Current Wage Developments, Producer Prices and Price Indexes, and *Occupational Outlook Quarterly,* among numerous other publications.

Department of State

Although it has far-flung responsibilities, the State Department—the senior executive department of the U.S. government—has remained one of the smallest departments in the cabinet. About one-third of its approximately nineteen thousand employees serve domestically; of the two-thirds serving abroad, slightly more than one-third are American citizens, and the rest are foreign nationals. Of the cabinet departments, State has the smallest budget even though it includes U.S. contributions to seventy-five multinational organizations and their affiliates. Americans employed by the department are members of either the Civil Service or the Foreign Service. Those in the Civil Service generally do not serve abroad, while Foreign Service personnel spend approximately 60 percent of their years of service in foreign countries.

History of the Department

The present-day Department of State had its beginnings in 1781, when Congress established a Department of Foreign Affairs, redesignated the Department of State in September 1789. During Secretary Thomas Jefferson's tenure (1789-1793), the department consisted of five clerks, two messengers, and a part-time translator of French. It maintained legations in London and Paris, a diplomatic agency in The Hague, and two consular missions. Only ten persons were added to the staff in the ensuing thirty years.

The department was reorganized by Secretary Louis McLane (1833-1834) into seven bureaus dealing with diplomatic, consular, internal, and servicing functions. That arrangement continued until 1870, when Secretary Hamilton Fish (1869-1877) split the diplomatic and consular bureaus into two geographically oriented units. In the early 1900s secretaries Elihu Root (1905-1909) and Philander C. Knox (1909-1913) reorganized the department into regional divisions, the basis for the contemporary structure. The 1924 Rogers Act combined the diplomatic and consular services in a single Foreign Service.

Throughout the 1920s and 1930s most of the State Department's work was carried out by its geographical divisions, which formulated policy and drafted instructions. Because of the small size of the divisions, it was relatively easy to conduct the nation's foreign policy. World War II, however, thrust the United States into the unambiguous position of world leader. Responding to the expansion of State's activities, Secretary Cordell Hull (1933-1944) regrouped related functions under individual assistant secretaries and established eleven coordinating offices.

According to author Martin Mayer, "The modern State Department is essentially the creation of George C. Marshall [1947-1949], who ... immediately saw what was wrong. No staff ... no planning: no real sense of who the other actors were, domestically." [34] Marshall put the undersecretary (who was Dean G. Acheson at the time) in charge of the daily operations of the department; staff wishing access to the secretary had to be cleared by him first. Marshall also established a Policy Planning Staff,

with George F. Kennan (later U.S. ambassador to the Soviet Union) in charge. Marshall's reorganization and the strength of the Policy Planning Staff (subsequently renamed the Policy Planning Council) gave the State Department preeminence in foreign policy making.

After the Hoover Commission on government reorganization recommended a thorough overhaul of the department in 1949, Secretary Acheson (1949-1953) rearranged the existing eighteen offices into five bureaus (four geographic and a Bureau of United Nations Affairs), as well as units dealing with economic, intelligence, public, and press affairs. The budgetary, personnel, and operating facilities were assigned to a deputy undersecretary. Eventually, there were six substantive and eight functional agencies.

During Dwight D. Eisenhower's first term the information service and foreign aid programs were taken away from State, and Congress reinstated the Foreign Agricultural Service in the Department of Agriculture. By 1953-1954, Sen. Joseph R. McCarthy's (R-Wis.) virulent accusations of communist penetration of the State Department had severely weakened its stature; recruitment into the Foreign Service came to a halt. In response, Secretary of State John Foster Dulles appointed a commission to examine the department's organization and personnel procedures. The commission recommended a sizeable expansion of the Foreign Service, achieved primarily by giving Foreign Service officer status to the department's Civil Service employees.

Another major reorganization occurred in 1970, following a period of intensive internal review by several task forces. Secretary William P. Rogers (1969-1973) phased in a number of managerial changes that strengthened the policy formulation process and assigned decision-making and managerial responsibilities to the secretary and assistant secretaries. Nonetheless, complaints continued to abound over what were considered an excessive number of meetings and the huge quantity of paperwork (including more than two million words of cable traffic a day) generated by the department.

Secretary's Position

The secretary of state, along with the secretaries of defense, Treasury, and justice, is generally considered a member of the president's inner cabinet, although the influence of the department has varied according to personalities and circumstances. President Harry S Truman, for example, relied heavily on the advice of Secretary Marshall in the postwar reconstruction of Europe. In the following years of mounting international tension, presidents continued to look to their secretaries for principal foreign policy leadership: Acheson under Truman, Dulles under Eisenhower, Dean Rusk (1961-1969) under presidents John F. Kennedy and Lyndon B. Johnson, and Henry A. Kissinger under Richard Nixon.

Before 1968, according to Mayer, "Presidents usually spent considerable time with their Secretaries of State—Dean Rusk estimated that he saw Kennedy more than two thousand times in the thousand days. Recently, and unfortunately, both President and Secretary have become too busy, and too tightly cosseted by their staffs." [35]

Recent secretaries have had their ups and downs in relations with the president. Jimmy Carter's first secretary of state, Cyrus R. Vance (1977-1980), brought to the administration broad experience in foreign policy and crisis management. He offered to foreign governments the reassurance of a well-known and widely respected figure in charge of U.S. diplomacy. It was primarily the president himself, however, who assumed the foreign policy initiative in reaching the major foreign policy achievement of his administration: the 1979 Camp David Peace Accords between Israel and Egypt.

Ronald Reagan's first secretary of state was Alexander M. Haig, Jr., a former army general and NATO commander known for his loyal service as President Nixon's White House chief of staff during the Watergate period. Haig remained controversial during his year and a half in office, declaring himself Reagan's foreign policy "vicar" and engaging in jealous turf fights over policy formulation with other administration figures. He suddenly resigned in June 1982, later saying that his departure was not entirely voluntary.

George P. Shultz—a former economics professor, corporate executive, and Nixon cabinet officer—succeeded Haig. Shultz changed both the style and substance of U.S. foreign policy, using a less aggressive posture and more quiet diplomacy.

Organization and Functions

The secretary of state is responsible for the overall direction, coordination, and supervision of U.S. foreign relations and for the interdepartmental activities of the U.S. government overseas. The secretary is the first-ranking member of the cabinet and a member of the National Security Council.

The secretary is assisted by a deputy secretary and four undersecretaries (security assistance, science, and technology; political affairs; economic and agricultural affairs; and management). The department's counselor is a principal officer, serving the secretary as a consultant on major foreign policy problems. The counselor conducts special international negotiations and consultations as directed by the secretary and provides guidance to the appropriate bureaus on such matters.

Also attached to the secretary's office are the U.S. ambassador to the United Nations, several ambassadors-at-large who undertake special missions, the chief of protocol, the special assistant for press relations, the executive secretariat, and the Policy Planning Council.

Regional Bureaus

Primary substantive responsibility in the department rests with the five regional bureaus (European and Canadian Affairs, African Affairs, East Asian and Pacific Affairs, Inter-American Affairs, and Near Eastern and South Asian Affairs), which are headed by assistant secretaries. These bureaus advise the secretary on the formulation of U.S. policies toward countries within their regional jurisdiction and guide the operations of the U.S. diplomatic establishments in those countries.

The Bureau of International Organization Affairs manages U.S. participation in the United Nations and its system of programs and agencies. The bureau also deals with international problems such as food production, air traffic safety, communications, health, human rights, education, and the environment. In addition, the bureau is responsible for U.S. participation in more than nine hundred international conferences, some hosted by the United States.

Functional Bureaus

The legal office is the principal adviser to the secretary, and through the secretary to the president, on all matters of international law arising in the conduct of U.S. foreign policy.

The remaining bureaus are divided by function. The Bureau of Administration provides supply, procurement, and administrative services for the department and for more than $3 billion worth of U.S. government-owned real estate in 240 cities abroad. Its security officers guard the department, protect visiting foreign dignitaries, and supervise security—provided by Marine security guards (numbering about 1,500) and about 150 State Department security agents—at U.S. embassies and consulates.

The Bureau of Economic and Business Affairs deals with international energy policy, international monetary developments, trade policy, assistance to U.S. business overseas, aviation, shipping, telecommunications, foreign investment, patents, trademarks, technology transfers, commodity matters, and other international economic concerns.

The Bureau of Intelligence and Research has three principal functions. First, it prepares current and long-range intelligence analyses for the department, overseas missions, and other government agencies. Second, it serves as the department's coordinator with other members of the U.S. intelligence community to assure conformity of their programs with U.S. foreign policy. And, third, the bureau manages the department's program of external research, which provides foreign policy expertise from outside the government.

The Bureau of Public Affairs, headed by an assistant secretary who also serves as spokesperson of the department, advises other bureaus in State on public opinion and arranges continuing contacts between department officials and the public through conferences, briefings, and speaking and media engagements. It produces and distributes publications (including the encyclopedic series, *The Foreign Relations of the United States*), films, and other information and educational materials on U.S. foreign policy.

The Bureau of Consular Affairs, under the direction of an assistant secretary, assists Americans who travel or live abroad. Its Passport Services office issues more than five million passports a year. Through 250 U.S. diplomatic and consular posts abroad, its Overseas Citizens Services assists Americans, ranging from distribution of federal benefits checks to help when sudden illness or death strikes. The Visa Services division oversees U.S. consular officers who interview foreign nationals applying to come to the United States to settle, work, study, or visit; they issue some six million nonimmigrant and some 300,000 immigrant visas annually.

The Politico-Military Affairs Bureau originates and develops policy guidance and provides general direction within the department on issues that affect U.S. security policies, military assistance, nuclear nonproliferation and conventional arms transfer policy, and arms control matters.

Established by Congress in 1974, the Bureau of Oceans and International Environmental and Scientific Affairs ensures that scientific, technological, and environmental developments are taken into account in the formulation and execution of U.S. foreign policy.

The Bureau of Human Rights and Humanitarian Affairs is concerned with human rights, asylum requests, and other humanitarian subjects, while the Bureau for Refugee

Programs administers refugee relief, care, and maintenance programs overseas and initial refugee reception programs within the United States.

Foreign Service

The United States has diplomatic relations with 155 countries. In some smaller countries where the United States does not maintain a mission, official contacts are channeled through embassies in neighboring countries or the United Nations. As of January 31, 1987, diplomatic and consular missions abroad included 141 embassies, eleven missions, seventy-three consulates general, twenty-nine consulates, one branch office, and forty consular agencies. Ambassadors are the personal representatives of the president as well as representatives of the Department of State and all other federal agencies. They have full responsibility for the implementation of U.S. foreign policy by all U.S. government personnel within their country of assignment, except those under military commands.

As chiefs of mission, each ambassador heads a "country team" which typically includes a deputy chief of mission; heads of political, economic, consular, and administrative sections; defense, agricultural, and foreign commercial service attachés; a public affairs officer; the director of the Agency for International Development (AID) mission; and, as needed, representatives of other agencies of the U.S. government.

Department of Transportation

Development of a coordinated national transportation policy—long a goal of Congress and the executive branch—eluded lawmakers in the early 1960s. Instead, Congress was, for the most part, content to extend existing programs, which President John F. Kennedy had described as "a chaotic patchwork of inconsistent and often obsolete legislation [evolving] from a history of specific actions addressed to specific problems of specific industries at specific times."

The search for integrated programs that would lead to a diversified transportation system was complicated by the fact that each mode of transportation had some vested interest in existing policies, regulations, and legislation—and each had its own spokespersons in the administration and Congress. They tended to oppose any changes that would alter these advantages, while often advocating changes designed to improve their own situations.

Kennedy's successor, Lyndon B. Johnson, nonetheless pursued the idea of establishing a transportation department, and Congress acceded to his wishes in 1966. As the president requested, Congress excluded from the new Department of Transportation (DOT) all economic regulatory and rate-setting activities conducted by existing federal agencies. The urban mass transportation programs administered by the Department of Housing and Urban Development (HUD) also were excluded pending further study of their logical place in the executive branch (they later were transferred to DOT). The final legislation substantially weakened the powers proposed for the secretary of transportation, effectively denying the secretary independent authority to coordinate or revise existing federal transportation policies and programs. This stemmed partly from the desire of Congress to retain direct influence over transportation activities and partly from the desire of various private transportation groups to preserve their relationships, built up over many years, with existing federal agencies.

The bill creating DOT established a National Transportation Safety Board—independent of the secretary and other units—to oversee accident investigations, determine the cause of accidents, and review license and certificate appeals. The existing separation of aviation safety functions was continued by transferring the Federal Aviation Agency's safety duties to the new Federal Aviation Administrator, whose decisions would be administratively final. The Civil Aeronautics Board's responsibilities, which included accident investigations, probable cause determination, and review of appeals, were given to the safety board. On other safety matters, the secretary was directed to enforce the 1966 auto and highway safety laws; the Federal Railroad and Federal Highway administrators (not the secretary) were given statutory authority over the safety functions transferred to them from the Interstate Commerce Commission; and the U.S. Coast Guard was to continue to enforce maritime safety.

Johnson named Alan S. Boyd, undersecretary of commerce for transportation, the first DOT secretary. Earlier, Boyd had been a member of the Civil Aeronautics Board, serving as chairman from 1961 to 1965. The Senate confirmed his appointment on January 12, 1967, and the department officially began operation on April 1.

The First Two Decades

With its inception, DOT assumed responsibility for administering the High Speed Ground Transportation Program transferred from the Department of Commerce. In July 1967 the Urban Mass Transportation Administration was shifted from HUD to DOT. During 1967 DOT issued the first thirteen national highway safety standards under the Highway Safety Act, and the first set of federal motor vehicle standards became effective that year.

In 1970 DOT and the Department of Defense announced their cooperation in a project called Military Assistance for Safety in Traffic. The 1970 Airport and Airways Development Act provided for a long-term airport/airway development project under the auspices of DOT but strictly supervised by Congress.

During the administration of Jimmy Carter, Congress enacted legislation to deregulate the airlines, railroads, and trucking. The new laws, for which DOT was the major overseer, pared away years of federal regulations that threatened the health of the industries and, in some cases, resulted in higher consumer costs. As for other major actions, in 1978 Congress provided nearly $54 million in aid for highway and mass transit programs administered by DOT. The controversial Chrysler Corporation Loan Guarantee Act of 1979 directed the secretary of transportation to prepare an assessment of the long-term viability of the corporation. Another hotly debated measure was the department's promulgation of final rules requiring recipients of DOT financial aid to make their facilities accessible to the handicapped. That was followed in 1979 by a ruling that all buses purchased after September 1, 1979, had to be accessible to the elderly and handicapped.

Other transportation highlights included passage of the 1980 Aviation Safety and Noise Abatement Act; passage in 1980 of the Staggers Rail Act, giving railroads more freedom in rate making and service options; authorization in 1981 of the Northeast Corridor Rail Improvement Project under the Federal Railroad Administration, and establishment in 1984 of the Office of Commercial Space Transportation.

Deregulation continued under Ronald Reagan with the sale of Conrail (the freight rail system). The president proposed cutting federal subsidies for Amtrak passenger service, phasing out mass transit subsidies, and returning responsibility for most roads, including the interstate system, to state and local governments. By the mid-1980s, however, DOT was focusing on combating terrorism and drug trafficking.

Organization and Functions

The secretary of transportation, assisted by a deputy secretary, oversees the nine operating administrations that compose the department, eight of which are concerned with a specific form of transportation. The secretary's office also develops and updates national transportation policy, prepares transportation legislation, issues licenses for commercial expendable space launch vehicle operations, and helps negotiate international transportation agreements. Reporting to the secretary are the Office of Civil Rights, the Contract Appeals Board, the Office of Small and Disadvantaged Business Utilization, the Office of Commercial Space Transportation, the general counsel, and the inspector general. Five assistant secretaries are assigned, respectively, to policy and international affairs, budget and programs, government affairs, administration, and public affairs.

Nine Operating Administrations

Created by Secretary of the Treasury Alexander Hamilton in 1790 to combat smugglers, the U.S. Coast Guard has seen its role and mission expand tremendously over the years. Coast Guard personnel go out on some seventy thousand search and rescue missions each year. They investigate and clean up oil spills, regulate operation of the U.S. merchant fleet, enforce U.S. maritime laws, operate the nation's only fleet of icebreakers, and help in the search for drug smugglers and illegal aliens. The Coast Guard maintains more than 45,000 navigational aids, which include buoys, lighthouses, and offshore towers. As one of the nation's five military services, the Coast Guard protects U.S. ports from sabotage, and it has participated in U.S. military conflicts abroad.

The principal mission of the Federal Aviation Administration (FAA) is to promote aviation safety while insuring efficient use of the nation's navigable airspace. The administration is responsible for issuing and enforcing safety rules and regulations; certifying aircraft, their quotas, aircraft components, air agencies, and airports; conducting aviation safety-related research and development; and managing and operating the national airspace system. FAA oversees approximately 710,000 licensed pilots, 274,000 mechanics, 14,000 air traffic controllers, and 43,000 flight engineers. It operates and maintains 24 air route traffic control centers, 400 airport traffic control towers, 316 flight service stations, 4 international flight service stations, 109 air route surveillance radars, 200 airport surveillance radars, and 851 instrument landing systems.

The Federal Highway Administration (FHWA) is re-sponsible for administering the federal aid program for highways, which, including the interstate system, make up a network of some 900,000 miles and carry about two-thirds of the nation's motor vehicle traffic. The FHWA also regulates and enforces federal requirements on the safety of trucks and buses engaged in interstate or foreign commerce, as well as the transport of hazardous cargoes.

The principal duties of the Federal Railroad Administration (FRA) are to issue standards and regulations designed to improve rail safety. It also provides policy guidance on legislative matters affecting rail transportation—such as the sale of Conrail, rail deregulation, and Amtrak (the passenger system)—and oversees the development of the northeast high-speed rail corridor between Washington, D.C., and Boston.

Created by Congress in 1966, the National Highway Traffic Safety Administration is authorized to issue motor vehicle safety standards and to investigate possible safety defects. In recent years the agency has waged a campaign against drunk drivers and for use of safety belts.

The Urban Mass Transportation Administration (UMTA) provides financial and planning assistance to the nation's public transit systems, including buses, subways, trolleys, commuter trains, and ferry boats. Although the federal government's involvement in mass transportation began in 1961, the existing $3 billion transit program started with passage of the 1964 Urban Mass Transportation Act. Between 1964 and 1987 the federal government invested more than $43 billion in the nation's transit systems.

Created by legislation in 1954, the St. Lawrence Seaway Development Corporation constructed the U.S. facilities of the St. Lawrence Seaway navigation project, operated jointly by the United States and Canada. The corporation continues to operate and maintain that part of the seaway between Montreal and Lake Erie, within the territorial limits of the United States, and it is responsible for developing the full seaway system from the western tip of Lake Superior to the Atlantic Ocean—a distance of twenty-three hundred miles.

The Maritime Administration (MARAD), which initially was excluded from DOT's purview, became part of the department in 1981. Like its predecessor agencies dating back to the creation of the United States Shipping Board in 1916, MARAD is responsible for developing and maintaining a merchant marine capable of meeting the nation's requirements for both commercial trade and national defense. The agency administers financial and technical programs, develops promotional and marketing programs, trains ships' officers at the U.S. Merchant Marine Academy at Kings Point, New York, negotiates bilateral maritime agreements, and maintains the National Defense Reserve Fleet.

In contrast to DOT's eight other administrations which focus on a single transportation sector, the purview of the Research and Special Programs Administration (RSPA) extends to all transportation modes. Established in 1977 by combining the functions of other offices, RSPA consists of an Office of Hazardous Materials Transportation and an Office of Pipeline Safety. Its Transportation Safety Institute designs and conducts training programs, and the Transportation Systems Center plans, develops, and manages programs in all fields of transportation research and development. RSPA is also responsible for ensuring that the nation's civil transportation system will continue to operate effectively during an emergency.

Department of the Treasury

Management of the monetary resources of the United States is the primary function of the Department of the Treasury. Among other responsibilities, it regulates national banks, assesses and collects income taxes and customs duties, manufactures coins and bills, determines international economic policy, reports the federal government's financial transactions, conducts international and domestic economic research, enforces tax and tariff laws, directs anticounterfeiting operations, and provides executive protection.

One of the oldest cabinet departments, Treasury was established by the first session of Congress on September 2, 1789. Yet many of its functions were carried out even before the signing of the Declaration of Independence; the Continental Congress issued paper money to finance the revolutionary war and appointed joint treasurers to oversee the effort.

The new republic's finances, however, remained in disarray until September 1789 when President George Washington appointed Alexander Hamilton to be the first secretary of the Treasury. Hamilton's shrewd financial policies resulted in renewed confidence in the Bank of the United States, which issued money in the government's name. As Treasury's first secretary, Hamilton established a precedent for the position's power in advising the president, as well as the controversy surrounding many of its holders. The department is not only intrinsically influential; its secretaries also have numbered among the president's closest advisers.

Bureau of Engraving

The Bureau of Engraving and Printing began operating in 1862, when the government started printing "greenback" currency to finance the Civil War. Today it issues annually more than 40 billion security documents, such as paper currency, postage stamps, and Treasury bonds.

Almost 150 years later, President Dwight D. Eisenhower was quoted as saying of his Treasury secretary: "In Cabinet meetings, I always wait for George Humphrey to speak. I sit back and listen to the others talk while he doesn't say anything. But I know that when he speaks, he will say just what I was thinking."

Evolution of the Department

Treasury's authority expanded considerably during the Civil War. The loss of customs revenues from the seceded southern states led to establishment of the Bureau of Internal Revenue, as well as the printing of paper currency and the institution of a national banking system. The growth of international trade following World Wars I and II resulted in a central role for Treasury in the 1944 Bretton Woods Conference, which established the International Monetary Fund and the postwar monetary system.

Many federal functions that originally resided in Treasury have been transferred over the years to other departments. For example, Treasury administered the Postal Service until 1829. The General Land Office, which was the core of the Interior Department, was part of Treasury from 1812 to 1849. Business activities were under Treasury's purview until the Department of Commerce and Labor was established in 1903. The functions of the Office of the Supervising Architect of the Treasury were transferred to the General Services Administration in 1949. The Coast Guard, the oldest seagoing armed service in the United States, was part of Treasury until its transfer to the Department of Transportation in 1967. Other marine interests initially administered by Treasury were passed on to other departments. The Bureau of the Budget was transferred from Treasury to the Executive Office in 1939.

Organization and Functions

Treasury is divided into two major components: the office of the secretary and the operating bureaus. The secretary, who is officially the second-ranking cabinet officer, has primary responsibility for formulating and recommending domestic and international financial, economic, and tax policy; participating in the preparation of broad fiscal policies that have general significance for the economy; and managing the public debt. As chief financial officer of the government, the secretary serves as chair of the cabinet Council on Economic Affairs and Senior Interagency Group on International Economic Policy and as U.S. governor of the International Monetary Fund, International Bank for Reconstruction and Development, Inter-American Development Bank, Asian Development Bank, and African Development Bank. The Treasury secretary is required by law to submit periodic reports to Congress on the government's fiscal operations, including an annual report.

The secretary is assisted by a deputy secretary, an undersecretary for finance, a general counsel, and an inspector general. Nine assistant secretaries are responsible for the following areas: economic policy, international affairs, fiscal operations and activities (including the Financial Management Service and the Bureau of the Public Debt), domestic finance, legislative affairs, management, tax policy, public affairs and public liaison, and enforcement (which oversees enforcement activities of the U.S.

Customs Service, Internal Revenue Service, U.S. Secret Service, Bureau of Alcohol, Tobacco and Firearms, Federal Law Enforcement Training Center, and Office of Foreign Assets Control).

The Office of the Treasurer of the United States was established September 6, 1777. Initially, the treasurer was responsible for the receipt and custody of government funds. Over the years, however, these duties have been dispersed throughout various Treasury bureaus. In 1981 the treasurer was assigned oversight of the Bureau of Engraving and Printing, the United States Mint, and the U.S. Savings Bond Division.

The Office of the Comptroller of the Currency, created February 25, 1863, is an integral part of the national banking system. The comptroller oversees the execution of laws related to nationally chartered banks (including trust activities and overseas operations) and promulgates rules and regulations governing their operations.

The Bureau of Alcohol, Tobacco and Firearms (ATF) was established on July 1, 1972, as successor to the Alcohol Tax Unit of the Bureau of Internal Revenue. ATF enforces federal laws that require excise taxes on alcoholic substances, control of firearms and explosives, and regulation of the tobacco industry.

In 1927 the Bureau of Customs was established as a separate agency within Treasury; in August 1973 it was redesignated the U.S. Customs Service. The Customs Service collects revenue from imports and enforces customs and related laws. Customs also administers the 1930 Tariff Act. As the principal border enforcement agency, the service's mission has been extended over the years to cover the administration and enforcement of some four hundred provisions of wide-ranging safety standards on behalf of more than forty federal agencies. In the seven customs regions and forty-four subordinate district or area offices in the fifty states, Virgin Islands, and Puerto Rico, there are approximately 240 ports of entry into the United States.

The Bureau of Engraving and Printing began operations in July 1862, when the government started printing "greenback" currency to finance the Civil War. It designs, prints, and finishes a large variety of security products, including all paper currency; U.S. postage, customs, and revenue stamps; Treasury bills, notes, and bonds; permits; and certificates of award. It is the largest printer of security documents in the world, issuing more than 40 billion security documents annually.

Responsibility for the government's cash management, credit management, debt collection programs, and central reporting and accounting systems originally rested with the Register of the Treasury. In 1920 those functions were transferred to the newly created Office of the Commissioner of Accounts and Deposits, which was renamed the Bureau of Government Financial Operations in 1974 and became the Financial Management Service (FMS) in 1984. FMS issues approximately 500 million Treasury checks and close to 250 million electronic fund transfer payments annually for federal salaries and wages, payments to suppliers of goods and services to the government, income tax refunds, and payments under major government programs such as Social Security and veterans' benefits.

The Bureau of Internal Revenue came into existence on July 4, 1862, to collect new income taxes—money that was used to pay for the Civil War. The Supreme Court declared the national income tax unconstitutional in 1894, but it was reinstated in 1913. Reorganized in 1953, the bureau was renamed the Internal Revenue Service (IRS).

The largest of Treasury bureaus, IRS employs more than ninety thousand persons in its Washington headquarters, seven regional offices, and sixty-two districts.

Congress created the Mint of the United States on April 2, 1792, and placed it in the State Department. In 1799 the Mint was made an independent agency, and in 1873 it became part of the Treasury as the Bureau of the Mint. It was placed under the supervision of the treasurer of the United States in 1981, and its name was changed to the United States Mint in 1984. The Mint's principal function is to produce coins and medals; it also has custody over Treasury gold and silver bullion.

Management of the national debt was consolidated into the Public Debt Service in 1920; it became a bureau in 1940. The primary responsibilities of the Bureau of the Public Debt include overseeing the management of the public debt, issuing U.S. securities, and managing receipts and expenditures. The department's Savings Bond Division, authorized in 1945 as successor to a number of World War II agencies, promotes and directs the sale and holding of U.S. savings bonds and notes. The U.S. treasurer administers the division and serves as its national director.

The Secret Service was created in 1865 to halt counterfeiting. It still pursues this goal but is better known as the agency that protects the president, a function it assumed after the assassination of President William McKinley in 1901. The Secret Service also protects the president's immediate family, the vice president and the vice president's immediate family, former presidents, former president's spouses and children under the age of sixteen, the president-elect and vice president-elect, presidential and vice-presidential candidates, and visiting heads of state.

Established in March 1970, the Federal Law Enforcement Training Center, located in Georgia, is an interagency training facility serving sixty federal law enforcement organizations, including the Secret Service, Customs, and ATF, as well as the FBI and other non-Treasury agencies.

Department of Veterans Affairs

Bills to elevate the Veterans Administration (VA) to cabinet-level status had been introduced in at least seventeen successive Congresses, but finally, fifty-eight years after it was created, legislation establishing the VA as the Department of Veterans Affairs (DVA) was signed into law October 25, 1988. Perhaps somewhat ironically, Ronald Reagan, who signed the authorizing legislation (PL 100-527), had stated as a presidential candidate that he would view his election "as a mandate to reduce the size of government...." [36] He also had advocated abolishing the Departments of Education and Energy, both of which were still in place at the end of his tenure. Reagan, however, in November 1987 had endorsed putting the VA—an agency with enormous political clout—in the cabinet. The DVA came into being on March 15, 1989, making it the fourteenth executive department and the fifth to be created since 1953. President George Bush named Edward J. Derwinski, a twelve-term member of the House of Representatives, as secretary.

Size and Functions

The VA was the largest of all federal independent agencies, providing the most comprehensive assistance and care for veterans of any nation. With more than 240,000 employees, the VA ranked in size below only the Defense Department and the U.S. Postal Service. Its budget, totaling more than $27.6 billion in fiscal year 1988, exceeded those of the Departments of Energy, the Interior, Justice, State, and Commerce combined and was the fifth largest among federal departments and agencies.

The functions the DVA assumed from the VA were essentially unchanged. They include administration of the following programs for veterans: disability compensation and pensions, education and training, medical care, medical research, home loan assistance, insurance, and national cemeteries. Under the DVA's purview is the largest health care system in the free world. Transferred to the DVA were 172 VA hospitals, 231 outpatient clinics, 58 regional offices, 117 nursing homes, 27 domiciliaries, and 189 "outreach" centers for Vietnam-era veterans. Its GI education programs have interacted with nearly every institution of higher education in the nation. The DVA operates 111 national cemeteries. The department also has significant ties to the U.S. housing and banking industries. In fiscal year 1987, the VA guaranteed 474,400 home loans for veterans, worth $34.7 billion.

History of the VA

Following the English precedent, the American colonies as early as 1636 enacted laws providing that returning disabled soldiers should be "maintained competently" by the colonies for the rest of their lives.[37] The Continental Congress, in an effort to encourage enlistment during the American Revolution, continued that policy, and, in fact, benefits were paid to veterans of the revolutionary war and their dependents until 1911.

In the meantime, Congress in 1789 passed a pension law that initially was administered by Congress and was subsequently transferred in 1818 to the secretary of war. In 1849, the Office of Pensions was moved from the War Department to the newly created Interior Department. During the Civil War, Congress authorized benefits for federal volunteers on the same basis as those already provided for the regular army. In his second inaugural address in March 1865, President Abraham Lincoln called upon Congress and the American people "to care for him who shall have borne the battle and for his widow, and his orphan" (the phrase subsequently became the VA's motto).

Early veterans legislation emphasized pensions, with direct medical and hospital care provided by states and localities. It was not until 1811 that Congress authorized the first medical facility for veterans, the U.S. Naval Home in Philadelphia, as a "permanent asylum for disabled and decrepit Navy officers, seamen and Marines." During the nineteenth century, other homes were established—among them the U.S. Soldiers Home—to provide care for the indigent and disabled veterans of the Civil War, Indian Wars, Spanish-American War, and Mexican War, and the discharged regular members of the armed forces. An honorable discharge from military service was one of the requirements for admission.

Congress greatly expanded veterans benefits after the United States entered World War I in 1917, establishing disability compensation, insurance for servicemen and veterans, a family allotment program for servicemen, and vocational rehabilitation for the disabled. With the exception of the latter, these programs were administered by the

Bureau of War Risk Insurance, which had been created in 1914. At the same time, another agency, the Public Health Service, also provided medical and hospital care.

Divided responsibilities for veterans among various departments and agencies proved unwieldy. Responding to the recommendations of a presidential study commission to consolidate functions in a single agency, Congress in 1921 established the United States Veterans' Bureau. Nonetheless, two other agencies also continued to administer veterans benefits: the Bureau of Pensions in the Interior Department and the National Homes for Disabled Volunteer Soldiers.

In 1930, Congress authorized the president further to "consolidate and coordinate government activities affecting war veterans." The three existing agencies became bureaus within the new Veterans Administration. Brig. Gen. Frank T. Hines, then head of the Veterans' Bureau, was named the first administrator of veterans affairs, a post he held until 1945.[38] Given its wide-ranging responsibilities, the new agency had a relatively small staff of 31,600.

The VA served about 4.7 million veterans during its first year; by the end of World War II, their numbers had swelled to almost 19 million. To deal with this challenge, VA facilities were substantially enlarged, and significant new programs, such as the GI bill (signed into law June 22, 1944), were established. Other new programs included vocational rehabilitation legislation (1943, expanded in 1980), establishment of a VA Department of Medicine and Surgery (1946), the Korean Conflict GI Bill (1952), creation of the Department of Veterans Benefits (1953), a new GI bill for veterans with service between 1955 and 1977 (1966), and a Veterans Educational Assistance Program for post-Vietnam-era veterans.

Debate over Establishing the DVA

Only a week after Reagan announced his support for a DVA, the House of Representatives on November 17, 1987, overwhelmingly passed its version of implementing legislation, and the Senate followed suit in July 1988. The action came despite a nonpartisan, congressionally mandated report that found "little evidence" such a move would improve government services for veterans. The report, by the National Academy of Public Administration (NAPA), concluded that "there is no compelling reason why the VA ... should be elevated to cabinet status." But at a March 15 Senate Governmental Affairs Committee hearing, during which the NAPA report was made public, Chairman John Glenn (D-Ohio) said if cabinet status for the VA was accompanied by management improvements at the agency, "then the case for elevation becomes very, very strong."

The NAPA report said the creation of a cabinet-level department would not "significantly improve access to the president, affect the adequacy of necessary resources or improve the organization, management and delivery of high-quality services and benefits." The NAPA report projected only "marginal" improvements in VA operations if the legislation were to become law. Furthermore, the report pointed out that an enlarged cabinet tended to "reduce its value to the president" and added that VA elevation could strengthen the argument for upgrading other federal agencies, such as the Social Security Administration. But NAPA stopped short of recommending against a Department of Veterans Affairs.

A second evaluation, also released at the March 15

hearing, criticized VA officials for "management inattention." The report, by the General Accounting Office, criticized the decentralized organization of VA services and said high-level VA managers "have not exercised enough oversight of the field facilities that deliver benefit and medical services to veterans."[39]

Proponents of placing the VA in the cabinet pointed out that the work of the agency reached far beyond the 27.4 million veterans in the United States. The VA also served millions of dependents and survivors of veterans. Altogether, they amounted to about one-third of the nation's population. Giving the agency a seat at the cabinet table would enhance its access to the president and improve its ability to defend itself during budget decisions, supporters maintained. They argued that giving the VA cabinet status would also allow better coordination of policy with other departments. "Veterans will no longer have to go through the back door of the White House" to focus the president's attention on their problems, said Rep. G. V. (Sonny) Montgomery (D-Miss.), chairman of the House Veterans Affairs Committee and a champion of cabinet status for the VA.[40]

During floor debate on the bill, however, Senate Veterans Affairs Committee chairman Alan Cranston (D-Calif.), said that Reagan, through executive order and without legislative action, could have had his VA chiefs attend cabinet sessions, as had occurred during the administration of his Democratic predecessor, Jimmy Carter.

Organization

Replacing the position of VA administrator is the secretary of the DVA, who is assisted by a deputy secretary. Before the establishment of the DVA, the VA's programs were administered by three separate departments—Veterans Benefits, Medicine and Surgery, and Memorial Affairs, which varied greatly in number of employees and budget. These departments were continued under the DVA.

The functions of the Department of Memorial Affairs were delegated to an assistant secretary. The Department of Medicine and Surgery was redesignated the Veterans Health Services Administration, headed by a chief medical director, and the Department of Veterans Benefits was renamed the Veterans Benefits Administration under a chief benefits director, who must be a medical doctor. Both directors are intended to be nonpolitical appointments but subject to Senate confirmation. The two officers are appointed for four years, and the president is required to notify Congress if either is removed from office before expiration of the four-year term. The existing Board of Contract Appeals continues to operate unchanged. Shortly after passing the DVA bill, however, Congress cleared legislation that would make the existing VA Board of Veterans' Appeals somewhat more independent by requiring the chair to be appointed by the president and confirmed by the Senate, among other changes.

Functions assigned to the associate deputy administrators were delegated to DVA assistant secretaries. They include budget and finance; personnel management; labor relations; planning; studies and evaluations; oversight; advisory functions regarding management; productivity and logistic support; information management; supervision of capital facilities and real property programs; equal opportunity; employment discrimination; procurement; and congressional, intergovernmental, public and consumer information and affairs. The responsibilities of the VA's

Office of General Counsel and the Office of Inspector General (IG) were unchanged under the new organization. The Senate had wanted to add 150-200 new IGs to the approximately 380 existing positions (the VA had the second smallest IG staff in the federal government), but the House opposed the increase. The final compromise would phase in 40 new IGs over fiscal years 1990-1991.

Notes

1. James D. King and James W. Riddlesperger, Jr., "Presidential Cabinet Appointments: The Partisan Factor," *Presidential Studies Quarterly* 14 (Spring 1984): 231.
2. Richard M. Pious, *The American Presidency* (New York: Basic Books, 1979), 936.
3. Nelson W. Polsby, "Presidential Cabinet Making: Lessons for the Political System," *Political Science Quarterly* 93 (Spring 1978): 19-20.
4. G. Calvin Mackenzie, *The Politics of Presidential Appointments* (New York: Free Press, 1981), 9.
5. John W. Macy, Bruce Adams, and J. Jackson Walter, *America's Unelected Government: Appointing the President's Team* (Cambridge, Mass.: Ballinger, 1983), 76-82.
6. David T. Stanley, Dean E. Mann, and Jameson W. Doig, *Men Who Govern: A Biographical Profile of Federal Executives* (Washington, D.C.: Brookings, 1967).
7. Linda Fisher, "Fifty Years of Presidential Appointments," in *The In-and-Outers: Presidential Appointees and Transient Government in Washington*, ed. G. Calvin Mackenzie (Baltimore: Johns Hopkins University Press, 1987), 28.
8. Ibid.
9. Stephen Hess, *Organizing the Presidency* (Washington, D.C.: Brookings, 1976), 28.
10. Ibid., 30.
11. Mackenzie, *The Politics of Presidential Appointments*, 12.
12. Harry S Truman, *1945, Year of Decisions* (New York: Signet, 1955), 364.
13. Dwight D. Eisenhower, *Mandate for Change* (New York: Signet, 1963), 137.
14. Hess, *Organizing the Presidency*, 62.
15. Mackenzie, *The Politics of Presidential Appointments*, 22.
16. Hess, *Organizing the Presidency*, 82.
17. David Halberstam, *The Best and the Brightest* (New York: Random House, 1972), 434.
18. Mackenzie, *The Politics of Presidential Appointments*, 39.
19. Ibid., 41.
20. Arthur M. Schlesinger, Jr., "Presidential War," *New York Times Magazine*, January 7, 1974, 28.
21. Mackenzie, *The Politics of Presidential Appointments*, 45.
22. Quoted in Dom Bonafede, "Cabinet Comment," *National Journal*, vol. 8 (December 11, 1976), 1784.
23. Mackenzie, *The Politics of Presidential Appointments*, 64.
24. R. Gordon Hoxie, "Staffing the Ford and Carter Presidencies," *Presidential Studies Quarterly* 10 (Spring 1984): 393.
25. Macy, Adams, and Walter, *America's Unelected Government*, 40.
26. Ross K. Baker, "Outlook for the Reagan Administration," in *The Election of 1980: Reports and Interpretations*, ed. Gerald Pomper (Chatham, N.J.: Chatham House, 1981), 164.
27. Richard A. Stubbing, with Richard A. Mendel, *The Defense Game* (New York: Harper and Row, 1986), 259-260.
28. *Washington Post*, October 7, 1978.
29. John G. Kester, "Thoughtless JCS Change Is Worse Than None," *Armed Forces Journal International* (November 1984): 113.
30. Richard Harris, *Justice: The Crisis of Law, Order, and Freedom in America* (New York: Dutton, 1970), 33-34.
31. Ibid., 161.
32. Jonathan Grossman, "The Origin of the Department of Labor," *Monthly Labor Review*, March 1973.

33. Janet Hook, "Brock Selected to Replace Donovan at Labor," *Congressional Quarterly Weekly Report,* March 23, 1985, 549.
34. Martin Mayer, *The Diplomats* (New York: Doubleday, 1983), 211.
35. Ibid., 240.
36. Quoted in *Congressional Quarterly Weekly Report,* October 19, 1988, A-21.
37. From *VA History in Brief* (Washington, D.C.: Government Printing Office, 1986).
38. Like the earlier Veterans' Bureau, the Veterans Administration originally used the apostrophe (Veterans' Administration), but the apostrophe eventually was dropped from the name.
39. The above quotations in this section come from Richard Cowan, "VA-Cabinet Plan Questioned, But Not Slowed," *Congressional Quarterly Weekly Report,* March 19, 1988, 749-750.
40. Quoted in Ben A. Franklin, "Congress Votes to Make the VA a Cabinet-Level Department," *New York Times,* October 19, 1988.

Selected Bibliography

Baker, Ross K. "Outlook for the Reagan Administration." In *The Election of 1980: Reports and Interpretations,* ed. Gerald Pomper. Chatham, N.J.: Chatham House, 1981.

Bonafede, Dom. "Cabinet Comment." *National Journal* Vol. 8 (December 11, 1976), 1784.

Eisenhower, Dwight D. *Mandate for Change.* New York: Signet, 1963.

Fisher, Linda. "Fifty Years of Presidential Appointments." In *The In-and-Outers: Presidential Appointees and Transient Government in Washington,* ed. G. Calvin Mackenzie. Baltimore: Johns Hopkins University Press, 1987.

Halberstam, David. *The Best and the Brightest.* New York: Random House, 1972.

Hess, Stephen. *Organizing the Presidency.* Washington, D.C.: Brookings, 1976.

Hoxie, R. Gordon. "Staffing the Ford and Carter Presidencies." *Presidential Studies Quarterly* 10 (Spring 1980): 378-401.

King, James D., and James W. Riddlesperger, Jr. "Presidential Cabinet Appointments: The Partisan Factor." *Presidential Studies Quarterly* 14 (Spring 1984): 231-237.

Mackenzie, G. Calvin. *The Politics of Presidential Appointments.* New York: The Free Press, 1981.

Macy, John W., Bruce Adams, and J. Jackson Walter. *America's Unelected Government: Appointing the President's Team.* Cambridge, Mass.: Ballinger, 1983.

Pious, Richard M. *The American Presidency.* New York: Basic Books, 1979.

Polsby, Nelson W. "Presidential Cabinet Making: Lessons for the Political System." *Political Science Quarterly* 93 (Spring 1978): 16-24.

Schlesinger, Arthur M., Jr. "Presidential War." *New York Times Magazine,* January 7, 1974, 28.

Stanley, David T., Dean E. Mann, and Jameson W. Doig. *Men Who Govern: A Biographical Profile of Federal Executives.* Washington, D.C.: Brookings, 1967.

Truman, Harry S. *1945, Year of Decisions.* New York: Signet, 1955.

Government Agencies
and Corporations

In addition to the fourteen cabinet departments the president is directly responsible for several other kinds of federal government agencies. Some of these agencies are autonomous and not part of any cabinet department, while others are part of the cabinet hierarchy but with significant power to operate largely as separate entities. No matter what kind of organizational relationship these agencies have to the rest of the executive branch, however, the president has direct legal responsibility for them—and often in fact exerts considerable control over them. Independent agencies are autonomous mainly because they are separated organizationally from the presidency.

These agencies have different objectives, powers, methods of determining their members, and organizations. Any similarity is derived from their existence largely outside the traditional lines of authority of the executive departments. Their independent or semi-independent structure results from either the desire of Congress to remove their operations from the control of the presidential hierarchy or presidential attempts to show concern for specific problems that could best be solved in an environment lacking political pressure. These agencies can be divided into three general categories: regulatory agencies, independent executive agencies, and government corporations.

Regulatory Agencies

Regulatory agencies and commissions regulate various aspects of the economy and, more recently, consumer affairs. The commerce clause of the Constitution (Article I, section 8) gives the federal government the legal authority "to regulate Commerce with foreign Nations, and among the several States . . . ." Although there is no universally agreed-upon definition of federal regulation, in 1977 the Senate Governmental Affairs Committee (then named the Government Operations Committee) defined a federal regulatory agency as "one which (1) has decision-making authority, (2) establishes standards or guidelines conferring benefits and imposing restrictions on business conduct, (3) operates principally in the sphere of domestic business activity, (4) has its head and/or members appointed by the president . . . and (5) has its legal procedures generally

By W. Craig Bledsoe and Richard A. Karno

governed by the Administrative Procedure Act." [1]

Regulatory agencies are either organizationally independent or part of an existing executive department. Independent regulatory agencies are governed by bipartisan commissions of five or more members. These commissioners usually serve lengthy, fixed terms, and they cannot be removed by the president. Among the major independent regulatory agencies are the Interstate Commerce Commission (ICC), Federal Reserve Board (FRB), National Labor Relations Board (NLRB), Federal Communications Commission (FCC), Federal Trade Commission (FTC), Civil Aeronautics Board (CAB), and Securities and Exchange Commission (SEC).

Agencies within an executive branch department serve under the authority of the department in which they are located. Heads of these agencies are subject not only to presidential appointment but also to presidential dismissal. Presidents may appoint and dismiss these agency heads either personally or through their department secretaries. Agencies within executive branch departments include the Food and Drug Administration (FDA), located in the Department of Health and Human Services, and the Occupational Safety and Health Administration (OSHA), located in the Department of Labor.

Although regulatory agencies oversee a variety of activities, they share certain jurisdictional and organizational characteristics. For example, all of these agencies have substantial federal authority to carry out various regulatory functions. Sometimes called quasi-agencies because they are empowered legally to perform quasi-legislative, quasi-executive, and quasi-judicial functions, they can issue rules that govern certain sections of the economy, oversee implementation of those rules, and adjudicate disputes over interpretation of the rules.

In creating these organizations Congress has attempted to protect their independence. For example, commissioners, who are appointed by the president, serve overlapping fixed terms, usually four to seven years. Even though they are political appointees, presidents cannot simply fire them. In 1935 the Supreme Court ruled that President Franklin D. Roosevelt unconstitutionally fired a member of the FTC. In *Humphrey's Executor v. United States* the Court held that presidents cannot remove regulatory commission members for ruling in ways that might displease the president or members of Congress. In a further attempt to ensure political independence from the president, Congress made these commissions bipartisan with limits placed on the number of appointees from any single political party. Generally, neither political party may have a majority of more than one. This organizational design makes these agencies and commissions independent of other executive organizations and places responsibility for the execution of their policies with the commissioners rather than the president.

Presumably, appointees to regulatory commissions should be not only experts in the policy area in which they have been chosen to oversee but also objective parties who would not favor one side over another in a policy dispute. In practice, however, regulatory agencies tend to develop reciprocal relationships with the interests they are supposed to regulate. Political scientist Samuel Huntington has suggested that regulatory agencies are inevitably "captured" by the interest groups they are supposed to be regulating.[2] Thus, the ICC would look out for the interests of the trucking industry, the FDA for the interests of drug manufacturers, and the Nuclear Regulatory Commission (NRC) for the interests of the nuclear industry.

Some regulatory agencies go through an inevitable life cycle. Regulatory agency scholar Marver H. Bernstein has argued that agencies are most aggressive when they are new. Over the years, however, they gradually lose their stamina and become captives of the interests they are supposed to regulate, or they become dormant. As public attention moves from the initial problem that prompted the regulation, the regulatory agency, out of public scrutiny, might become free to operate as it wishes.[3] Even if a regulatory life cycle exists, however, some agencies have been spurred on to new innovative action by the public. In the 1950s and 1960s, for example, the FDA became much more aggressive about drug testing after the public expressed concern about unsafe drugs.

While the original mandate of regulatory activity was primarily economic regulation, modern regulatory agencies undertake regulation that goes beyond the traditional economic motives, moving more and more into the area of social concerns. Although these social concerns usually are related to economic activities, their scope is different from traditional regulation in that they touch upon issues that are of importance to individual consumers. For this reason regulatory activity is divided into economic regulation and social regulation.

Economic Regulation

In 1887 the federal government undertook its first major regulation of a private sector of the economy when Congress, exercising its constitutional right to regulate interstate commerce, created the Interstate Commerce Commission. According to political scientist Robert E. Cushman, "The Interstate Commerce Commission was an innovation not because it was endowed with a new type of power, but because it represented a new location of power in the federal system."[4]

Ironically, Congress initially did not intend to make the Interstate Commerce Commission independent of the control of the executive branch. During the original congressional debate on creation of the ICC, matters of independence and presidential control were never considered. Congress first placed the ICC in the Interior Department, which subjected its budget, staff, and internal management to control by an executive department. Two years later, Congress gave the ICC control over its own affairs.

It was only several years after it achieved independence that the ICC gained any real measure of power. Initially, it lacked the power to do anything more than issue cease-and-desist orders to stop railroads from violating provisions of the Interstate Commerce Act of 1887. It had neither the authority to set or adjust railroad shipping rates nor any coercive power to enforce its rulings. Moreover, in the early years the courts conscientiously reviewed ICC orders, often substituting their own judgments favoring the railroads for those of the commission. It soon became obvious to the railroads that they could circumvent the ICC by appealing judgments to the courts.

Gradually the ICC became politically and organizationally independent. In 1906 Congress passed the Hepburn Act, which gave the commission final rate-making powers and the authority to adjust rates that the ICC deemed unreasonable or unfair. And in 1910, with the passage of the Mann-Elkins Act, Congress strengthened the commission's enforcement ability by authorizing it to suspend and investigate new rate proposals and to set original rates.

Abandoning the idea that the ICC might be able to handle the regulation of all commerce, Congress created a network of new regulatory agencies patterned after the ICC. In 1913, for example, the Federal Reserve System began to govern banking and regulate the supply of money. The following year saw creation of the Federal Trade Commission to regulate business practices and control monopolistic behavior. Between 1915 and 1933, the beginning of Franklin Roosevelt's administration, Congress set up seven other regulatory agencies, including the Tariff Commission (1916), Commodities Exchange Authority (1922), Customs Service (1927), and Federal Power Commission (1930).

After the Great Depression and beginning with Roosevelt's "New Deal," an extraordinary flood of regulatory programs passed Congress. Between 1932 and 1938 eight major regulatory agencies were set up to handle problems created by the economic crisis of the depression. These included several agencies that have become mainstays in the American way of life. For example, the Federal Home

Sue Klemens

The Interstate Commerce Commission, the nation's oldest regulatory agency, regulates interstate surface transportation within the United States.

Loan Bank Board (FHLBB) was set up in 1932 to regulate federally chartered savings and loan associations; they were a source of private funds for building and buying homes. The Federal Deposit Insurance Corporation (FDIC) was created by the Banking Act of 1933 to regulate state-chartered, insured banks that were not members of the Federal Reserve System and to provide federally guaranteed insurance for bank deposits. And the Securities and Exchange Commission was founded in 1934 to protect the public against fraud and deception in securities and financial markets. Finally, the Wagner Act of 1935 created the National Labor Relations Board to prevent "unfair labor practices" and to protect the right of collective bargaining.

Social Regulation

While the New Deal was the true beginning of large-scale federal regulation of the economy, it also provided the foundation for the many social regulatory agencies that characterized the 1960s and 1970s. As New Deal programs expanded the scope of the federal government, use of the federal government to solve the nation's economic and social problems became accepted. By the mid-1960s the federal government was providing medical care, educational aid, nutritional help, urban renewal, and job training, among other services. And by the mid-1970s social activism had grown to such an extent that many consumer and environmental groups had called for a new wave of regulation intended to achieve certain social goals such as clean air and consumer protection. Congressional Quarterly's *Federal Regulatory Directory* divides these social regulatory agencies into four areas of concern: regulations to protect consumers, environmental protection, workplace safety, and energy regulation.[5]

By the early 1970s the well-defined consumer movement had begun to have a significant impact on American life. Consumers were very vocal in their cries for protection against false advertising and faulty products. Organized groups were demanding safer and better products and lower prices for food, fuel, and medical care. Earlier, in 1965, Ralph Nader had more or less launched consumerism as a political movement with the publication of his book *Unsafe at Any Speed,* which attacked the automobile industry's poor safety record. Through Nader's efforts and those of other consumer advocates interested in automobile safety, the National Highway Traffic Safety Administration (NHTSA) was created within the Department of Transportation in 1970. With its authority to set automobile safety and fuel efficiency standards, the agency represents one of the early efforts at consumer legislation. The Consumer Product Safety Commission (CPSC) represents an independent consumer protection agency. With its passage of the Consumer Product Safety Act in 1972, Congress gave the commission the task of protecting consumers against unreasonable risks of injury from hazardous products.

Advocates of a cleaner environment were also part of the consumer movement; the creation of the Environmental Protection Agency (EPA) in 1970 stemmed directly from their efforts. Set up as an independent regulatory agency, EPA was charged with supervising and protecting the nation's environment, including its air, water, land, and noise. In its short history EPA has become one of the most controversial of all federal agencies, largely because of its wide-ranging responsibilities and the costs of the programs that it advocates to clean up the environment.

Workplace safety was another concern of the consumer movement. Consumers wanted to minimize hazards in the workplace by establishing guidelines for improving safety and health on the job. Established as an agency within the Labor Department in 1970, the Occupational Safety and Health Administration was charged with promulgating and enforcing worker safety and health standards. It is authorized to conduct unannounced on-site inspections and to require employers to keep detailed records on worker injuries and illnesses. OSHA thus has considerable regulatory power that it can wield in carrying out its quasi-legislative, quasi-executive, and quasi-judicial functions.

By the 1970s the United States found itself repeatedly confronted with the dual problems of a dwindling energy supply and the rising costs of energy. In an attempt to protect consumers from growing energy problems, Congress created a number of agencies designed to alleviate some of the difficulties. In 1973 it established the Federal Energy Administration (FEA) to control short-term fuel shortages, and in 1974 the Energy Research and Development Administration (ERDA) with the mandate to develop nuclear power and new energy sources. Also in 1974 Congress created the Nuclear Regulatory Commission to regulate nuclear safety. All of these agencies, except the NRC, were abolished in 1977 when their functions were moved to the newly created Department of Energy.

Methods of Regulation

Regulatory agencies use a variety of techniques to carry out their mandates. In fact, the method that each agency uses may be limited by the legislation that created the agency in the first place. For example, Congress may find an issue of such importance that it tells the agency exactly how to regulate the area of concern. For issues of lesser importance, Congress may give the agency a free hand to use whatever regulatory methods it believes appropriate.

One of the most common methods of regulation is the required disclosure of consumer information. For example, the Food and Drug Administration requires manufacturers of a variety of food products to list the ingredients of their product, and often the product's nutritional value. In 1977, in an extreme form of public disclosure, the Consumer Product Safety Commission banned Tris, a flame retardant used in children's sleepwear, because the product contained carcinogens. In less severe action, the agency might require labels on some products warning consumers of the risks attached to product use. Health warnings on cigarette packages and containers of artificially sweetened soft drinks are some of the best-known examples.

The most extreme form of regulation is mandatory licensing—that is, specific professions and businesses must obtain licenses to practice their trade, to take certain actions, or own certain goods. In most cases failure to obtain the license results in civil or criminal action. Licenses usually are required when the consumer is unable to determine the qualifications of the individuals offering their services. Various federal agencies and commissions license everything from radio and television stations to nuclear power plants. Licensing requires a massive amount of red tape, but for successful applicants it provides some economic benefit in that it allows them to practice their trade or provide their service while protecting their interests by keeping the unqualified out.

When information about certain products cannot be conveniently provided to consumers or the potential harm of a product is very high, agencies often will set standards to which the company must comply. Failure to maintain the standards could result in legal penalties. Agencies can impose two kinds of standards. Performance standards require simply that minimum goals be met, but no guidelines are given on the method or methods to be used. Thus, EPA could require a specific city to meet minimum air pollution standards without reference to how that city achieves those standards. Specification standards, in contrast, spell out exactly how certain requirements are to be met. EPA would tell a city exactly what kind of equipment to use to reduce pollution.

Standards are only as effective as the agency's ability to enforce them. One method of enforcing regulatory rules or standards is taxation—historically a tool of regulation. Higher taxes often are imposed on companies or persons who refuse to comply with the rules. The tariffs placed on imported goods to protect American manufacturers were early examples of a regulatory tax. More recently taxes have been imposed on automobiles that use fuel less efficiently than others.

Other economic incentives are used by regulatory agencies to encourage certain types of behavior. Tax credits, for example, frequently are offered to firms to encourage investment in capital equipment. Colleges and universities receive research grants to conduct needed agricultural research. Farmers receive price supports to encourage them to grow particular crops. In each case, the government regulates by giving or withholding economic benefits.

Some agencies have the power to recall consumer products that could harm their users. *Consumer Reports* estimates that between 1973 and 1980 the Consumer Product Safety Commission recalled more than 120 million products in more than twenty-six hundred separate actions, resulting in about eighty recalls a week. From the time automobile recalls began in 1966 to 1980 over eighty-six million automobiles, trucks, vans, and other vehicles were recalled. Recalls do not always result, however, in effective regulation. Whether the product is corrected is usually left up to the consumer.

Independent Executive Agencies

Independent executive agencies are similar to independent regulatory agencies in that they are not part of a specific cabinet department. But unlike regulatory agencies, they are normally considered to be part of the presidential hierarchy and report to the president. The most important examples of these agencies are the National Aeronautics and Space Administration (NASA) and the General Services Administration (GSA).

Many of these agencies were created in an effort to avoid bureaucratic inertia, often resulting from the failure of existing agencies to accomplish their objectives. In 1964, for example, the Johnson administration created the Office of Economic Opportunity (OEO) to help implement its "Great Society" programs. By locating OEO in the Executive Office of the President and not in a specific department, the White House was able to exert more control over its operation and ensure that the administration's antipoverty objectives were carried out. Similarly, NASA was lo-

Florida Department of Commerce

NASA is a civilian agency that controls U.S. aeronautical and space activities. In 1958 the first American satellite went into orbit, and eleven years later, *Apollo II* completed the first successful manned flight to the moon.

cated outside the control of a specific department to help expedite its formation and operation, free from the traditional demands of departmental control. In addition, it was set up apart from the Defense Department to demonstrate that the U.S. space program would be controlled by civilians rather than the military.

Often independent agencies are born out of vested interests. Members of Congress and interest groups want to guarantee that these agencies are responsible to their wishes. In addition, presidents and Congress often want these agencies free from the traditional constraints and methods of old-line departments. For example, in an effort to challenge directly actions detrimental to the environment, Congress made the EPA independent of old-line departments that might have traditional environmental interests.

With some degree of independence from hierarchical executive control, independent executive agencies can maneuver more openly in ways that will maximize their objectives. This kind of freedom, however, often means that independent agencies will have few allies in the executive branch, possibly diminishing their overall influence on the development of executive policy. Some agencies have been quite successful in their independent status by developing new coalitions with groups not traditionally represented by executive departments. For example, the Civil Rights Commission, established in 1957 as a bipartisan, six-member independent agency, used its autonomous organizational status to become a constructive critic of federal civil rights policies. Between 1959 and 1970, by successfully forging coalitions outside the executive branch, the commission was able to get over two-thirds of its recommendations either enacted into law or included in executive orders.

Executive independence can result, however, in overlapping jurisdictions and conflicts between the independent agencies and existing executive organizations. Until it was replaced by the Office of Personnel Management in 1978, the Civil Service Commission's independence made it an easy target for groups seeking to influence particular aspects of federal personnel policy. An interviewee in a Brookings Institution report noted the difficulty of placing responsibility within the commission: "Well, we think it works first for its congressional committees, second for the status of employees, third for the American Legion in support of veterans' preference laws, fourth for the civil service employees' unions, and possibly fifth for the President." [6] The attempt to remove politics from the federal personnel selection process therefore resulted in just the opposite; politics became a primary factor in determining federal job selection.

Government Corporations

A third type of agency, which operates either autonomously or semiautonomously of the regular departmental structure, is the governmental corporation. Even though investors in them cannot buy stock and collect dividends, these organizations operate much like a private corporation that sells a service. Government corporations usually provide a service for a public need that the private sector has found too expensive or unprofitable to undertake.

Three of the best-known government corporations are the Tennessee Valley Authority (TVA), created in 1933 to develop electric power and navigation in the Tennessee Valley region; the National Railroad Passenger Corporation, or Amtrak, the nation's passenger train service; and the U.S. Postal Service. Several successful government corporations have been based on the TVA model. Comsat, for example, is a modern government corporation which sells time-sharing on NASA satellites. The Postal Service became a government corporation only recently. Originally created in 1775 by the Continental Congress with Benjamin Franklin as its postmaster general, this longtime cabinet department assumed its corporate status in 1970. In urging reorganization of the Postal Service, President Richard Nixon argued that by freeing the agency from the direct control of the president and Congress, and the resulting bipartisan pressure, it could operate more efficiently.

By giving them a corporate charter Congress has given these corporations greater latitude in their day-to-day operations than that given other agencies. As corporations, federal agencies can acquire, develop, and sell real estate and other kinds of property, acting in the name of the corporation rather than the federal government. They have the power as well to bring a lawsuit on behalf of the corporation, and they can be sued. Also like private corporations, these agencies are headed by a bipartisan board of directors or board of commissioners. Often a corporation such as the Postal Service will have a single head who is supplemented by a board. Corporation heads and members are appointed by the president and approved by the Senate. They serve long, staggered terms to prevent any one president from controlling the corporation.

Government corporations are not dependent on annual appropriations as are other executive departments and agencies. Their earnings may be retained by them and deposited directly back into their operations. Consequently, they are less subject to financial control by the president or Congress, and they are free of the annual process of defending their estimates for the fiscal year before the Office of Management and Budget (OMB), the president, and Congress. Even so, their operations are reviewed annually by all three, using a review process that tends to be less demanding since they are not requesting appropriations. Because some government corporations have difficulty operating in the black, Congress is committed to providing long-term appropriations for their operations. For example, Congress has promised the Postal Service a fifteen-year funding program.

Government corporations also are free to provide some of their own financing. The Postal Service not only uses revenues that it generates from its own activities, but it is also empowered to borrow money by issuing bonds.

Compared to their modern counterparts, the original government corporations had more independence, as well as much more fiscal freedom than other agencies and departments so that they could realize their goals. Almost unheard of until the New Deal, government corporations became particularly important during World War II as a means of accomplishing specific tasks such as developing raw materials. They operated almost identically to private corporations. Initially, Congress gave them independent funding, which they sustained through their revenues.

In 1945, however, Congress passed the Government Corporation Control Act, which sought to make these agencies more accountable to the president and Congress. While preserving some of the previous independence of government corporations, the act attempted to control them in unique ways. It provided that Congress must first authorize the corporate form of organization, specifying what the corporation may and may not do. Congress may modify the authority or responsibilities of the corporation, or even dissolve it. And if it chooses Congress may withhold working capital.

Sometimes the federal government takes over an ailing corporation in an effort to insure its survival. Amtrak, the nation's railway service, is a prime example. Although Amtrak is a losing proposition in terms of its multibillion dollar federal subsidy, Congress decided that the survival of passenger train service in the United States is in the public interest.

Styles and Methods of Appointment

Almost all independent and semi-independent agency heads and commissioners are selected according to Article II, section 2, of the Constitution, which states that the president "shall nominate, and by and with the advice and consent of the Senate, shall appoint Ambassadors, other public Ministers and Consuls, Judges of the Supreme Court and all other Officers of the United States. . . ." The Founders decided, however, to permit the president or heads of the departments to appoint such "inferior officers" as they thought proper. Thus, the heads of a few regulatory agencies within the departments, such as the Food and Drug Administration, are not appointed by the president but by the secretary of the department in which the agency resides. In either case appointees must be approved by the Senate. Once the Senate has confirmed a nominee, it may not reconsider the nomination.

The president has the power to remove for any reason the heads of agencies within the executive branch, but independent agency heads and commissioners usually may be removed only for inefficiency, neglect of duty, or misconduct. Even though removal is rare, it occasionally occurs. In 1975 President Nixon removed the chairman of the Civil Aeronautics Board, Robert D. Trimm, for "incompetence." Trimm resigned involuntarily out of respect for the office of the president. If he had chosen to fight his removal, the Nixon administration would have had to submit proof of Trimm's incompetence.

Although the Constitution does not specify qualifications for agency heads and commissioners, Congress has required statutorily that appointees to certain agencies meet certain criteria. For example, the act creating the Federal Reserve Board requires its members to be a fair representation of financial, agricultural, industrial, commercial and geographical interests. Similarly, appointments to the Federal Aviation Administration must be not only qualified administrators but also civilians with aviation experience.

One of the requirements for most agencies, especially regulatory, is that they have no more than a simple majority of commissioners from the same political party. Ironically, then administrations pay more attention to nominees from the opposition party than from their own. According to executive branch scholar William E. Brigman, "By careful scrutiny every administration has managed to find members of the opposition party, or registered independents, who are supportive of administration goals." [7] By choosing members of the opposition party who agree with their views, presidents are able to bypass the intent of bipartisanship. Richard Nixon, for example, once attempted to nominate the Tennessee leader of "Democrats for Nixon" to a Democratic slot on a commission. When the Democratic-controlled Senate refused to confirm the nominee, Nixon successfully appointed him as an independent. Although bipartisan representation may exist in terms of numbers, rarely does a true minority party view exist in an agency or commission.

Because presidents are authorized to name the heads of most agencies and commissions, they usually take this opportunity to appoint someone from their own party. Presidents may decide to replace existing chairs. If they name one of the sitting commissioners as the new commission head, the retiring chair does not have to leave the commission until his or her term of appointment has expired. Many, however, decide to leave anyway. The terms of most heads of agencies and commissions are fixed. For example, the chair of the Federal Reserve Board serves a four-year term, while a new chair of the Civil Aeronautics Board is named each year.

Selection and Nomination

Appointees to independent agencies and regulatory commissions represent 20.3 percent of all major executive appointments made by the president. Thus, the task of selecting these personnel is one of the president's most important jobs.[8]

As for most presidential appointments, the president relies heavily on others—such as advisers or a formal personnel office—to help search for, screen, and recommend potential appointees. Presidents are presented then with several choices, and they often make the final decision themselves; however, this may mean simply affirming the selection of their advisers.

Few presidents have played active roles in the process of selecting and nominating appointees to independent agencies and regulatory commissions, but President Gerald R. Ford paid attention to almost every such appointment. Yet even Ford did not meet with the nominees. That privilege was reserved for the nominated chairs.

Even though presidents take very little time with the appointment of commissioners, their selection and nomination is one of the most important sources of influence that presidents have over independent agencies and regulatory commissions. Despite the organizational independence of these agencies, every administration has sought to control them. The process of influence appears to be a simple matter of appointing ideologically pure partisans, but factors other than political philosophy must be considered because of the difficulty encountered in measuring partisan purity and loyalty in potential nominees.

Traditionally, most presidents have viewed agency seats as important political rewards and have instructed their advisers to use them as such. Agency vacancies thus have become an important way to pay political debts and not necessarily the best way to influence policy.

Few people are nominated who are not politically acceptable to the White House. Although a potential appointee's educational background, geographical representation, and party loyalty are all important, political connections may be the most important presidential consideration. Congressional sponsorship has been particularly useful to appointees. In a study of thirty-eight appointments to four regulatory agencies over a fifteen-year period, the Senate Governmental Affairs Committee found that congressional sponsorship most often determined selection of the nominee.[9] And very few administrations do not first consult with members of Congress and special-interest groups to obtain some type of informal clearance for the nominee.

Whether regulatory commissioners should come from the industries that they are supposed to regulate is one of the more controversial questions confronting the appointment process. The most logical place to turn for experts on the interest to be controlled is that interest itself. But appointing someone who has such an association leaves the commissioner open to a conflict-of-interest charge.

Most presidents, however, at least check with the interests to be regulated, whether they be traditional interest groups or consumer groups. Political scientist Louis Kohlmeier, Jr., has argued that every recent president has run some kind of check with the regulated interest before appointing a regulator. "Almost no president has ever sent up for Senate confirmation a name to which industry takes vigorous exception. . . . All presidents have run checks with industry before picking regulators, fundamentally because all have looked upon regulation more or less as industry's preserve." [10] Yet there are often pressures in the other direction as well. Because presidents want to avoid confirmation fights, they usually have their aides consult with key public-interest groups. According to presidential appointments scholar G. Calvin Mackenzie, "The appointment of regulatory commissioners . . . rarely aroused much interest or controversy before 1970. But the growing political prominence of a number of self-declared public interest

U.S. Postal Service

The Postal Service was created in 1775 with Benjamin Franklin as the first postmaster general. In 1987 postal workers handled 154 billion pieces of mail.

groups sharply increased the conflict engendered by these appointments in the decade that followed.... The likely effect ... is that the president's freedom of choice will be circumscribed." [11]

Presidential Use of Appointments

Recent presidents have looked upon the appointment of a strong and loyal agency or commission chair as the most effective method for influencing agency policies. Consequently, presidents pay close attention to the selection of commission chairs. Since 1969, when President Richard Nixon finally gained control over the last holdout, the president has had the power to name the agency or commission chair. With the exception of the Federal Communications Commission and the Interstate Commerce Commission, which have resisted attempts at consolidating power within their chairs, there are very few collegial decisions within the agencies and commissions. Chairs have power over budgets and personnel, and they have more information than the other commissioners. They therefore wield substantial powers in the direction and control of their agencies. Brigman wrote: "Realizing that a strong chairman can accomplish the administration's goals without explicit intervention, thereby preserving the fiction of regulatory independence, the White House pays much more attention to the selection of chairmen than it does to ordinary commissioners." [12]

The desire of presidents to control a regulatory commission often stems from their philosophy of regulation and the role of government in general. By appointing agency heads and commissioners that share their philosophical views, presidents are best able to leave their imprint on the government. Regulation itself represents the expanding role of government in an individual's life. The presidencies of Jimmy Carter and Ronald Reagan point to two different views of the role of regulation, reflected in their desire to control the philosophy of the regula-

tory agencies and commissions through the appointment process.

Even though President Carter expressed an interest in reducing regulation through several of his appointments to executive branch and regulatory posts, he still appointed a significant number of "activists" to head agencies concerned with consumer protection and health and safety standards. For example, he appointed Michael Pertschuk, who had been instrumental in developing the Consumer Product Safety Commission, as chairman of the Federal Trade Commission. Pertschuk pushed the FTC into an activist position on the issues of television advertising directed at children and automobile advertisements that promoted more driving during periods of gas shortages. Carter also named Joan Claybrook, former director of Ralph Nader's public-interest group Congress Watch, as director of the National Highway Traffic Safety Administration. During her tenure, NHTSA proposed the mandatory installation of automatically inflating airbags in automobiles. In addition, Carter appointed to CPSC some of its most activist commissioners, making that commission the most energetic in its history.

President Reagan, in contrast, made extensive use of the appointment process to promote his policy of attacking the expanding role of the federal government. Many of his appointments to executive branch regulatory agencies and independent agencies and commissions were nominees who shared his philosophy of hostility to governmental regulations and controls. By appointing Thorne Auchter to head the Occupational Safety and Health Administration, Reagan instilled in OSHA a philosophy sympathetic to businesses who complained of high regulatory costs. Reagan's appointment of Raymond Peck as NHTSA's administrator created in that agency a philosophy of deregulation of the automobile industry, reversing the support for mandatory airbags expressed during the Carter administration. And his appointment of S. R. Shad, a vice president of E. F. Hutton and Company, to head the Securities and Exchange Commission narrowed the SEC's view of its role in the regulation of the marketing of new securities. This contrasted greatly with an agency that had an independent and aggressive staff that traditionally had sought tough enforcement of disclosure requirements and antifraud provisions.

Agency Profiles

The following agency profiles describe the sixty-three independent establishments, government corporations, and quasi-official agencies, as defined in the *U.S. Government Manual*, in existence as of January 1989. Unless stated otherwise the following rules apply to each agency: the agencies do not have a bipartisanship requirement of its governing body; a new president can replace the agency head at the beginning of a new administration; and the governing body serves at the discretion of the president.

ACTION

Established in 1971 by executive order, ACTION is the center for federal volunteer programs, resources, and initiatives. The organization is headed by a director and a deputy director who are appointed by the president with Senate confirmation, as is an associate director for Domestic and Anti-Poverty Operations. Terms of office are not fixed, and appointees serve at the discretion of the president and may be replaced by an incoming president.

ACTION is headquartered in Washington, D.C., and maintains nine regional offices and forty-eight state or district offices. ACTION programs are carried out in all fifty states, Puerto Rico, the Virgin Islands, and the District of Columbia. Programs supported by ACTION involve more than 397,000 volunteers who serve full time or part time for up to two years. Some volunteers receive stipends; others receive no remuneration.

Volunteers in Service to America (VISTA) is the oldest program in ACTION. VISTA's goal is to alleviate poverty in the United States. Volunteers serve on a full-time basis and work through locally sponsored community projects. ACTION provides VISTA volunteers with a basic subsistence allowance for housing, food, and incidentals. More than half of VISTA's programs are designed to serve young people.

In the Foster Grandparents Program, low-income volunteers sixty years old and over provide companionship and guidance to mentally, physically, or emotionally handicapped children and those in the juvenile justice system. In 1987, more than twenty-three thousand seniors participated in the Foster Grandparent Program. The Retired Senior Volunteer Program (RSVP) is the largest ACTION program, with 365,000 volunteers. RSVP places retirees aged sixty and over with nonprofit organizations and public agencies in need of volunteer services. Funding and technical assistance are provided by ACTION and local communities. The Senior Companion Program was established in 1974 under the Domestic Volunteer Service Act. Under the program, low-income persons aged sixty or over provide care and companionship to other adults, particularly the homebound elderly.

ACTION also operates the National Center for Service Learning, a student volunteer program. The center provides free training, resource materials, and on-site consultation to high school, college, and community staff personnel who direct, plan, and develop student volunteer programs. Young Volunteers in Action consists of volunteers aged fourteen to twenty-two, who participate in projects such as tutoring homebound students, serving in parks and recreation centers, assisting in hospitals, and aiding disaster-relief efforts. Volunteers may be eligible for academic credit for their work. The Office of Voluntarism Initiatives administers programs that support local self-reliance through volunteer initiatives and that encourage citizen participation in volunteer projects.

ACTION has primary responsibility for carrying out the federal drug abuse prevention effort through its Drug Prevention Program. The program sponsors drug-use education and prevention efforts and disseminates information on the health effects of drugs and on various prevention methods.

Administrative Conference of the United States

The Administrative Conference of the United States is a permanent, independent federal agency that recommends improvements in the administration of regulatory, benefit, and other government programs. Established by the Administrative Conference Act of 1964, the Administrative

Conference is headed by a chair who is appointed to a five-year term by the president, with Senate confirmation. A council, which acts as an executive board, consists of the chair and ten other members appointed by the president for three-year terms. Additional members numbering not fewer than sixty-four or more than eighty are drawn from government and the private sector to serve two-year terms. Members representing the private sector are appointed by the chair, with council approval.

The Administrative Conference provides a forum for agency officials, private lawyers, university professors, and other experts in administrative law and government to study procedural problems and to develop improvements. The entire membership meets at least once each year. Membership is divided into six standing committees: adjudication, administration, governmental processes, judicial review, regulation, and rule making. The committees study subjects selected by either the chair, the council, or the assembly. The assembly has authority to approve, reject, or amend any recommendations presented by the committees. Although the final recommendations of the Administrative Conference are nonbinding, the chair is authorized to encourage departments and agencies to adopt the proposed changes.

African Development Foundation

The African Development Foundation (ADF) is an independent public corporation created by Congress to provide development assistance to indigenous nongovernmental African groups and individuals. Congress authorized ADF in 1980 as a complement to U.S. foreign aid programs; its aim is to deliver economic assistance directly to African communities and grass-roots organizations. Aid is awarded primarily for farming, education, husbandry, manufacturing, and water management projects. In the legislation that created ADF, Congress required that the corporation's beneficiaries design and implement their own projects. Since 1984 ADF has funded more than one hundred projects in nineteen countries. The foundation is governed by a seven-member board of directors appointed by the president with Senate confirmation. Board members serve staggered terms ranging from two to six years. By law five members are chosen from the private sector and two are from the government.

The goal of ADF is to make local communities responsible for their own development through programs appropriate for their needs and to give priority to objectives established by the community. ADF also seeks to demonstrate the value of local or traditional methods, so as to avoid social and economic disruption caused by the introduction of new equipment or production systems.

Because its purpose is to provide grass-roots assistance, ADF requires that a basic level of community organization be in place at the time a request is made. In addition, a proposed project must involve the community at large, and the community must comprehend the responsibilities of implementing the project and its recurring costs. Communities requesting ADF aid also must demonstrate the skill and capacity to manage project funds effectively.

In addition to funding grass-roots development activities, ADF supports applied research conceived and executed by Africans. ADF's field staff includes African Regional Liaison Officers (RLOs) who serve as liaisons between ADF and applicants in each of ADF's five African regions. RLOs provide technical support, assist ADF in monitoring projects, and provide information about funding procedures. Country Resource Facilitators provide the same support in those countries in which they are resident.

American Battle Monuments Commission

The American Battle Monuments Commission (ABMC) is responsible for commemorating the services of American armed forces where they have served since the United States entered into World War I on April 6, 1917. A small independent agency, ABMC oversees the design, construction, operation, and maintenance of permanent U.S. military burial grounds in foreign countries. ABMC also controls the design and construction of U.S. military monuments and markers in foreign countries by U.S. citizens and organizations both public and private.

Created by Congress in 1923, ABMC administers, operates, and maintains twenty-four permanent U.S. military burial grounds, twelve separate monuments, and four memorials in twelve countries worldwide. The policy-making body of the commission comprises eleven members who are appointed by the president for an indefinite term and serve without pay. The board members and their elected chair serve at the pleasure of the president. New appointments can immediately be made by an incoming president. A professional staff of full-time civilian employees consists of U.S. citizens and foreign nationals from countries where ABMC installations are located. Field offices in Paris and Rome supervise operations in Europe and the Mediterranean. The superintendents of the cemeteries in Mexico City, Corozal, Panama, and Manila report directly to the Washington office.

The commission provides assistance in locating grave and memorial sites and general information on travel and accommodations for visitors. For immediate family traveling overseas specifically to visit a grave or memorial site, the commission provides letters authorizing "non-fee" passports and other services at the grave site.

Appalachian Regional Commission

The Appalachian Regional Commission (ARC) administers a comprehensive program for the economic development of the Appalachian region. Created by the Appalachian Regional Development Act of 1965, the commission consists of fourteen members, including the thirteen sitting governors of states within the Appalachian region and a federal chair, appointed by the president and subject to Senate confirmation. A cochair also is appointed. The federal cochair serves at the pleasure of the president. Members' terms run concurrent with their terms as governor.

The Appalachian region, as defined by the Appalachian Regional Development Act as amended, includes all of West Virginia and parts of New York, Pennsylvania, Maryland, Virginia, Ohio, Kentucky, Tennessee, North Carolina, South Carolina, Georgia, Alabama, and Mississippi. It incorporates 397 counties, covers a total of 195,000 square miles, and has a current population of more than twenty million.

Federal efforts to revitalize the economy of the Appalachian region had been considered as early as 1902. The region had been poor and underdeveloped even though it is rich in resources. By 1964 per capita income in many areas of the region was less than half the national average, and education levels in the region were far below the national average.

Board for International Broadcasting

The Board for International Broadcasting (BIB) is an independent federal agency chartered to oversee the operations of the nonprofit radio corporation Radio Free Europe/Radio Liberty (RFE/RL). Radio Liberty broadcasts to the Soviet Union, and Radio Free Europe broadcasts to Poland, Romania, Czechoslovakia, Hungary, Bulgaria, and the Baltic states. Both programs operated as separate entities from the early 1950s until 1976, when they merged to create Radio Free Europe/Radio Liberty, Inc. RFE/RL has a statutory mission to further the open communication of information and ideas in Eastern Europe and the Soviet Union. In terms of broadcast hours, it is the leading external broadcaster to those areas.

The main function of BIB is to "assess the quality, effectiveness, and professional integrity" of RFE/RL's broadcasts "within the context of the broad foreign policy objectives of the United States." Established in 1973, the board is composed of nine members including a chair, who are appointed by the president with Senate confirmation. No more than five members may be from the same political party, and members serve three-year terms. The chief operating executive of RFE/RL is chosen by the board and becomes an ex officio, nonvoting member of BIB. All members of the board serve at the pleasure of the president.

In addition to its oversight responsibilities, the board develops long-range strategies for REF/RL and conducts studies to determine the most efficient allocation of resources. The board administers grants awarded to REF/RL and procures specialized electronic equipment for the company. Under the board's guidance, REF/RL provides news, political analysis, and cultural programs in twenty-two languages, using five transmitter relay stations. In 1985, Radio Free Afghanistan, a new service of Radio Liberty, went on the air. The service broadcasts seven hours a week to Afghanistan in that country's principal language, Dari.

Central Intelligence Agency

The Central Intelligence Agency (CIA) is an independent agency established by the National Security Act of 1947 to coordinate the nation's intelligence activities and to correlate, evaluate, and disseminate intelligence that affects national security. The CIA is responsible for the production of political, military, economic, biographical, sociological, and scientific and technical intelligence to meet the needs of national policy makers.

The CIA is headed by a director and a deputy director who are appointed to an indefinite term by the president with Senate confirmation and serve at the discretion of the president. The director of the CIA is designated as the director of central intelligence (DCI). In addition to heading the CIA, the DCI heads the intelligence community and is the primary adviser to the president and the National Security Council on national foreign intelligence matters. The director of the CIA is not a cabinet-level position. One exception, however, was William Casey, who was appointed by President Ronald Reagan, and designated as a cabinet officer.

In addition to the DCI's office staff, the intelligence community consists of the CIA, the National Security Agency, the Defense Intelligence Agency, the offices within the Department of Defense responsible for collection of specialized national foreign intelligence, the Bureau of Intelligence and Research of the Department of State, and the intelligence elements of the military services, the Federal Bureau of Investigation, and the Departments of Treasury and Energy.

In 1949 the National Security Act was amended by the Central Intelligence Agency Act. The legislation permits the CIA to use confidential fiscal and administrative procedures, and it exempted the agency from certain limitations on expenditure of federal funds. The act allows CIA funds to be included in the budgets of other agencies and then transferred to the CIA without regard to the restrictions placed on the initial appropriation. The amount of CIA funds held by other agencies is classified. The 1949 act also exempted the CIA from having to disclose its organization, functions, number of personnel, and the names, titles, and salaries of its employees.

The CIA conducts covert activities abroad in support of U.S. foreign policy objectives. These actions are executed so that the role of the U.S. government is not apparent or acknowledged publicly. Only the president can authorize covert actions upon the recommendation of the National Security Council. Upon initiating a covert action, the DCI must notify the intelligence oversight committees of Congress.

The agency has no law enforcement or security functions either at home or abroad. The CIA is expressly prohibited by presidential executive order from routinely engaging in the domestic use of electronic, mail, or physical surveillance, monitoring devices, or unconsented physical search. These restrictions can be lifted only under the most extraordinary conditions of concern for the national welfare and only with the approval of the U.S. attorney general.

Oversight of the CIA is conducted by the Intelligence Oversight Board. The board consists of three voluntary members appointed by the president from the public sector. Board members serve indefinite terms at the discretion of the president. The chair of the board is also a member of the president's Foreign Intelligence Advisory Board.

Commission of Fine Arts

The Commission of Fine Arts was established by Congress in 1910 to advise the government on matters pertaining to the arts and the architectural development of Washington, D.C. The commission, comprising seven members including a director who are appointed by the president for four-year terms, was initially authorized to advise on statues, fountains, and monuments within the District of Columbia. Subsequent executive orders and acts of Congress have greatly expanded the commission's duties to include the preservation of places of national interest and approval of architectural designs of government buildings.

The commission also reviews plans for private structures within the district and advises on building height limits and architectural standards in the Old Georgetown and Shipstead-Luce areas. Land to be acquired as parkland

in the District of Columbia, Maryland, and Virginia also falls under commission responsibility.

The commission's members advise on matters of art and architectural development when requested to do so by the president or by a member of Congress. Contracting officers of the federal and district governments also are directed to call for the commission's advice on such matters. Among the more significant reviews by the commission are the Mall, the Lincoln Memorial, the Federal Triangle, the National Gallery of Art, and the Vietnam Veterans Memorial. The commission is not required by law to be bipartisan, and members serve at the pleasure of the president.

Commission on the Bicentennial of the U.S. Constitution

Established by Congress in July 1985, the Commission on the Bicentennial of the U.S. Constitution promotes and coordinates activities to commemorate the Constitution, adopted at the Constitutional Convention on September 17, 1787. Through national, state, and local events, it seeks to increase awareness and understanding of the country's founding document.

The commission comprises twenty-three members, twenty of whom are appointed by the president. The chief justice of the United States, the president pro tempore of the Senate, and the Speaker of the House of Representatives, or their designees, are also members. Commission members, including the chair, serve for the life of the commission. Senate confirmation of the chair was not required. A staff director manages the commission. The commission receives funds from corporate sponsors as well as from the federal government.

Nationwide bicentennial activities included a high school essay contest; a traveling exhibition of the Constitution, Magna Carta, and other historic documents; and distribution of more than 300 million copies of the Constitution. The commission recognized cities, towns, and counties—termed "Designated Bicentennial Communities"—that formed a body to plan local events celebrating the Constitution. Before it disbands in December 1991, the commission also will mark bicentennials of the Bill of Rights, the formation of the first federal government, and the first Congress.

Commission on Civil Rights

Established by the Civil Rights Act of 1957, the Commission on Civil Rights is an independent, fact-finding agency that monitors developments in civil rights under the Constitution. The Civil Rights Act of 1983 increased the commission's membership from six to eight commissioners, four of whom are appointed by the president and four by Congress. Not more than four members may be of the same party. With the approval of a majority of the commission, the president designates a chair and a vice chair from among its members.

Commissioners serve either six- or three-year-terms and can be removed by the president only for neglect of duty or malfeasance in office. A full-time staff director oversees the day-to-day activities of the commission. The chair is appointed by the president with the commission's approval and serves at the pleasure of the president. An incoming president can appoint a new chair at any time.

The commission assesses the laws and policies of the federal government to determine the nature and extent of denial of equal protection under the law on the basis of race, color, religion, sex, national origin, age, or handicap, and it submits reports to the president and to Congress. Areas of study include employment, voting rights, education, and housing.

In its fact-finding capacity, the commission may hold hearings and issue subpoenas for the production of documents and the attendance of witnesses at such hearings. Subpoenas may be issued in the state in which the hearing is being held and within a fifty-mile radius of the site. The commission maintains advisory committees and consults with representatives of federal, state, and local governments and private organizations. The commission lacks direct enforcement powers but refers complaints to appropriate government agencies for action.

Advisory committees are located in each state and in the District of Columbia. Each committee comprises citizens familiar with local and state civil rights issues. The members serve without compensation and assist the commission with its fact-finding, investigative, and information dissemination functions. Three regional offices coordinate the commission's regional operations and assist the state advisory committees in their activities. The offices are staffed by a director, equal opportunity specialists, researchers, attorneys, and other administrative personnel.

The commission maintains a library that serves as a national clearinghouse for civil rights information and conducts studies of discrimination against certain groups, including women, blacks, Hispanics, eastern and southern Europeans, and Asian and Pacific island Americans.

Commodity Futures Trading Commission

The Commodity Futures Trading Commission (CFTC) is an independent regulatory agency established in 1975 to administer the Commodity Exchange Act of 1936. Congressional legislation established the CFTC in 1974 for four years. This mandate was renewed in 1978, 1982, and 1986.

The purpose of the commission is to ensure that futures markets function smoothly. Oversight regulation is needed to guard against manipulation, abusive trade practices, and fraud. Specific responsibilities of the commission include regulating commodities exchanges, approving futures contracts, registering commodities traders, protecting customers, and monitoring information. The commission has three major operating units: the Divisions of Economic Analysis, Enforcement, and Trading and Markets. The CFTC serves as a disseminator of knowledge about commodities markets. It publishes weekly commodity reports, *Monthly Commitments of Traders* reports, and relevant books and pamphlets. It also provides training courses to people in the field.

The CFTC is headed by five commissioners who are appointed by the president with the consent of the Senate. They serve staggered five-year terms, and no more than three commissioners can be of the same political party. The president designates one commissioner as chair. A majority vote by the commissioners is required for major policy decisions and committee actions.

In 1981, the CFTC registered the National Futures Association (NFA) as an industrywide self-regulatory organization. The NFA safeguards the interests of public and commercial users of futures markets by establishing codes of conduct and offering advice. If a dispute arises between customers and sellers, the NFA can provide arbitration. In 1982, Congress passed a law requiring the NFA and the CFTC to begin actively sharing regulatory responsibilities.

Consumer Product Safety Commission

The Consumer Product Safety Commission (CPSC) is an independent regulatory agency established by Congress to protect consumers from unreasonable risks of injury associated with consumer products. Created by the 1972 Consumer Product Safety Act (CPSA), in response to the consumer movement, the CPSC comprises five commissioners, not more than three of whom may be members of the same political party. Commissioners are appointed to seven-year terms by the president, with Senate confirmation. The president also designates one of the commissioners to serve as chair. The chair and commissioners can be removed by the president for neglect of duty or malfeasance, but for no other reason. A newly elected president, however, can appoint a new chair.

In addition to the Consumer Product Safety Act, the CPSC administers the Flammable Fabrics Act, the Federal Hazardous Substances Act, the Poison Prevention Packaging Act of 1970, and the Refrigerator Safety Act. The commission's statutory mandate provides a broad range of regulatory authority over consumer products. CPSC responsibilities include development of uniform safety standards, bans on unsafe products, safety test methods and testing devices, and development of consumer and industry education programs. Consumer products not regulated by the CPSA include boats, cars, planes, food, drugs, cosmetics, pesticides, medical devices, alcohol, tobacco, and firearms. Standards set by the CPSC preempt any differing state or local law; however, states and localities may set different standards that produce a greater degree of consumer protection without undue burden on interstate commerce.

The CPSC currently uses two advisory bodies to implement its legislative mandate. The Toxicological Advisory Board is composed of members qualified in scientific disciplines relating to toxicology. The board gives the commission scientific and technical advice on precautionary labeling for hazardous substances.

The commission also can create a Chronic Hazard Advisory Panel to advise the commission about the risk of cancer, birth defects, or gene mutations associated with consumer products. The panels, formed when the commission perceives a need, consist of seven members appointed from a list of scientists nominated by the president of the National Academy of Sciences.

Responsibility for correcting potentially hazardous products belongs primarily to manufacturers, who are required to certify that the consumer products they produce meet all applicable safety standards issued under the CPSA. They must allow the CPSC to test products for compliance and inspect and investigate their factories. If a manufacturer fails to comply with a standard or certification requirement, charges may be brought against the company by the Justice Department of the commission in U.S. district court.

Environmental Protection Agency

The Environmental Protection Agency (EPA) is an independent regulatory agency responsible for implementing the federal laws designed to protect the environment. EPA was created in 1970 through an executive reorganization plan that consolidated components of five executive departments and independent agencies into a single regulatory agency.

The agency is directed by an administrator and a deputy administrator appointed by the president with Senate confirmation. Nine assistant administrators manage specific environmental programs or direct other EPA functions. The agency's general counsel and its inspector general also are named by the president with Senate confirmation. The agency has ten regional administrators across the country. All governing members of EPA are appointed to no fixed term and serve at the pleasure of the president.

EPA administers nine comprehensive environmental protection laws that authorize the agency to protect the public health and welfare from harmful effects of pollutants and toxic substances. The Clean Water Act authorizes EPA to restore and maintain the "chemical, physical, and biological integrity of the Nation's waters." Under the Safe Drinking Water Act of 1974, EPA establishes national standards for drinking water from both surface and ground water sources. The fundamental objective of the Clean Air Act is the protection of the public health and welfare from harmful effects of air pollution. Regulation of current and future waste management and disposal practices was authorized by the Resource Conservation and Recovery Act. In 1980 Congress passed the Comprehensive Environmental Response, Compensation, and Liability Act, also called the "Superfund." The Superfund program provides EPA with a trust fund of $8.5 billion to respond to conditions or sites that pose a danger to human health or the environment.

EPA's Office of Pesticide Programs administers two statutes regulating pesticides. The Federal Insecticide, Fungicide, and Rodenticide Act governs the licensing or registration of pesticide residue levels in food or feed crops. The Toxic Substances Control Act authorizes EPA to identify and control chemicals that pose an unreasonable risk to human health or the environment. In addition, EPA administers the Marine Protection, Research, and Sanctuaries Act and the Uranium Mill Tailings Radiation Control Act.

The agency maintains a research office that provides data in six major research areas: engineering and technology, environmental processes and effects, monitoring systems and quality assurance, health effects, health and environmental assessment, and exploratory research. For technical advice and review, EPA relies on its Science Advisory Board, consisting of eminent non-EPA scientists. Congress created the board to advise the agency on scientific issues and to review the quality of EPA scientific research.

Enforcement of EPA regulations is supported by state agencies and the agency's National Enforcement Investigation Center in Denver, Colorado. The agency also maintains a criminal investigation unit with specialized training in criminal law enforcement techniques. The agency enforces its regulations through compliance promotion, administrative money penalties, negotiated compliance schedules, and judicial enforcement entailing criminal proceedings.

Equal Employment Opportunity Commission

The Equal Employment Opportunity Commission (EEOC) is an independent agency established in 1965 to eliminate employment discrimination based on race, color, religion, sex, or national origin. EEOC is composed of five commissioners, not more than three of whom may be of the same political party. The commissioners are appointed by the president and confirmed by the Senate for staggered five-year terms. The president designates one member to serve as chair and another to serve as vice-chair. The general counsel also is nominated by the president and confirmed by the Senate for a four-year term. The chair is responsible for the administration of the commission. The five-member commission decides equal employment opportunity policy and approves all litigation undertaken by the commission. The general counsel is responsible for conducting all commission litigation. All appointees to EEOC serve at the pleasure of the president.

The commission was created by Title VII of the Civil Rights Act of 1964. The Equal Employment Opportunity Act of 1972 extended the commission's jurisdiction to include state and local governments, public and private educational institutions, public and private employment agencies, and private businesses that ship or receive goods across state lines and employ fifteen or more persons. EEOC jurisdiction also covers labor unions with fifteen or more members and joint labor-management committees for apprenticeships and training.

The commission has authority to investigate, conciliate, and litigate charges of discrimination in employment. It also has the authority to issue guidelines, rules, and regulations and to require employers, unions, and others covered by Title VII to report regularly the race, ethnic origin, and sex of their employees and members. In cases where a charge of discrimination cannot be conciliated, EEOC has the authority to file a lawsuit in federal district court to force compliance with Title VII.

In addition to administering Title VII, EEOC enforces the Equal Pay Act of 1963, which requires equal pay for equal work, and the Age Discrimination in Employment Act of 1967. In 1978, the Pregnancy Discrimination Act amended the Civil Rights Act of 1964 to prohibit discrimination on the basis of pregnancy, childbirth, or related medical conditions.

EEOC also administers Executive Order 12067, which requires oversight and coordination of all federal equal employment opportunity regulations, practices, and policies. Responsibility regarding handicap discrimination in federal employment was transferred to the commission from the former Civil Service Commission. Employees of the U.S. Congress are not under the protection of the EEOC because the Congress exempted itself from the provisions of Title VII.

Export-Import Bank of the United States

The Export-Import Bank (Eximbank) is an independent, corporate agency that stimulates foreign trade by supporting export financing of U.S. goods and services. Founded in 1934, Eximbank was intended to increase foreign trade during the Great Depression. The agency's first

Agencies and Corporations 119

loan in 1935 financed the Cuban government's purchase of silver from U.S. mines. Eximbank also financed construction of the Burma Road in the late 1930s and the Pan American Highway through Latin America in the 1940s. After World War II, Eximbank helped U.S. companies participate in the reconstruction of Europe and Asia. Eximbank supports U.S. exports by neutralizing the effect of export credit subsidies from other governments and absorbing risks the private sector will not accept.

Eximbank's board of directors consists of five full-time members appointed for four-year terms by the president with Senate confirmation. One member is appointed by the president to serve as chair. All members of the board serve at the discretion of the president. In addition, the secretary of commerce and the U.S. trade representative serve as ex officio, nonvoting members. The board is responsible for Eximbank's activities and policies and approves support for individual transactions.

The bank is organized into two main operating divisions. The International Lending Division manages, administers, and coordinates Eximbank's medium-term and long-term international lending and guarantee activities. Eximbank's loans provide competitive fixed-interest-rate financing for U.S. exports facing foreign competition that is backed with subsidized official financing. Evidence of foreign competition is not required for exports produced by small businesses where the loan amount is $2.5 million or less. Eximbank extends direct loans to foreign buyers of U.S. exports and intermediary loans to fund parties that lend to foreign buyers.

The Insurance and Banking Division is divided into a United States division and an insurance division. The U.S. division is responsible for loans and guarantees to U.S. borrowers, specifically the Working Capital Guarantee Program, which helps small companies obtain pre-export financing from commercial lenders. In addition, Eximbank provides loans and guarantees to American companies competing for domestic sales against foreign firms backed by unfairly subsidized financing from a foreign export credit agency.

The insurance division is responsible for Eximbank's export credit insurance programs. The agency's Foreign Credit Insurance Association provides credit insurance policies for nonpayment on export credit transactions that cover political and commercial risks. Political risks include war, cancellation of an existing export or import license, expropriation, confiscation of or intervention in the buyer's business, and transfer risk (failure of foreign government authorities to transfer the foreign currency deposit into dollars). Commercial risks cover nonpayment for reasons other than specified political risks.

Eximbank's policies are coordinated with overall U.S. government foreign and economic policies and do not normally support sales to Communist countries. To be eligible for Eximbank support, 50 percent of goods or services exported must be of U.S. manufacture.

Farm Credit Administration

The Farm Credit Administration (FCA) is an independent financial regulatory agency established in 1933 to oversee the Farm Credit System. FCA was created in response to the need for increased lending to rural farmers unable to obtain credit from bankers headquartered in large U.S. cities.

FCA is administered by a three-member, full-time board of directors appointed by the president with Senate confirmation. The directors serve staggered terms of two, four, and six years, and not more than two members can be of the same political party. The president also selects one member to serve as chair and as the agency's chief executive officer. Board members can be removed for neglect of duty or malfeasance, but for no other reason. New appointments including the chair can be made immediately by an incoming president. As head of FCA, the board provides for the examination and regulation of and reporting by institutions within the Farm Credit System, a nationwide network of agricultural lending institutions and their service organizations. The Farm Credit System comprises three types of banks: the Federal Land Banks, the Federal Intermediate Credit Banks, and the Banks for Cooperatives. In addition to the FCA board, the agency is organized under offices of Examination, General Counsel, Internal Audit, Congressional and Public Affairs, Analysis and Supervision, and Administration.

In 1916 Congress passed the Federal Farm Loan Act, which divided the country into twelve farm credit districts and created and funded a Federal Land Bank in each of them. The land banks make long-term farm mortgage loans through local Federal Land Bank Associations. Loans can be made to farmers, ranchers, commercial fishers, rural homeowners, and people operating farm-related businesses and legal entities. Federal Land Banks hold more than 40 percent of all outstanding farm real estate debt in the United States.

In 1923 Congress passed the Agricultural Credits Act, establishing and funding twelve Federal Intermediate Credit Banks. The banks provide short- and intermediate-term loan funds to Production Credit Associations and other financing institutions serving agricultural producers.

The Production Credit Associations, established in 1933 by the Farm Credit Act, also provide short- and intermediate-term loans. Loans are made to farmers, ranchers, rural homeowners, producers and harvesters of aquatic products, and to people operating certain farm-related businesses. Most loans are for operating purposes and mature within a year. The associations also grant intermediate-term loans of up to ten years to agricultural producers and up to fifteen years for commercial fishers.

The Farm Credit Act also established thirteen Banks for Cooperatives to provide financing for agricultural cooperatives. The banks participate with the district banks on loans that exceed their individual lending capacities. They also participate in international lending activities that benefit U.S. cooperatives.

In its regulatory capacity, the FCA has a broad range of authority, including the power to issue cease-and-desist orders, levy civil money penalties, and remove officers and directors of system institutions. The FCA also is responsible for direct examination of the Federal Land Bank Associations and the Production Credit Association. Although it is a federal agency, the expenses of the FCA are paid by the Farm Credit Banks.

Federal Communications Commission

The Federal Communications Commission (FCC) is an independent regulatory agency charged with regulating interstate and international communications by radio, television, wire, satellite, and cable. Established by the Communications Act of 1934, the FCC assumed regulatory authority previously exercised by the Federal Radio Commission (which was abolished), the secretary of commerce, and the Interstate Commerce Commission. FCC jurisdiction covers the fifty states, the District of Columbia, and the possessions of the United States.

The FCC is composed of five commissioners, not more than three of whom may be members of the same political party. The commissioners are nominated by the president and confirmed by the Senate for staggered seven-year terms. The terms are arranged so that no two expire in the same year. The president also designates one of the members to serve as chair. The chair can be removed for neglect of duty or malfeasance, but for no other reason unless replaced by an incoming president.

The commissioners supervise all FCC activities, delegating responsibilities to staff units, bureaus, and committees. The FCC allocates bands of frequencies to nongovernment communications services and assigns frequencies to individual stations. The commission also licenses and regulates stations and operators. It regulates the technical aspects and equal employment practices of cable systems and monitors competition in the cable industry.

The FCC does not regulate the broadcast networks or programming practices of individual stations, but it does have rules governing obscenity, slander, and political broadcasts. The FCC has no authority over government communication or other forms of communications media, including movies, newspapers, and books.

The four bureaus that conduct most FCC regulatory activities are Mass Media, Common Carrier, Private Radio, and Field Operations. The Mass Media bureau regulates AM, FM, and television broadcast stations and related facilities. The bureau also administers and enforces cable television rules and licenses private microwave radio facilities used by cable systems. The Common Carrier bureau regulates common carriers of wire and radio communications including telephone, telegraph, and satellite companies. The Private Radio bureau regulates radio stations providing communications services to businesses, individuals, nonprofit organizations, and state and local governments. Field Operations detects violations of radio regulations, monitors transmissions, inspects stations, investigates complaints of radio interference, and issues violation notices.

The FCC maintains a chief scientist and general counsel to act on international matters and to assist in regulatory functions. The chief scientist advises the commission on technical, engineering, and scientific matters. The general counsel advises the commission on legal issues, coordinates its legislative program, and represents the commission in court.

Federal Deposit Insurance Corporation

The Federal Deposit Insurance Corporation (FDIC) is an independent agency that provides insurance to bank depositors and serves as the federal regulator and supervisor of insured state banks that are not members of the Federal Reserve System. The FDIC was established by the Banking Act of 1933 to provide protection against mounting bank failures that followed the stock market crash of October 1929. The corporation insures funds of bank depositors up to $100,000. Separate $100,000 coverage is provided to holders of Keogh Plan Retirement Accounts and Individual Retirement Accounts.

Management of the corporation is carried out by a three-member board of directors, two of whom are appointed by the president with Senate confirmation for six-year terms. One of these appointed directors is designated by the president to be chair. Board members can be removed for neglect of duty or malfeasance but for no other reason, although the president may appoint another director as chair at any time. The comptroller of the currency, who serves ex officio as the board's third member, also is appointed by the president with Senate confirmation for a five-year term. Only two members of the board may be members of the same political party.

Many states require state-chartered banks that are not members of the Federal Reserve System to apply to the FDIC for federal insurance coverage. The FDIC examines banks to determine the adequacy of their capital structure, prospects for future earnings, the general character of each bank's management, and the needs of the community in which each bank is located. National banks and state banks that are members of the Federal Reserve System receive FDIC insurance with their charters and do not require investigation by the corporation.

At year-end 1985, the FDIC employed 1,542 bank examiners at 105 offices throughout the nation. Corporation examiners conduct about ten thousand bank examinations and investigations each year and issue reports on their findings. Each examination report outlines any unacceptable banking practices or violations of law and suggests corrective steps. Usually, the FDIC then attempts to work with the bank management informally by obtaining its approval of a corrective agreement or by privately issuing a proposed notice of charges and a proposed cease-and-desist order. If, after a meeting with the bank and the appropriate state supervisory authority, the bank does not consent to comply with the proposed order, the FDIC will initiate formal proceedings by publicly issuing the notice of charges and holding a hearing before an administrative law judge.

The FDIC also can terminate a bank's insurance if it finds the bank has been conducting its affairs in an unsound and unsafe manner. When insurance is terminated, existing deposits, less subsequent withdrawals, continue to be insured by the FDIC for two years. If a bank becomes insolvent, the FDIC attempts to arrange a deposit assumption, in which another bank takes over many of the assets of the failed bank and assumes both insured and uninsured deposits. If such a transaction cannot be arranged, the FDIC pays off all depositors to the insured maximum limit.

The FDIC receives no annual appropriations from Congress. Funding is provided from assessments on deposits held by insured banks and from interest on the required investment of its surplus funds in government securities. The FDIC can withdraw up to $3 billion from the Treasury to augment its Deposit Insurance Fund, but this option never has been exercised. Depositors in failed FDIC-insured banks have recovered about 99.4 percent of their total deposits from January 1, 1934, through December 31, 1984.

Federal Election Commission

The Federal Election Commission (FEC) is an independent regulatory agency created in 1975 to administer and enforce the provisions of the Federal Election Campaign Act of 1971. The commission comprises six members appointed by the president and confirmed by the Senate. The commissioners serve staggered six-year terms, and no more than three commissioners may be members of the same political party. The chair and vice-chair must be members of different political parties and are elected annually by their fellow commissioners. The chair can be removed only by impeachment and cannot be replaced by the president until the chair's term expires. The clerk of the House of Representatives and the secretary of the Senate serve as nonvoting members of the commission.

There were several attempts to reform campaign financing before the Federal Election Campaign Act of 1971. As early as 1907, Theodore Roosevelt recommended public financing of federal elections and a ban on private contributions, with little success. The Corrupt Practices Act of 1925 attempted to force public disclosure of campaign finances; but, because it was not specific and inclusive, it was difficult to enforce.

The Federal Election Campaign Act of 1971, as amended, requires the disclosure of sources and uses of funds in campaigns for any federal office, limits the size of individual contributions, and provides for partial public financing of presidential elections. The act was amended in 1974 and 1976 to establish public financing of presidential primary elections, limits on campaign contributions, and an independent body to oversee the campaign finance law.

Any candidate for federal office and any political group or committee formed to support a candidate must register with the FEC and file periodic reports on campaign financing. Individuals and committees making expenditures on behalf of a candidate must also file reports.

Contributions from national banks, corporations, labor organizations, government contractors, and nonresident foreign nationals are prohibited. Also prohibited are contributions of cash in excess of $100, contributions from one person given in the name of another, and contributions exceeding legal limits.

FEC staff members review the reports for omissions, and, if any are found, they request additional information from the candidate or committee. If the missing information is not supplied, the FEC has the authority to seek a conciliation agreement, to impose a fine, or to sue for the information in U.S. district court. These procedures also apply to cases in which the FEC discovers a violation of campaign finance law. If any matter involves willful violations, the commission may refer the case to the Justice Department.

The commission also administers provisions of the law covering the public financing of presidential primaries and general elections.

Federal Emergency Management Agency

The Federal Emergency Management Agency (FEMA) is an independent agency responsible for the federal government's civil emergency preparedness, mitigation, and response activities in both peace and war. The agency headquarters are in Washington, D.C. The director of FEMA is appointed by the president with consent of the Senate and serves at the pleasure of the president.

In 1979 a presidential directive consolidated five federal agencies to form FEMA and transferred closely allied functions from other departments to the new agency. The former federal agencies that make up FEMA are: the Defense Civil Preparedness Agency, the Federal Disaster Assistance Administration, the Federal Preparedness Agency, the Federal Insurance Administration, and the United States Fire Administration. Other programs transferred to FEMA include the community preparedness for weather emergencies, Earthquake Hazard Reduction, dam safety coordination, and oversight of the Federal Emergency Broadcast System. In addition, two new functions were added to the agency's responsibilities—coordination of emergency warnings and federal response to consequences of terrorist incidents.

FEMA's National Preparedness Directorate develops and coordinates federal programs to ensure that government at all levels is able to respond to and recover from national emergencies. Its responsibilities include arrangements for succession to office and emergency organization of departments and agencies. The agency assesses national mobilization capabilities and develops programs for resource management during national and civil emergencies.

The State and Local Programs and Support Directorate provides funding, technical assistance, supplies, equipment, and training for state and local emergency programs. The directorate administers the President's Disaster Relief Program, which provides supplemental federal assistance when the president declares an emergency or major disaster. Requests for assistance under this program are made by the governor of the affected state and are directed to the president before being sent to the FEMA regional director. FEMA then evaluates the damage and assistance requirements and makes recommendations to the president. Direct disaster assistance can be extended to state and local governments and to individual victims and their families.

FEMA's National Flood Insurance Program provides insurance coverage to participating communities and works with local government officials to reduce future flood damage through floodplain management. FEMA also administers the National Earthquake Hazards Reduction program, which publishes seismic resistance design codes and construction methods. The United States Fire Administration seeks through education and research programs to lower loss of life and property because of fire. FEMA maintains the National Emergency Training Center in Emmitsburg, Maryland, which conducts education programs in hazard mitigation, emergency preparedness, fire prevention and control, disaster response, and long-term disaster recovery. There are ten FEMA regional offices nationwide. Each office is headed by a regional director who reports to the FEMA director and is responsible for all FEMA programs in the region.

Federal Home Loan Bank Board

The Federal Home Loan Bank board is an independent agency responsible for all federal regulation of the thrift industry. The board is one of three components of the Federal Home Loan Bank System and adopts the policies and regulations that guide the system. The other elements of the bank system are the twelve regional (district) federal home loan banks and the individual savings institutions that make up the thrift industry.

The bank system originated with the Federal Home Loan Bank Act passed by Congress in 1932. The act was a response to the Great Depression, which had undermined the nation's banking system and created a need for a reserve credit system to ensure the availability of funds for home financing.

The bank board comprises a governing panel that makes policy and an independent federal agency that carries out board policy in regulating, monitoring, and supervising the bank system. The board panel is composed of three members appointed by the president and confirmed by the Senate to four-year terms. The president designates one member of the panel as chair. Board members serve at the discretion of the president, and no more than two board members may belong to the same political party. An incoming president can appoint a new chair at any time.

The board members meet in formal session as often as necessary and adopt or amend regulations affecting the thrift industry and individual thrift institutions. The board also decides when to close or merge failing institutions, directs the policy of the Federal Savings and Loan Insurance Corporation (FSLIC), and regulates the twelve district banks. The bank board also governs the Federal Home Loan Mortgage Corporation, which operates a secondary or resale market for conventional home mortgages or mortgages not insured by a federal agency.

The agency is self-supporting, and its operating costs are paid from a U.S. Treasury account funded by assessments on the twelve district banks and by assessments on the FSLIC. The board creates new savings institutions by granting federal charters, grants new FSLIC deposit insurance, directs how associations must keep their books, and invests assets.

The district banks operate within guidelines established by the bank board and assist in carrying out the board's responsibilities. Each district bank is wholly owned by the member thrift institutions in its area. The banks are located throughout the United States and provide thrifts with additional funds and services. Certain district bank employees are empowered by the bank board to act as the board's agents, examining thrift institutions and supervising corrective measures when problems are found.

The bank system's third component consists of its member thrift institutions, which number more than three thousand. The majority of these institutions are savings and loan associations, and one-half of these are federally chartered and thus subject to all bank board regulations. State-chartered thrift institutions that carry FSLIC insurance are subject to some regulation by the bank board in addition to state regulations. Other bank board regulations apply to all members of the bank system.

Federal Labor Relations Authority

The Federal Labor Relations Authority (FLRA) is an independent agency established to administer Title VII of the Civil Service Reform Act of 1978. The FLRA is chartered to serve as a neutral third party in the resolution of labor-management disputes arising among unions, employees, and federal agencies. The FLRA is charged with resolution of labor-managements disputes among all employees, both U.S. citizens and foreign nationals of the Panama Canal area.

The authority comprises three full-time members appointed by the president with Senate confirmation and removable only for cause. Not more than two members may be of the same political party, and one member is desig-

nated by the president to serve as chair. Members serve staggered five-year terms, and an incoming president can appoint a new chair. The president also appoints a general counsel to a term of five years. The general counsel has direct responsibility for the investigation of alleged unfair labor practices and the filing and prosecuting of complaints.

The Federal Service Impasses Panel is an entity within the FLRA whose function is to assist in resolving negotiation impasses between agencies and unions. If the parties are unable to reach a settlement after assistance from the panel, the panel may hold hearings and take whatever action it deems necessary to resolve the impasse. The panel consists of a chairman and six other members appointed by the president. The panel is not bipartisan by law, and members serve five-year terms.

Specifically, the FLRA is empowered to determine the appropriateness of organizations representing federal employees. The authority supervises or conducts elections of labor organizations by employees and sets criteria for representation of national federal labor organizations. The authority also conducts hearings to resolve complaints of unfair labor practices and exceptions to awards granted by federal arbitrators.

Federal Maritime Commission

The Federal Maritime Commission (FMC) is an independent regulatory agency established by executive order in 1961 to replace the Federal Maritime Board as regulator of the ocean commerce of the United States. The order abolished the board and transferred its responsibility for promoting the nation's merchant marine to the Transportation Department's Maritime Administration.

The FMC has five members who are appointed by the president with Senate confirmation. No more than three of the commissioners may be members of the same political party. The president designates one of the commissioners to serve as chair at the president's discretion. Members serve five-year terms.

The FMC consists of six offices directly responsible to the chair: the offices of the managing director, the secretary, equal employment opportunity, policy planning and international affairs, the general counsel, and administrative law judges. Six bureaus report to the director of programs and are responsible for trade monitoring, domestic regulation, economic analysis, hearing investigations, and administration.

As required by the Shipping Acts of 1916 and 1984, the commission regulates the rates charged for shipping in domestic commerce, monitors the rates in foreign commerce, and licenses ocean freight forwarders. The commission also regulates the formation by shipping companies of rate-setting cartels (conferences) that would otherwise be in violation of antitrust statutes (the ocean carrier conferences were exempted from antitrust laws by both acts).

Other responsibilities of the FMC include review of rates filed by common carriers and investigation of charges of discriminatory practices in ocean commerce. The commission does not have the authority to approve or disapprove general rate increases or individual commodity rates in U.S. foreign commerce except for certain foreign government-owned carriers. Charges of discriminatory treatment are investigated and resolved by administrative proceedings conducted by FMC staff.

Federal Mediation and Conciliation Service

The Federal Mediation and Conciliation Service (FMCS) is an independent federal agency created to prevent and to minimize labor-management disputes having a significant effect on interstate commerce or national defense. Created by the Labor-Management Relations Act of 1947 (also known as the Taft-Hartley Act), FMCS is headed by a director who is appointed by the president with Senate confirmation. The director serves an indefinite term at the discretion of the president. An incoming president can appoint a new director at any time.

The FMCS objective is to prevent or minimize work stoppages by providing free mediation to labor-management disputes in both the public and private sectors of the economy. Collective bargaining, mediation, and voluntary arbitration are the processes encouraged by FMCS mediations for settling labor-management issues. FMCS does not mediate labor-management disputes in the railroad and airline industries, which fall under the jurisdiction of the National Mediation Board.

The Labor-Management Relations Act requires parties to notify FMCS thirty days before a contract termination or modification date so that mediation services may be proffered. If, in the opinion of the president, a threatened or actual strike may imperil the national health or safety, a board of inquiry, appointed from an agency list of arbitrators, may be appointed to submit a report on the dispute. After receiving the report, the president can seek to enjoin the strike for not more than eighty days.

FMCS offers five types of technical assistance programs: Labor Management Committees, training, Relationship by Objectives, consultation/liaison, and conferences and seminars. Labor Management Committees are cooperative efforts by disputing parties directed at improving specific work site problems, including safety and health, organization of work quality, productivity, and absenteeism. The committees also address common issues such as worker training and retraining and introduction of new technology.

Relationship by Objectives programs are usually implemented only when labor-management relations have deteriorated to the point that negotiators face difficulty proceeding. In these programs FMCS mediators attempt to analyze and restructure existing labor-management relationships and determine objectives agreeable to both parties.

Parties having disputes under collective bargaining agreements fall under the responsibility of the FMCS Division of Arbitration Services. FMCS maintains a roster of qualified private citizens experienced in the collective bargaining process. Upon request, FMCS will furnish a panel of these arbitrators from which the parties select the one most mutually acceptable to hear and provide a final decision on their particular dispute. In most cases a panel of arbitrators is provided only on joint request of the disputing parties.

To encourage cooperation among disputing parties FMCS regulations provide that information obtained by mediators in the course of the duties shall not be subsequently revealed in judicial, arbitrable, or administrative hearings. The Labor-Management Cooperation Act of 1978 empowered FMCS to provide financial assistance to eligible applicants for the establishment and operation of labor-management committees. The committees focus on such issues as enhancing labor relations, improving economic development, and increasing productivity.

Federal Reserve System

The Federal Reserve System (the "Fed") is an independent regulatory and monetary policy-making agency established by the Federal Reserve Act in 1913. The Fed is the nation's central bank and is charged with making and administering policy for the nation's credit and monetary affairs. It also has supervisory and regulatory power over banking in general and over state-chartered banks that are members of the system.

By buying and selling government securities, it influences the supply of credit and the level of interest rates, in turn strongly affecting the pace of economic activity and the overall price level. The Fed also regulates credit activities, collects economic data, and oversees the activities of bank holding companies.

The Fed consists of five major parts: the board of Governors, the Federal Open Market Committee, the twelve Federal Reserve banks, the Federal Advisory Council, and the member banks of the system. The Fed is administered by a board of seven governors who are nominated by the president and confirmed by the Senate. Governors are appointed to a single fourteen-year term. One member is designated by the president to serve as chair for a four-year term and can be reappointed. All appointees serve at the pleasure of the president.

The board's primary function is the formulation of monetary policy. It has authority to approve proposed changes in the discount rate, to change reserve requirements, to set margin requirements for financing of securities traded on national security exchanges, and to set maximum interest rates on time and savings deposits of its member banks.

The Federal Open Market Committee (FMOC) is composed of seven board members plus the president of the New York Reserve Bank. Four other voting positions rotate among the eleven remaining Reserve bank presidents. The committee establishes the extent to which the Fed buys and sells government and other securities. Purchases and sales of securities in the open market are undertaken to supply the credit and money needed for long-term economic growth, to offset cyclical economic swings, and to accommodate seasonal demands of businesses and consumers for money and credit. The committee also oversees the system's operations in foreign exchange markets.

The operations of the Fed are conducted through a nationwide network of twelve Federal Reserve banks and twenty-five branches. Each Reserve bank is an incorporated institution with its own board of directors. Under supervision of the Board of Governors, they determine interest rates the bank may charge on short-term collateral loans to member banks and on any loans extended to nonmember institutions.

The Federal Advisory Council consists of one member from each of the Federal Reserve districts. The council meets in Washington, D.C., at least four times a year. It confers with the Board of Governors on economic and banking matters and makes recommendations regarding the affairs of the system.

The Fed receives no funding from Congress. Interest

paid on government securities purchased by the Fed constitutes about 94 percent of the Fed's earnings. In addition, the Fed earns money from the fees it charges for its services, from interest on its discount window loans, and from its foreign currency operations.

Federal Retirement Thrift Investment Board

The Federal Retirement Thrift Investment Board is an independent agency responsible for establishing policies for the investments, management, and administration of the Thrift Savings Plan (TSP) for federal employees. Created by the Federal Employees' Retirement System Act of 1986, the board consists of five part-time members who are appointed by the president with consent of the Senate. The president designates one member as chair. A sixth member is appointed by the board as executive director, responsible for the management of the agency and TSP.

The board operates TSP solely for the benefit of the participants and their beneficiaries. Investments in the plan and earnings on those investments cannot be used for any other purpose. The plan is a tax-deferred retirement savings and investment plan chartered by Congress to provide federal employees with the same savings and tax benefits that many private corporations offer their employees. Because TSP is a defined contribution plan, the amount employees and their agencies may contribute to an account is established by law. Plan benefits are determined by the amount contributed and the earnings on the contributions. TSP is one of the three parts of the Federal Employees' Retirement System (FERS). FERS employees may invest up to 10 percent of their salary and are eligible for up to 5 percent in employer matching contributions.

The plan began operation on April 1, 1987, with $148 million invested in retirement savings accounts for 563,000 federal and postal employees. As of September 1988 thrift savings fund investments totaled $2.2 billion with 1.3 million participants.

Federal Trade Commission

The Federal Trade Commission (FTC) is an independent agency created to regulate interstate commerce in the United States. The FTC is headed by five commissioners who are nominated by the president and confirmed by the Senate for seven-year terms. One commissioner is designated chair by the president, and no more than three of the commissioners may be members of the same political party. Commissioners are removable only for cause. The chair serves at the discretion of the president but remains a commissioner if removed as head of the commission. An incoming president can appoint a new chair at any time.

Established in 1914 by the Federal Trade Commission Act, the FTC was created to act as the federal government's chief trustbuster. That same year, Congress passed the Clayton Antitrust Act, giving the FTC broad powers to define and prohibit unfair methods of competition and specific business activities tending to lessen competition or create monopolies. Consumer protection was added to the FTC's responsibilities in 1938 through passage of the Wheeler-Lea Amendment to the original FTC act.

In 1974, the Magnuson-Moss Warranty/Federal Trade Commission Improvement Act empowered the FTC to issue trade regulation rules (TRR). TRRs have the force of law and can apply to an entire industry or only to industries in a specific geographical region. The Bureau of Competition handles investigations and actions related to anticompetitive behavior. The Bureau of Consumer Protection handles consumer issues and problems.

Once the FTC determines that a company has engaged in illegal activities, it either negotiates an agreement with the company voluntarily to stop the practice, or it initiates adjudicative proceedings to order the practice stopped. The FTC also can order violators to make restitution to consumers harmed by their actions.

At the request of a business or an individual, the FTC may issue an advisory opinion on whether a practice violates FTC restrictions. The opinions define the limits of the law as they relate to that particular business practice. Advisory opinions may be overturned by the commission, which then must give the individual or business originally affected by the opinion a reasonable amount of time to alter practices to conform to the new ruling.

In complaints alleging anticompetitive or anti-consumer practices, the FTC initiates adjudicative proceedings. Before beginning a proceeding, the FTC conducts an investigation to determine whether charges of illegal behavior should be brought. The party charged is notified and given thirty days to respond to the complaint. If the respondent decides not to dispute the charge, the illegal practice must be stopped. The respondent also may dispute the charge in a hearing before an administrative law judge. If a respondent fails to comply with an FTC cease-and-desist order or TRR, the commission can obtain a court order imposing a penalty of $10,000 a day for each rule or order the respondent ignores. Further failure to comply can result in contempt-of-court charges.

The FTC operates an outreach program to apprise businesses of laws and regulations. The commission also publishes pamphlets and other materials for consumers to warn them of fraudulent practices and to inform them of their rights under the law.

General Services Administration

The General Services Administration (GSA) is an independent central management agency responsible for federal procurement, property, and telecommunications services. Established in 1949, GSA, with more than twenty-four thousand employees nationwide, services congressional, judicial, and executive agencies and many of their international facilities. GSA's principle components are the Federal Supply Service (FSS), the Federal Property Resources Service (FPRS), the Public Buildings Service (PBS), and the Office of Information Resources Management (OIRM). The director of GSA is appointed by and serves at the pleasure of the president.

The Federal Supply Service purchases and distributes goods and services for government use. Goods include office supplies, industrial items, and scientific and medical equipment. Services supplied by GSA include use of prenegotiated contracts for freight and household moves and for maintenance and repair of government items. FSS controls a fleet management system consisting of eleven centralized, computerized maintenance and repair control centers across the country. The system oversees GSA's motor pool of eighty-five thousand vehicles and manages the government's federal travel program.

The Federal Property Resources Service sells surplus government land, buildings, and other materials or distributes those items between federal agencies. Unneeded real property can be donated to state and local governments. FRPS also controls the emergency stockpiles of strategic and critical materials. GSA manages the stockpile under the policy guidance of the Federal Emergency Management Agency.

Federal workspace is controlled by the Public Buildings Service, which functions as owner, developer, and property manager of federal work sites, including office buildings, laboratories, and warehouses. PBS provides space by constructing new buildings, purchasing existing buildings, or leasing workspace.

The Office of Information Resources Management combines several previously separate GSA organizations. OIRM provides federal agencies with products and services covering telecommunications, data processing, office automation, and information management. The GSA-run Federal Telecommunications System is the largest private phone system in the world.

GSA also assists other federal agencies in developing acquisition policies. In conjunction with the Department of Defense and the National Aeronautics and Space Administration, GSA developed the Federal Acquisition Regulation, the primary regulation used by all executive agencies for procuring supplies and services.

GSA also issues the Federal Information Resources Management Regulations governing telecommunications, automated data processing, and records management. GSA operates Business Services Centers in twelve major cities across the country to provide information to anyone interested in doing business with the federal government. Public inquiries are handled by GSA Federal Information Centers. Federal publications are promoted and distributed to the public by the GSA's Consumer Information Center in Pueblo, Colorado.

Inter-American Foundation

The Inter-American Foundation (IAF) is an independent government corporation established to promote assistance programs in Latin America and the Caribbean. Created in 1969, the IAF was granted authority to conduct its affairs independently of other U.S. foreign policy agencies. The IAF is based in Rosslyn, Virginia, and is governed by a nine-member board of directors appointed by the president and confirmed by the Senate. Six members of the board are drawn from the private sector and three from the government. The president appoints one member as chair. All members of the board can be removed for neglect of duty or malfeasance but for no other reason.

The IAF supports local and private development efforts through grants and educational programs. The majority of IAF grants go to grass-roots organizations such as agricultural cooperatives, community associations, and small urban enterprises. Other grants are awarded to large organizations that work with local groups, providing credit, technical assistance, training, and marketing services. Funding comes from congressional appropriations and the Social Progress Trust Fund administered by the Inter-American Development Bank.

The IAF awards fellowships to doctoral and masters degree candidates at U.S. universities to conduct field work on grass-roots development issues. Fellowships also are awarded to scholars from Latin America and the Caribbean wishing to study development issues at U.S. universities. In 1986 the IAF inaugurated an Office of Learning and Dissemination to document and evaluate projects conducted through IAF grants. The office's findings are made available through seminars and conferences. In addition, the IAF publishes a quarterly journal in three languages, which reports on projects and issues affecting IAF countries.

Interstate Commerce Commission

The Interstate Commerce Commission (ICC) is an independent federal agency responsible for regulating interstate surface transportation within the United States. Established by the Interstate Commerce Act of 1887, the ICC is the nation's oldest independent regulatory agency. The ICC was created to regulate the rapidly expanding railroad industry and in the ensuing years assumed responsibility for the burgeoning trucking industry.

During the 1970s and early 1980s Congress passed legislation aimed at deregulating the transportation industry. The new legislation greatly reduced the budget and responsibilities of the commission and the number of commissioners was reduced from seven to five. The commissioners are appointed by the president with Senate confirmation to five-year terms. No more than three commissioners can be of the same political party. The chair, who is designated by the president and serves at the pleasure of the president, coordinates and organizes the commission's work and acts as its representative in legislative matters.

The ICC maintains jurisdiction over for-hire companies providing surface transportation in the United States. Companies regulated by the ICC include interstate railroads, trucks, buses, household movers, some inland water carriers, freight forwarders, transportation brokers, and commodity pipelines that carry resources other than oil, water, or natural gas. Not falling under ICC jurisdiction are domestic and international air traffic, ships in international trade, oil and gas pipelines, and transportation companies that operate entirely within a single state.

The ICC has authority to settle controversies over rates and charges among competing and similar modes of transportation and shippers and receivers of freight. In addition, the ICC rules upon applications for mergers, consolidations, and acquisitions and approves the sale of carriers.

Businesses entering interstate transportation must obtain operating authority from the ICC specifying routes that may be served and types of freight to be handled. Authority is granted on a temporary or permanent basis depending on need. A carrier may apply to purchase existing authority from another carrier.

Carriers operating under ICC authority are required to file with the commission a tariff schedule, or lists of rates and charges, which must be adhered to by law. The ICC cannot set rates charged by carriers but can approve or disapprove rate schedules filed by companies. If rates are challenged, or if the ICC on its own determines they are unfair, it can suspend their effectiveness pending an investigation and hearing. If for any reason the rates are found to be unlawful, the commission can order them canceled. If a carrier fails to comply, the commission may ask for a court order enforcing the rulings. Further failure to comply may result in civil or criminal penalties.

Cases requiring a formal proceeding are heard by ICC administrative law judges. Upon completion of formal hearings and arguments the administrative law judge may issue an initial report, which may be appealed to the commission. Informal cases or "modified procedures" are those with limited or no opposition and are presided over by the ICC's Office of Proceedings. Decisions of the Office of Proceedings may be appealed to the commission.

The ICC has special responsibilities in several fields of transportation. The agency's Rail Services Planning Office oversees the restructuring of sections of the railroad network and allows railroads greater flexibility in adjusting their rates. In addition, the agency sets guidelines and rules to ensure that fair prices are charged by household movers and that customers are aware of legal protections.

Legal Services Corporation

The Legal Services Corporation (LSC) is a nonprofit, independent organization established by Congress to provide financial support for legal assistance in noncriminal matters to persons unable to afford such assistance. Established by the Legal Services Corporation Act of 1974, the LSC assumed responsibility for the nation's legal services program from the Office of Economic Opportunity. The creation of the LSC was an attempt by Congress to depoliticize the provision of legal services. LSC was chartered as a private corporation with a bipartisan board and with restrictions on lobbying and political advocacy. Funding for LSC is provided by Congress and by outside sources, such as interest earned on participating lawyers' trust accounts.

In keeping with its independent status, LSC officers and employees are not considered officers and employees of the federal government. LSC financial statements are audited by an independent firm of certified public accountants and included in the corporation's annual report, which is submitted to Congress. The LSC is governed by an eleven-member board of directors appointed by the president with Senate confirmation. Board members serve three-year terms and can be removed only for cause. By law no more that six members may be of the same political party. The board selects a chair from among its members by a vote of seven or more directors.

The board is authorized to provide financial assistance to qualified programs furnishing legal assistance to eligible clients. The maximum income level prescribed by the corporation for eligible clients is 125 percent of the official poverty threshold. Each program's board of directors, taking local living costs into account, sets its own financial eligibility standards for clients and cannot go beyond the corporation level without LSC approval. Eligibility is determined primarily by family income, fixed debts and obligations, medical bills, child care expenses, liquid and non-liquid assets, and seasonal income variations.

The corporation is responsible for ensuring that recipient programs provide services efficiently and effectively and that all recipients comply with the Legal Services Corporation Act, the terms of appropriations bills, and all rules and regulations issued by the corporation. Oversight of recipient programs is provided by advisory councils established in each state. Each state's advisory council consists of nine members appointed by the governor from among the attorneys admitted to practice in the state. The advisory council is charged with notifying the LSC of any apparent violation of the provisions of the LSC act.

Merit Systems Protection Board

The Merit Systems Protection Board (MSPB) is an independent quasi-judicial agency created to safeguard against partisan politics in federal merit systems and to protect employees against unlawful abuses by agency management. The board was established in 1979 by the Civil Service Reform Act of 1978. The act abolished the Civil Service Commission and divided its responsibilities among the MSPB, the Office of Personnel Management (OPM), and the Federal Labor Relations Authority. In addition to its Washington, D.C., headquarters, the board maintains regional offices in eleven major cities around the country.

Operating under bipartisan leadership, the board consists of a chair, a vice-chair, and one other member. No more than two of its three members may be from the same political party. Board members are appointed by the president with Senate confirmation and serve overlapping, non-renewable, seven-year terms. An independent special counsel to the board is also appointed by the president with Senate confirmation to a five-year term. Both the special counsel and the board members may be removed only for inefficiency, neglect of duty, or malfeasance in office. The chair can be removed by the president without cause but remains a board member unless cause for dismissal is shown.

The Reform Act established merit system principles for federal employment that include the selection and promotion of employees based on merit, through fair, open competition and equal pay for work of equal value in the private sector. In addition, the principles guarantee employee constitutional rights, protection for whistle-blowers, and rights of privacy. The Reform Act also outlines a number of prohibited personnel practices, including discrimination and coercion of an employee to participate in political activities.

The board hears and decides appeals brought by employees concerning agency actions and reviews cases of discrimination. The board also reviews employment regulations established by OPM to determine if they conflict with established personnel principles and cases brought by the special counsel, who investigates prohibited personnel practices such as reprisals against whistle-blowers and violations of the Freedom of Information Act. Discrimination complaints that do not involve adverse actions, such as removal, demotion, or suspension of more than fourteen days, go to the Equal Employment Opportunity Commission. Cases involving examination ratings and classification decisions are reviewed by the Office of Personnel Management.

The board conducts special studies of particular merit systems to measure compliance with established principles. If the board finds an agency in violation of the Reform Act the agency has fifteen days to show evidence of compliance, a schedule for full compliance, and a statement of actions completed, in progress, or remaining.

National Aeronautics and Space Administration

After the Soviet Union launched Sputnik I, the world's first artificial satellite, on October 4, 1957, Congress and the administration of President Dwight D. Eisenhower agreed to combine the government's existing individual space efforts into one agency, which would manage the national space program. The National Aeronautics and Space Act of 1958 created the National Aeronautics and Space Administration (NASA), a civilian agency chartered to exercise control over U.S. aeronautical and space activities.

NASA is headed by an administrator who is charged with responsibility for all functions and authorities assigned to the agency. The administrator is appointed by the president with Senate confirmation to an indefinite term and serves at the pleasure of the president. The NASA Advisory Council advises the NASA administrator on the agency's aeronautics and space plans, programs, and issues. Council members are chosen by the administrator from the scientific community to serve at the pleasure of the administrator.

The problem of launch vehicles occupied much attention in NASA's first years, and on January 31, 1958, the first American satellite, *Explorer 1,* went into orbit. On April 12, 1961, however, the Soviet Union achieved the first successful manned space mission. NASA responded on May 5, 1961, with the *Freedom 7* Mercury spacecraft. On May 25, 1961, President John F. Kennedy addressed a joint session of Congress and called for a national goal of "landing a man on the moon and returning him safely to Earth" within a decade. The U.S. manned space program continued with the Gemini series in 1965-1966, and on July 20, 1969, *Apollo 11* completed the first successful manned flight to the moon.

In addition to space flight, NASA is responsible for many other scientific research programs, including studies in the fields of space science, aeronautics, solar system and planetary science, astrophysics, life science, and earth science. NASA employs more than twenty-two thousand people in fourteen space flight centers, research centers, and other installations throughout the United States.

The agency's Washington, D.C., headquarters determines programs and projects, establishes management policies, procedures, and performance criteria, evaluates progress, and reviews and analyzes the agency's aerospace program.

Following the explosion of the space shuttle *Challenger,* a presidential committee organized to study the accident issued a report recommending nine changes in the agency's organization and operations. The recommendations included creating an office of Safety, Reliability, Maintainability and Quality Assurance, which would report directly to the administrator. Three separate committees of the National Research Council were organized to provide oversight of space shuttle redesign efforts, including redesign and testing of the shuttle's booster rocket O-rings, whose failure was determined to be the cause of the *Challenger* explosion.

National Archives and Records Administration

The National Archives and Records Administration is responsible for identifying, preserving, and making available to the federal government and to the people of the United States all forms of government records not restricted by law that have been determined to have sufficient historical, informational, or evidential value to warrant being preserved.

The National Archives was first established as an independent agency in 1934. In 1949 the archives was incorporated into the newly established General Services Administration and renamed the National Archives and Records Service. In 1984 Congress once again established the archives as an independent agency renaming it the National Archives and Records Administration.

The archives is headed by the archivist of the United States, who is appointed by the president with Senate confirmation to no fixed term. The archivist can be removed only for cause. In addition to the agency's regular staff, the archives' major organizational elements are the offices of Management and Administration, the National Archives, Public Programs, Records Administration, Federal Register, Presidential Libraries, and Federal Records Centers.

Daily operations of the archives are managed by the office of Management and Administration. The office's responsibilities include the agency's budget, property, personnel, and security and safety management.

The office of the National Archives oversees the reference and maintenance of permanently valuable records in the National Archives in Washington, D.C., and eleven field branches throughout the country.

The Public Programs office oversees public outreach programs that include distribution of audiovisual materials, workshops, lectures, exhibitions, volunteers, ceremonial events, and publications such as *Prologue,* the quarterly journal of the National Archives.

The office of Records Administration determines the appropriate disposition of all federal records including those produced by federal agencies. These records include microforms, maps, charts, drawings, photographs, motion pictures, sound recordings, and electronic and paper records. The office reviews the retention periods proposed by each agency for its documents and determines how documents will be handled once they are no longer held by the agencies.

The Records Administration office also indentifies records of continuing value to be preserved in the National Archives. These records may document the organization, policies, and activities of the federal government or contain information of high research value.

The office of the Federal Register publishes the official text of laws, administrative regulations, and presidential documents. It publishes the daily *Federal Register,* the *Code of Federal Regulations,* the *United States Government Manual,* the *Weekly Compilation of Presidential Documents,* the *Public Papers of the Presidents,* and the *Codification of the Presidential Proclamations and Executive Orders.* The office also is responsible for publication of slip laws, the *United States Statutes at Large,* and the *Privacy Act Compilation,* and it ensures the accuracy of the official count of electoral college votes for president and vice president.

As of 1988, the office of Presidential Libraries maintained nine presidential libraries and museums dedicated to preserving and displaying records of presidents Herbert C. Hoover, Franklin D. Roosevelt, Harry S Truman, Dwight D. Eisenhower, John F. Kennedy, Lyndon B. Johnson, Richard Nixon, Gerald R. Ford, and Jimmy Carter.

The current estimate of the holdings in the National Archives is 1.5 million cubic feet of records, not including records held by the presidential libraries. Archive records include 3 billion paper documents, 91 million feet of motion pictures, 5.2 million still photographs, 1.6 million maps, 173,000 video and sound recordings, 9.7 million aerial photographs, and 3,600 reels of computer tape.

National Capital Planning Commission

The National Capital Planning Commission (NCPC) is the central development planning agency for the federal government in the Washington area. Established in 1924 as a park planning agency, NCPC's role was expanded under the National Capital Planning Act of 1952 to include central planning for the federal and District of Columbia governments. In 1973, the National Capital Planning Act was amended by the D.C. Home Rule Act, which made the mayor of the District of Columbia the chief planner for the District.

NCPC prepares the federal components of the Comprehensive Plan for the National Capital (the District of Columbia and federal property within the region), which is a statement of goals, policies, and guidelines for the future development of the national capital. In addition to work facilities for federal employees, historic preservation, and parks within the region, NCPC is responsible for reviewing plans for all new federal buildings in the area. NCPC also prepares and submits annually to the Office of Management and Budget a five-year Federal Capital Improvements Program that contains land acquisitions and development proposals from all federal agencies. NCPC planning activities cover the national capital region, which includes the District of Columbia and Prince George's and Montgomery counties in Maryland, and Arlington, Fairfax, Prince William, and Loudoun counties in Virginia.

The commission consists of five appointed and seven ex officio members. Three citizen members are appointed by the president and two by the mayor of the District of Columbia. Presidential appointees include one resident from Maryland and Virginia and one from anywhere in the United States. The two mayoral appointees must be District residents. Ex officio members include the secretaries of defense and interior, administrator of the General Services Administration, the D.C. mayor, chair of the D.C. city council, chair of the Senate Committee on Governmental Affairs, and chair of the House Committee on the District of Columbia. The president designates a chair from among the twelve members.

National Credit Union Administration

The National Credit Union Administration (NCUA) is an independent agency created to regulate the nation's federal credit unions. NCUA approves or disapproves applications for federal credit union charters and examines federal credit unions to determine their financial condition. NCUA issues charters to credit unions whose applications are approved and supervises credit union activities.

Established by a 1970 amendment to the Federal Credit Union Act of 1934, NCUA is based in Washington, D.C., and maintains six regional offices nationwide. Before 1970, administration of the original Federal Credit Union Act was shifted among several federal agencies. The Financial Institutions Regulatory and Interest Rate Control Act of 1978 reorganized NCUA and replaced the agency's single administrator with a three-member governing board. Board members are appointed by the president with Senate confirmation to six-year terms. The president designates one member to serve as chair, and not more than two

members may be of the same political party. Board members can be removed only for cause. An incoming president may, however, appoint another member as chair.

A credit union is a cooperative association designed to promote thrift among its members. Membership in a credit union is limited to persons having a common bond of occupation or association and to groups within a well-defined neighborhood, community, or rural district. The credit union accumulates a fund from savings to make loans to members for useful purposes at reasonable interest rates. Credit unions are managed by a board of directors and committees made up of members of the credit union. After expenses and legal reserve requirements are met, most of the earnings of a credit union are returned to the members in the form of dividends on share holdings. There are two types of credit unions: federal credit unions, chartered by NCUA, and state credit unions, chartered by state agencies. In 1987 the federal credit union system consisted of 9,566 credit unions with total assets of $104 billion.

Federal credit unions pay an annual operating fee to NCUA and provide the agency with financial reports at least annually. NCUA also regulates the operations of the Central Liquidity Facility (the central bank for loans) and administers the National Credit Union Share Insurance Fund (NCUSIF). All federally chartered credit unions are insured by NCUSIF, which was authorized in 1970. Insurance coverage for member accounts was increased from $40,000 to $100,000 in 1980. The fund also insures member accounts in 60 percent of state-chartered credit unions.

National Foundation on the Arts and Humanities

The National Foundation on the Arts and the Humanities is an independent agency established by Congress in 1965 to promote progress and scholarship in the humanities and the arts in the United States. The foundation consists of the National Endowment for the Arts, the National Endowment for the Humanities, the Federal Council on the Arts and the Humanities, and the Institute of Museum Services.

Each endowment is itself an independent agency and is governed by its own council comprising a chair and twenty-six members who are appointed to four-year terms by the president with Senate confirmation. Council members, chosen for their expertise in the arts or humanities, advise the chair on policies and procedures and review applications for financial support. Members can be removed only for cause.

The National Endowment for the Arts was created to support American arts and artists. The endowment awards matching grants to nonprofit, tax-exempt arts organizations of outstanding quality and both matching and non-matching fellowships to artists of exceptional talent. By law, the agency also provides a minimum of 20 percent of its program funds in matching grants to state arts agencies and to regional arts organizations. Programs receiving endowment funds include dance, design arts, folk arts, literature, media arts, music, opera-musical theater, theater, and visual arts. Funding of endowment programs is guided by advisory panels of private citizens who are artists or recognized experts in their particular field. The council reviews the panel decisions and makes final recommendations on grants and policy to the chair. The endowment budget for fiscal year 1987 was more than $165 million.

The National Endowment for the Humanities was created to support research, education, and public programs in the humanities. According to the legislation that created the endowment, the term *humanities* includes, but is not limited to, the study of history, philosophy, languages, linguistics, literature, archaeology, jurisprudence, comparative religion, ethics, the social sciences that employ historical or philosophical methods, and the history, criticism, and theory of arts. The endowment provides grants through five divisions—Education Programs, Fellowships and Seminars, General Programs, Research Programs, and State Programs—and two offices, the Office of Challenge Grants and Office of Preservation. The 1986 budget for the National Endowment for the Humanities was $134.7 million.

The Federal Council on the Arts and Humanities consists of twenty members, including the two endowment chairs and the director of the Institute of Museum Services. Membership is made up of heads of federal agencies whose service with the council is determined by their agency position. The council is designed to coordinate the activities of the two endowments and related programs of other federal agencies. The Institute of Museum Services is an independent agency established by Congress in 1976 to assist museums in maintaining, increasing, and improving their services to the public. The institute makes grants to museums subject to policy directives and priorities set by the National Museum Services Board. The board comprises fifteen nonvoting members appointed by the president with Senate confirmation to indefinite terms, and four ex officio, nonvoting members. Members serve at the discretion of the president.

National Labor Relations Board

The National Labor Relations Board (NLRB) is an independent federal agency created in 1935 to administer the National Labor Relations Act (the Wagner act), the nation's principal labor relations law. NLRB has five board members including a chair who are appointed by the president, with Senate confirmation, to staggered five-year terms. The board also has a general counsel who is appointed to a four-year term. By law the board is bipartisan, and the president can reappoint or remove members for neglect of duty or malfeasance in office, but for no other cause.

As chief administrator of the National Labor Relations Act, NLRB seeks to reduce interruptions in commerce caused by industrial strife. In its statutory assignment, NLRB determines and implements, through secret-ballot elections, the choice of employees whether to be represented by a union and, if so, by which one. The act also is intended to prevent unfair labor practices by either employers or unions. It outlaws practices such as interference with employees' freedom to organize and bargain collectively, domination of unions, antiunion discrimination, and refusal to bargain. In 1947, the Taft-Hartley Act added prohibitions against various union practices such as intimidation of employees and restraint or coercion of neutral employers. In 1959, the act was again amended, and steps were taken to eliminate gaps between federal and state jurisdiction in labor relations disputes.

The five-member board acts primarily as a quasi-judicial body in deciding cases brought before it by one of its thirty-three regional offices or sixteen field offices throughout the country. The general counsel is responsible for the investigations and prosecution of charges of violations of the act. NLRB does not bring action on its own but responds to charges or petitions filed by employees or employers.

Charges are initially investigated by regional or field office staff who then determine whether formal proceedings are warranted. If so, the parties involved are encouraged to reach a voluntary settlement. If the case cannot be settled, a formal complaint is issued and the case is heard before an NLRB administrative law judge. The administrative law judge's decision may be appealed to the board; if left unchallenged, it becomes the order of the board. In cases of representation disputes, the thirty-three regional directors are authorized to process all petitions, rule on contested issues, and direct elections or dismiss the request. Actions of the regional directors are subject to review by the board on limited grounds.

Since its establishment, NLRB has processed more than 350,000 cases alleging unfair labor practices and has conducted more than 250,000 secret-ballot employee self-determination elections.

National Mediation Board

The National Mediation Board (NMB) is an independent agency that governs collective bargaining and representation disputes in the airlines and railroads as prescribed by the Railway Labor Act of 1926. Established in 1934, the NMB comprises three members appointed by the president with Senate confirmation. Members serve staggered three-year terms, and not more than two members may be of the same political party. The position of chair, which is decided by the board, rotates annually among the three members. Board members serve at the pleasure of the president.

The NMB administers the Railway Labor Act, the oldest extant labor relations statute in the United States. The act is intended to maintain a free flow of commerce in the railroad and airline industries and to ensure the right of employees to organize and bargain collectively through representatives of their own choosing. Originally enacted to cover only the railroad industry, the act was extended in 1936 to include the nation's airlines.

The NMB is the only federal labor relations agency authorized to handle both mediation and representation disputes. Since its inception the board has resolved more than fifty-five hundred representation issues and nearly twelve thousand rail and air mediation cases. The board mediates contract disputes between employees and the carriers over wages, rules, and working conditions. These are known as "major disputes." When negotiations reach a stalemate, either party may request mediation by the board, or the board may intervene in negotiations at its own initiative. Once the NMB becomes involved in a dispute, the status quo must be maintained until the board decides to release the parties from negotiations. If the NMB is unsuccessful in its mediation efforts, the disputing parties are urged to submit to voluntary arbitration for final and binding settlement. If arbitration is rejected by either party, a thirty-day "cooling-off" period begins during which the parties must continue to maintain the status quo and refrain from self help. If the dispute continues and threatens to interrupt interstate commerce and deprive sections of the country of essential transportation services, the NMB can notify the president who may then appoint an emergency board. The president's board has thirty days to investigate the dispute and report its findings, which are nonbinding. If either side rejects the findings, neither party may act, except to reach an agreement, for thirty more days. If after that time an agreement still has not been reached, the parties are then legally free to act.

Representation disputes involving labor organizations and railroad or airline employees also fall under NMB jurisdiction. The board is authorized to determine the appropriate crafts or classes of rail or airline employees and to designate an employee representative through secret ballot among the employees or through other appropriate methods.

The National Railroad Adjustment Board in Chicago is authorized by the NMB to mediate "minor disputes," which are disagreements over the interpretation and applications of existing contracts between individual carriers and employees.

National Railroad Passenger Corporation (Amtrak)

The National Railroad Passenger Corporation (Amtrak) is an operating railroad corporation whose capital assets are owned by the U.S. government through the Department of Transportation. In 1986 Amtrak carried 20.3 million travelers over more than five billion passenger miles. Created in 1970 by the Rail Passenger Service Act, Amtrak began operation on May 1, 1971, with a $40 million appropriation from Congress. At that time, railroads carried less than 7 percent of the intercity passenger traffic in the United States with less than 450 trains in operation. Before the creation of Amtrak, highway and air transportation systems in the United States were beginning to be overwhelmed by the growing need for transportation between the nation's major population centers. With thousands of miles of existing tracks and rights-of-way into major population centers, the nation's rail facilities were viewed by some as an economical form of transportation when compared with the costs of constructing new highways and airports.

The new corporation inherited, however, an antiquated system of locomotives, passenger cars, and other railroad assets. The Amtrak fleet consisted of twenty- to thirty-year-old steam-heated cars, and the average age of Amtrak's locomotives was seventeen years. For the first two years of operation, Amtrak was almost totally dependent on private railroads from which they leased equipment and facilities. When created, Amtrak assumed responsibility for managing intercity passenger train service over twenty-three thousand route miles connecting twenty-one major population centers. In 1973 Amtrak received its first new equipment, and in 1976 the corporation acquired a major portion of the busy 455-mile Northeast Corridor between Washington, D.C., and Boston, as well as two important feeder lines. Also in 1976, Congress passed the Railroad Revitalization and Regulatory Reform Act, which authorized spending $2.5 billion to rebuild the Northwest Corridor. The corporation continued to upgrade its facilities, and by 1982 all fifteen hundred of Amtrak's cars were new or rebuilt.

Management of Amtrak was assigned to a board comprising nine members. They include the president of Amtrak, who is appointed by the board, and the secretary of transportation. Three members are appointed by the president of the United States with Senate confirmation: one of the three is selected from a list recommended by the Railway Labor Executives Association; one is selected from among the governors of the states with an interest in rail transportation; and one is selected as a representative of business connected with rail transportation. Two additional members are selected by the president from a list recommended by commuter agencies that provide service over the Amtrak-owned Northeast Corridor; and two members are selected annually by the Department of Transportation, which is the preferred stockholder of the corporation. Board members serve staggered one- to two-year terms and can be removed only for cause. The board of directors meets ten times each year at Amtrak's Washington, D.C., headquarters. Meetings consist of a closed session for the discussion of personnel and proprietary matters and a session open to the media and interested persons.

National Science Foundation

The National Science Foundation (NSF) is an independent federal agency established to promote and advance scientific progress in the United States. Created by the National Science Foundation Act of 1950, the NSF was an outgrowth of the important contributions made by science and technology during World War II. Since its inception the NSF has provided financial and other support for research, education, and related activities in science, mathematics, and engineering. The NSF is headed by a director, who is appointed by the president, and a twenty-four-member governing board; all are appointed for indefinite terms and serve at the pleasure of the president. Board members include scientists, engineers, educators, and industry officials.

Each year the NSF receives thousands of proposals for research and graduate fellowships from academic institutions, private research firms, industrial laboratories, and major research facilities and centers. The NSF staff is divided into grant-making divisions covering various disciplines and fields of science and engineering. Outside advisers from the scientific community serve on formal committees or as ad hoc reviewers of the proposals. Applicants receive verbatim, unsigned copies of reviews of their proposals and can appeal final decisions, which are made by NSF staff members. Awardees are wholly responsible for doing their research and preparing the results for publication. The NSF does not assume responsibility for research findings or their interpretation.

Specific fields of research funded by the NSF are the mathematical and physical sciences, all fields of engineering, biological and environmental sciences, the social sciences and economics, behavioral and neural sciences, computer and information science, atmospheric, earth, and ocean sciences, and engineering education. The NSF does not support projects in clinical medicine, the arts and humanities, commerce, or social work.

The NSF does not conduct research itself but funds large-scale cooperative facilities for scientists and engineers. National and regional facilities supported by the NSF include research centers for physics, astronomy and atmospheric sciences, supercomputer centers, oceanographic vessels, and Materials Research Laboratories. In addition, the NSF manages a long-term U.S. scientific research program in Antarctica.

Other NSF programs include funding of cooperative research efforts between industry, government, and academics and outreach programs with state government and private organizations. The NSF also monitors resources for science and engineering and publishes analyses and statistical studies on the supply and demand for personnel and funding in those fields. In 1985, the NSF sponsored the first National Science and Technology Week. The annual event includes science fairs, competitions, and public access to research facilities, lectures, and other activities.

National Transportation Safety Board

The National Transportation Safety Board (NTSB) is an independent agency authorized to investigate transportation accidents and to formulate safety recommendations. Established by the Department of Transportation Act of 1966, the NTSB was made entirely independent of the Department of Transportation by the Independent Safety Board Act of 1974.

The safety board is composed of five members appointed by the president with Senate confirmation. Members serve five-year terms, and the president designates two members to serve as chair and vice-chair for two-year terms. No more than three members can be of the same political party, and all serve at the pleasure of the president.

The board is authorized to investigate and determine the probable cause of air, rail, highway, and marine accidents. The board also investigates pipeline accidents involving a fatality or substantial property damage. The NTSB assembles investigative teams, or "Go-Teams," that are dispatched to accident scenes. The Go-Teams consist of board personnel skilled in various types of accident investigation and may include a board member. The Go-Team gathers data from the accident or through interviews with witnesses. For accident investigations requiring off-site engineering studies or laboratory tests, the board operates its own technical laboratory. The laboratory has the capability to read out "black boxes" containing aircraft cockpit voice recorders and flight data recorders. The laboratory's metallurgists can determine whether failures resulted from a design flaw, from overloading, or from deterioration in static strength through fatigue or corrosion.

Following an accident, the board may hold a public hearing to collect additional information. A board member presides over the hearings, and witnesses testify under oath. Upon completion of the fact-finding phase, the data is reviewed at NTSB headquarters where the "probable cause" of the accident is determined. The final accident report is then presented to the full five-member board for discussion and approval at a public meeting in Washington.

To increase safety, the board makes a safety recommendation as soon as a problem is identified, without necessarily waiting until an investigation is completed and the probable cause of an accident determined. Each recommendation designates the person or party expected to take action, describes the action the board expects, and clearly states the safety need to be satisfied. The Department of Transportation is required to respond to each board recommendation within ninety days. The board also is empowered to conduct special studies that go beyond examination of a single accident to broader transportation and safety problems.

Nuclear Regulatory Commission

The Nuclear Regulatory Commission (NRC) was established by the Energy Reorganization Act of 1974 to regulate the civilian uses of nuclear materials in the United States. When President Gerald R. Ford signed the legislation creating the NRC in 1975 the commission formally took over the nuclear regulatory and licensing functions of the Atomic Energy Commission (AEC), which was abolished.

The NRC is headed by five commissioners appointed by the president and confirmed by the Senate. No more than three commissioners may be of the same political party. Commissioners serve five-year terms with one commissioner appointed by the president to serve as chair. The chair directs the day-to-day operations of the agency and is responsible for the commission's response to nuclear emergencies. Commission members can be removed only for cause.

The NRC's Office of Nuclear Reactor Regulation licenses nuclear reactors used for testing, research, and power generation. A construction permit must be granted before construction can begin on a nuclear facility, and an operating license must be issued before fuel can be loaded and the reactor started. The office reviews license applications to determine what effect the proposed facility will have on the environment and whether it can be built and operated without undue risk to public safety and health. Applicants are investigated to determine whether they are properly insured against accidents. No application to construct a new nuclear plant has been filed since 1979.

Public hearings on applications for construction permits are mandatory. Hearings are conducted by the Atomic Safety and Licensing Board in communities near proposed nuclear facilities. Notices of these hearings are published in the *Federal Register* and the local newspaper and are posted in the nearest public document room. Interested parties can petition for the right to participate in the public hearings.

The Office of Nuclear Material Safety and Safeguards ensures that public health and safety, national security, and environmental factors are considered in the licensing and regulation of nuclear facilities. Safeguards also are reviewed and assessed against possible threats, thefts, and sabotage. The Office of Nuclear Regulatory Research administers the commission's research program. In 1980 it merged with the Office of Standards Development. Their combined functions include developing and recommending nuclear safety standards in the construction of nuclear power plants and preparing standards for the preparation of environmental impact statements. The Office of Inspection and Enforcement inspects nuclear facilities to determine whether they are constructed and operated in compliance with license provisions and NRC regulations. Analysis of operating data, enforcement of NRC regulations, and special projects are controlled by separate offices within the agency.

After the accident at Pennsylvania's Three Mile Island nuclear power plant on March 28, 1979, President Jimmy Carter appointed a commission to study government and industry safety practices in nuclear energy. The conclusions of the commission led to a reorganization of the NRC in 1980, in which greater responsibility for directing the commission's response to nuclear emergencies was transferred to the office of the chair.

The new plan also provided that the executive directo

for operations for the agency report directly to the chair. Formerly, supervision of the operating staff was left to the collective commission.

Occupational Safety and Health Review Commission

The Occupational Safety and Health Review Commission (OSHRC) is an independent, quasi-judicial agency created to review contests of citations or penalties prescribed by the Occupational Safety and Health Administration (OSHA). Established in 1971 by the Occupational Safety and Health Act of 1970, the review commission is based in Washington, D.C., and is independent of OSHA and the Department of Labor. The commission comprises three members who are appointed by the president, with Senate confirmation, and their administrative staff. Members are appointed for staggered six-year terms.

After the issuance of citations or penalties by OSHA, the employer is notified in writing and a period of time is allocated to correct the violation. The employer then has fifteen days to contest the assessment. If the employer does not contest the citations or penalties, they become the final order of the commission. If a citation is contested, the review commission usually holds a hearing before an OSHRC administrative law judge. The judge's decision becomes final thirty days after the commission receives it, unless a petition for discretionary review is filed. Decisions also can be reviewed at the discretion of one or more commission members. Penalties imposed by the commission range from fines up to $1,000 for "other than serious violations" to $10,000 and/or imprisonment for up to six months for willful violation resulting in the death of an employee.

In fiscal year 1985, the review commission received 1,360 cases of which 1,165 were resolved without a hearing. In addition to the Washington, D.C., office, review commission judges are stationed in four regional offices.

Office of Personnel Management

The Office of Personnel Management (OPM) is an independent agency that sets and carries out personnel policies for the federal work force. OPM was created by the Civil Service Reform Act of 1978, replacing the U.S. Civil Service Commission, which had been established in 1883 by the Pendleton Act. The Reform Act also established the Office of Government Ethics within OPM to direct executive branch policies toward preventing conflicts of interest by executive branch personnel.

Headquartered in Washington, D.C., OPM has approximately 6,500 permanent employees and maintains ten regional offices nationwide. In 1986, OPM personnel policies covered a work force of 2.1 million federal employees. The director of OPM is appointed by the president with Senate confirmation and serves as chief adviser on personnel policies governing civilian employment in executive branch agencies and some legislative and judicial agencies. The director is appointed to a four-year term and can be removed only for cause. An incoming president can appoint a new director at any time.

As the U.S. government's central personnel agency, OPM is responsible for recruiting and examining federal employees, providing development and training programs,

classifying jobs, investigating personnel to support its selection and appointment processes, evaluation of agency personnel programs, and overseeing pay administration. Positions covered by OPM include the federal civil service from General Schedule grades one through fifteen and Wage Grade (blue-collar) positions. The agency also administers the Qualifications Review Board examining process for career Senior Executive Service appointments.

OPM oversees federal employee retirement and insurance programs and enforces government policies on labor relations and affirmative action. OPM is chartered to administer federal employment under a merit system based on knowledge and skills through the Merit Systems Protection Board.

OPM's Incentive Awards program gives cash and honors to employees who provide suggestions that improve government operations and whose performance is judged superior. OPM also administers the Presidential Rank Awards program for recognition of sustained high-quality accomplishment of career members of the Senior Executive Service.

Panama Canal Commission

The Panama Canal Commission manages, operates, and maintains the Panama Canal under the Panama Canal Treaty of 1977. The treaty abolished the former canal organization—the Panama Canal Company and the Canal Zone Government. Two years later Congress passed the Panama Canal Act of 1979, which established the commission as the managing agency of the Panama Canal until the year 2000 when the treaty expires. At that time the entire facility will be turned over to the government of Panama, which is committed to keeping the canal open and efficient to international marine traffic.

The commission is supervised by a nine-member board. Five members are U.S. nationals appointed by the president with Senate confirmation. Four members are Panamanian nationals proposed by their government for appointment by the U.S. president. The commission administrator is a U.S. citizen, and the deputy administrator is a Panamanian citizen. Beginning in 1990, the positions will be reversed. The U.S. administrator serves at the pleasure of the president.

The canal is approximately fifty-one miles long and runs across the Isthmus of Panama connecting the Pacific and Atlantic oceans. In 1987, 677,521 vessels, of which more than 80 percent were oceangoing commercial class, transited the canal. A canal on the Isthmus of Panama was first proposed by King Charles I of Spain in 1534. In 1880 the French under Count Ferdinand de Lesseps, the builder of the Suez Canal, began work on the Panama Canal; but disease and financial problems ended the French effort almost twenty years later. In 1903, shortly after Panama's independence from Colombia, Panama and the United States signed a treaty by which the United States, under President Theodore Roosevelt's administration, undertook to construct the canal. The project was completed eleven years later at a cost of $387 million.

Peace Corps

The Peace Corps is an independent agency created by executive order in 1961 to help developing countries meet their basic needs for health care, food, shelter, and education. The corps trains volunteers to participate in its programs in Latin America, Africa, Asia, and the Pacific. Peace Corps volunteers offer skills in a variety of fields including education, health, nutrition, agriculture, forestry, and rural development. The goals of the Peace Corps as set by Congress are: to help developing countries to meet their needs for trained workers, to help promote a better understanding of Americans on the part of the peoples served, and to help promote a better understanding of other peoples on the part of Americans.

The corps is headed by a director who is appointed by the president with Senate confirmation. There is no fixed term, and the director serves at the discretion of the president.

The Peace Corps's overseas operations are administered through three regions comprising twenty-five nations in sub-Saharan Africa, nineteen countries in Central and South America and the Caribbean, and nineteen nations in North Africa, the Near East, Asia, and the Pacific. Africa is the Peace Corps's largest area of operations; almost half of the corps' volunteers are stationed there. In 1986 the Peace Corps had nearly six thousand volunteers in programs worldwide. The average age of the volunteers was twenty-nine years old, and almost 10 percent of the volunteers were fifty years of age or older.

The idea of the Peace Corps originated in 1960 when Sen. Hubert H. Humphrey (D-Minn.) introduced a bill calling for establishment of a "Peace Corps." Although Congress defeated the bill, less than four months later in a campaign speech at the University of Michigan, presidential candidate John F. Kennedy questioned his audience whether they would be willing to volunteer their services overseas as representatives of the United States. The idea became a presidential directive soon after Kennedy's election and was funded out of the White House. In 1961 Congress approved funds and legislation formally establishing the Peace Corps with the mandate to "promote world peace and friendship."

In 1971 President Nixon created ACTION to incorporate various federal voluntary organizations, including the Peace Corps, under one umbrella agency. After complaints from the corps' leadership that the corps had lost its identity, President Carter in 1979 signed legislation granting the Peace Corps special independence within ACTION.

Volunteers must be U.S. citizens, at least eighteen years old, and medically qualified. There is no upper age limit. If married, an applicant must serve with his or her spouse. Although they participate in a U.S. agency program, Peace Corps volunteers are not officials of the U.S. government and have no diplomatic privileges. All volunteers receive intensive, short-term technical and language training. They also are offered cultural studies of the history, customs, and the social and political systems of the host country. The normal tour of duty is twenty-four months following three months of training. Volunteers receive a monthly allowance for rent, food, travel, and all medical needs. A readjustment allowance of $175 a month is set aside, payable on completion of service.

Pennsylvania Avenue Development Corporation

The Pennsylvania Avenue Development Corporation (PADC) was established by Congress in 1972 to plan the development and use of the area adjacent to Pennsylvania Avenue between the U.S. Capitol and the White House. The legislation that created the PADC charged the corporation with creating a plan for developing and administering the area in a manner "suitable to its ceremonial, physical and historic relationship to the legislative and executive branches of the federal government." The corporation's Pennsylvania Avenue Plan includes oversight responsibilities of the government buildings, monuments, memorials, and parks in and around the area.

A board of directors comprising fifteen voting members and seven nonvoting members heads the PADC. Eight of the voting members are appointed by the president to serve six-year terms. Seven other voting members representing specific public interests include heads of federal agencies, the mayor of the District of Columbia, and the city council chair (or designees of the mayor and council chair). All voting members can be removed only for cause. The seven nonvoting members are advisory officials expert in or responsible for cultural, historic, or planning activities in the District. The chair of the corporation is appointed by the president.

The PADC maintains three operating committees: Cultural Affairs, Design, and Affirmative Action. The legislation that created the PADC provides for various powers, including review and approval authority over public and private development. The corporation also has authority to construct and to rehabilitate buildings, to manage property, and to establish restrictions, standards, and other requirements that ensure conformance to the plan. According to the PADC plan, by 1992 the area will contain 8.3 million square feet of office space, 825,000 square feet of retail space, 2,500 hotel rooms, and 1,200-1,500 residential units.

Pension Benefit Guaranty Corporation

The Pension Benefit Guaranty Corporation (PBGC) was created by Title IV of the Employee Retirement Income Security Act of 1974. PBGC ensures that participants in the pension plans it insures will receive their benefits in the event that the plan does not have sufficient funds to pay. PBGC also may force a plan to terminate if the agency determines that the pension fund is in trouble. In 1988, nearly forty million workers participated in more than 112,000 covered plans.

PBGC is a nonprofit corporation wholly owned by the federal government. It is financed by premiums levied against covered pension plans, the assets of plans it places into trusteeship, and investment income. The corporation is administered by a board of directors and an executive director. The board comprises the secretaries of labor, commerce, and the Treasury; the labor secretary serves as chair. A seven-member advisory committee made up of two labor representatives, two business representatives, and three public members advises the corporation.

PBGC coverage is mandatory for single-employer, private defined pension plans—plans whose benefits are determined by using a formula including factors such as age, length of service, and salary. The agency also protects the pension benefits of the approximately eight million participants in multiemployer pension plans. Multiemployer plans are based on collective bargaining agreements involving a union and two or more employers.

Postal Rate Commission

The Postal Rate Commission (PRC) is an independent regulatory agency established to consider proposed changes in postal rates, fees, and mail classifications and to issue recommended decisions to the governors of the Postal Service. The PRC was created by the Postal Reorganization Act of 1970, which also changed the old Post Office Department into the U.S. Postal Service.

The commission consists of five members appointed by the president and confirmed by the Senate and can be removed only for cause. Members serve six-year terms, and no more than three may be members of the same political party. The president designates one of the commissioners as chair. A vice-chair is elected annually by the commissioners. An incoming president can appoint a new chair.

In addition to reviewing proposed changes in rates and classifications, the PRC considers changes in the nature of available postal service and customers' appeals of Postal Service decisions to close or consolidate post offices. The PRC also investigates complaints concerning postal rates, fees, and mail classifications or services.

After receiving a rate proposal and supporting testimony from the Postal Service, the PRC issues public notice of the filing and appoints an officer of the commission, who is a staff member of the PRC's Office of the Consumer Advocate, to represent the interest of the general public before the commission. After a discovery period and public hearings, during which the commission receives oral and written testimony, the PRC issues a written recommendation, which is then forwarded to the Postal Service governors. The governors may either accept the decision, in which case the proposed rate is implemented, or reject the decision and return it for reconsideration by the commission. The governors also may allow the commission's recommendation to stand, but under protest. In this case the rate proposal will be implemented under protest, while the decision either undergoes judicial review by the Postal Service or is returned for reconsideration. Decisions on mail classifications (which are official definitions of the different services available from the Postal Service) and proposed changes in postal services undergo similar reviews by both the PRC and the Postal Service governors.

Railroad Retirement Board

The Railroad Retirement Board (RRB) is an independent agency created to administer retirement and unemployment programs for the nation's railroad employees. The board, which is based in Chicago, is made up of three members who are appointed by the president with Senate confirmation. Members serve staggered five-year terms. By law, one member is appointed upon recommendations made by railroad labor organizations, one upon recommendations of railroad employers, and the third member, the chair, is in effect independent of the employees and employers and represents the public interest. The president also appoints an inspector general for the board who reports directly to the chair. Board members serve five-year terms and can be removed only for cause.

The function of the board is to determine and pay benefits under the retirement-survivor and unemployment-sickness programs. The board maintains lifetime earnings records for covered employees, a network of field offices to handle claims, and examiners to adjudicate the claims.

The railroad retirement system is based on three federal laws: the Railroad Retirement Act, the Railroad Unemployment Insurance Act, and the Railroad Retirement Tax Act. The original Railroad Retirement Act of 1934 set up the first retirement system for nongovernment workers to be administered by the federal government before being declared unconstitutional. A federal district court held that neither employees nor their employers could be compelled to pay railroad retirement taxes. However, the act evolved into the Railroad Retirement Carriers' Taxing Acts of 1935, and the RRB began awarding annuities in 1936. The act was further amended in 1937 to establish the railroad retirement system. In 1946 and 1951 the act was again amended to coordinate in certain areas with the Social Security system. In 1974 Congress adopted a two-tier system of benefits that would provide amounts equal to Social Security benefits and other industrial pension systems. The system was designed to phase out dual railroad retirement/Social Security benefits being collected by railroad employees. With several modifications the two-tier system remains intact today.

From 1936 when the board first began issuing benefits, through September 1986, benefits under the railroad retirement system have been awarded to 1.6 million retired employees, and 2.9 million survivors. During the same period, over $89 billion was paid in benefits of all types.

Securities and Exchange Commission

The Securities and Exchange Commission (SEC) is an independent, quasi-judicial regulatory agency created in 1934 to administer federal securities laws. The commission is composed of five members, not more than three of whom may be of the same political party. The commissioners are nominated by the president and confirmed by the Senate for staggered five-year terms. The president also designates one of the members to serve as chair. A general counsel serves as the chief legal officer for the commission. Commission members serve five-year terms at the discretion of the president.

The origins of the SEC may be traced to the stock market crash of October 29, 1929. The crash and the ensuing economic depression focused public attention on reported stock manipulations and unscrupulous trading during the 1920s. A Senate investigation of securities trading eventually prompted the passage of the Securities Act of 1933, also known as the "truth-in-securities" bill. The act required anyone offering securities for sale in interstate commerce or through the mails to file information with the Federal Trade Commission (FTC) on the financial condition of the issuing company. The following year Congress passed the Securities Exchange Act of 1934, which created the SEC and transferred to it the functions that had been assigned to the FTC under the 1933 law. The 1934 act required companies whose securities were traded on national exchanges to file periodic financial reports. The measure also required that exchanges and over-the-counter dealers and brokers conduct business in line with principles of fair and equitable trade.

The SEC maintains four divisions with specific areas of responsibility for various segments of the federal securities laws. The Division of Corporation Finance has the overall responsibility of ensuring that disclosure requirements are met by publicly held companies registered with the commission.

The Securities Exchange Act requires the registration of "national securities exchanges" (those have a substantial trading volume) and of brokers and dealers who conduct an over-the-counter securities business in interstate commerce. Exchanges establish their own self-regulatory rules, although the commission, through its Division of Market Regulation, may alter or supplement them if it finds that the rules fail to protect investors. The division also examines applications from brokers and dealers to determine if they conform to business practices and standards prescribed by the commission.

Since 1934, Congress has passed three additional securities measures, including the Public Utility Holding Company Act of 1935, the Investment Company Act of 1940, and the Investment Advisers Act of 1940. Administration of these acts is the primary responsibility of the commission's Division of Investment Management.

Investigation and enforcement of securities laws is the primary responsibility of the commission's Division of Enforcement. Although most investigations are conducted through informal inquiry, the commission has the authority to issue subpoenas requiring sworn testimony and the production of books, records, and other documents pertinent to the subject under investigation. If the investigations show possible fraud or other violation, the securities laws provide several courses of action or remedies. The commission may apply for a civil injunction enjoining those acts or practices alleged to violate the law or commission rules. If fraud or other willful violation is indicated, the commission may refer the facts to the Department of Justice with a recommendation for criminal prosecution. The commission also may, after a hearing, issue orders that suspend or expel members from exchanges, censure firms or individuals, or bar individuals from employment with a registered firm.

Selective Service System

The Selective Service System is an independent agency that provides personnel to the armed forces in emergencies and administers the alternative service program for conscientious objectors. The legislation under which the agency operates is the Military Selective Service Act. The Selective Service was originally mandated by the Selective Service Act of 1948, which ordered that men be selected for the draft on a fair and equitable basis consistent with the maintenance of an effective national economy. The act replaced the expired Selective Training and Service Act of 1940, which was the first peacetime draft in U.S. history.

The last draft calls were issued in 1972, and the president's authority to conscript men into the armed forces expired on July 1, 1973. Mandatory registration continued until 1975 when it was suspended; it was reinstated in the summer of 1980 by the Military Selective Service Act. The act states that male U.S. citizens and male aliens residing in the United States, who are between the ages of eighteen and twenty-six are required to register with the Selective Service within thirty days of their eighteenth birthday. Failure to register or otherwise comply with the act is, upon conviction, punishable by a fine or imprisonment, or both. According to the act, a person who knowingly counsels, aids, or abets another to fail to comply with the act is subject to the same penalties.

The director of the Selective Service is appointed by the president and confirmed by the Senate. The director is appointed to an indefinite term and serves at the discretion of the president. The staff of 270 full-time employees is composed of civilians and active duty military officers. Approximately 725 National Guard and Reserve officers conduct monthly drills under the jurisdiction of the Selective Service System and could be called up to active duty in an emergency.

The Selective Service System headquarters is in Washington, D.C. The agency maintains six regional headquarters throughout the country in addition to offices in each state. Additional offices are in New York City, the District of Columbia, Guam, Puerto Rico, the Virgin Islands, and the Northern Mariana Islands. Local boards are allocated to counties or corresponding political subdivisions.

The local boards make judgments about registrant claims for deferment or exemption from military service if a draft is resumed. The local board members are the only officials permitted to make initial decisions about claims of conscientious objections, hardship, or religious ministry. The local board also can review claims denied by the area office for other classifications or student postponements if a registrant requests a review.

District appeal boards are maintained in areas corresponding to federal judicial districts. The boards review and affirm or change any decision appealed to it from any local board in its area. Members of both the local boards and the district appeal boards are civilians appointed by the president, who serve without pay. If a claim for classification is denied by the district appeal board by less than a unanimous vote, the registrant can appeal to the president through the National Selective Service Appeal Board. Decisions of the National Appeal Board are final.

Small Business Administration

The Small Business Administration (SBA) is an independent federal agency that provides both new and established small businesses with financial assistance, management counseling, and training. Created by the Small Business Act of 1953, the authority of SBA was expanded by the Small Business Investment Act of 1958. The act authorized SBA to aid, counsel, and assist the interests of small businesses in order to promote free, competitive enterprise. The agency's Office of Advocacy works to ensure that a fair proportion of the total purchases and contracts for supplies and services for the government be placed with small business enterprises.

SBA is headed by an administrator and a deputy administrator. The administrator, the agency's chief counsel for advocacy, and its inspector general are appointed by the president with Senate confirmation. The deputy administrator is appointed by the administrator. The appointees serve at the discretion of the president under no fixed term.

Most SBA aid is in the form of guarantees of loans made by banks. In particular, loans are provided to assist small businesses that have sustained substantial economic injury from sources such as: major natural disasters; urban renewal or highway construction programs; construction programs conducted with federal, state or local funds; and the closing or reduction in operation of major federal military installations. SBA also makes loans to businesses to assist them in meeting requirements imposed by federal laws and by federal air and water pollution standards. In addition, loans are provided to homeowners who have suffered economic injury as a result of natural disasters. Special programs expand and promote ownership of businesses by women and minorities.

SBA licenses, regulates, and lends to small business investment companies (SBICs). These companies provide venture capital to small businesses in the form of equity financing, long-term loans, and management services. SBA determines SBIC loan requirements, approves SBIC charters and articles of incorporation, reviews specific terms of financing and interest rates to be charged, and enforces regulations and penalties regarding investments.

Two pieces of legislation affecting SBA were signed into law in 1980. Both acts are intended to aid small businesses that cannot absorb the costs of regulation compliance. The Regulatory Flexibility Act requires the federal government to anticipate and reduce the impact of federal regulations on small business. The Small Business Investment Incentive Act exempts certain small- and medium-sized businesses from the registration requirements of securities laws.

Smithsonian Institution

The Smithsonian Institution, which encompasses the world's largest museum complex, is an independent trust establishment devoted to public education, research, and national service in the arts, sciences, and history. The Smithsonian complex comprises the National Zoological Park and fourteen museums and galleries—thirteen in Washington, D.C., and one in New York City. Nine of the museums are on the National Mall between the U.S. Capitol and the Washington Monument. The institution also maintains research facilities in nine states and the Republic of Panama.

The institution is governed by a board of regents, which is composed of the vice president of the United States, the chief justice of the United States, three members of the Senate, three members of the House of Representatives, and nine citizen members, nominated by the board and approved by Congress in a joint resolution signed by the president. The chief justice traditionally has served as chancellor of the institution, and the chief executive officer is the secretary, who is appointed by the board.

In 1829, James Smithson, a British scientist, drew up his will naming his nephew, Henry James Hungerford, as beneficiary. The will stipulated that should Hungerford die without heirs (as he did in 1835), the estate would go to the United States "to found at Washington, under the name of the Smithsonian Institution, an establishment for the increase and diffusion of knowledge among men." Smithson's fortune—105 bags containing approximately 100,000 gold sovereigns worth more than $500,000—was brought to the United States in 1838. Eight years later, on August 10, 1846, an act of Congress signed by President James K. Polk established the Smithsonian Institution. James Smithson never visited the United States. He died in Genoa, Italy, in 1829 where he was buried in a small English cemetery. In 1904, when the burial ground was to be displaced by the enlargement of a quarry, his tomb and remains were escorted to the United States by Alexander Graham Bell, and reinterred in the original Smithsonian building.

The original building, commonly known as "the Castle," was completed in 1855 and today houses the institution's administrative offices and the Visitor Information and Associates Reception Center. The Castle also serves as headquarters for the affiliated Woodrow Wilson International Center for Scholars. Other Smithsonian facilities include the Arts and Industries Building, which serves as a showplace for items from the institution's collections in the fields of history, technology, and air and space; the Arthur M. Sackler Gallery, which is the museum of Near Eastern and Asian art; the Freer Gallery of Art; the Hirshhorn Museum and Sculpture Garden, which is devoted to the exhibition, interpretation, and study of modern and contemporary art; the National Air and Space Museum; the National Museum of African Art; the National Museum of American History; the National Museum of Natural History; and the Cooper-Hewitt Museum in New York City, which is the only museum in the United States devoted exclusively to the study and exhibition of historical and contemporary design.

Smithsonian research facilities include the Archives of American Art, the international Environmental Science Program, the Smithsonian Astrophysical Observatory, the Environmental Research Center, and the Tropical Research Institute. In addition to the Smithsonian trust funds, which include endowments, donations, and other revenues, the Institution receives an annual appropriation from Congress.

State Justice Institute

The State Justice Institute is a private, nonprofit corporation created to further the development and improvement of the administration of justice in the state courts. Established by the State Justice Institute Act of 1984, the institute is based in Alexandria, Virginia. It is administered by a board of directors consisting of eleven members appointed by the president, with consent of the Senate, to three-year terms. By law the board membership comprises six judges, a state court administrator, and four members of the public, of whom no more than two may be of the same political party. The board may remove its own members only for cause.

The board of directors selects a chair from among its membership to act as governor of the institute's quarterly meetings. The board also selects an executive director, an ex officio member who manages the daily business of the institute.

The institute's statute contains fourteen broad areas of interest including education for judges and support personnel of state court systems, access to a fair and effective judicial system, and coordination and cooperation of the state courts with the federal judiciary. The institute provides grants and funds cooperative agreements with individuals or organizations interested in carrying out innovative programs. All funding for the institute and its programs is authorized by Congress. Interested parties submit concept papers to the institute for review. Those chosen by the board of directors may receive grants from the institute of up to $300,000, although grants of more than $200,000 are unusual. In 1987, the institute awarded eighty-two grants totaling $8.6 million.

Tennessee Valley Authority

The Tennessee Valley Authority (TVA) is an independent corporate agency of the federal government, charged with responsibility for developing the resources of the Tennessee Valley region. Established by Congress in 1933, TVA serves ninety-one thousand square miles in the southeast United States comprising parts of seven states—Tennessee, Alabama, Mississippi, Kentucky, Virginia, North Carolina, and Georgia. TVA is responsible for providing for flood control and improving navigation on the Tennessee River, producing electric power, and promoting agricultural, economic, and industrial development.

TVA is headed by a three-member board of directors appointed by the president with Senate confirmation. Directors serve staggered, nine-year terms, and one director is designated as chair by the president. The daily affairs of TVA are administered by a general manager, who is responsible to the board of directors.

The three major administrative offices of TVA are in Muscle Shoals, Alabama, and Knoxville and Chattanooga, Tennessee. A small liaison staff is in Washington, D.C., and seven district offices are located throughout the Tennessee Valley region. Day-to-day operations of TVA are conducted by three divisions: Power and Engineering, Natural Resources and Economic Development, and Agricultural and Chemical Development.

The Office of Power and Engineering is responsible for the overall electrical supply program in the TVA area. The office oversees the design, construction, and daily operation and maintenance of the TVA power system, the nation's largest. The TVA electric power system serves more than seven million consumers through 160 municipal and cooperative power distributors. The power system is self-supporting from revenues from power sales. Other TVA programs, such as fertilizer development and flood control, are funded by Congress.

The Office of Natural Resources and Economic Development manages programs designed to use and protect the natural resources of the Tennessee Valley area. Programs include reservoir land use, aquatic plant control, and water conservation, development, and management.

Through TVA facilities, the Office of Agricultural and Chemical Development researches and develops new fertilizers and fertilizer manufacturing processes. The office is chartered to improve and preserve agricultural resources and to encourage soil conservation in the Tennessee Valley area.

United States Arms Control and Disarmament Agency

The United States Arms Control and Disarmament Agency (ACDA) is an independent government agency mandated by Congress to formulate, implement, and support arms control and disarmament policies. The agency has four main tasks: to prepare for and manage U.S. participation in negotiations on disarmament and arms control, to conduct research, to participate in verifying compliance with existing agreements, and to disseminate information on arms control and disarmament to the public.

ACDA is headed by a director and deputy director who are appointed by the president with Senate confirmation. The appointees serve an unspecified term at the discretion of the president. The offices of director and deputy director advise the president, the National Security Council, the secretary of state, and other senior government officials on arms control and disarmament matters.

Before ACDA was created, disarmament negotiations

usually were handled by the State Department's Office of United Nations Affairs. While campaigning for president, John F. Kennedy proposed the establishment of the U.S. Arms Control Research Institute. The new agency, which was renamed as a result of a compromise between the Kennedy administration, the Senate, and the House, was signed into law in 1961.

ACDA maintains four bureaus and four offices. The Strategic Programs Bureau (SP) develops, for presidential approval, arms control policy, strategy, tactics, and language for ongoing arms limitation talks with the Soviet Union. The bureau provides analysis and support for negotiations on the U.S. Strategic Defense Initiative. SP also provides agency representatives and advisers for delegations to negotiations for the Strategic Arms Reduction Talks and the Defense and Space Talks.

The Multilateral Affairs Bureau develops arms control policy, strategy, tactics, and language for ongoing multilateral arms limitations negotiations and provides organizational support, delegation staffing, and advice for multilateral negotiations.

The Bureau of Verification and Intelligence is responsible for policies and studies dealing with the verifiability of provisions of current and projected arms control agreements. The bureau also provides operations analysis, intelligence, and computer support for all ACDA's activities.

The Bureau of Nuclear Weapons Control performs ACDA work on nuclear nonproliferation issues, arms and technology transfers, arms control impact studies, defense economics and economics of arms control, military expenditure recording and analysis, and weapons analyses.

The Office of General Counsel is responsible for all matters of domestic and international law relevant to ACDA's work and provides advice and assistance in drafting and negotiating arms control treaties and agreements. Other ACDA offices include the Office of Public Affairs, which coordinates the agency's dissemination of public information; the Office of Congressional Affairs, which coordinates ACDA's contacts with Congress on all matters relating to arms control; and the Office of Administration, which has responsibility for the daily operation of the agency and its negotiating staffs in Geneva, Stockholm, and Vienna.

United States Information Agency

The United States Information Agency (USIA) is an independent agency responsible for the U.S. government's overseas information, educational exchange, and cultural programs. Its director reports to the president and receives policy guidance from the secretary of state. The director, deputy director, and four associate directors are appointed by the president with Senate confirmation and serve at the discretion of the president.

USIA originated as the Voice of America (VOA) in 1942 during World War II. The Smith-Mundt Act established the information program as a long-term, integral part of U.S. foreign policy in 1948, and in 1953 Congress created USIA. The State Department retained control over educational and cultural affairs until 1978.

In 1988 USIA had 204 posts in 127 countries. Overseas posts are maintained at U.S. diplomatic missions and are grouped in five geographical areas: Africa; Europe; East Asia and the Pacific; the American Republics; and North Africa, the Near East, and South Asia. Each post reports to an area office in the agency's Washington, D.C., headquarters. USIA officers overseas engage in political advocacy of American foreign policy objectives. In addition to its radio service, the Voice of America, the agency uses personal contacts with foreign leaders and films, videotapes, magazines, and direct satellite to carry out its mission. USIA also maintains a library open to the public in many of its overseas posts.

The chief of the agency's program in any country is the public affairs officer (PAO), who usually has the diplomatic designation of counselor of the embassy for public affairs. PAOs advise U.S. ambassadors on issues of public affairs diplomacy and the public articulation of U.S. policies.

Program direction and administrative responsibilities of USIA are held by the agency's Washington office. U.S.-based personnel conduct the broadcasting operations of the Voice of America and the Television and Film Service and produce agency publications, films, exhibits, and other support materials for field posts. USIA's Washington office is also responsible for advising the president and others in the official foreign affairs community on the implications of foreign opinion for the United States. USIA provides opinion analyses on international issues as well as daily summaries of foreign media treatment of U.S. actions and policies.

The Voice of America is the global radio network of USIA. It broadcasts 1,003 hours each week in forty-two languages and is heard by more than 100 million adults at least once a week. USIA's WORLDNET is an interactive international television service that provides direct communication on international issues between U.S. spokespersons and foreign leaders and journalists. USIA also sponsors educational exchange programs including the Fulbright Program, which operates in 120 countries and awards more than 3,500 scholarships each year.

United States Institute of Peace

The United States Institute of Peace is an independent, federal, nonprofit corporation created to develop and disseminate knowledge about the peaceful resolution of international conflict. Established in 1984, the institute is governed by a bipartisan fifteen-member board of directors. Board members are appointed by the president with Senate confirmation and serve at the discretion of the president. Members of the board include the director of the U.S. Arms Control and Disarmament Agency, the assistant secretary of state for human rights and humanitarian affairs, the president of the National Defense University, and the assistant secretary of defense for international security policy. The president of the board is the only nonvoting member.

The institute maintains a program of grants to nonprofit organizations and to public institutions and individuals researching the nature and processes of peace, war, and international conflict management. The institute also administers an internal research and studies program and a fellowship program for scholars and practitioners of conflict management. Other activities include an education and public information program and a research library program. The institute produces a biennial report to Congress and the president and the *United States Institute of Peace Journal*. All funding for the institute and its activities is appropriated by Congress.

United States International Development Cooperation Agency

The United States International Development Cooperation Agency (IDCA) was established by Congress in 1979 to plan and coordinate U.S. policy on economic issues affecting developing countries. The director of IDCA is intended to serve as principal international development adviser to the president and to the secretary of state. The agency's mission requires that the director of IDCA and senior agency staff participate in a wide range of interagency activities.

IDCA incorporates the Agency for International Development, the Trade and Development Program, and the Overseas Private Investment Corporation. Responsibility for U.S. participation in multilateral development banks is shared by the director of IDCA and the secretary of the Treasury. The director of IDCA also shares policy responsibility for the Food for Peace Program with the Department of Agriculture. The agency guides U.S. participation in certain programs of the United Nations (UN) and the Organization of American States (OAS), including the UN Development Program, the UN Children's Fund, the World Food Program, and the OAS Technical Assistance Funds.

As head of the primary policy-making agency for U.S. assistance programs, the director of IDCA is a member of the National Advisory Committee on International and Monetary Affairs, the Trade Policy Committee, and the Advisory Committee on Agricultural Assistance. The director also chairs the Development Coordination Committee, a broad interagency body that coordinates development and development-related policies and programs.

United States International Trade Commission

The United States International Trade Commission is an independent, quasi-judicial agency that investigates the effect of U.S. foreign trade on domestic production, employment, and consumption. Created by Congress in 1916 as the United States Tariff Commission, the agency acquired its present title under the Trade Act of 1974.

The commission comprises six members appointed by the president, with Senate confirmation for terms of nine years, unless appointed to fill an unexpired term. A commissioner who has served for more than five years is not eligible for reappointment. No more than three commissioners may be of the same political party. The chair is designated by the president and serves a two-year term. No chair may be of the same political party as the preceding chair. The chair and vice-chair also must belong to different parties.

As a fact-finding agency, the commission has broad powers to study and investigate all aspects of U.S. foreign trade, the competitiveness of U.S. products, and foreign and domestic customs laws. It does not set policy, although its technical advice forms a basis for economic policy decisions on U.S. international trade. The commission conducts three types of investigations. It examines whether increasing imports cause serious injury to U.S. industry and whether importers are infringing on U.S. patents, copyrights, or trademarks. The commission may initiate an investigation or arrange one after receiving a complaint.

After receiving a petition from an industry representative or from the Commerce Department, the commission also investigates whether there are reasonable indications that U.S. industries are threatened or materially injured by imports that are subsidized or sold in the United States at prices lower than foreigners would charge in their home market (a practice known as "dumping"). At the same time, the Commerce Department examines whether those subsidies or pricing practices are unfair. If both preliminary investigations are affirmed, the commission must conduct a final investigation to determine whether a U.S. industry is being materially injured or threatened by unfairly priced imports. If the commission finds that such harm is occurring, the Commerce Department must order that a duty be placed on the imports equal to the amount of the unfair subsidy or price. That duty cannot be lifted by the president.

United States Postal Service

Established on July 26, 1777, at the meeting of the Second Continental Congress in Philadelphia, the United States Postal Service (USPS) is the second oldest department or agency of the U.S. government. By 1780 the new Post Office Department consisted only of a postmaster general, a secretary/comptroller, three surveyors, one inspector of dead letters, and twenty-six post riders. When the seat of government and postal headquarters were moved to Washington, D.C., in 1880, officials were able to carry all postal records, furniture, and supplies in two wagons. In 1987 the U.S. Postal Service employed more than 750,000 people and handled 154 billion pieces of mail. In that year USPS had operating revenues exceeding $31 billion and more than 29,000 post offices nationwide.

The growth of the USPS during its long history reflects the rapid expansion of the nation and has been marked by both great successes and great difficulties. Benjamin Franklin was appointed the first postmaster general of the new nation, and the methods and organization of mail delivery that he created remained intact for almost two hundred years. By 1966, however, years of financial neglect and lack of centralized control had left the Post Office Department unable to deal efficiently with the increasing demands of the modern era.

The problems led Winton M. Blount, postmaster general under President Richard Nixon, to propose in 1969 a reorganization of the Post Office Department. Reforms passed by Congress less than a year later failed to rectify the situation, however, and on March 16, 1970, approximately 152,000 postal employees in 671 postal locations began a work stoppage. The department and leaders of the seven unions representing the postal employees met to try to agree on a plan for reorganization. That plan was submitted to Congress, and on August 12, 1970, President Nixon signed into law the most comprehensive postal legislation since the founding of the Republic.

The new organization, renamed the United States Postal Service, began operating on July 1, 1971, under the vested authority of a board of governors. The board comprises eleven members, nine of whom are appointed by the president on a bipartisan basis with advice and consent of the Senate. The nine members in turn appoint a tenth member of the board, the postmaster general, who serves as the chief executive officer of the Postal Service. The nine members and the postmaster general appoint the deputy postmaster general, who serves as the eleventh member of the board. The new legislation also established an independent postal rate commission of five members, appointed by the president, to recommend postal rates and classifications for adoption by the board of governors. *(See "Postal Rate Commission," p. 134, in this chapter.)*

Notes

1. *Federal Regulatory Directory, 1983-1984* (Washington, D.C.: Congressional Quarterly Inc., 1983), 3.
2. Samuel Huntington, "The Marasmus of the ICC," *Yale Law Journal* 61 (April 1952): 467-509.
3. Marver H. Bernstein, *Regulating Business by Independent Commission* (Princeton, N.J.: Princeton University Press, 1955).
4. Robert E. Cushman, *The Independent Regulatory Commissions* (New York: Oxford University Press, 1941), 19.
5. *Federal Regulatory Directory, 1983-1984*, 16-20.
6. Marver H. Bernstein, *The Job of the Federal Executive* (Washington, D.C.: Brookings, 1958), 172.
7. William E. Brigman, "The Executive Branch and the Independent Regulatory Agencies," *Presidential Studies Quarterly* 11 (Spring 1981): 251.
8. Linda Fisher, "Fifty Years of Presidential Appointments," in *The In-and-Outers: Presidential Appointees and Transient Government in Washington,* ed. G. Calvin Mackenzie (Baltimore: Johns Hopkins University Press, 1987), 4.
9. *Federal Regulatory Directory, 1983-1984*, 37.
10. Louis Kohlmeier, Jr., *The Regulators: Watchdog Agencies and the Public Interest* (New York: Harper and Row, 1969).
11. G. Calvin Mackenzie, *The Politics of Presidential Appointments* (New York: Free Press, 1981), 82-83.
12. Brigman, "The Executive Branch," 249.

Selected Bibliography

Bernstein, Marver H. *Regulating Business by Independent Commission.* Princeton, N.J.: Princeton University Press, 1955.
_____. *The Job of the Federal Executive.* Washington, D.C.: Brookings, 1958.
Brigman, William E. "The Executive Branch and the Independent Regulatory Agencies." *Presidential Studies Quarterly* 11 (Spring 1981): 244-261.
Cushman, Robert E. *The Independent Regulatory Commissions.* New York: Oxford University Press, 1941.
Federal Regulatory Directory, 1983-1984. Washington, D.C.: Congressional Quarterly Inc., 1983.
Fisher, Linda. "Fifty Years of Presidential Appointments." In *The In-and-Outers: Presidential Appointees and Transient Government in Washington,* ed. G. Calvin Mackenzie. Baltimore: Johns Hopkins University Press, 1987.
Huntington, Samuel. "The Marasmus of the ICC." *Yale Law Journal* 61 (April 1952): 467-509.
Kohlmeier, Louis, Jr. *The Regulators: Watchdog Agencies and the Public Interest.* New York: Harper and Row, 1969.
Mackenzie, G. Calvin. *The Politics of Presidential Appointments.* New York: Free Press, 1981.

Presidential Commissions

Since the birth of this nation, presidents have been appointing commissions to probe subjects that normally are beyond the daily scope of presidential advisory organizations. Twentieth-century presidents have relied on commissions to gather information and to focus public attention on specific problems.

Although commissions can be created either by the president or by Congress, they are usually placed within the executive office. Carl Marcy, an early scholar of presidential commissions, has noted that commissions "grow out of the inadequacies in the executive departments or in Congress, or, in some instances, they develop because of the unusual nature of the problem to be met." [1] In recent years the number and variety of presidential commissions have increased tremendously. Yet often they have been ridiculed by presidential scholars and the press for their sometimes meaningless objectives and empty conclusions. In truth, not all presidential commissions have worked well; some, however, have proven valuable and important.

Presidents have no specific constitutional grant of authority to appoint commissions. They usually justify such a step, however, by pointing to the general grant of authority in the Constitution that directs the president to "take care that the laws be faithfully executed" and "from time to time give to the Congress information on the State of the Union, and recommend to their consideration such measures as he shall judge necessary and expedient" (Article II, section 3). President John Tyler (1841-1845), in naming a presidential commission to investigate corruption in the New York City Customhouse, was the first president to justify such action by pointing to his constitutional authority to do so. Tyler asserted that the information collected by the commission was for his use as president, but that it probably would find its way to Congress in the form of proposed legislation. He argued: "The expediency, if not the necessity, of inquiries into the transactions of our customs houses, especially in cases where abuses and malpractices are alleged, must be obvious to Congress." [2] His constitutional justification of presidential commissions has stood up over the years.

Although it is generally recognized that presidents have the power to establish presidential commissions, they often seek congressional approval anyway. One reason may be the funds required to operate and staff a presidential

commission. Presidents often seek public funds for financing commission activities through legislation, which Congress routinely passes. Some presidential commissions, however, are created by an executive order of the president and are financed by emergency, executive, or special projects funds, which are spent at the president's discretion. President Herbert C. Hoover (1929-1933), who significantly expanded the use of presidential commissions by appointing sixty-two during his first sixteen months in office, reportedly raised at least $2 million in private funds to finance them.

Presidential commissions date back to the administration of George Washington (1789-1797), who appointed a commission to investigate the Whiskey Rebellion. In this incident a group of liquor distillers in western Pennsylvania threatened the nation with civil disorder over the federal liquor tax. Washington, perplexed over a situation potentially divisive to the young nation, took the problem to a group of distinguished citizens; he clearly had confidence in their findings. In his sixth annual address to the Congress, Washington flatly stated: "The report of the commissioners marks their firmness and abilities, and must unite all virtuous men." [3]

Most nineteenth-century presidents used commissions to meet the specific needs of their administrations. President Martin Van Buren (1837-1841), for example, appointed a commission to examine the European postal systems. Strong presidents have used commissions freely. Andrew Jackson (1829-1837) appointed two commissions just to check up on the actions of the Navy.

The use of presidential commissions is nevertheless primarily a twentieth-century phenomenon. The first serious study of commissions found that some one hundred commissions had been appointed up to 1940. [4] A more recent study indicated that another forty-four were appointed between 1945 and 1970. [5] Since 1970 their numbers have increased greatly. In the late 1980s the White House Personnel Office listed about 250 commissions or special committees. [6] These commissions ranged from the President's Council on Physical Fitness and Sports to the President's Committee on the Arts and Humanities to the Presidential Commission on the Human Immunodeficiency Virus Epidemic (AIDS Commission).

Over the years presidential commissions have played significant roles in many policy areas. Recent commissions have investigated business regulation, tariffs, government waste, defense spending, the space program, Social Security,

By W. Craig Bledsoe

Although presidential commissions are largely a twentieth-century phenomenon, they date back to George Washington's administration, when he appointed a commission to investigate the Whiskey Rebellion.

Library of Congress

the Iran-contra affair, and government reorganization. Theodore Roosevelt (1901-1909) introduced the use of commissions for substantive policy advice to the president. Inspired by the royal commissions used extensively in Great Britain to investigate policy questions, Roosevelt appointed a number of commissions during his administration, including the Aldrich Commission, whose recommendations led to establishment of the Federal Reserve System. Herbert Hoover himself, after his retirement from the presidency, headed two important commissions on government reorganization appointed by Presidents Harry S Truman and Dwight D. Eisenhower, respectively. Presidential commissions also have been sent overseas to supervise national elections and investigate the stability of foreign governments. In 1917, for example, after the overthrow of Czar Nicholas II, President Woodrow Wilson sent a special commission to Russia to find out how democratic the regime of Aleksandr Fyodorovich Kerensky would be.

Although the objectives of presidential commissions have varied, most have been important to presidential decision making, and many have contributed significantly to the development of government policy. For example, Franklin D. Roosevelt's most notable commission, the President's Committee on Administrative Management (Brownlow Commission), developed the blueprint for the Executive Office of the President. *(See Executive Office of the President: White House Office chapter.)*

Types of Presidential Commissions

Presidential commissions fall into three broad categories: permanent federal advisory organizations, ad hoc or blue ribbon commissions, and White House conferences.

Permanent Federal Advisory Organizations

When presidents want advice from sources outside the White House staff and the cabinet, they often establish a permanent advisory organization—committee, commission, council, board, or task force—within the executive branch. These organizations formulate and coordinate recommendations for the president on specific policy issues over an indefinite period of time. A permanent advisory organization is either given independent status, placed in the Exec-

utive Office of the President (EOP), or placed in the department to which it is most germane. *(See Table 1.)* For example, the Advisory Committee for Trade Negotiations, the Presidential Board of Advisors on Private Sector Initiatives, and the President's Committee on the Arts and Humanities are officially located in EOP. Both the National Advisory Committee on Oceans and Atmosphere and the President's Export Council are located in the Department of Commerce. The Advisory Committee on Federal Pay has independent organizational status.

Permanent advisory organizations usually have the right to review and question presidential initiatives and programs. Congress may give these organizations large grants of authority, and it usually specifies membership qualifications and the terms of office for members. Because permanent advisory organizations often are set up in response to interest group pressure, their composition is likely to reflect the respective groups. Normally, qualifications for advisory organization membership are couched in language open to broad interpretation, but statutory provisions usually make interest group representation mandatory. The Federal Council on the Aging, for example, must have members representative of older Americans and national organizations that have an interest in the aging.

Although permanent advisory organizations are designed to facilitate presidential decision making, presidents sometimes view them as an uninvited burden. For example, the National Council on Marine Resources and Engineering Development (1966-1971), established to develop a comprehensive program of marine science exploration, was forced upon Lyndon B. Johnson's administration by interest groups trying to protect their industry. Both Presidents Johnson and Richard Nixon often clashed with the council. Thus, when Nixon took office he dismantled the group by moving its functions into existing departments. Presidential scholar Richard M. Pious has described the effects of these organizations: "The president has little time to consider their proposals and may wall himself off from officials who run them. He may become impatient with long-range planning and irritated at lack of consideration for his political problems." [7]

Ad Hoc Commissions

Ad hoc commissions investigate particular issues or related policy questions. They consist of three or more members, who are appointed directly by the president for a specified period of time. A commission is considered ad hoc

Library of Congress

President Hoover significantly expanded the use of presidential commissions, appointing sixty-two during his first sixteen months in office.

Table 1 Presidential Advisory Organizations, 1987

Organization [a]	Location	Organization [a]	Location
Advisory Committee on Federal Pay	Independent	President's Advisory Council on Mediation and Conciliation	FMCS
Advisory Committee for Radio Broadcasting to Cuba	EOP	President's Board of Advisors on Private Sector Initiatives	EOP
Advisory Committee for Trade Negotiations	EOP	President's Cancer Panel	HHS
Advisory Council on Dependents Education	DOD	President's Commission on Americans Outdoors	DOI
Advisory Council on Education Statistics	DED	President's Commission on Executive Exchange	EOP
Advisory Council on Historic Preservation	EOP	President's Commission on White House Fellowships	EOP
Commission of Fine Arts	Independent	President's Committee on the Arts and the Humanities	EOP
Commission on Presidential Scholars	DED	President's Committee on Employment of the Handicapped	DOL
Employee Retirement Income Security Act Advisory Council (ERISA)	DOL	President's Committee on Mental Retardation	HHS
Federal Council on the Aging	HHS	President's Committee on the National Medal of Science	EOP
Federal Council on the Arts and Humanities	EOP	President's Council on Integrity and Efficiency	EOP
Intergovernmental Advisory Council on Education	DED	President's Council on Physical Fitness and Sports	HHS
Missing Children's Advisory Board	DOJ	President's Economic Policy Advisory Board	EOP
National Advisory Committee on Oceans and Atmosphere	DOC/NOAA	President's Export Council	DOC
National Advisory Council on Adult Education	DED	President's Foreign Intelligence Advisory Board	EOP
National Advisory Council on Child Nutrition	USDA	President's National Security Telecommunications Advisory Committee	EOP
National Advisory Council on Continuing Education	DED	President's Physical Evaluation Board	Army
National Advisory Council on Indian Education	DED	President's Task Force on Legal Equity for Women	EOP
National Advisory Council on Maternal, Infant and Fetal Nutrition	USDA	South Florida Task Force and National Narcotics Border Interdiction System	EOP
National Advisory Council on Women's Educational Programs	DED	U.S. Arms Control General Advisory Committee	USACDA
National Agricultural Research and Extension Users Advisory Board	USDA	U.S. Sentencing Commission	DOJ
National Cancer Advisory Board	HHS	United States Advisory Commission on Public Diplomacy	USIA
National Commission for Employment Policy	DOL		
National Council on Educational Research	DED		
National Council on Vocational Education	DED		
National Highway Safety Advisory Committee	DOT		
National Volunteer Advisory Council	EOP		
Presidential Academic Fitness Program	DED		
Presidential Advisory Commission on Small and Minority Business	SBA		

Source: Charles B. Brownson and Anna L. Brownson, eds., *1987 Federal Staff Directory* (Mt. Vernon, Va: Congressional Staff Directory, Ltd., 1987), 46-47.

Note: DED-Department of Education; DOC-Department of Commerce; DOD-Department of Defense; DOI-Department of the Interior; DOJ-Department of Justice; DOL-Department of Labor; DOT-Department of Transportation; EOP-Executive Office of the President; FMCS-Federal Mediation and Conciliation Service; HHS-Department of Health and Human Services; NOAA-National Oceanic and Atmospheric Administration; SBA-Small Business Administration; USACDA-U.S. Arms Control and Disarmament Agency; USDA-U.S. Department of Agriculture; USIA-U.S. Information Agency.

a. Active as of 1987.

when it has a termination and reporting date not more than three years after its creation. Created either by executive order, by congressional legislation, or by joint action, ad hoc commissions are purely advisory with no power to implement their findings or recommendations, which are published and made available to the public. At least one member of an ad hoc commission must not be from the executive branch. Members, however, may be from Congress, the federal judiciary, or state or local governments, or they may be private citizens. Many ad hoc commissions have been composed entirely of private citizens.[8]

Ad hoc commissions are sometimes called blue ribbon commissions when their members have distinguished

records in the public or private sector. Thus, in this way national leaders in business, agriculture, science, technology, and other important fields, who otherwise might not accept permanent positions in the federal government or might not make a suitable permanent adviser, are able to serve in a temporary but official advisory capacity to the president. A 1979 study of the effect of ad hoc commissions on presidential policy making found that of the thirteen hundred commissioners studied "over 60 percent were prestigious members of some national elite at the time of their appointment." [9]

Ad hoc commissions usually are asked to examine a particular problem and to offer advice on how to deal reasonably with that problem. According to political scientist David Flitner, Jr., such commissions are either procedure oriented, situation oriented, or crisis oriented.[10] Procedure-oriented commissions examine the operating procedures of existing agencies before recommending improvements in their efficiency or making judgments about their overall utility. These commissions have examined, among other things, postal procedures, criminal code reform, and general government operations. For example, the 1980 Grace Commission on More Effective Government examined the efficiency of virtually all federal government operations in the United States.

Situation-oriented commissions investigate broad areas of vital concern to large sectors of the population. These commissions include the Commission on Law Enforcement and the Administration of Justice (Katzenbach Commission), the Commission on Obscenity and Pornography (Lockhart Commission), the Commission on Population Growth and the American Future (Rockefeller Commission), and the National Commission on Marijuana and Drug Abuse (Shafer Commission).

As their name implies, crisis-oriented commissions arise from a particular event or crisis. Such a commission may or may not investigate the more fundamental cause underlying the crisis. Examples of crisis-oriented commissions include the President's Commission on the Assassination of President Kennedy (Warren Commission), the National Advisory Commission on Civil Disorders (Kerner Commission), the National Commission on the Causes and Prevention of Violence (Eisenhower Commission), the President's Commission on Campus Unrest (Scranton Commission), and the AIDS Commission.

White House Conferences

The White House conference is another means of going beyond the traditional executive branch advisory bodies. Invitees to such a conference (often as many as several hundred attend) usually meet for several days to discuss a specific topic. Like ad hoc commissions, White House conferences are temporary and must report back to the president on the subject of their investigation.

Customarily, a small organizational committee is convened first to prepare an agenda for the conference itself. The 1980 White House Conference on Families, for example, followed the administrative work of the National Advisory Committee to the White House Conference on Families, which was established in June 1979 to guide and assist the chair of the conference.

Most conferences meet only once or in a series of panels or committees that make recommendations to the entire conference. Another small committee usually writes the report of the conference.[11]

The White House Conference on International Cooperation, held in late 1965, was typical of this kind of conference. Called in recognition of the International Year of Cooperation, designated by the United Nations, the conference was designed to promote a dialogue between private citizens and government officials on international problems and prospects for world peace. A National Citizen's Commission on International Cooperation, composed of 230 members working in thirty separate committees, was convened to lay the groundwork for the conference. In addition to these committees, other government and private experts were added as the committees went about their deliberations. All together more than a thousand persons from various areas of expertise took part in the overall discussions before the final conference was held in December 1965. Although all the committees did not come together until the final conference, each put in many hours in their separate meetings. For example, the Committee on Culture and Intellectual Exchange divided itself into twelve committees and held six meetings of the full committee, and the Arms Control and Disarmament Committee held four full committee meetings with many of its members meeting regularly in smaller groups. The final conference produced a report entitled "Blueprint for Peace," which contained over four hundred recommendations.[12]

Paul Hosefros, *New York Times*

The 1987 three-member Tower Commission investigated the White House's involvement in the Iran-contra affair. From left: Edmund Muskie, Sen. John Tower, and Gen. Brent Scowcroft.

The Commissioners

Although White House conferences tend to be large affairs, most presidential commissions are relatively small, with between fifteen and twenty-five members. The size of a commission usually depends on its scope and possible political impact. For example, one of the smallest recent ad hoc commissions was the three-member President's Special Review Board, or Tower Commission, which in 1987 investigated the White House's involvement in the Iran-contra affair. One of the largest was the twenty-four-member Commission on Population Growth and the American Future, established during the early 1970s to study the effects of population growth on the United States. The more narrowly defined the commission's topic, the more likely it is that the commission will be small. The 1970 President's Commission on Campus Unrest, founded to study disorder and violence on college and university campuses, had only nine members. The larger commissions usually are given more time to conduct their operations. *(See Table 2.)*

The appointment of commissioners is related to how the commission was established. If a president establishes a commission by executive order, the president is responsible for appointing all members of the commission. If Congress at the request of the president or through its own initiative establishes a commission through statutory law within the presidency, appointment power is divided among several sources with the president having the majority of appointments. The two Hoover-chaired Commissions on the Organization of the Executive Branch of Government of 1949 and 1955 are good examples of presidential commissions established by statutory law with appointment power divided among different sources. Both commissions were set up by a unanimous vote of Congress. Each commission had twelve members—four appointed by the president, four by the vice president, and four by the Speaker of the House. Of these, at least two members had to come from the private sector and two from the public sector. Moreover, appointments had to be based on proportional partisan representation. The first Hoover Commission comprised six Democrats and six Republicans; the second, five Democrats and seven Republicans. The Commission on Population Growth and the American Future had a congressionally mandated membership composed as follows:

> (1) two members of the Senate who shall be members of different political parties and who shall be appointed by the President of the Senate;
> (2) two members of the House of Representatives who shall be members of different political parties and shall be appointed by the Speaker of the House of Representatives; and
> (3) not to exceed twenty members appointed by the President.[13]

Most commissions represent a number of constituencies. According to Frank Popper, a scholar of presidential commissions, "A commission generally includes at least one businessman, labor leader, lawyer, educator, editor, farmer, woman, Negro, Protestant, Catholic, Jew, Easterner, Midwesterner, Southerner, Westerner, federal government official, congressman, member of a previous administration, enlightened amateur, and friend of the president."[14] Even though many of these constituencies may be represented by one person, most major sectors of American society will

Table 2   Number of Commissioners on Recent Presidential Commissions

Commission	Number of commissioners
President's Commission on the Assassination of President Kennedy	7
President's Commission on Law Enforcement and the Administration of Justice	19
National Advisory Commission on Civil Disorders	11
National Commission on the Causes and Prevention of Violence	13
Commission on Obscenity and Pornography	18
President's Commission on Campus Unrest	9
Commission on Population Growth and the American Future	24
National Commission on Marijuana and Drug Abuse	13

Source: David Flitner, Jr., *The Politics of Presidential Commissions* (Dobbs Ferry, N.Y.: Transnational Publishers, 1986), 45-46.

be represented on a single commission. Presidents customarily attempt to maintain bipartisanship on commissions; to do otherwise would completely discredit the results of the commission's investigation.

Commission appointments usually are not considered political plums, but most commissioners tend to be well known, with outstanding records in either public or private service. Representatives of the private sector are primarily attorneys, college professors, and other professionals. *(See Table 3.)*

Some scholars see the elite nature of commissions as a positive characteristic that allows them to forge a consensus among various elite interests. Daniel Bell, a member of the National Commission on Technology, Automation, and Economic Progress (1964-1965) has written: "The distinctive virtue of the government commission arrangement is that there is a specific effort to involve the full range of elite or organized opinion in order to see if a real consensus can be achieved."[15] Popper has noted that most commissioners are more like each other than like their constituents.

> [Commission members] know, or know of, each other. They are primarily administrators, and they are used to working in committees. They have already succeeded in their careers, and their commission service is an honor rather than a steppingstone. They do not really need the nominal payment they get for their commission service. Some have national power, and all share what may be called the conservatism of personal success.[16]

Although elites are represented on commissions, leaders of some interest groups are not. And because of the nature of elite representation, representatives of most minority groups are seldom on the rosters of commissions. For example, of the 114 members of the commissions listed in Tables 2 and 3, only 12 were women.[17] *(See Tables 2 and 3.)*

Any group that is out of the mainstream of American politics is not represented at all. Political scientists

Thomas E. Cronin and Sanford E. Greenberg noted that during the Eisenhower, Kennedy, and Johnson administrations, presidential commissions were "extraordinarily skewed in composition in favor of the best educated and the professionally well established." [18]

Elite participation on commissions is so complete that often the same names appear on commission rosters again and again. In seeking bipartisanship, both Democratic and Republican presidents often appoint the same people. And ad hoc commissions have been especially popular ways for former government officials to return to the policy-making process. From 1950 to 1970 seven individuals served on three commissions each and twenty-five on two commissions each. [19] Over the years Milton Eisenhower, President Eisenhower's brother, served on some twenty commissions. Among those officials who served on more than one commission during the Reagan administration (1981-1989) were former senator John G. Tower (R-Texas) and former secretary of state Edmund S. Muskie (National Commission on the Public Service and the President's Special Review Board), retired Air Force lieutenant general Brent Scowcroft (Commission on Defense Management and President's Special Review Board), former astronaut Neil Armstrong (*Challenger* Commission and National Commission on Space), former Virginia governor Charles S. Robb (National Commission on the Public Service and National Bipartisan Commission on Central America), and business executive J. Peter Grace (President's Private Sector Survey

Table 3   Number of Commissioners by Profession

Profession	Number of commissioners
Attorney	15
Professor	14
U.S. representative	10
U.S. senator	10
Clergy	7
Medical	6
University president or dean	5
Business	4
Federal judge	4
Police	3
State government (not governor)	3
Cabinet member or official	2
Former governor	2
Housewife	2
Labor leader	2
Newspaper publisher or editor	2
Political action group	2
Private foundation official	2
Race relations group	2
Research, research institute	2
State judge	2
Student	2
Governor	1
Civic leader	1
Author	1
Mayor	1
University fellow	1
Cannot be determined	5

Source: David Flitner, Jr., *The Politics of Presidential Commissions* (Dobbs Ferry, N.Y.: Transnational Publishers, 1986), 46.

on Cost Control, Peace Corps Advisory Council, and Presidential Commission on World Hunger).

The tendency to appoint former government officials to commissions has created an "established class of commissioners who are tapped repeatedly for service." [20] A Johnson aide explained:

> There is a problem that the same damn names turn up time after time. It is as hard as the devil to find new people. There was a lot of talk about finding that bright young man in Iowa in the Kennedy Administration. They didn't find him. There is really a sort of a liberal house establishment. The same people keep turning up on the same problems. You have a deuce of a time trying to reach out to get outside of the major cities.

This situation results in what presidential commission critic Thomas R. Wolanin has described as a "ho-hum-those-guys-again" attitude from the public, which reduces the effectiveness and persuasiveness of a commission's work. [21]

Selection Process for Commission Members

Shortly after the decision has been made to establish a commission, a presidential aide usually is put in charge of developing a list of potential nominees. Political considerations almost always are part of the deliberations that go into formulating a list of members. One Johnson aide described the process:

> After we had a topic, we'd make up a list of the general skills and areas we wanted represented, but no names. The lists were a lot alike. We'd check with the appropriate departments, the Budget Bureau, and the Civil Service Commission. They'd suggest specific names which would go to the president. He would add, subtract, or substitute names or categories. He'd add the people we wanted for general wisdom-at-large delegates. When he didn't like a list, he'd say things like "That guy's been on everything lately," or "Everyone's from New York and Texas. See if you can spread it out a little." [22]

Most administrations have maintained lists of people who were recommended for appointment to various federal positions, or who came to the attention of the White House because of their distinguished accomplishments. In addition to consulting these files, presidential aides also consult various constituent groups. Sometimes people in these groups themselves volunteer, or groups submit names for consideration. Certain groups will be asked to submit names, especially if their support is crucial to the successful operation of the commission. The Kennedy administration, for example, wanted the support of both political parties for an investigation into the increasing costs of campaign financing. It thus asked the Republican National Committee to submit a list of names for the President's Commission on Campaign Costs (1961-1962). In addition, former cabinet members and other former presidential appointees frequently turn up on commissions because nominees often are chosen from lists of people who have served on previous commissions, who held positions in past administrations, or who testified at congressional hearings in the relevant area. [23]

Once the list of potential appointees has been narrowed, it is given to the president for final approval. As in most presidential appointments the amount of interest that individual presidents show in the final selection process varies. President Johnson, for example, paid meticulous attention to his commission appointments. Other presidents have given little attention to final decisions on commission personnel, especially if the commission is of minor importance. If the commission is politically important, however, presidents may intervene just before the final selection is made by deleting or adding names for personal or political reasons. For example, at the final selection point President John F. Kennedy added one of his personal friends to the list of nominees for the President's Commission on Campaign Costs. One of Kennedy's assistants explained, "He was conservative as hell but the president respected him. Kennedy had served in the House with him and may have served on the same committee with him." [24]

Selection Process for Commission Chairs

Because the chairs of commissions serve as the public symbols of their groups (their names may even be used as a shorthand way of referring to a commission), selection of the chair is an important presidential decision. The most famous example of this is probably the President's Commission on the Assassination of President Kennedy, which became known as the Warren Commission after its chairman, Chief Justice Earl Warren. Similarly, the Kerner Commission (named after former Illinois governor Otto Kerner) and the Grace Commission (named after industrialist Peter Grace) both represent commissions that became better known by the names of their chairs. The heads of commissions assume most of the responsibility for the operation of their groups. They publicize their commission's work by testifying before congressional committees, giving speeches, making television appearances, and writing articles about the commission's investigation. Presidents also may ask chairs to play a role in the selection of other commission members.

Most important, however, commission heads are responsible for leading their commissions to a consensus and producing a report with specific recommendations at the conclusion of their investigations. The chair sets the tone for the commission and its success or failure. Because chairs preside at meetings, they are in a distinctive position to provide the commission with leadership. Indeed, as Wolanin has noted, they can exercise social leadership and facilitate the process of producing the commission's report: "The role of the chairman is most often primarily political, producing agreement, and administrative, producing a report, rather than substantive." [25] Lloyd M. Cutler, executive director of the 1968-1969 National Commission on the Causes and Prevention of Violence (also known as the Eisenhower Commission on Violence), has described the importance of an effective chair:

> Our chairman was Dr. Milton Eisenhower, an able and devoted man who ... was the key to the success of the entire commission. Dr. Eisenhower was a man with whom all of the commissioners were ready to agree even though they might disagree a great deal with one another. It was his presence and his continuing force on the commission that I think led to the largely unanimous reports that were filed. He is also quite a draftsman in his own right and ... every word in this report was at least reviewed and edited by Dr. Eisenhower and a very large number of those words were written in the first instance by him. [26]

Commission chairs should have multidimensional qualities. According to Flitner, "The chairman must, ideally, exhibit the integrity and fairness of a judge, the administrative skills of an executive, and the intellectual abilities of a scholar." [27] President Johnson had to make a very thoughtful decision about his selection of a chair for the Commission on the Assassination of President Kennedy. In his memoirs Johnson commented on the politically sensitive appointment and his choice for the post:

> The Commission had to be bipartisan, and I felt that we needed a Republican chairman whose judicial ability and fairness were unquestioned. I don't believe that I ever considered anyone but Chief Justice Earl Warren for chairman. I was not an intimate of the Chief Justice. We had never spent ten minutes alone together, but to me he was the personification of justice and fairness in this country.... We had to bring the nation through that bloody tragedy, and Warren's personal integrity was a key element in assuring that all the facts would be unearthed and that the conclusions would be credible. [28]

The most important characteristics sought in a commission chair are national prominence and a reputation for fairness.

Although few potential nominees eventually refuse to chair a commission, presidents may have difficulty persuading some of their selections to serve. When Johnson asked Milton Eisenhower to chair the Commission on Violence, for example, Eisenhower proved somewhat reluctant. Johnson "persuaded" him by pointing out that a press conference already was scheduled for that day to announce the appointments to the commission. Most potential appointees end up agreeing to serve as chair because, as one commission member put it, "You just don't say no to the President of the United States." [29]

Commission Staff

One of the first and most important responsibilities of a commission chair is selection of the commission's staff. The staff provides the support services necessary to carry out the commission's mandate and does most of the commission's work. This includes collecting data, preparing briefings, coordinating meetings, and working out differences of opinion among commission members. Staffers usually are younger and not as well known as commissioners. They tend to be lawyers or academics, and they often come from federal agencies working in the commission's area of interest. Staffers not recruited from federal agencies most often come from universities, private industries, research firms, and private law practices.

Generally, a commission's staff is divided into four components: executive director, subordinate staff, consultants, and general counsel.

Executive Director

Although presidents may designate a commission's executive director, most often this task is left to the newly appointed commission chair, who may confer with the president or with other commission members. Most executive directors are known by someone in the White House or the federal agency that advocated creation of the commission. The executive director, perhaps with the assistance of the commission chair, is generally responsible for recruiting other staff members. If the staff is large, the higher-level staff members may recruit their own staff. In almost all cases, however, recruitment of staff members occupies a major portion of the executive director's initial time and efforts. Recruitment is especially difficult for executive directors of short-lived ad hoc commissions. Few potential staffers are willing to leave their permanent jobs for positions that will last no longer than a few months. Lloyd Cutler, executive director of the Eisenhower Commission on Violence, reportedly spent ten weeks of the eighteen-month commission lining up thirty-one staff members.[30]

In addition to hiring staff the executive director serves as mediator between the staff and the commission. According to political commentator Elizabeth Drew, the relationship between the commission and the staff is usually one of mutual contempt.

> The staff is often composed of young, less experienced people who still think that the world can and should be changed; the commissioners know better.... [In addition] the commissioners, being important people, are not very interested in chewing things over with a lot of young staff members.... So the policy alternatives go up from the staff, and the policy directives come down from the commission, and seldom do the twain meet, except in the person of the exhausted, whipsawed executive director.[31]

Executive directors thus serve not only as administrators but also as diplomats who must motivate and fashion the work of the commission. Popper observed that executive directors

> must prevent commissioners from taking the commission in contradictory or irrelevant directions. He has the nearly impossible task of making commissioners and staff members regard the commission as a cohesive group, and not as a fragmented and temporary collection of individuals. But above all, he must infuse the commissioners and staff with a sense of urgency.[32]

Executive directors are responsible as well for overseeing and coordinating the entire operation of their commissions. They are, above all, administrators, and they devote much of their time to activities that have little to do with the substance of the commission's work. The rest of the staff researches and writes the report. Drew noted that much of the job of an executive director is

> begging for money from executive agencies, which have their own problems, ... cutting through civil service regulations so that the staff can be hired before the commission expires; arguing with the General Services Administration over office space and typewriters and with the Government Printing Office over how long it will take to print the report.[33]

Subordinate Staff

Past commission staffs have ranged in size from just a few staffers to well over a hundred. To some extent the size of the staff depends on the scope of the investigation—the narrower the scope, the smaller the staff. The Warren Commission, which conducted a very narrow investigation using the resources of the Federal Bureau of Investigation, had a relatively small staff of only 27. The Kerner Commission on Civil Disorders had a much broader scope and a staff of 115. No hard and fast rule can be applied to staff size, however. The most important determinant of the size

of a commission's staff is the commission's operational budget, and that frequently is a political consideration. Popper has written:

> The fact that some technical commissions have a small staff often means that the president does not really want much substantive advice from them; he is doing little more than showing concern for a specialized group. If he had wanted more from them, he would have given them more money to hire larger staffs. Such funds are given to the small, highly publicized commissions from which he expects broad political impact.[34]

Not all commissions have the same positions. Staff titles may include: deputy or associate director, administrative officer, editorial officer, public affairs officer, and director of research.[35] Staff members usually are chosen for their competence in the areas relevant to the work of the commission. The staff director also tries not to rely too heavily on any one source of staff, thereby promoting the objectivity and independence of the staff in the eyes of the public. Finally, to establish political credibility staff appointees often have ties to important constituencies with which the commission must deal.[36]

Consultants

Commissions often use outside consultants and researchers—individuals, consulting firms, or "think tanks"—to supplement the work of the permanent staff. The 1967 President's Commission on Postal Organization relied on Arthur D. Little, Inc., a consulting firm in Cambridge, Massachusetts, for most of its research, and the Eisenhower Commission on Violence (1968-1969) hired the Louis Harris organization to take several polls. Consultants write most of the technical supplements that accompany a commission's final report, and they are free to disagree with the overall findings of the commission.[37] At least two ad hoc commissions used consulting organizations exclusively: the National Advisory Commission on Libraries (1969-1970) used nine private firms, and the President's Commission on an All-Volunteer Armed Force (1969-1970), three outside firms.[38]

Although consultants provide commissions with a variety of talents, commissioners and staffers often question their work. But, in fact, faced with time constraints, many consultants feel rushed and uncomfortable with their own efforts. Nevertheless, their work is an important part of a commission's effort. According to Popper, "The consultant's work, regardless of its quality and its pertinence to the report, is fundamentally valuable to a commission, not for its intellectual merits or policy proposals, but because it involves the appropriate academic, professional, and technical communities in the work of the commission." [39]

General Counsel

The complexity of the legal issues encountered by most commissions requires the services of legal counsel. Commissions having a large number of attorneys on staff may not appoint a general counsel, but this is the exception rather than the rule. Depending on the nature of a commission's investigation, its general counsel may consist of only one attorney or an entire legal staff. The Warren Commission, for example, had in addition to its regular staff of twenty-seven a fourteen-member legal team to investigate the assassination of President Kennedy. The general counsel is usually consulted on any legal questions that arise during the commission's investigation.

How Commissions Operate

Permanent commissions operate much like any federal agency; they carry out their investigations and business on an ongoing basis, funded by annual congressional appropriations. Ad hoc commissions, in contrast, operate under quite different circumstances because of the money and time constraints arising from their temporary status.

Ad hoc commissions must work toward a deadline. President Johnson called on the Kerner Commission, for example, to produce a preliminary report in March 1968, just seven months after the commission was established. Thus, as sociologist Amitai Etzioni has observed, "More than anything else, commissions are part of government by fire-brigade." [40] After forming, commissions spend much of their time hiring staff. They then organize to distribute the workload, investigate their area of concern, and report their findings, and they finally disband without any means of implementing their findings or recommendations. Whether good or bad, temporary ad hoc commissions are a stopgap method of solving problems. James F. Campbell, general counsel to the Eisenhower Commission on Violence, viewed the fast pace of ad hoc commissions in a positive light.

> It's a very hectic pace ... but at least one is thinking, deliberating, researching, and so on. You have the same kind of pace in the executive branch to "put out fires," and to meet budget deadlines, and to get something up to the Hill. The pace is just as fast there and there's no time for thinking or deliberating or writing or researching.... At least with commissions one is "hectically thinking." [41]

Commissions have varied in how often they meet. The Kerner Commission, for example, had a reputation for hard work and met a total of forty-four days over its lifetime of seven months. The mid-1960s President's Commission on Law Enforcement and the Administration of Justice had a more typical pace of only nineteen days over seventeen months. Meetings usually are held on weekends for the convenience of the participants and rarely take place more than once a month. Attendance also varies from commission to commission. Small, highly publicized commissions might have a normal attendance as high as 80 percent. Some commissions, however, rarely have more than 50 percent of their commissioners at a given meeting. [42] Wolanin found that most commissioners and staff members did not find poor attendance to be a problem; in fact, they found attendance at commission meetings adequate for exercising commission responsibilities. Although attendance at subcommittee meetings and hearings also tends to vary from commission to commission, it generally is considered good. [43]

Some passive members may attend commission meetings but not participate actively in commission proceedings. Most commissioners who attend meetings, however, participate in the debates and deliberations of the commission. Popper has reported that the commissioners who make the most useful contributions have the greatest sense of urgency about the commission's topic. [44] Just their ap-

pointment to the commission indicates that most commissioners have a generally high interest and involvement in the subject of the commission and therefore the commission's work. The impact of this active involvement is reflected in the writing of the report. According to one staff member of the National Commission on Technology, Automation, and Economic Progress, "The report went through fourteen bloody drafts, and I mean bloody. You couldn't recognize the relation between the first two drafts and the final report. This indicates the impact that the commissioners had." [45]

Wolanin has divided the approaches of commissioners to their work into two categories: the commissioner as statesman or stateswoman and the commissioner as constituency representative. Commissioners with the first perspective view the problem under investigation in terms of the public interest; those representing constituencies view their work primarily in terms of its impact on their clientele. As one labor leader explained, "When I serve [on a commission], I do so as an individual citizen, but always with the thought of labor's viewpoint, of course.... I just sit as a member and discuss the report, in particular how it affects the workers." [46]

Most commissioners are statesmen or stateswomen because of their initial objectivity, which usually figures in their selection for the commission, or because of their growth during the commission's investigation. Commissioners apparently undergo a period of learning which leads to their advocacy of positions that they ordinarily might oppose. Flitner called this phenomenon "collegial intellectual growth among commissioners," reflecting an exposure to facts that dispel the commissioner's preconceptions. He quoted Milton Eisenhower, whose Commission on Violence made eighty-one nearly unanimous recommendations: "It was a revelation to me.... We freed our minds of all preconceptions. When we started we couldn't agree on anything." [47]

Commissions carry out their investigations differently. Some commissions divide themselves into study groups or task forces that investigate specific areas within the broader scope of the commission. The 1967 Commission on Pornography, for example, had four study groups: (1) legal, (2) traffic and distribution, (3) effects, and (4) positive approaches. Each area was assigned commissioners, staff, consultants, and advisers. Some commissions do not use task forces at all. The Eisenhower Commission on Violence, for example, did not assign its commissioners to task forces. Instead, it allowed its staff the freedom to work on task force problems, and the commission then reviewed the staff's work. [48]

In addition to their private meetings and deliberations, commissions often hold hearings. With the exception of the final report, hearings are the most visible activity of a commission, and they allow commissioners to become better acquainted with their subject. Hearings may be open or closed. Closed hearings are primarily for informational purposes. The Warren Commission heard direct testimony from 94 witnesses in closed testimony. Its legal staff heard testimony from 395 others and received sixty-one sworn affidavits. These witnesses provided commissioners and staffers with a wealth of information from a variety of perspectives otherwise unavailable. Hearings generally allow a commission to be more thorough and impartial. According to Popper, "There is a general agreement, even among commissioners, that hearings inform commissioners so that, by the time the report is being written, their knowledge of the commission's subject is often comparable to the staff's." [49]

Public hearings also allow commissions to establish legitimacy and to generate publicity. Political scientist Martha Derthick found that members of the President's Commission on Campus Unrest "knew that by making hearings public, whatever value they might have as sources of information would be lost." The commission held public hearings anyway, however, "to demonstrate that it would listen to diverse opinions." [50] Howard Shuman, executive director of the National Commission on Urban Problems (1967-1968), has pointed out the dramatic effect of its public hearings:

> Among the best things the Commission did was to hold hearings in the ghettos of the major cities of the country.... The best testimony received was from the ordinary citizens. It had a fire and a spirit which was unmatched by the experts we heard.... The hearings and inspections provided a common experience for the members of our commission and united them as no other action could have done. [51]

Most presidential commission hearings receive more publicity than their congressional counterparts. For example, in investigating the ghetto racial riots of the summer of 1967, the Senate Permanent Subcommittee on Investigations, chaired by Democratic senator John L. McClellan of Arkansas, found the possible causes of the riots to be conspiracies, the involvement of antipoverty workers, and the moral degeneracy of the rioters. Public hearings conducted by the National Advisory Commission on Civil Disorders, an ad hoc presidential commission created to investigate the same problem, found no evidence of conspiracy, no misconduct on the part of antipoverty workers, and no evidence of the moral degeneracy of the rioters. Although the two investigations came to different conclusions, the Commission on Civil Disorders received greater publicity than McClellan's Senate investigation and its report became more widely accepted. [52]

For any commission, all of the staff work, investigations, public and private hearings, subcommittee meetings, and full commission deliberations are conducted with the goal of the final report in sight. Reports have varied in length from the three-page letter to the president produced by the President's Commission on the World's Fair (1959) to the six-volume report produced by the National Commission on Higher Education (1946-1947). Reports often include appendices of technical reports, subcommittee studies, and hearing transcripts.

Wolanin found that commissions generally use one of three methods in producing a report. [53] According to the most common method, subcommittees of commissioners review the data, and the staff for each group then produces position papers. After reviewing these papers, the subcommittees make recommendations to the full committee. The full commission then reviews the subcommittees' reports and recommendations, making revisions and producing a mutually acceptable final report. The second method frequently used by commissions is similar to the first, except that the subcommittees do not make detailed reports and recommendations to the full commission. Instead, all the subcommittees meet together acting as a committee of the whole, which undertakes all revisions, itself. This method is generally used by smaller commissions with narrowly defined mandates. According to the third and least used method, the commission makes policy decisions and then directs the writing of the report to conform to its decisions.

As the writing of the final report looms ever larger on the commission's agenda, tensions rise among the staff and the commissioners. Reports often go through draft after draft with certain commissioners seemingly impossible to satisfy. Some chapters of the final report of the Warren Commission reportedly went through twenty drafts. Staffers often spend day and night working on the final report and endure endless criticism from all sides. In describing this growing tension among the staff and commissioners, Popper recalled the words of a journalist who worked with several commissions:

> All the strands of activity and hostility always come together in the writing. The first few commission meetings haven't done anything more than introduce the commissioners to each other. They size up each other. Then in the next few meetings, attendance drops off and the staff begins to show its strength. Then the staff trots out its early drafts, and all of a sudden the swing members, the ones with open minds and without ideological preconceptions, assert themselves. They make worthwhile, influential suggestions about the drafts. Apparently vulnerable people like women and clergymen can pull a lot of weight here. Finally, in the last few meetings, the staff produces drafts all over the place, the homework swamps the commissioners, and the staff sneaks in everything they think they can get away with. They get away with a lot, because by this time the commissioners have fourteen chapters to read in two days, and it's too late to change anything anyway. [54]

In their final reports, however, commissions seek accommodations and compromise. Efforts also are made to ensure that relations among commissioners and staffers do not fragment beyond repair. A strong, competent chair is likely to intervene and call for more temperate rhetoric from commissioners. For example, Nicholas Katzenbach, chair of the President's Commission on Law Enforcement and the Administration of Justice, helped produce a unified report through his ability to negotiate compromise positions when serious conflicts developed among staffers and commissioners. [55]

Commissions often seek unanimity in their reports because they believe that it instills more legitimacy in their work. According to Martha Derthick, this goal leads to inaccuracies in reports. "Commissions frequently decide that it would be best not to confuse the nation with divided counsel. Since the commissioners usually are divided on important issues, this guarantees that a large number of these issues will be fudged." [56]

Although dissenting footnotes could be added to the final report, they usually do not appear. Instead, commissions seek consensus, and "consensus can nearly always be made to cover up differences." [57] For example, the Warren Commission was divided on whether President Kennedy and Texas governor John B. Connally were hit by the same bullet. Three commissioners believed that both men had been hit by the same bullet, while three others believed that the men were hit by different bullets.

In seeking a unanimous report, the commission entered into a debate over adjectives. One commissioner wanted the report to state that there was "compelling" evidence that the same bullet had hit both Kennedy and Connally. The commission finally compromised on the adjective "persuasive." The issue was never really settled by the commission.

Functions of Commissions

Although ostensibly used to supplement standard presidential advisory procedures, presidential commissions serve a variety of functions. Some scholars have argued that commissions serve no useful purposes and should not be a part of the presidential advisory system. Others have argued, somewhat skeptically, that presidents use commissions for their own purposes—that is, either to generate support for existing policies or to postpone effective action by passing the problem off on a presidential commission. Elizabeth Drew has listed eight rather cynical reasons for appointing a commission:

1. To obtain the blessing of distinguished men for something you want to do anyway.
2. To postpone action, yet be justified in insisting that you are working on the problem.
3. To act as a lightning rod, drawing political heat away from the White House.
4. To conduct an extensive study of something you do need to know more about before you act, in case you do.
5. To investigate, lay to rest rumors, and convince the public of the validity of one particular set of facts.
6. To educate the commissioners, or get them aboard on something you want to do.
7. Because you can't think of anything else to do.
8. To change the hearts and minds of men.[58]

Another factor further complicates trust in the efficacy of commission work: once a commission's report is written, presidents can choose either to follow or to ignore the report's recommendations. They sometimes choose to ignore them, fueling the fires of the critics. Sen. Edward M. Kennedy (D-Mass.) has characterized commissions as "so many Jiminy Crickets chirping in the ears of deaf presidents, deaf officials, deaf congressmen, and perhaps a deaf public."[59]

What functions do commissions actually serve? The conventional wisdom is that presidents appoint commissions to avoid confronting an issue, to delay action, or to divert public attention. Yet research indicates that most presidents heed and act favorably on the reports they receive from their commissions.[60] Commissions serve a variety of other purposes, however, besides merely providing presidents with advice. Several scholars have identified these functions, and political scientist George T. Sulzner has classified them into two general categories. Functions in the first category generally relate to solving problems. They include investigating, defining, and recommending action on specific problems and generating public demands for such action. Functions in the second category relate to presidential management of conflict. They include consensus building and pacifying political groups.[61] Each use of presidential commissions may go beyond the purely advisory function for which the commission was nominally created. Presidents may, and often do, use commissions to manage conflict during their administrations.

The first and most obvious function of commissions is to provide presidents with the information needed to make informed decisions. Although some scholars have inpugned this motive, most presidents appoint commissions to facilitate the fact-finding activities of the executive branch. According to Wolanin, "Most commissions are formed because the president wants to act but is not sure how, or is not sure that important segments of public opinion, congressional leadership, or executive branch agencies are

ready to support him."[62] In fact, commission recommendations are usually accepted and often implemented. For example, President Truman's response to the growing demand for action against the outbreak of black lynchings in the fall of 1946 was appointment of the President's Committee on Civil Rights in late 1946 to look into civil rights violations across the nation. In his memoirs, Truman explained that he took this action "because of repeated antiminority incidents immediately after the war in which homes were invaded, property was destroyed, and a number of innocent lives were taken. I wanted to get the facts behind these incidents of disregard for individual and group rights which were reported in the news with alarming regularity...."[63] The final report of the commission eventually forced congressional consideration and implementation of its various proposals.

Presidents often turn to presidential commissions to obtain information about a problem that regular presidential advisory mechanisms are unable to handle. Flitner has reported that a primary function of commissions is "surmounting the pathologies of organizational complexity: for avoiding duplication of effort and circumventing bureaucratic obstacles."[64] Some presidential commissions are able to bring together resources, skills, and information in a way that is unachievable by other advisory agencies of the executive branch. For example, the President's Private Sector Survey on Cost Control (1982-1983), or the Grace Commission, was composed entirely of private sector appointees, who were charged with recommending where the government could spend its money more efficiently. The 170 members of the Grace Commission issued a report that proposed 2,478 cost-cutting measures, which in theory would have saved the government $425 billion. Judging from the bureaucratic and congressional debate that ensued over the proposals, it is doubtful that any other executive branch advisory mechanism could have produced such a report. Four years after the report was issued only about thirteen hundred of its recommendations were in place, reportedly saving the government almost $39 million.

In addition to their advisory function, presidential commissions allow presidents to manage conflict by building a consensus for their programs. As many critics have charged, presidents use commissions to sell their programs to the country. Political commentator Harlan Cleveland has observed that "Commissions can . . . help the president build support for what he has already decided to do."[65] And according to Daniel Bell, the ability of presidents to use commissions to build consensus has become so pronounced that there is a danger that presidents may use commissions primarily to manipulate public opinion.[66] Other observers believe, however, that presidents can use commissions to focus the nation's attention on problems that otherwise would not gain legitimacy.

The very presence of "blue ribbon" commissioners, who represent a variety of interests, lends credibility to a commission's work. As an example, Etzioni pointed to the composition of the National Commission on the Causes and Prevention of Violence, which refocused the national dialogue on the causes and prevention of violent behavior: "If ten wise men drawn from such a cross-section of the nation support a set of conclusions, the country is more likely to go along with them than if these conclusions are advocated by ten experts."[67] Similarly, the National Bipartisan Commission on Central America (1984) gave the Reagan administration a report that essentially upheld the administration policy of increased military assistance to El

Salvador and continued aid to the Nicaraguan rebels. Because of its distinguished commissioners, headed by former secretary of state Henry Kissinger, and its bipartisan character, including former Democratic National Committee chairman Robert Strauss, criticism of the final report was muted.

Increasingly, however, the blue ribbon nature of some commissions has been questioned, leaving some final commission reports suspect. For example, the composition of the 1988 Presidential Commission on the Human Immunodeficiency Virus Epidemic (AIDS Commission) apparently offended both ends of the political spectrum. The Reagan administration nominated appointees representing various interests in the AIDS crisis. Liberals, however, were offended by the participation of such conservatives as state representative Penny Pullen of Illinois, who authored a mandatory AIDS testing bill, and conservatives were outraged by the inclusion of an avowed homosexual, New York geneticist Dr. Frank Lily. The medical community complained, as well, noting that not enough medical personnel were represented. As a result, the commission's final report did not receive the widespread support enjoyed by most other commission reports.

The symbolic functions of commissions can be the most useful to presidents in managing conflict. The very creation of a commission sends signals to various groups and individuals that the administration is concerned about a specific problem. According to Flitner,

> By their existence, commissions symbolize the highest cognizance and concern over a situation. Commissions communicate that the president is aware of a situation and will begin a process of directing attention to it. This implies a search for facts and answers and willingness to give the disaffected members of society a "fair hearing." . . . In short, commissions represent the fact that the president is at least doing something.[68]

In many respects the creation of the AIDS Commission was a symbolic response of the Reagan administration to the growing AIDS crisis. Similarly, in late 1987 in response to demands by public service groups, President Reagan appointed the National Commission on the Public Service to conduct a two-year study of the morale of federal bureaucrats.

Some critics charge that the symbolic function of commissions undermines effective policy making by allowing presidents to delay action. Cleveland has contended: "On the whole, presidential commissions are probably better adapted to smothering problems with well-publicized inaction than to paving the way for novel action."[69] This assessment may have been true in some cases, but overall it does not seem to be the motivation behind most presidential commissions.

Delay does occur, however. Sulzner has suggested that the delay that results from the appointment of commissions is an integral part of the policy-making process by which government adapts to emerging social problems. It promotes political pacification through a cooling-off period. "Frequently, commissions hold public hearings where they solicit representative testimony from diverse sources, and these hearings can serve as outlets for the airing of grievances. Moreover, the opportunity for expression may have cathartic effects for the interests involved that may be as rewarding to them as the provision of concrete remedies."[70]

Over the years some commissions have been abused or ignored in their efforts. Commission recommendations often do not become policy; sometimes they do. The final report of the Commission on Law Enforcement and the Administration of Justice is generally credited with having prompted the passage of the Safe Streets Act of 1968, for example. But more than just making policy recommendations, commissions have served other important, although often symbolic, functions. According to Flitner,

> They have affected the attitudinal atmosphere of society. They have helped demythologize subjects such as the conspiracy theory or riot origins and the assumption that increasing population growth is necessarily advantageous. Commissions have helped lower the emotional content of certain issues, such as marijuana use. . . . Commissions have altered the terms in which issues are discussed and, although they have by no means either reached or convinced everyone of their findings, they have spread awareness to all levels of society, a not undesirable function in a democracy.[71]

Notes

1. Carl Marcy, *Presidential Commissions* (New York: King's Crown Press, 1945), 97.
2. Ibid., 8.
3. Quoted in Elizabeth B. Drew, "On Giving Oneself a Hotfoot: Government by Commission," *Atlantic Monthly,* May 1968, 45.
4. Marcy, *Presidential Commissions,* 8.
5. Frank Popper, *The President's Commissions* (New York: Twentieth Century Fund, 1970), 66-67.
6. Bill Whalen, "Commissions: The Mixed Ones Often Are More Productive," *Washington Times,* October 6, 1987.
7. Richard M. Pious, *The American Presidency* (New York: Basic Books, 1979), 164.
8. Alan L. Dean, "Ad Hoc Commissions for Policy Formulation," in *The Presidential Advisory System,* ed. Thomas E. Cronin and Sanford E. Greenberg (New York: Harper and Row, 1969), 101-102.
9. Terrence R. Tutchings, *Rhetoric and Reality: Presidential Commissions and the Making of Public Policy* (Boulder, Colo.: Westview, 1979), 12.
10. David Flitner, Jr., *The Politics of Presidential Commissions* (Dobbs Ferry, N.Y.: Transnational Publishers, 1986), 28-29.
11. Thomas R. Wolanin, *Presidential Advisory Commissions: Truman to Nixon* (Madison, Wis.: University of Wisconsin Press, 1975), 10.
12. Henry Fairlie, "Government by White House Conference: Two Views," in Cronin and Greenberg, *The Presidential Advisory System,* 144-149.
13. Flitner, *The Politics of Presidential Commissions,* 45.
14. Popper, *The President's Commissions,* 15.
15. Daniel Bell, "Government by Commission," in Cronin and Greenberg, *The Presidential Advisory System,* 121.
16. Popper, *The President's Commissions,* 18.
17. Flitner, *The Politics of Presidential Commissions,* 46.
18. Cronin and Greenberg, *The Presidential Advisory Commission,* xix.
19. Popper, *The President's Commissions,* 17.
20. "The Commission: How to Create a Blue Chip Consensus," *Time,* January 19, 1970, 20.
21. Quoted in Wolanin, *Presidential Advisory Commissions,* 85.
22. Quoted in Popper, *The President's Commissions,* 20.
23. Wolanin, *Presidential Advisory Commissions,* 82-83.
24. Quoted in ibid., 83.
25. Ibid., 123.
26. Quoted in Flitner, *The Politics of Presidential Commissions,* 50-51.
27. Ibid., 50.

28. Lyndon Baines Johnson, *The Vantage Point—Perspectives on the Presidency, 1963-1969* (New York: Popular Library, 1971), 26.
29. Wolanin, *Presidential Advisory Commissions,* 84.
30. Popper, *The President's Commissions,* 22.
31. Drew, "On Giving Oneself a Hotfoot," 48.
32. Popper, *The President's Commissions,* 24.
33. Drew, "On Giving Oneself a Hotfoot," 48.
34. Popper, *The President's Commissions,* 22.
35. Flitner, *The Politics of Presidential Commissions,* 59.
36. Wolanin, *Presidential Advisory Commissions,* 108.
37. Popper, *The President's Commissions,* 24.
38. Tutchings, *Rhetoric and Reality,* 27.
39. Popper, *The President's Commissions,* 26.
40. Amitai Etzioni, "Why Task Force Studies Go Wrong," *Wall Street Journal,* July 9, 1968, 18.
41. Quoted in Flitner, *The Politics of Presidential Commissions,* 63.
42. Popper, *The President's Commissions,* 27.
43. Wolanin, *Presidential Advisory Commissions,* 112.
44. Popper, *The President's Commissions,* 28.
45. Quoted in Wolanin, *Presidential Advisory Commissions,* 113.
46. Ibid., 121.
47. Flitner, *The Politics of Presidential Commissions,* 79-80; quote on p. 80.
48. Ibid., 65-66.
49. Popper, *The President's Commissions,* 37.
50. Martha Derthick, "On Commissionship—Presidential Variety," Brookings Reprint No. 245 (Washington, D.C.: Brookings, 1972), 627, 636.
51. Quoted in Flitner, *The Politics of Presidential Commissions,* 77.
52. Popper, *The President's Commissions,* 36-37.
53. Wolanin, *Presidential Advisory Commissions,* 110-111.
54. Popper, *The President's Commissions,* 31-32.
55. Flitner, *The Politics of Presidential Commissions,* 87.
56. Derthick, "On Commissionship," 629.
57. Popper, *The President's Commissions,* 33.
58. See Drew, "On Giving Oneself a Hotfoot," 45-47.
59. Quoted in Flitner, *The Politics of Presidential Commissions,* 2.
60. Thomas E. Cronin, "On the Separation of Brain and State: Implications for the Presidency," in *Modern Presidents and the Presidency,* ed. Marc Landy (Lexington, Mass.: Lexington Books, 1985), 60-61.
61. George T. Sulzner, "The Policy Process and the Uses of National Governmental Study Commissions," in *Perspectives on the Presidency: A Collection,* ed. Stanley Bach and George T. Sulzner (Lexington, Mass.: D. C. Heath, 1974), 207.
62. Wolanin, *Presidential Advisory Commissions,* 193.
63. Harry S Truman, *Memoirs* (Garden City, N.J.: Doubleday, 1955-1956), 2: 180.
64. Flitner, *The Politics of Presidential Commissions,* 180.
65. Harlan Cleveland, "Inquiry into Presidential Inquirers," in *The Dynamics of the American Presidency,* ed. Donald B. Johnson and Jack L. Walker (New York: Wiley, 1964), 292.
66. Bell, "Government by Commission," 121.
67. Etzioni, "Why Task Force Studies Go Wrong," 18.
68. Flitner, *The Politics of Presidential Commissions,* 180.
69. Cleveland, "Inquiry into Presidential Inquirers," 292.
70. Sulzner, "The Policy Process," 216.
71. Flitner, *The Politics of Presidential Commissions,* 180-181.

Selected Bibliography

Bach, Stanley, and George T. Sulzner, eds. *Perspectives on the Presidency: A Collection.* Lexington, Mass.: D. C. Heath, 1974.
Bell, Daniel. "Government by Commission." In *The Presidential Advisory System,* ed. Thomas E. Cronin and Sanford E. Greenberg, 117-123. New York: Harper and Row, 1969.
Cleveland, Harlan. "Inquiry into Presidential Inquirers." In *The Dynamics of the American Presidency,* ed. Donald B. Johnson and Jack L. Walker, 291-294. New York: Wiley, 1964.
Cronin, Thomas E. "On the Separation of Brain and State: Implications for the Presidency." In *Modern Presidents and the Presidency,* ed. Marc Landy, 51-63. Lexington, Mass.: Lexington Books, 1985.
Cronin, Thomas E., and Sanford E. Greenberg, eds. *The Presidential Advisory Commission.* New York: Harper and Row, 1969.
Dean, Alan L. "Ad Hoc Commissions for Policy Formulation." In *The Presidential Advisory System,* ed. Thomas E. Cronin and Sanford E. Greenberg, 101-116. New York: Harper and Row, 1969.
Derthick, Martha. "On Commissionship—Presidential Variety." Brookings Reprint No. 245. Washington, D.C.: Brookings, 1972.
Drew, Elizabeth B. "On Giving Oneself a Hotfoot: Government by Commission." *Atlantic Monthly,* May 1968, 45-49.
Etzioni, Amitai. "Why Task Force Studies Go Wrong." *Wall Street Journal,* July 9, 1968, 18.
Fairlie, Henry. "Government by White House Conference: Two Views." In *The Presidential Advisory System,* ed. Thomas E. Cronin and Sanford E. Greenberg, 144-149. New York: Harper and Row, 1969.
Flitner, David, Jr., *The Politics of Presidential Commissions.* Dobbs Ferry, N.Y.: Transnational Publishers, 1986.
Johnson, Donald B., and Jack L. Walker, eds. *The Dynamics of the American Presidency.* New York: Wiley, 1964.
Landy, Marc, ed. *Modern Presidents and the Presidency.* Lexington, Mass.: Lexington Books, 1985.
Marcy, Carl. *Presidential Commissions.* New York: King's Crown Press, 1945.
Popper, Frank. *The President's Commissions.* New York: Twentieth Century Fund, 1970.
Sulzner, George T. "The Policy Process and the Uses of National Government Study Commissions." In *Perspectives on the Presidency: A Collection,* ed. Stanley Bach and George T. Sulzner, 206-218. Lexington, Mass.: D. C. Heath, 1974.
"The Commission: How to Create a Blue Chip Consensus." *Time,* January 19, 1970, 20.
Tutchings, Terrence R. *Rhetoric and Reality: Presidential Commissions and the Making of Public Policy.* Boulder, Colo.: Westview, 1979.
Whalen, Bill. "Commissions: The Mixed Ones Often Are More Productive." *Washington Times,* October 6, 1987.
Wolanin, Thomas R. *Presidential Advisory Commissions: Truman to Nixon.* Madison, Wis.: University of Wisconsin Press, 1975.

Index

Acheson, Dean G., 63, 64, 72, 97
Ackley, Gardner, 45
Acquired Immune Deficiency Syndrome (AIDS) Commission, 141, 144, 152
ACTION, 113-114, 133
Adams, Bruce, 28-30, 70, 76
Adams, John, 58, 65
Adams, Sherman, 5, 13, 14, 18-19, 40, 65
Ad hoc commissions. *See* Presidential commissions
Administration Office, ACDA, 137
Administration Office, EOP, 11, 53-54
Administrative Conference Act of 1964, 114
Administrative Conference of the United States, 114
Administrative politics, 19, 66. *See also* Presidential commissions
Advisers. *See* Staff and advisers; White House Office
Advisory Board on Economic Growth and Stability, 44
Advisory organizations. *See* Presidential commissions
Aeronautics Division, Commerce Department, 79
Afghanistan, 115
African Development Bank, 101
African Development Foundation, 114-115
Age Discrimination in Employment Act, 118
Agencies
   executive agencies, 107, 110-111
   government corporations, 107, 111
   See also Regulatory agencies; specific agency names
Agency for International Development, 99, 138
Agency for Toxic Substances and Disease Registry, 88
Agricultural Adjustment Act, 77, 78
Agricultural Credits Act of 1923, 119
Agricultural Society, U.S., 77
Agriculture Department (USDA), 76-78, 90, 97, 138
Agriculture policy, 78
Air Corps, 80
Air Force Department, 80
Airport and Airways Development Act of 1970, 99
Alcohol, Drug Abuse, and Mental Health Administration, 88
Aldrich Commission, 142
Allen, Richard, 21

American Battle Monuments Commission, 115
American Medical Association, 86
American Printing House for the Blind, 84
American Samoa, 92
Amtrak, 100, 111, 130
Anderson, Martin C., 41
Anderson, Robert B., 44
Andrus, Cecil D., 91
Antarctica, 130
Antitrust Division, Justice Department, 94
Appalachian Regional Commission, 115
Appalachian Regional Development Act of 1965, 115
Appointment power and process
   cabinet and subcabinet, 69-76
   commissioners on presidential commissions, 145-147
   Executive Office of the President, 25-32
   regulatory agencies, 107-108, 111-113
   White House staff, 12, 15-16
Apollo 11, 127
Archives of American Art, 136
Archivist of the United States, 127
Armed Forces Policy Council, 82
Arms Control and Disarmament Agency, U.S. (ACDA), 137, 138
Armstrong, Neil, 146
Army Department, 80
Arnold, Peri E., 40
Arthur, Chester A., 2, 95
Arthur D. Little, Inc., 148
Arthur M. Sackler Gallery, 136
Arts and Industries Building, 136
Ash, Roy L., 34, 40
Asian Development Bank, 101
Atlantic Monthly, 35
Atomic Energy Commission, 131
Attorney general, 63, 92, 93
Auchter, Thorne, 113
Automobile industry, 109
Aviation industry, 99, 100, 129-130
Aviation Safety and Noise Abatement Act of 1980, 99

Babcock, Orville E., 2
Baker, Howard H., Jr., 13, 21
Baker, James A., III, 13, 15, 20-21, 46
Baker, Richard A., 65
Baker, Ross K., 76
Baldrige, Malcolm, 76
Ball, George W., 66
Banking Act of 1933, 109, 120

Banking and finance
   agriculture loans, 119
   credit union regulation, 128
   FDIC protection, 120
   SBA assistance, 135
   thrift regulation, 121-122
Bankruptcy administration, 94
Bankruptcy Code, 94
Banks for Cooperatives, 119
Barden-LaFollette Act of 1943, 86
Barnard, Henry, 83
Bell, Alexander Graham, 136
Bell, Daniel, 33, 34, 145, 151
Bell, Griffin B., 63, 93
Bell, Terrel H., 83-84
Bennett, William J., 84
Benson, Ezra Taft, 78
Bentsen, Lloyd M., Jr., 49
Berle, Adolph A., Jr., 2
Berman, Larry, 33-35
Bernstein, Marver H., 108
Bilingual Education and Minority Languages Affairs, Office of, 84
Bledsoe, W. Craig, 25, 57, 69, 107, 141
Block, John R., 76, 78
Blount, Winton M., 74, 139
Blue ribbon commissions, 143. *See also* Presidential commissions
Board for International Broadcasting, 115
Board of Contract Appeals, 104
Board of Veterans' Appeals, 104
Bowles, Chester, 73
Boyd, Alan S., 99
Brady, Nicholas F., 65
Bretton Woods agreement, 101
Brigman, William E., 112, 113
Brock, William E., III, 48, 96
Brookings Institution, 34, 70, 71, 111
Brown, Harold, 63, 81-82
Brownell, Herbert, Jr., 72-73
Brownlow, Louis D., 2, 33
Brownlow Commission, 2-3, 30, 33, 142
Brownlow Report, 3, 22
Brzezinski, Zbigniew, 14, 38, 39
Buchanan, Patrick, 7
Budget Act of 1974, 32, 36
Budget and Accounting Act of 1921, 33
Budget Circular 49, 33
Budget politics, 32-34, 36
Building and Housing Division, Commerce Department, 79
Bulletin of Labor, 95
Bundy, McGeorge, 6, 14, 38, 65, 66, 73

Bureaucracy
   civil service system, 132
   See also Appointment power and process
Bureaucratic politics, 19, 66
Bureau for Refugee Programs, 98-99
Bureau of Administration, 98
Bureau of Agricultural Economics, 77
Bureau of Alcohol, Tobacco, and Firearms,
   102
Bureau of the Budget (BOB), 101
   origin and development, 32-33
   role expansion, 3, 30, 33-34
Bureau of Consular Affairs, 98
Bureau of Customs, 102
Bureau of Economic Analysis, 79
Bureau of Economic and Business Affairs,
   98
Bureau of Employment Security, 86
Bureau of Engraving and Printing, 102
Bureau of Export Administration, 79
Bureau of Human Rights and Humanitar-
   ian Affairs, 98
Bureau of Indian Affairs, 90, 91
Bureau of Intelligence and Research, 98,
   116
Bureau of Internal Revenue, 101, 102
Bureau of International Organization Af-
   fairs, 98
Bureau of Labor Statistics, 96
Bureau of Land Management, 91
Bureau of Mines, 79, 91
Bureau of Nuclear Weapons Control, 137
Bureau of Oceans and International Envi-
   ronmental and Scientific Affairs, 98
Bureau of Pensions, 103
Bureau of Politico-Military Affairs, 98
Bureau of Public Affairs, 98
Bureau of the Public Debt, 101, 102
Bureau of Public Roads, 79
Bureau of Reclamation, 91
Bureau of Verification and Intelligence,
   137
Bureau of War Risk Insurance, 103
Burns, Arthur F., 8, 44
Bush, George
   administrative politics, 13, 65, 84, 85, 102
   vice presidency, 53
Business and industry regulation. *See* spe-
   cific industries
Business Liaison, Office of, 80
Business Services Centers, 125
Butz, Earl L., 78

Cabinet
   alternatives to, 66
   holdovers, 65
   members, 57
   origin and development, 57-61
   pay and perquisites, 70
   presidential appointments, 69-76
   role and function, 61-66
   subcabinet, 69
   vice president membership, 60
   White House liaison, 5, 10
   White House staff conflicts, 62, 65
   See also specific cabinet secretaries
Cabinet departments
   current units, 69
   presidential appointments, 69-76
   supercabinet proposal, 19, 66
   See also specific departments
Califano, Joseph A., 6, 14, 18, 40, 87
Campaign finance reform, 120-121

Campbell, James F., 149
Camp David Accords, 98
Cannon, James M., 41
Caribbean countries, assistance programs,
   125
Carlucci, Frank C., 38, 82
Carter, Jimmy
   administrative style, 20, 38, 41
   appointment politics, 29-30, 71
   bureaucratic politics, 31, 53, 82-85, 89,
      91, 96, 113, 131, 133
   cabinet politics, 61-63, 70, 75-76, 81, 104
   deregulation efforts, 99, 113
   economic policy, 45-46
   presidential library, 127
   foreign policy, 97-98
   science policy, 50
   staff, appointments and role, 1, 8-9, 12-
      16, 20
   trade policy, 48
Casey, William J., 116
Cavazos, Lauro F., 65, 84
Census Bureau, 79
Center for Statistics, 84
Centers for Disease Control, 88
Central Intelligence Agency (CIA), 37, 115-
   116
Central Intelligence Agency Act of 1949,
   116
Challenge Grants, Office of, 129
Challenger Commission, 146
Challenger space shuttle, 127
Chase, Salmon P., 59
Cheney, Richard, 13, 20
Chief of staff, 12-13
Child Abuse Prevention and Treatment
   Act, 87
Chronic Hazard Advisory Panel, 117
Chrysler Corporation Loan Guarantee Act
   of 1979, 99
Civil Aeronautics Administration, 79
Civil Aeronautics Board, 99, 107, 112
Civil Division, Justice Department, 94
Civilian Radioactive Waste Management,
   Office of, 86
Civil Rights, Office for, 84
Civil Rights Act of 1957, 116
Civil Rights Act of 1964, 93, 118
Civil Rights Act of 1983, 116
Civil Rights Commission, 110-111, 116-117
Civil Rights Division, Justice Department,
   94
Civil rights issues, 151
Civil Service, State Department, 97
Civil Service Commission, U.S., 111, 132
Civil Service Reform Act of 1978, 122, 126,
   132
Civil service system, 132. *See also* Appoint-
   ment power and process
Clark, John D., 43
Clark, Ramsey, 92
Clark, William P., 15, 20, 21, 91
Clay, Lucius, 72
Claybrook, Joan, 113
Clayton Antitrust Act of 1914, 124
Clean Air Act, 118
Clean Water Act, 118
Cleveland, Grover, 2, 95
Cleveland, Harlan, 151, 152
Clientele politics. *See* Interest group
   politics
Clifford, Clark M., 4, 13, 39
Coal Mine Health and Safety Act of 1969,

88
Coast Guard, 99-101
Cohen, Benjamin V., 66
Cohen, Wilbur J., 74
Coleman, Norman J., 77
Coleman, William T., Jr., 75
Colm, Gerhard, 43
Commerce and Labor Department, 78
Commerce Department, 48, 78-80
Commercial Space Transportation, Office
   of, 100
Commission chairs, 147
Commission of Fine Arts, 116
Commission on the Bicentennial of the
   Constitution, 54, 116
Commission on Defense Management, 146
Commission on Economy and Efficiency,
   33
Commission on Obscenity and Pornogra-
   phy (Lockhart), 144, 149
Commission on the Organization of the
   Executive Branch of the Government
   (first Hoover Commission, 1949), 43, 80,
   145
Commission on the Organization of the
   Executive Branch of the Government
   (second Hoover Commission, 1955), 145
Commission on Population Growth and the
   American Future (Rockefeller), 144, 145
Commissions
   in general. *See* specific commission
      names
   presidential. *See* Presidential
      commissions
Committee of Style, 57
Committees
   congressional. *See* Congressional
      committees
   in general. *See* specific committee names
Commodities Exchange Authority, 108
Commodity Exchange Act of 1936, 117
Commodity Futures Trading Commission,
   117
Communications Office, 8, 14
Community Relations Service, 93
Comprehensive Environmental Response,
   Compensation, and Liability Act of 1980,
   118
Comptroller of the Currency, 102
Comsat, 111
Congested Production Areas, Committee
   for, 30
Congressional Affairs, Office of, ACDA,
   137
Congressional Budget and Impoundment
   Control Act of 1974, 32, 36
Congressional Budget Office (CBO), 32
Congressional committees. *See* specific
   committee and subcommittee names
Congressional Relations, Office of (OCR),
   4-5
Congressional staff, 12
Connally, John B., 45
Connelly, Matthew, 5
Conrail, 100
Conscription, 135
Conservation and Renewable Energy, Of-
   fice of, 86
Constituency politics. *See* Interest group
   politics
Consultants, 148
Consumer Affairs, Office of, 31
Consumer Information Center, 125

Consumer movement, 109
Consumer Product Safety Act of 1972, 109, 117
Consumer Product Safety Commission, 109, 110, 113, 117
Consumer Reports, 110
Coolidge, Calvin, 2
Cooper-Hewitt Museum, 136
Cooperative Extension Service, 77
Cortelyou, George B., 2
Cost of Living Council, 45
Council for Rural Affairs, 31
Council for Urban Affairs, 31
Council of Economic Advisers (CEA), 28
    organization and functions, 25, 46-47
    origins and development, 4, 30, 34, 42-46
Council of National Defense, 59
Council on Economic Affairs, 101
Council on Environmental Quality (CEQ), 31, 51-53, 90
Council on International Economic Policy, 31
Council on Natural Resources and Environment, 52
Counterfeiting, 102
Cox, Archibald, 92
Cranston, Alan, 104
Credit union regulation, 128
Criminal Division, Justice Department, 94
Cronin, Thomas E., 11, 12, 60, 63, 64, 146
Cuba, 66
Cushman, Robert E., 108
Customs Service, 101, 102, 108
Cutler, Lloyd N., 12, 13, 147, 148

Daily National Intelligencer, 90
Dawes, Charles G., 33
Dean, John W., III, 19
Deaver, Michael K., 15, 20-21
Defense and Space Talks, 137
Defense Department (DOD), 99
    appointee resignations, 71
    budget process, 35
    composition and size, 80
    GAO audit, 82
    intelligence activities, 116
    organization and functions, 82
    origins and development, 37, 80-82
Defense expenditures, 72
Defense Intelligence Agency, 116
Defense Mobilization, Office of, 30, 49
Defense Reorganization Act of 1958, 81
Defense Secretary, 63, 82
Defense Waste and Transporation Management Program, 86
Democratic National Committee (DNC), 75
Department of Transportation Act of 1966, 131
Departments. See Cabinet departments; specific departments
Department secretaries. See Cabinet; specific secretaries
Deregulation, 99-100, 113
Derthick, Martha, 150
Derwinski, Edward J., 102
Dillon, C. Douglas, 66, 73
Director for Mutual Security, Office of, 30
Discrimination cases, 126
District of Columbia, 128, 133
District of Columbia Home Rule Act, 128
Dodge, Joseph M., 34
Domestic Council, 8, 14, 31, 34, 40-41, 46

Domestic policy adviser, 6, 8, 14
Domestic Policy Staff, 39, 41
Domestic Volunteer Service Act, 114
Donnelly, Harrison, 25
Donovan, Raymond J., 76, 96
Douglas, Lewis W., 33
Downey, Thomas J., 35
Draft, military, 135
Drew, Elizabeth, 148, 151
Drug Abuse Policy, Office of, 31
Drug Abuse Prevention, Special Action Office for, 31
Drug Enforcement Administration (DEA), 94
Drug Prevention Program, 114
Duberstein, Kenneth, 13
Dubridge, Lee A., 49-50
Dulles, John Foster, 5, 63, 73, 97
Duncan, Charles W., 84
Dunlop, John T., 75
Durkin, Martin P., 64, 73

Early, Stephen T., 2, 3
Economic Affairs, Office of, 79
Economic Analysis Bureau, 79
Economic Development Administration, 80
Economic Opportunity, Office of (OEO), 25, 31, 110
Economic Opportunity Council, 31
Economic policy, 42-47
Economic Policy Council, 41, 45, 46
Economic Policy Group, 41
Economic Regulatory Administration, 85
Education, Office of, 83, 86, 87
Educational Research and Improvement, Office of, 84
Education Department, 82-84
Edwards, James B., 76, 85
Ehrlichman, John D., 8, 14, 19, 35, 40-41, 45, 62
Eisenhower, Dwight D.
    administrative politics, 34, 39-40, 44, 126, 146
    administrative style, 16, 18-19, 30-31, 38
    appointment politics, 26, 27
    bureaucratic politics, 81, 86
    cabinet politics, 60, 62-65, 72-73, 97, 101
    foreign policy, 37
    presidential library, 127
    science policy, 49-50
    staff, 4-5, 14
    trade policy, 47
Eisenhower, Milton, 146, 147, 149
Eisenhower Commission on Violence, 144, 147-149, 151
Eizenstat, Stuart E., 41
Election financing reform, 120-121
Elementary and Secondary Education, Office of, 84
Elementary and Secondary Education Act, 84
Ellsworth, Henry L., 77
El Salvador, 151-152
Emancipation Proclamation, 59
Emergency management, 121
Emergency Preparedness, Office of, 31
Employee Retirement Income Security Act of 1974, 133
Employment Act of 1946, 34, 42, 43
Employment and Training Office, 96
Employment regulation, 95-97
Employment Standards Administration (ESA), 96

Energy Department, 84-86, 90, 109, 116
Energy Information Administration, 85
Energy policy, 84-86, 109
Energy Reorganization Act of 1974, 131
Energy Research and Development Administration, 84, 109
Energy Resources Council, 31
Environmental Defense Fund v. Thomas, 36
Environmental Protection Agency (EPA), 52, 90, 109, 110, 118
Environmental Quality, Council on (CEQ), 31, 51-53
Environmental Quality, Office of (OEQ), 52-53
Environmental Quality Improvement Act of 1970, 52
Environmental regulation, 51-53, 109
Environmental Research Center, 136
Environmental Science Program, 136
Environment and Public Works Committee, Senate, 36
Equal Employment Opportunity Act of 1972, 118
Equal Employment Opportunity Commission, 118, 126
Equal Pay Act of 1963, 118
Etzioni, Amitai, 149, 151
European Community (EC), 47
Ewing, Oscar R., 86
Executive agencies, 107, 110-111
Executive and Legislative Reorganization Subcommittee, House, 34
Executive Expenditures Committee, House, 43
Executive Office for United States Attorneys, 94
Executive Office of the President (EOP)
    Administration Office, 53-54
    appointment process, 25-32
    components and organization, 1, 25
    establishment, 3, 25, 33
    functions, 25
Executive Order 8248, 3
Executive Order 11541, 35
Executive Order 11991, 53
Executive Order 12028, 53
Executive Order 12067, 118
Executive Order 12188, 48
Executive Order 12291, 36
Executive Order 12498, 36
Explorer I, 127
Export-Import Bank of the United States, 118-119

Family Farmer Bankruptcy Act of 1986, 94
Family Support Administration, 88
Farm Credit Act, 77, 119
Farm Credit Administration, 78, 119
Farm Credit System, 119
Farmers Home Administration, 78, 89
Farm policy, 78
Farm Security Administration, 78
Federal Acquisition Regulation, 125
Federal Advisory Council, 123
Federal Aviation Administration (FAA), 79, 99, 100, 112
Federal Bureau of Investigation (FBI), 93, 94, 102, 116
Federal Bureau of Prisons, 94
Federal Communications Act, 120
Federal Communications Commission (FCC), 79, 107, 113, 119-120

Federal Contract Compliance Programs, Office of, 96
Federal Corrupt Practices Act of 1925, 121
Federal Council on the Arts and Humanities, 128, 129
Federal Credit Union Act of 1934, 86, 128
Federal credit union regulation, 128
Federal Deposit Insurance Corporation, 109, 120
Federal Election Campaign Act of 1971 (FECA), 121
Federal Election Commission (FEC), 120-121
Federal Emergency Management Agency, 121, 125
Federal Employees Retirement System, 124
Federal Employees Retirement System Act of 1986, 124
Federal Energy Administration, 84, 85, 109
Federal Energy Regulatory Commission, 85
Federal Farm Loan Act of 1916, 119
Federal Hazardous Substances Act, 117
Federal Highway Administration, 100
Federal Home Loan Bank Act of 1932, 121
Federal Home Loan Bank Board, 108-109, 121-122
Federal Home Loan Mortgage Corporation, 122
Federal Housing Administration, 88
Federal Information Centers, 125
Federal Information Resources Management Regulations, 125
Federal Insecticide, Fungicide, and Rodenticide Act, 118
Federal Intermediate Credit Banks, 119
Federalism, 90
Federalist No. 70, 57
Federal Labor Relations Authority, 122, 126
Federal Land Bank Associations, 119
Federal Land Banks, 119
Federal Law Enforcement Training Center, 102
Federal Maritime Administration, 122
Federal Maritime Commission, 122
Federal Mediation and Conciliation Service, 123
Federal Open Market Committee, 123
Federal Political Personnel Manual, 29
Federal Power Commission, 84, 108
Federal Procurement Policy, Office of, 36
Federal Property Council, 31
Federal Property Resources Service, 124, 125
Federal Radio Commission, 120
Federal Railroad Administration, 100
Federal Records Centers, Office of, 127
Federal Register, Office of the, 127
Federal Regulatory Directory (Congressional Quarterly), 109
Federal Reserve Act of 1913, 123
Federal Reserve Board, 107, 112
Federal Reserve System, 108, 123-124, 142
Federal Retirement Thrift Investment Board, 124
Federal Savings and Loan Insurance Corporation, 122
Federal Security Agency, 83, 86
Federal Service Impasses Panel, 122
Federal Supply Service, 124
Federal Telecommunications System, 125
Federal Trade Commission (FTC), 107, 108, 124, 134
Federal Trade Commission Act of 1914, 124
Feigenbaum, Edward D., 29
Feldstein, Martin S., 46
Fenn, Dan, Jr., 28
Fielding, Fred F., 41
Finance Committee, Senate, 90
Financial disclosure, 70
Financial Institutions Regulatory and Interest Rate Control Act of 1978, 128
Financial Management Service, 101, 102
Finch, Robert H., 74
Fiscal policy, 32-34, 36
Fish, Hamilton, 97
Fish and Wildlife Service, 91
Flammable Fabrics Act, 117
Flanigan, Peter M., 74
Flash, Edward S., Jr., 42
Flexner, James Thomas, 57, 58
Flitner, David, Jr., 144, 147, 149, 151, 152
Food and Drug Act of 1906, 77, 88
Food and Drug Administration (FDA), 77, 86, 88, 107-109, 111
Food for Peace Program, Office of, 31, 78, 138
Food Stamp Program, 78
Ford, Gerald R., 131
    administrative politics, 31, 38, 41, 45, 85
    administrative style, 8-9, 16, 20
    appointment politics, 29, 112
    cabinet politics, 61, 66, 75, 81
    law enforcement, 93
    presidential library, 127
    science policy, 50
Foreign Agricultural Service, 97
Foreign Assets Control, Office of, 102
Foreign Intelligence Advisory Board, 116
Foreign Operations Administration, 30
Foreign Relations of the United States, The (State Department), 98
Foreign Service, 97, 99
Forest Service, 77
Forrestal, James V., 72, 80
Fossil Energy, Office of, 86
Foster Grandparents Program, 114
Frank, Jerome, 72
Franklin, Benjamin, 57, 111, 137
Freedom of Information Act, 126
Freedom 7, 127
Freeman, Orville L., 78
Freer Gallery, 136
Fulbright Program, 138

Gallatin, Albert, 59
Gallaudet University, 84
Gardner, John W., 63, 74
Garfield, James A., 59
General Accounting Office (GAO), 32, 82, 104
General Agreement on Tariffs and Trade (GATT), 47
General Counsel, Office of, ACDA, 137
General Counsel, Office of, DVA, 104
General counsel, presidential commissions, 148-149
General Land Office, 90, 101
General Services Administration (GSA), 101, 110, 124-125, 127
Geological Survey, U.S., 91
GI bills, 103
Global Issues Working Group, 53
Goodwin, Richard, 40
Gordon, Kermit, 34, 45
Governmental Affairs Committee, Senate, 37, 107, 112
Government Corporation Control Act of 1945, 111
Government corporations, 107, 111
Government Ethics, Office of, 132
Government National Mortgage Association (GNMA), 88, 90
Government Operations Committee, Senate, 38, 107
Government Reports, Office of, 30
Grace, J. Peter, 146, 147
Grace commissions, 144, 146, 147, 151
Graham, William R., 50
Grant, Ulysses S., 2
Great Society, 31, 87
Greenberg, Sanford E., 146
Greenspan, Alan, 45
Grossman, Jonathan, 95
Guam, 92
Gulick, Luther, 2

Hagerty, James C., 4, 14
Haig, Alexander M., Jr., 13, 19-20, 64, 98
Haiti, 1097
Halberstam, David, 74
Haldeman, H. R. (Bob), 8, 13, 16, 19
Hamilton, Alexander, 58, 101
Handicap discrimination, 118
Hardin, Clifford M., 74, 78
Harding, Warren G., 33
Hargrove, Erwin C., 43-46
Harriman, W. Averell, 4, 73
Harris, Patricia, 89
Harris, Richard, 92
Harrison, Benjamin, 2
Hatch Agricultural Experiment Stations Act of 1887, 77
Hathaway, Stanley K., 70
Hauge, Gabriel, 44
Hayes, Rutherford B., 2
Hazardous Materials Transportation, Office of, 100
Head Start program, 87
Health, Education, and Welfare Department (HEW), 63, 83, 86-87
Health and Human Services Department (HHS), 86-88
Health Care Financing Administration, 88
Health Resources and Service Administration, 88
Heclo, Hugh, 64
Heller, Walter W., 44, 45
Helms, Jesse, 76
Hepburn Act of 1906, 108
Herrington, John S., 85
Herter, Christian A., 47
Hess, Stephen, 26, 28, 30, 33, 41, 44, 45, 60, 62, 66, 71, 73
Hickel, Walter J., 61, 64, 65, 74, 90-91
High Speed Ground Transportation Program, 99
Highway Safety Act, 99
Hill, A. Alan, 53
Hills, Carla A., 75, 1117
Hines, Frank T., 103
Hirshhorn Museum and Sculpture Garden, 136
Historic Preservation Fund, 91
Hobby, Oveta Culp, 86
Hodel, Donald P., 85, 91
Hodgson, Godfrey, 62

Holifield, Chester E., 40
Hollings, Ernest F., 8
Hoover, Herbert C., 2, 65, 79, 127, 141, 142
Hoover Commission (first, 1949), 43, 80, 145
Hoover Commission (second, 1955), 145
Hopkins, Harry L., 904, 3, 15, 71
Hornig, Donald F., 50
House and Home Finance Agency, 89
House of Representatives, 12
Housing and Urban Development Department (HUD), 88-90
Houston, David F., 77
Howard University, 84
Howe, Louis McHenry, 2
Hoxie, R. Gordon, 58, 59, 76
Huberman, Benjamin, 50
Hufstedler, Shirley M., 83
Hughes, Howard, 903
Hull, Cordell, 71, 97
Human Development Services, Office of, 87
Humphrey, George M., 63, 101
Humphrey, Hubert H., 133
Humphrey's Executor v. United States, 107
Hungerford, Henry James, 136
Huntington, Samuel, 108

Ickes, Harold L., 59, 71, 90
Immigration and Naturalization Service (INS), 94
Improvements in the Administration of Justice, Office for, 93
Independent executive agencies, 107, 110-111,
Independent regulatory agencies. *See* Regulatory agencies; specific agency names
Independent Safety Board Act of 1974, 130
Indian Education Act, 84
Information Agency, U.S. (USIA), 137-138
Information and Regulatory Affairs, Office of (OIRA), 36-37, 46
Information Office, USDA, 77
Information Resources Management, Office of, 124, 125
Ink, Dwight A., Jr., 40
Inspection and Enforcement, Office of, 131
Inspector General, Office of, DVA, 104
Institute of Museum Services, 128, 129
Institute of Peace, U.S., 138
Intelligence community, 116
Intelligence Oversight Board, 116
Intelligence Policy and Review, Office of, 93
Interagency Toxic Substances Data Committee, 53
Interagency Trade Organization, 47
Inter-American Development Bank, 101, 125
Inter-American Foundation, 125
Interest group politics
    policy-making influence, 108, 110, 142, 145
    White House management, 9, 12, 14-15
Intergovernmental Relations, Office of, 31
Interior Department, 90-92, 101
Internal improvements issue, 90
Internal Revenue Service (IRS), 94, 102
International Bank for Reconstruction and Development, 101
International Criminal Police Organization-United States National Central Bureau (INTERPOL-USNCB), 94
International Development Cooperation Agency, U.S., 138
International Monetary Fund, 101
International monetary system, 101
International Trade Administration, 79
International Trade Commission, U.S., 138-139
International Year of Cooperation, 144
Interstate Commerce Commission (ICC), 107, 108, 113, 125-126
Interstate Commerce Commission Act of 1887, 125
Investigations, Senate Permanent Subcommittee on, 150
Investment Advisers Act of 1940, 135
Investment Company Act of 1940, 135
Iran-contra affair, 21, 37, 38

Jackson, Andrew, 2, 59, 62, 141
James, E. Pendleton, 31, 76
Jay, John, 57
Jefferson, Thomas, 58
Job Corps, 96
Job Training Partnership Program, 96
Johnson, Andrew, 1-2, 83, 95
Johnson, Lyndon B.
    administrative activities, 66, 149
    administrative style, 18, 38, 40
    appointment politics, 16, 28, 146, 147
    bureaucratic politics, 12, 31, 34, 87-89, 95, 99, 110, 142
    cabinet politics, 60, 62, 63, 65, 74, 97
    economic policy, 45
    presidential library, 127
    science policy, 50
    staff, 1, 6-7, 14, 15, 18
    trade policy, 47
Johnson, Richard G., 50
Johnson, Robert, 1-2
Joint Chiefs of Staff (JCS), 80, 82
Joint Economic Committee, 42, 44
Joint Economic Report Committee, 42-44
Jones, Jesse H., 61-62
Jones, Roger, 33
Jordan, Hamilton, 13, 20, 30, 61, 62, 75, 76
Judiciary Act of 1789, 92
Justice Assistance Act of 1984, 94
Justice Department, 58, 63, 92-95, 135
Justice Management Division, 93
Justice Programs, Office of, 94

Karno, Richard A., 107
Katz, James Everett, 50, 51
Katzenbach, Nicholas, 150
Katzenbach Commission, 144, 149, 150, 152
Kendall, Amos, 2
Kennan, George F., 97
Kennedy, David M., 74
Kennedy, Edward M., 151
Kennedy, John F.
    administrative style, 38, 40, 66
    appointment politics, 26, 28, 34, 44-45, 146, 147
    assassination investigation, 144, 147-150
    bureaucratic politics, 31, 87-89, 99, 137
    cabinet politics, 60, 62, 63, 65, 73, 96, 97
    defense policy, 81
    domestic policy, 50, 127
    economic policy, 79
    foreign policy, 133
    presidential library, 127
    speeches, 15
    staff, 1, 5-6, 12-15, 17-18, 65
    trade policy, 47
Kennedy, Robert F., 63, 66, 73
Kerensky, Aleksandr Fyodorovich, 142
Kerner, Otto, 147
Kerner Commission on Civil Disorders, 144, 147-150
Kessel, John H., 41
Kessler, Frank, 62-63, 66
Kester, John G., 82
Keyserling, Leon, 4, 43-44
Keyworth, G. A., II, 50
Killian, James R., 50
Kirkland, Lane, 96
Kirschten, Dick, 41, 42
Kissinger, Henry A., 97, 152
    national security adviser, 8, 14, 15, 19, 37-40
Kitchen cabinet, 59
Kleindienst, Richard G., 92
Knights of Labor, 95
Knox, Franklin, 71
Knox, Henry, 57, 58
Knox, Philander C., 97
Kohlmeier, Louis, Jr., 112
Korean War, 30, 60
Kreager, H. Dewayne, 30

Labor and Human Resources Committee, Senate, 76, 96
Labor Department, 78, 95-97
Labor-Management Cooperation Act of 1978, 123
Labor-Management Office, 96
Labor-Management Relations Act of 1947 (Taft-Hartley Act), 34, 123, 129
Labor Management Reporting and Disclosure Act, 96
Labor relations, 122, 123, 128-129
Laird, Melvin R., 74, 81
Lamont, Daniel, 2
Lance, Thomas Bertram, 30-31, 35
Land and Natural Resources Division, Justice Department, 94
Land and Water Conservation Fund, 91
Landis, James, 72
Laski, Harold J., 62
Latin America, 125. *See also* specific countries
Law enforcement agencies and officers, 117, 118, 124, 125, 132, 134
Learning and Dissemination, Office of, 125
Legal Counsel, Office of, 93
Legal Policy, Office of, 93
Legal Services Corporation, 126
Legal Services Corporation Act of 1974, 126
Legislative Affairs, Office of (Justice Department), 93
Legislative Affairs, Office of (White House), 14
Levi, Edward H., 75
Lewis, Drew, 76
Liaison Services, Office of, 94
Libraries, 54, 127
Light, Larry, 41
Lily, Frank, 152
Lincoln, Abraham, 59, 103
Lipshutz, Robert J., 13
Lobbying, presidential efforts, 14
    See also Interest group politics
Loeb, William, Jr., 2
Los Angeles Times Magazine, 1081
Louis Harris organization, 147

Lovett, Robert A., 72
Lyng, Richard E., 78
Lynn, James T., 35

McCarthy, Joseph R., 97
McCarthy, Timothy J., 908
McClellan, John L., 150
McCone, John A., 66
McCracken, Paul W., 45
McCulley, Richard T., 28
McFarlane, Robert C., 38
McIntyre, James T., 35
McIntyre, Marvin H., 2, 3
McKay, James C., 93
Mackenzie, G. Calvin, 26, 29, 70, 73-75, 112
McKinley, Ida Saxton, 2
McKinley, William L., 2
McLane, Louis, 97
McLaughlin, Ann Dore, 96
McNamara, Robert S., 63, 64, 66, 73, 74, 81
McTague, John P., 50
Macy, John W., 28-30, 70, 76
Madison, James, 58, 59, 90
Magnuson-Moss Warranty/Federal Trade Commission Improvement Act of 1974, 124
Malek, Frederic V., 26, 29, 75
Management and Administration, Office of, 127
Management and Budget, Office of (OMB), 25, 32, 34-36
Manchester, William, 28
Mann-Elkins Act of 1910, 108
Marcy, Carl, 141
Marine Hospital Service, 87
Marine Protection, Research, and Sanctuaries Act, 118
Maritime Administration, 79, 100
Markets, Office of, USDA, 77
Marsh, John O., Jr., 29
Marshall, F. Ray, 65, 96
Marshall, George C., 63, 72, 97
Martin, William McChesney, 44
Mathews, F. David, 75
Mayer, Martin, 97
Mayo, Robert P., 40
Meat Inspection Act of 1906, 77
Media, 8, 14
Medicaid, 87, 88
Medicare, 87, 88
Medicine and Surgery Department, 104
Meese, Edwin, III, 10, 15, 20-21, 63, 93
Mellon, Andrew W., 65
Memorial Affairs Department, 104
Mendel, Richard A., 82
Merchant Marine Academy, U.S., 100
Merit Systems Protection Board (MSPB), 126
Merriam, Charles E., 2
Military Assistance for Safety in Traffic, 99
Military Selective Service Act of 1980, 135
Miller, James C., III, 35
Minerals Management Service, 91
Mine Safety and Health Administration, 96
Minority Business Development Agency, 80
Mint, U.S., 102
Mitchell, John N., 63, 74, 92
Moley, Raymond, 2
Montgomery, G. V., 104
Monthly Labor Review, 95
Moore, Frank, 26

Morley, Samuel A., 43-46
Morris, Gouverneur, 57
Morton, Rogers C. B., 29
Moyers, Bill, 15
Moynihan, Daniel P., 8
Multilateral Affairs Bureau, ACDA, 137
Muskie, Edmund, 146

Nader, Ralph, 109
Nathan, Richard P., 64
National Academy of Public Administration (NAPA), 70-71, 103
National Academy of Sciences, 50, 117
National Advisory Commission on Civil Disorders (Kerner), 144, 147-150
National Advisory Commission on Libraries, 148
National Aeronautics and Space Act of 1958, 127
National Aeronautics and Space Administration (NASA), 50, 110, 126-127
National Air and Space Museum, 136
National Archives, Office of, 127
National Archives and Records Administration, 127
National Association of Manufacturers, 78
National Bipartisan Commission on Central America, 146, 151-152
National Bureau of Standards, 79
National Capital Planning Act of 1952, 128
National Capital Planning Commission, 128
National Center for Health Services Research and Health Care Technology Assessment, 87-88
National Center for Health Statistics, 88
National Center for Service Learning, 114
National Citizens Commission on International Cooperation, 144
National Commission on the Causes and Prevention of Violence (Eisenhower), 144, 147-149, 151
National Commission on Higher Education, 150
National Commission on Marijuana and Drug Abuse (Shafer), 144
National Commission on the Public Service, 146, 152
National Commission on Space, 146
National Council on Marine Resources and Engineering Development, 142
National Credit Union Administration, 128
National Credit Union Share Insurance Fund, 128
National Defense Reserve Fleet, 100
National Defense University, 138
National Education Association, 83
National Endowment for the Arts, 128
National Endowment for the Humanities, 128, 129
National Environmental Policy Act of 1969, 52
National Foundation on the Arts and Humanities, 128-129
National Futures Association, 117
National Guard, 135
National Highway Traffic Safety Administration, 100, 109, 113
National Homes for Disabled Volunteer Soldiers, 103
National Institute of Mental Health, 88
National Institute on Alcohol Abuse and Alcoholism, 88

National Institute on Drug Abuse, 88
National Institutes of Health (NIH), 88
National Labor Relations Act (Wagner Act), 109, 129
National Labor Relations Board (NLRB), 107, 109, 129
National Library of Medicine, 87
National Mediation Board, 129-130
National Museum of African Art, 136
National Museum of American History, 136
National Museum Services Board, 129
National Oceanic and Atmospheric Administration, 79
National Park Service, 91-92
National Park System, 91
National Railroad Adjustment Board, 130
National Railroad Passenger Corporation (Amtrak), 100, 111, 130
National Register of Historic Places, 92
National Research Council, 127
National Resources Planning Committee, 30
National Science and Technology Policy, Organizations, and Priorities Act of 1976, 49
National Science and Technology Week, 131
National Science Foundation, 31, 49, 50, 130-131
National Science Foundation Act of 1950, 130
National Security Act Amendments of 1949, 80, 116
National Security Act of 1947, 4, 37, 80, 115
National security adviser, 13-14, 37, 39
National Security Agency, 116
National Security Council (NSC), 20, 30, 116, 137
  foreign-policy-making role, 8, 38
  Iran-contra affair, 38
  membership, 4, 37
  organization and functions, 25, 38-39, 62
  origins and development, 4, 5, 18, 37-38
  staff, 37
National Selective Service Appeal Board, 135
National Technical Information Service, 79
National Technical Institute for the Deaf, 84
National Telecommunications and Information Administration, 80
National Tourism Policy Act of 1981, 79
National Transportation Safety Board, 99, 131
National Zoological Park, 136
Native Americans services, 87, 90, 91, 96
Natural Resources Department (proposed), 84
Naval Home, U.S., 103
Naveh, David, 42
Navy Department, 80
Nessen, Ronald H., 9
Neustadt, Richard E., 17, 33
New Frontier, 6
New Republic, 73
News media, 8, 14
Newton, Isaac, 77
New York Times, 69
Nicaragua, 152. See also Iran-contra affair

Nicholas II (czar of Russia), 142
Nitze, Paul, 66
Nixon, Richard
    administrative activities, 52, 133
    administrative style, 19-20, 39-41
    appointment politics, 28-29, 71, 112, 113
    budget politics, 87
    bureaucratic politics, 31, 34-35, 38, 66,
        84-85, 90, 96, 111, 142
    cabinet politics, 61-65, 74-75, 81, 97
    economic policy, 45
    law enforcement authority, 92
    presidential library, 127
    science policy, 50
    staff, 7-8, 12-16
    trade policy, 47-48
    Watergate scandal, 8, 92
North, Oliver L., 38
Northeast Corridor Rail Improvement
    Project, 100
Northern Mariana Islands, 92
Nourse, Edwin G., 4, 43
Nuclear Material Safety and Safeguards,
    Office of, 131
Nuclear Materials Production Program, 86
Nuclear Reactor Regulation, Office of, 131
Nuclear Regulatory Commission (NRC),
    108, 109, 131-132
Nuclear Regulatory Research, Office of,
    131
Nuclear Waste Policy Act of 1982, 86

Occupational safety and health, 88, 109,
    132
Occupational Safety and Health Act of
    1970, 132
Occupational Safety and Health Adminis-
    tration (OSHA), 96, 107, 109, 113
Occupational Safety and Health Review
    Commission, 132
Ocean commerce, 122
O'Donnell, Kenneth P., 5
Office of. See specific office names
Offices and Service Division, Justice De-
    partment, 93
Okun, Arthur M., 45, 47
Old Age, Survivors, and Disability Insur-
    ance (OASDI), 87, 88
Old Age and Survivors Insurance (OASI),
    87
Older Americans Act of 1965, 87
Omnibus Crime Control and Safe Streets
    Act of 1968, 152
Open Skies proposal, 5
Organization for Economic Cooperation
    and Development, 46
Organization of American States, 138
Overman Act of 1918, 72
Overseas Private Investment Corporation,
    138

Packard, David, 81
Packers and Stockyards Act of 1921, 77
Panama, 136
Panama Canal, 132
Panama Canal Commission, 132
Panama Canal treaties, 132
Panic of 1893, 78
Paperwork Reduction Act of 1980, 36
Pardon Attorney, Office of, 93
Patent and Trademark Office, 80
Patent Office, 77, 79, 80, 90
Patterson, Robert P., 72

Pay and perquisites, 70
Peace Corps, 132-133
Peace Corps Advisory Council, 146
Peck, Raymond, 113
Pendleton, George H., 59
Pennsylvania Avenue Development Cor-
    poration, 133
Pension Benefit Guaranty Corporation
    (PBGC), 133
Pension Office, 90
Pensions and retirement, 124, 133-134
Pentagon. See Defense Department
Perkins, Frances, 71, 95
Permanent advisory commissions. See
    Presidential commissions
Personnel Management, Office of (OPM),
    126, 132
Personnel Office, White House, 15, 16, 29
Persons, Wilton B. (Jerry), 13, 18
Pertschuk, Michael, 113
Pierce, Samuel R., Jr., 76, 89
Pinckney, Charles Cotesworth, 57
Pious, Richard, 25, 62, 69, 142
Pipeline Safety, Office of, 100
Planning and Evaluation, Office of, 10, 20
Poindexter, John M., 38
Poison Prevention Packaging Act of 1970,
    117
Policy Development, Office of (OPD), 11,
    14, 20, 39-42
Policy Planning Council, 97, 98
Policy Planning Office (PPO), 29, 75-76
Polk, James K., 90, 136
Polsby, Nelson W., 69-70
Popper, Frank, 145, 148-150
Porter, Roger, 42
Postal Rate Commission, 134
Postal Reorganization Act of 1970, 134
Postal Service, U.S., 111, 134, 139
Post Office Department, 101, 134
Postsecondary Education, Office of, 84
Powderly, Terence, 95
Powell, Jody L., 62
Pregnancy Discrimination Act of 1978, 118
Preservation, Office of, 129
Presidential Commission on the Human
    Immunodeficiency Virus Epidemic, 141,
    144, 152
Presidential commissions, 141-153
    ad hoc commissions, 142-144
    appointment of commissioners, 145-147
    constitutional authority, 141
    functions, 151-152
    funding, 141
    historical background, 141-142
    methods of operation, 149-150
    permanent advisory organizations, 142
    staff, 147-149
    White House conferences, 144
    See also specific commission names
Presidential libraries, 127
Presidential transition period, 26
President's Advisory Committee on Gov-
    ernment Organization (Rockefeller), 34
President's Commission on an All-Volun-
    teer Armed Force, 148
President's Commission on the Assassina-
    tion of President Kennedy (Warren), 144,
    147-150
President's Commission on Campaign
    Costs, 146, 147
President's Commission on Campus Unrest
    (Scranton), 144, 145, 150

President's Commission on Law Enforce-
    ment and the Administration of Justice
    (Katzenbach), 144, 149, 150, 152
President's Commission on Postal Reorga-
    nization, 148
President's Commission on World Hunger,
    146
President's Commission on the World's
    Fair, 150
President's Committee on Administrative
    Management (Brownlow), 2-3, 30, 33, 142
President's Committee on Civil Rights, 151
President's Private Sector Survey on Cost
    Control (Grace), 146, 151
President's Science Advisory Committee
    (PSAC), 49-50
President's Special Review Board, 146
Press, Frank, 50
Price, Raymond, 8
Production Credit Associations, 119
Productivity, Technology and Innovation,
    Office of, 79
Professional Responsibility, Office of, 93-
    94
Public Affairs, Office of, ACDA, 137
Public Buildings Service, 124, 125
Public Health Service, 86, 87, 103
Public Health Service Act of 1944, 87
Public Liaison, Office of (OPL), 14-15
Public politics, 12
Public Programs, Office of, 127
Public Utility Holding Company Act of
    1935, 135
Pullen, Penny, 152

Quadriad, 45

Radio Division, Commerce Department, 79
Radio Free Afghanistan, 115
Radio Free Europe, 115
Radio Liberty, 115
Rail Passenger Service Act of 1970, 130
Railroad industry
    Amtrak, 100, 111, 130
    regulation, 99-100, 125-126, 129-130
Railroad Retirement Act of 1934, 134
Railroad Retirement Board, 134
Railroad Retirement Carriers' Tax Acts of
    1935, 134
Railroad Retirement Tax Act, 134
Railroad Revitalization and Regulatory Re-
    form Act of 1976, 130
Railroad Unemployment Insurance Act,
    134
Railway Labor Act of 1926, 129
Railway Labor Executives Association, 130
Randolph, Edmund, 58
Reagan, Ronald
    administrative style, 16, 20-21, 31, 38, 41-
        42
    appointment politics, 31-32, 50, 71, 76,
        93, 113, 151-152
    budget politics, 35, 36
    bureaucratic politics, 83, 85, 89, 91, 96,
        100, 102, 104
    cabinet politics, 61, 63, 64, 66, 98
    defense policy, 82
    economic policy, 46
    environmental policy, 53
    staff, 1, 10-11, 14-16
    trade policy, 48, 49
Records Administration, Office of, 127
Redfield, William C., 79

Redford, Emmette S., 28
Reedy, George E., 60
Refrigerator Safety Act, 117
Regan, Donald T., 13, 21, 46, 76
Register of the Treasury, 102
Regulatory agencies
   appointment of commissioners, 107-108,
    111-113
   constituency politics, 108
   independent status, 107
   methods of regulation, 109-110
   structure and functions, 107-109
   See also specific agencies
Regulatory Analysis Review Group, 46
Regulatory Flexibility Act of 1980, 136
Regulatory reform, 36-37, 46, 99-100, 113
Removal power. See Appointment power
  and process
Reorganization Act of 1939, 72
Reorganization Act of 1949, 72
Reorganizational authority, 72
Reorganization Plan No. 1 (Carter), 41, 53
Reorganization Plan No. 2 (Kennedy), 50
Reorganization Plan No. 2 (Nixon), 34, 40
Reorganization Plan No. 9 (Eisenhower),
  44
Report of the President's Special Review
  Board (Tower Commission Report), 21
Research and Special Programs Adminis-
  tration, 100
Resettlement Administration, 78
Resource Conservation and Recovery Act,
  118
Retired Senior Volunteer Program
  (RSVP), 114
Retirement plans, 124, 133-134
Richardson, Elliot L., 64, 81, 92
Richardson, Warren, 76
Robb, Charles S., 146
Robertson, Stephen L., 1
Robinson, David Z., 51
Rockefeller, Nelson A., 5, 41, 50
Rockefeller Committee, 34
Rogers, William K., 2
Rogers, William P., 8, 38, 64, 74, 97
Rogers Act of 1924, 97
Rollings, Daniel G., 2
Romney, George W., 74
Roosevelt, Franklin D.
  administrative style, 17, 25
  appointment politics, 2, 26-27, 107
  bureaucratic politics, 30, 33, 39, 72, 79,
   86, 142
  cabinet politics, 59, 62, 71-72
  presidential library, 127
  staff, 2-3, 13, 15
Roosevelt, Theodore, 2, 78, 95, 121, 132,
  142
Root, Elihu, 97
Roper, Daniel C., 71
Rosenman, Samuel I., 3, 13
Rostow, Walt W., 38
Roth, William V., Jr., 37
Roybal, Edward R., 41
Rumsfeld, Donald, 13, 20, 29
Rural Development Program, 78
Rural Electrification Administration, 78
Rusk, Dean, 63, 66, 73, 74, 97
Rusk, Jeremiah M., 77

Safe Drinking Water Act of 1974, 118
Safety, Reliability, Maintainability and
  Quality Assurance, Office of, NASA, 127

Safire, William, 7
St. Lawrence Seaway Development Cor-
  poration, 100
Saulnier, Raymond J., 44
Savings Bond Division, Treasury Depart-
  ment, 102
Saxbe, William B., 92
Schlesinger, Arthur M., Jr., 60, 62, 74
Schlesinger, James R., 81, 84
Schultze, Charles L., 34, 45-46
Schwellenbach, Lewis B., 72
Science adviser, 49-51
Science Advisory Committee, 49
Science and Technology, Office of (OST),
  31
Science and Technology Policy, Office of
  (OSTP), 49-51
Scientific research funding, 129-130
Scowcroft, Brent, 38, 146
Scranton, William O., 29
Secretary of. See specific department
  names
Secret Service, 102
Securities Act of 1933, 134
Securities and Exchange Commission
  (SEC), 107, 109, 113, 134-135
Securities Exchange Act of 1934, 134, 135
Securities regulation, 134-135
Selective Service Act of 1948, 135
Selective Service System, 135
Selective Training and Service Act of 1940,
  135
Senate staff, 12
Senior Community Service Employment
  Program, 96
Senior Companion Program, 114
Senior Interagency Group on International
  Economic Policy, 101
Seward, William H., 59
Shad, S. R., 113
Shipping Act of 1916, 122
Shipping Act of 1984, 122
Shultz, George P.
  labor secretary, 74
  OMB director, 35, 40-41
  secretary of state, 63, 64, 76, 98
  Treasury secretary, 45, 64
Shuman, Howard E., 150
Slemp, C. Bascom, 2
Small Business Act of 1953, 135
Small Business Administration (SBA), 135-
  136
Small Business Investment Act of 1958,
  135
Small Business Investment Incentive Act
  of 1980, 136
Smith, Harold, 33
Smith, Robert, 59
Smith, William French, 93
Smith-Lever Agricultural Extension Act of
  1914, 77
Smith-Mundt Act, 137
Smithson, James, 136
Smithsonian Astrophysical Observatory,
  136
Smithsonian Institution, 136
Social Progress Trust Fund, 125
Social Security, 87, 134
Social Security Administration, 86, 88
Social Security Board, 86
Soil Bank Program, 78
Soil Conservation and Domestic Allotment
  Act, 78

Soil Conservation Service, 78
Soldiers Home, U.S., 103
Solicitor General, 93
Sorensen, Theodore C., 5, 6, 13-15, 28, 40,
  65, 66
Soviet Union, 50, 127
Space Council, 31
Space exploration program, 126-127
Special Action Office for Drug Abuse Pre-
  vention, 31
Special Counsel, White House, 13
Special Education and Rehabilitative Ser-
  vices, Office of, 84
Special Representative for Trade Negotia-
  tions, Office of, 31, 47
Speechwriters, 15
Sprinkel, Beryl W., 46
Sputnik I, 5, 50
Staff and advisers
  congressional staff, 12
  presidential commissions' staff, 147-149
  See also White House Office
Staggers Rail Act of 1980, 99
Standards Development, Office of, 131
Stans, Maurice H., 34, 74
State, Secretary of, 63, 97-98
State Department, 57-58, 97-99, 116, 137
State Justice Institute, 136
State Justice Institute Act of 1984, 136
States' rights issues, 90
Stedman, John R., 13
Steelman, John Roy, 4, 30
Stein, Herbert, 45
Stevenson, Adlai E., II, 73
Stever, H. Guyford, 50
Stimson, Henry L., 63-64, 71
Stockman, David, 35, 36
Strategic Arms Reduction Talks, 137
Strategic Defense Initiative (SDI), 82, 137
Strategic Programs Bureau, ACDA, 137
Strauss, Robert, 152
Stubbing, Richard A., 80, 82
Subcommittees. See specific subcommittee
  names
Sulzer, William, 95
Sulzner, George T., 89, 151
Summerfield, Arthur E., 73
Sununu, John H., 13
Superfund, 118
Supervising Architect of the Treasury, Of-
  fice of, 101
Supplemental Security Income (SSI), 88
Supreme Court, 93
Surface Mining, Office of, 91
Surface Mining Control and Reclamation
  Act of 1977, 91
Survey of Current Business, 79
Sylvis, William, 95

Taft, Robert A., 26, 73
Taft, William Howard, 33, 78, 95
Taft-Hartley Act of 1947, 34, 123, 129
Talent Hunt, 28
Talent Inventory Program, 29-30
Tariff Act of 1930, 102
Tariff Commission, 108
Task Force on Regulatory Reform, 53
Task forces, 66
Tax Division, Justice Department, 94
Taylor, Maxwell, 66
Telecommunications, Office of, 80
Telecommunications Policy, Office of, 31,
  80

Telecommunications regulation, 119-120
Television and Film Service, 138
Tennessee Valley Authority, 111, 136-137
Thompson, Llewellyn, 66
Thompson, Margaret C., 25, 69
Thornburgh, Dick, 65, 93
Three Mile Island accident, 131
Tobin, James, 45
Tower, John G., 146
Tower Commission, 145
Tower Commission Report, 21
Toxicological Advisory Board, 117
Toxic Substances Control Act, 118
Trade Act of 1974, 48, 136
Trade and Development Program, 138
Trade Expansion Act of 1962, 47
Trade policy, 47-49, 79, 136-137
Trade Representative, U.S., 31, 47-49
Transition period, 26
Transportation Department, 99-100
Transportation regulation, 99-100, 125-126,
  130
Transportation Safety Institute, 100
Transportation Systems Center, 100
Travel and Tourism Administration, U.S.,
  79
Travel Service, U.S., 79
Treasury, U.S., 91
Treasurer of the United States, 102
Treasury Act of 1789, 58
Treasury Department, 57-58, 90, 116
Treasury Secretary, 63, 101, 138
Trimm, Robert D., 112
Troika, 45
Tropical Research Institute, 136
Trucking industry, 99, 125
Truman, Harry S
  administrative politics, 30, 37-39, 43, 49,
    151
  administrative style, 17
  appointment politics, 27
  bureaucratic politics, 86
  cabinet politics, 59-60, 62-64, 72, 97
  defense policy, 80
  presidential library, 127
  staff, 4, 13, 15
Trust Territory of the Pacific, 92
Tugwell, Rexford G., 2
Tumulty, Joseph P., 2
Tyler, John, 141

Udall, Morris K., 90
United Nations programs, 138
United States agencies and corporations.
  See other part of title
United States Attorneys' Bulletin, 94
United States Attorneys' Manual, 94
United States Marshals Service, 94
United States Mint, 102

Unsafe at Any Speed (Nader), 109
Uranium Mill Tailings Radiation Control
  Act, 118
Urban Development Action Grants, 89
Urban Mass Transportation Act of 1964,
  100
Urban Mass Transportation Administra-
  tion, 99, 100
U.S. Savings Bond Division, 102

Valenti, Jack, 15
Van Buren, Martin, 141
Vance, Cyrus R., 38, 63, 66, 97
Veterans Administration, 89, 102-104
Veterans' Affairs Department (DVA), 102-
  104
Veterans Benefits Administration, 104
Veterans Benefits Department, 104
Veterans' Bureau, 103
Veterans Educational Assistance Program,
  103
Veterans Health Services Administration,
  104
Vice president, 60
Vinton, Samuel F., 90
Virgin Islands, U.S., 92
VISTA (Volunteers in Service to America),
  114
Vocational and Adult Education, Office of,
  84
Voice of America, 137, 138
Volpe, John A., 19, 74

Wage and price controls, 45
Wagner Act, 109, 129
Walker, Robert J., 90
Wallace, Henry A., 64, 71
Walter, J. Jackson, 28-30, 70, 76
War Department, 57-58
War Information, Office of, 30
War Mobilization, Office of, 30
War on Poverty, 31
War Refugee Board, 30
Warren, Earl, 147
Warren Commisison, 144, 147-150
Washington, George, 1, 57, 58, 63, 141
Washington Post, 82
Watergate scandal, 8, 92
Watkins, James D., 85
Watson, Jack H., Jr., 13, 20, 29, 30, 61, 76
Watt, James G., 76, 85, 91
Wayne, Stephen J., 39
Ways and Means Committee, House, 90
Weaver, Robert C., 74, 89
Webb, James E., 33-34
Webster, William H., 93
Wedtech Corporation, 93
Weidenbaum, Murray, 46
Weinberger, Caspar W., 82

Wells, William G., Jr., 51
Wexler, Anne, 14-15
Wheeler, Earle G., 81
Whiskey Rebellion, 141
Whiskey Ring scandal, 2
Whistleblowers' protection, 126
White House Communications Office, 8, 14
White House Conference on Families, 144
White House Conference on International
  Cooperation, 144
White House conferences, 144. See also
  Presidential commissions
White House Office, 1-23
  cabinet conflicts, 62, 65
  cabinet liaison, 5, 10
  chief of staff, 12-13
  congressional liaison, 14
  contemporary operation, 11-12
  counsellor to the president, 10
  criticism, 21-22
  domestic policy adviser, 6, 8, 14
  interest group politics, 9, 12, 14-15
  media liaison, 8, 14
  national security adviser, 13-14
  organizational styles, 16-21
  origins and development, 1-11
  political party management, 10
  presidential secretaries, 2
  press secretary, 14
  special counsel, 13
  speechwriters, 15
  staff profiles, 16
  staff selection, 15-16
White House Personnel Office, 15, 16, 29,
  75
Wiesner, Jerome B., 50
Wildavsky, Aaron B., 21-22
Willis, Charles F., Jr., 27
Willkie, Wendell L., 15
Wilson, Charles E., 18, 81
Wilson, James, 77
Wilson, William B., 95
Wilson, Woodrow
  administrative politics, 78-79, 95, 142
  appointment politics, 2
  cabinet politics, 59, 62
Wirtz, W. Willard, 96
Wolanin, Thomas R., 146, 147, 149-151
Woodin, William H., 71
Woodrow Wilson International Institute
  for Scholars, 136
World Commission on Environment and
  Development, 53
World Food Program, 138
WORLDNET TV service, 138
Wright, Carroll D., 95

Yeutter, Clayton K., 47-49
Young Volunteers in Action, 114

Ziegler, Ronald L., 8, 14